The Politics of
Canadian
Foreign Policy

The Politics of Canadian Foreign Policy

SECOND EDITION

Kim Richard Nossal

Department of Political Science
McMaster University

Prentice-Hall Canada Inc., Scarborough, Ontario

Canadian Cataloguing in Publication Data

Nossal, Kim Richard
  The politics of Canadian foreign policy

2nd ed.
Includes bibliographical references and index.
ISBN 0-13-684119-8

1. Canada - Foreign relations administration.
2. Canada - Politics and government.   3. Canada -
Foreign relations.   I. Title.

JX1729.N68 1989   327.71   C89-093313-8

Prentice-Hall, Inc., Englewood Cliffs, New Jersey
Prentice-Hall International, Inc., London
Prentice-Hall of Australia, Pty., Ltd., Sydney
Prentice-Hall of India Pvt., Ltd., New Delhi
Prentice-Hall of Japan, Inc., Tokyo
Prentice-Hall of Southeast Asia (Pte.) Ltd., Singapore
Editora Prentice-Hall do Brasil Ltda., Rio de Janeiro
Prentice-Hall Hispanoamericana, S.A., Mexico

ISBN 0-13-684119-8

Production Editor: Linda Collins
Cover Design: Nightlight Graphics
Production Coordinator: Sandra Paige
Composition: Darlene Simpson

1 2 3 4 5 WP 93 92 91 90 89

Printed and bound in Canada by Webcom

Contents

3. Power and Foreign Policy   45

Part II: The Domestic Setting   85

4. Society and Foreign Policy   87

5. Dominant Ideas   127

Part III: The Governmental Setting   158

6. The Political Executive   161

7. The Bureaucracy   203

8. The Legislature 231

9. The Provinces and Foreign Policy 255

Preface to the Second Edition

In the fall of 1983, when the first edition of this book was completed, the international system was marked by crisis and Canadian politics by the prospect of change. Internationally, relations between East and West had sunk to a new low after a Soviet fighter shot down Korean Air Lines flight 007, provoking a new round of harshness and recrimination. In March, President Ronald Reagan had outlined the Strategic Defense Initiative, which promised a new generation of destabilizing strategic weapons. In Canada, the 32nd Parliament was coming to an end, as was the long tenure of Pierre Elliott Trudeau as prime minister; Brian Mulroney, who had just ousted Joe Clark as leader of the Progressive Conservative party, was feeling his way in international affairs. The domestic foreign policy agenda was dominated by concerns about international peace and stability, typified by the debate over cruise missile testing.

By the summer of 1988, when this edition was completed, the international environment had changed considerably. The rise of Mikhail Gorbachev as General Secretary of the Communist Party of the Soviet Union was transforming both Soviet politics and foreign policy. Soviet troops were in the process of withdrawing from Afghanistan; Iran and Iraq had agreed to a United Nations-supervised ceasefire; the Vietnamese were pulling out of Kampuchea; South Africa was disengaging from Angola. The Reagan administration was in its waning days. There were also changes in the Canadian environment. The Progressive Conservative government of Brian Mulroney was celebrating its fourth year in office. The foreign policy debate was dominated by the Canada-United States free trade agreement negotiated and signed by the Mulroney government.

The marked differences between 1983 and 1988 point out the importance of both change and continuity in the politics of Canadian foreign policy, and why an understanding of that context is critical for placing the decisions that shape Canada's place in the world in a firmly political context. This book seeks to examine that context. Its purpose is to identify who makes the decisions that define Canada's role in world politics, and under what conditions those decisions are made. It thus examines the impact of international and domestic politics on foreign policy behaviour, and explores the ways in which the external and domestic environments constrain and impel Canadian foreign policy-makers. The book also explores the governmental setting of foreign policy—the interplay of the executive, the bureaucracy, the legislature, and the provincial government in the shaping of foreign policy.

* * *

I owe numerous people a debt of gratitude for their help with this book. I am grateful not only to Prentice-Hall's reviewers, including Douglas A. Ross and Cranford Pratt, but to all those colleagues who offered their comments and criticisms on the first edition; their suggestions prompted a reworking of a number of aspects, as they will see. My thanks to Linda Collins and Monica Schwalbe of Prentice-Hall Canada for guiding this edition through to completion. To Lori Farrell goes my appreciation—and a new steel-reinforced keyboard.

Those who are inveterate readers of footnotes will know what debts I owe to James Eayrs, John W. Holmes, and C.P. Stacey. All students of Canadian foreign policy depend on their historical research and their reflections of the craft of state in Canada, and I am no exception. To Jim Eayrs and John Holmes, I also owe the special thanks of a former student. Mr. Holmes, who taught me so much about Canadian foreign policy, passed away as this edition was being completed; his warmth, wit, and wisdom will be sorely missed.

Hamilton, Ontario
August 1988

CHAPTER ONE

Analyzing Foreign Policy

INTRODUCTION

A country's foreign policy usually presents itself as formless and unconnected, a wide range of seemingly discrete and episodic issues and events that tumble, in kaleidoscopic fashion, into our consciousness briefly, and then are gone. The pressing issues of the day—relayed by a few columns of type in the daily papers, or by the ubiquitous 20-second clip of spot analysis on the nightly news—capture our attention, provoke our interest and perhaps our emotions, but only briefly. Today's issues are quickly replaced by new and more pressing concerns, demanding of our full attention. But these, in turn, become old hat, quickly forgotten, and if remembered at all, considered vaguely irrelevant in today's changed world. Little thought tends to be given to the longer-term coherence of the current events of foreign policy, or their connections with the past. Even less thought is devoted to putting these issues into a broader analytical perspective, or to understanding what forces shape the numerous foreign policy concerns that appear on the agenda.

The purpose of this chapter is to suggest a way in which Canada's foreign policy can be analyzed methodically. It does not pretend to offer a formal model, much less a theory, of foreign policy-making. Such an enterprise is well beyond its scope, though the discussion below owes an obvious intellectual debt to the work of those scholars who have sought to render the study of foreign policy more systematic.[1] This introductory chapter does, however, propose to examine a number of analytical issues and to offer a framework for analysis: a set of guideposts to how we might think about Canadian foreign policy, how we might organize and filter observations about Canada's international behaviour, and how we can better understand the determinants and sources of foreign policy in Canada. In essence, it seeks to answer two questions: what is foreign policy, and what determines a state's course in international politics?

WHAT IS FOREIGN POLICY?

It may, at first blush, appear odd that we should begin with so elementary a question. There are, however, two main areas of definitional confusion. First, the term "foreign policy" itself has numerous meanings, and it is necessary to identify these. Second, there is little agreement about what subject matter appropriately falls into the category of foreign policy, and what is appropriately excluded.

Foreign policy, Don Munton has complained, is a term that is used in so many ways that "it is seldom clear whether it refers to actions, goals, decisions, objectives, strategies, interests, orientations, initiatives, attitudes, plans, undertakings, or whatever."[2] The plaint is not overdrawn; the term *is* used in all those frequently inconsistent ways, by the practitioners of statecraft themselves, by academics who study their behaviour, and by the general public. But however maddening to the student of foreign policy, whose very enterprise demands placing a premium on definitional clarity, the problem cannot be satisfactorily resolved. It is true that one could propose a more precise definition, and insist that all other definitions of the term were wrong, but this would defy common usage, if not common sense. Rather, the multifaceted usage of the term in common parlance has to be lived with.

This said, however, there is some utility in drawing at least one minimal distinction between foreign policy and other phenomena. The word "policy" connotes the actions, goals, and decisions of authoritative political actors—or, more commonly, governments. To note that foreign policy lies only in the realm of governments (and only those governments with the authority to make foreign policy) is to make a critical distinction. For it excludes from consideration the foreign behaviour of non-governmental or transnational actors, such as interest groups, firms, and non-governmental organizations. It is not that these actors do not play an important role in international politics; nor that such groups do not have significant impact on the formulation and execution of the international behaviour of governments; nor do not have international policies that they pursue. They do. But foreign policy, properly speaking, is concerned with the explanation of the behaviour of those who have the capacity to exercise supreme political authority over a given set of issue areas, for a given people in a given territory. That is why we exclude the external policies of governments like that of Toronto. The members of the City Council of Toronto may declare their city a nuclear-free zone, as indeed they have done. But this declaration commands no authority, and has no effect—for the simple reason that municipal governments are not empowered to decide such matters, even for those who live within their boundaries. Such a decision can be, and has been, overridden by the legitimate authority on such matters, the federal government. (Compare, for example, the authority— and the effects—of a comparable decision by the government of New Zealand, which *is* empowered to make the country a nuclear-free zone.) But that is why, in the case of Canadian foreign policy, we must include the provincial governments in a consideration of foreign policy—for the provinces do have such competence in certain areas.

If we follow this distinction with trying to define the foreign nature of governmental behaviour, we run into the second difficulty with the term "foreign policy." And that is the lack of agreement on what policy matters are to be included in "foreign" policy, and what are to be excluded. The difficulty is that other policy areas are defined in purely functional terms: fisheries policy, correctional policy, industrial policy and so on. While there will inevitably be overlaps between policy areas, a functional delineation makes differentiation relatively easy. However, foreign policy suggests a delineation on fundamentally geopolitical terms: foreign policy begins where the territorial jurisdiction of the state ends. A dictum common in American foreign policy is that "politics stops at the water's edge"—a prescription that domestic political differences should be subordinated when dealing with the outside world. For some, therefore, "foreign" policy is likened to any other type of governmental policy—the programs and instruments used by governments to achieve their political objectives. It is not so much "foreign policy" as it is "policy that is foreign," the argument runs, in the sense that foreign policy is assumed to be little more than the external dimension of domestic policy, the projection of the government's interests beyond the boundaries of the state.[3] Thus, any aspect of governmental policy that extends beyond the geopolitical boundary is, *ipso facto*, foreign policy.

There is, however, a dissenting view that "foreign" policy is essentially a functional, not a geographical, category. In other words, foreign policy has its own distinct subject matter, just like other functional policy areas. Morgenthau is the most unabashed proponent of this view. International *politics*, he argues, is not the same as international *relations*. International politics is about power. Thus, only when a state's behaviour is directed towards the maintenance or expansion of its power is it acting politically. Not all foreign policy behaviour, he claims, is political. He cites the kind of international activities that are part of a country's foreign relations, but not its foreign policy: negotiation of extradition treaties, trading in goods and services, providing humanitarian assistance, and promoting one's culture abroad.[4]

A less exclusionary perspective would focus not so much on power alone, but the associated elements of power politics. In this view, the proper realm of foreign policy is the realm of "high" politics. This is what Rudyard Kipling termed the "Great Game" of international politics: the juggling, conspiring and, if necessary, fighting that states engage in for dominance and control in an anarchic system. Leaders of states balance and counter-balance power, aligning and combining, to avoid the inexorable consequences of losing power: domination, conquest, enslavement, or death at the hands of their rivals.[5] But international politics is also an arena in which states cooperate with one another in limited ways, erecting in the process the rudimentary elements of what Hedley Bull has termed an "anarchical society."[6] Foreign policy is thus mainly concerned with three dominant questions of high politics: international order, peace, and war.

This realist perspective has been roundly criticized by some who claim that such thinking is outmoded, more properly belonging to an earlier and putatively less complex era, when dynasts and their plenipotentiaries played the "sport of kings."[7] Things have changed, they say. Nuclear weapons have made war and the use of force impractical; society is more complex; the rate of change is more dramatic; the forces of technology and capitalist exchange have led to the emergence of a global economy that ties all states closely together; communications have been revolutionized, creating a "global village." We are living in an interdependent world, where issues of "high" politics have given way in importance to the "low" issues of international relations: the distribution of wealth, the exchange of goods, services and knowledge, the protection of the environment, the maintenance of adequate global food supplies and health, and the management of international communications. To exclude from the area of foreign policy these profound transformations taking place in the international system is, in this view, atavistic and anachronistic.[8]

Between the exclusionary realists and the power-deprecating *interdependentistas* there is, of course, a middle ground. It has been expressed well by two British students of foreign policy and international relations, Steve Smith and Michael Smith. Noting that the international system today features a "fluctuating agenda of diplomatic, military, economic and social concerns which are difficult to disentangle," they conclude that

> Perspectives on foreign policy in these conditions must take account of complexity and paradox. Policy content is neither wholly diplomatic and military nor entirely economic and social; it is not as completely dominated by "high politics," as claimed by some theorists, but it is not thoroughly permeated by "low politics" as claimed by others... "Foreign policy" appears now to be an umbrella term for attempts by governments to influence or manage events outside the state's boundaries....[9]

Such an in-between perspective commends itself to an examination of Canadian foreign policy largely because governments in Ottawa have traditionally been concerned about both high and low politics. They have never been able to avoid the rivalries of the great powers, nor the systemic wars into which the global community has been plunged since 1867. Canadian governments have always been concerned with peace, war, and international order. And they have never been able to escape a concern with the low politics of economics, trade, the environment, and social affairs. Canada's relationship with the United States has ensured that low politics will always be as much a priority of foreign policy as high politics.

In the examination of Canadian foreign policy presented in this book, we will, following Smith and Smith, be focussing on issues of both high and low politics. However, it should be noted that it is beyond the purview of the discussion here to examine the politics of policy-making in the more specialized areas of Canada's external policy. Cultural policy, immigration and refugee policy, international development assistance, international finance and monetary policy, and trade policy are all ably treated elsewhere.[10] We will also, *pace* Professor Munton, define foreign policy widely to refer to the external objectives of the Canadian government, its orientation to the international system, its relations with other governments, its positions and attitudes on world politics, and its actions, programs, and decisions.

WHAT DETERMINES FOREIGN POLICY?

Explaining a country's foreign policy, James Rosenau has suggested, requires one to be exceedingly "venturesome," for the foreign policy analyst must take into account not only what happens at the international level, but also be familiar with the pattern and context of domestic politics, and with the nature, structure, and process of government. In short, "those who study foreign policy must, perforce, concern themselves with politics at every level."[11] Because foreign policy is forged in the nexus of three political environments—international, domestic, and governmental—it cannot be analyzed unless each level of politics is examined. It is within these three spheres that the sources, or the determinants, of a state's foreign policy are to be found.

The International Setting

The first important source of foreign policy for any state is the international setting, or what is sometimes known as the "external environment." There are two distinct, but interrelated, aspects to the international setting. The first is the environment in which the state must operate. The second is the condition in which the state finds itself in that environment. An assessment of the external environment must address a number of general questions about the nature of the international system itself. What is the nature of the political units comprising the system (i.e., what political form do the units take)? How many states are there within the system? What is the distribution of power among them (i.e., how many "poles of power" exist within the system)? Is it unifocal, bipolar, tripolar or multipolar? What is the nature of the international order? What is the degree and nature of cooperation and institutionalization within the system? The effects of all these factors on a particular state's foreign policy will be considerable. For example, the polarity of the system is likely to make a difference to the general orientation of any particular state's foreign policy behaviour since polarity has an impact on stability and peace. Likewise, the degree and strength of international institutions will have a comparable impact, for strong institutionalization is likely to offer greater opportunities for active diplomacy aimed at strengthening international order.

A consideration of the condition in which the state finds itself in this system would include: the state's geographic location, its status relative to other states, its external economic linkages, its alignments in international politics, and its capabilities and power. It will be obvious that these are "external" sources only in the sense that these attributes of the state, when they interact in the context of international politics, have an effect on that state's behaviour. It will also be obvious that these factors tend to be the givens, or *relative invariants*, in a state's foreign policy, in the sense that every foreign policy-maker must confront them without being able to change them easily or rapidly. To a brief examination of each of these factors we now turn.

Location.　Most students of foreign policy begin with the obvious aspect of setting, the state's location in the international system. Location refers not only to its physical or geographic location, but also to its location in a broader political sense. The importance of geographic location is clear. Not only does it determine some of the attributes of capability, such as arable land and natural resources, but it also determines neighbourhood and the state's security. Clearly, a state with no neighbours will have a different set of foreign policy concerns than a state with numerous other states on its borders; a state physically remote from others will have a different view of security than a state surrounded by either security-conscious or expansionist neighbours. Likewise, distance or proximity to the centres of great power rivalry will condition a state's foreign policy, if not its very existence. Contiguity to a great power brings with it complexities for foreign policy, as Afghanis, Canadians, Mexicans, Poles, and Vietnamese have discovered.

But location also refers to a state's location in the international hierarchy, and the impact that has on foreign policy outcomes. A superpower such as the Soviet Union will obviously have a different perspective on international politics than a microstate like Tonga. Soviet foreign policy will inevitably reflect its global concerns and its global reach; the pattern of its international relationships will reflect its status at the apex of the international hierarchy. Tongan foreign policy, by contrast, will be primarily limited to the South Pacific, to relations with its neighbours and the dominant powers within the region. Likewise, regional "great" powers—or those at the apex of regional hierarchies—will have foreign policy concerns very different from the smaller powers in their immediate vicinity, as the foreign policies of India, Brazil, and South Africa demonstrate.

Economic structure. A state's economic structure and complexity, and its location within the economy of the international system, will bear heavily on the pattern of its international relations, its capacity for independence in foreign policy, and its weaknesses and strengths. A state with a minimally developed economy, or a single-crop economy, will have different international priorities than a state with a highly mixed and relatively strong economic structure. Such issues as dependence (or lack of it) on international trade, financial flows, technology, or natural resources like food, fuel, or raw materials will also have a bearing on foreign policy orientations. Diversification (or lack of it) of the state's trade will also affect its role in international politics.

Alignment. A state's alignment in international politics will have a profound influence on its foreign policy. First, alignment brings with it the advantages of the enhanced physical security that comes with membership in a collective. But it also brings obligations that limit its capacity for independent action. Alliances protect, but they also constrain. Moreover, alignments are inertial: once aligned, a state will find it exceedingly difficult to realign. Finally, friendship brings with it an automaticity to one's adversaries or enemies: for small states in particular, the adversaries of their friends become their adversaries.

Capability. Another factor in the external realm is capability: what kinds of resources a state has to act in international politics. Relative to others in the international system, what is its population? its wealth? its level of development? its industrial structure? its level of urbanization? its capacity to apply military force or economic coercion? How dependent or vulnerable is it, economically or militarily?

Power. The factors of geographic location, status, economic structure, alignment, and capability all have a crucial impact on the final element of the international setting: a state's power. In international politics, where there is no sovereign to arbitrate disputes, and only a loose arrangement of rules to which states attach themselves, each state must seek to maximize its goals as best it can. All states must rely on power to achieve the one goal that all independent political entities, whether tribal kingdoms or nation-states, universally pursue: the capacity to make decisions for themselves. A careful consideration of power as a critical determinant of both a state's subsidiary foreign policy goals and its capacity to attain them is integral to understanding its foreign policy.

The Domestic Setting

Some theorists of international politics assert the primacy of external sources of foreign policy over all others. They argue that the nature of the international system itself drives the behaviour of states, and that therefore, the domestic setting of foreign policy is of little importance. A cogent proponent of such a view is Kenneth Waltz, who likens the systemic forces of the international system to the systemic forces of a market: firms operating in a market have structural constraints that ensure that they act in a manner to ensure their survival; those which do not go bankrupt. Likewise, in international politics, Waltz argues, units which do not act according to the international system's requirements will perish. The structure of the international environment, therefore, determines the general behaviour of states.[12]

As a theory applied to the interactions of states as a whole, Waltz's structural realism has much to commend it. But it was intended to explain—that is, predict—international politics at a macro level. As he readily acknowledges, his theory is not meant as a micro theory of foreign policy decision-making: it is not intended to predict the exact course of a particular state's foreign policy. That, he suggests, would be like expecting the law of gravity to predict the exact path of a leaf falling from a tree.

This book, by contrast, is interested in the path of the leaf: understanding the external behaviour of a particular state at a particular time in history. It is for this reason that we cannot ignore the impact that domestic politics has on the international policies of the government in Ottawa. In considering the impact of the domestic setting of Canadian foreign policy, we have to be sensitive to a number of possible explanatory variables. We have to take into account the nature, composition, and background of Canadian society, and particularly the historical cleavages within the Canadian polity. As we will see, the uneasiness of the relationship between francophones and anglophones has not surprisingly frequently inserted itself into foreign policy questions over the course of Canadian history. Likewise, we must be aware of the political form of the Canadian community and the impact it has on the foreign policy behaviour of decision-makers in Ottawa. Representative government means that Canada's governors are made accountable to the citizenry through the device of periodic elections. We will thus examine the degree to which the "electoral connection" plays a part in the determination of external policy. Finally, we must pay heed to the role and impact of societal demands for particular directions in foreign policy behaviour.

Such demands emanate in two distinct ways. First, there is the unorganized and largely uncoordinated expression of opinions about international affairs and the proper policies that the Canadian government should pursue. This manifests itself either as "elite opinion" or, more broadly, "public opinion." On the other hand, organized interests will articulate particular demands. How the demands of both organized and unorganized interests are aggregated and managed by the government will affect the course of foreign policy. In short, we have to begin by recognizing that in the context of the Canadian case, foreign policy decision-making is not the sport of kings as it was in dynastic Europe, and that the domestic political environment will affect those decisions.

However, it should be noted that conclusions drawn from evidence about the impact of domestic politics on the foreign policy behaviour of the Canadian government will largely depend on the initial working assumptions one brings to the analysis. There are three broad schools of thought in empirical democratic theory[13] about how to analyze the relationship between the governors and the governed, or, to use the terminology employed in the literature, between the state and society. Each of these approaches employs very different assumptions.

The liberal-pluralist approach assumes that the state is essentially little more than a referee, reacting to numerous demands made by individuals, interests, and groups in society, adjudicating between conflicting demands, and making political decisions based on a "marketplace" calculus of what policies will be supported by the greatest number.[14]

Marxist approaches, by contrast, assume that the behaviour of the democratic state is tightly bound to the capitalist mode of production and to the inherent conflict between the dominant or hegemonic class—those who control capital—and other classes in society. The two main variants of the Marxist approach employ somewhat different approaches, however. Instrumental Marxists see the state merely as the governing instrument of the bourgeoisie, always making decisions that serve the interests of the capitalist class. Structural Marxists, by contrast, have a more sophisticated view of the relations between the bourgeoisie and the state in capitalist society. Most importantly, structuralists see the state as being relatively autonomous from those who actually own and control capital. The state's dominant interest, in this view, is the long-term maintenance of the capitalist system itself, not the short-term enrichment of individual capitalists. Thus, the state seeks to be as autonomous as possible in order to mediate inter-class conflict, frequently embracing in the process policies (such as social welfare policies) that are not in the short-term interests of individual capitalists. However, to the extent that such policies forestall disaffection or revolution, and give the system legitimacy in the eyes of other classes, they save greedy capitalists from themselves, and are thus in the long-term interests of the capitalist system. However, while structural and instrumental Marxism differ in perspective, the focus of both variants is on the tendency of the state to act in the interests of the dominant class in capitalist societies, the owners of capital.[15]

The unifying theme of the variants of liberal and Marxist theories of the democratic state is that the state's behaviour is understandable only by reference to the interest of society. The statist approach, however, assumes a rather different relationship between state behaviour and societal interests. It turns Winston Churchill's assertion that, in a democratic society, politicians and bureaucrats "are proud to be the servants of the state and would be ashamed to be its masters" around somewhat by assuming that state officials in fact both serve the state and are its masters. Statism argues that the state, consisting of a group of men and women charged with making authoritative decisions for the polity, are not mere automata, robotically pursuing the interests dictated to them by others. Rather, they will have their own conceptions of the national interest, conceptions that will include a calculus about their own personal interests, those of the institution, department or agency to which they are attached, and the interests of the government as a whole. They certainly will have their own ideas about how best to achieve these. Statism further assumes that the policy preferences embraced by the state as a whole may differ considerably from the interests and preferences being articulated by individuals, groups, organizations, and classes in society. Moreover, statist theory asserts, where there is a clash between the state's preferences and those of society, it is the state that has both the willingness and the capacity to ensure that state preferences prevail over those of society.[16]

It is clear that these contending paradigms offer starkly different predictions about the importance of domestic sources as an explanation of Canadian foreign policy-making.[17] Statism predicts little or no impact: foreign policy will be explained by either external or governmental sources, or both. Marxist variants predict that the key explanatory variable in foreign policy will be either the interests of the capitalist class or the interests of the capitalist system writ large. The liberal-pluralist approach predicts a maximal role for domestic sources: the interests, preferences, and demands of individuals and groups in society will be reflected in foreign policy behaviour. Thus the prism employed to analyze foreign policy is significant, for it will have an inevitable impact on one's conclusions about the importance of the domestic sources of Canadian foreign policy.

The Governmental Setting

The international and domestic environments, it can be argued, set the parameters within which the government makes foreign policy decisions. External and domestic factors will establish the general boundaries of viable policy options. But it is within and by government that the decisions that establish a state's course in international politics are made. But while the government makes decisions in the name of the state, it is not a unitary, monolithic actor, thinking, moving, and speaking with any singularity of purpose. Within the government apparatus, there are competing conceptions of the national interest, contending views on which course to follow. Moreover, these diverging opinions articulated by officials, both elected and bureaucratic, are heavily influenced by their position within the government structure. And decisions made by the government are not necessarily based on assumptions of pure means-end rationality: frequently, decision outcomes are the product of saw-offs and compromises by officials from different parts of the government negotiating on a particular foreign policy issue. As Graham T. Allison showed two decades ago,[18] foreign policy decisions are the outcome of governmental politics.[19]

Because the process of decision-making will so markedly affect the decisions themselves, we must examine the governmental setting of foreign policy making, and the politics within the state apparatus that influences those outcomes. The institutional and organizational structures that exist for the making of authoritative decisions; the lines of authority within those institutions; and the political relationships within and between different organizations of government—these must all be examined. Politics within the executive (between cabinet ministers, between the cabinet and the bureaucracy, and between departments and agencies of government), and between the executive and those members of the legislature not in cabinet, both in the House of Commons and the Senate, will be important in explaining policy.

There is, in Canada's case, one additional aspect to the governmental setting that must be examined: the impact of the federal structure on the conduct of foreign policy. The constitutions of most federal states do not allow a legitimate role in international affairs for the subnational units in the federation. In Canada, however, the Constitution Acts 1867-1982 are silent on the question of whether the federal government has exclusive jurisdiction in all matters of foreign policy. Consequently, we must examine the politics between levels of government and the impact this has on foreign policy behaviour.

Within the context of the governmental setting, particular attention should be paid to those who actually make foreign policy decisions for Canada. The individuals who occupy key decision-making roles—notably the prime minister and the secretary of state for external affairs (as Canada's foreign minister is styled)—will exert a personal influence on the direction of policy.

Settings as Determinants

The discussion in this chapter—laying out the nexus and identifying the three political settings in which policy is made—is intended as no more than a guide to the analysis of Canada's foreign policy. The framework itself has no explanatory (that is, predictive) capability, though when applied to particular aspects of foreign policy can help illuminate causality. Certainly no attempt has been made to replicate Rosenau's exercise of hypothesizing the "relative potencies" of the different sources of foreign policy.[20] This is quite purposeful, for it is important to keep in mind that across the broad span of foreign policy issues, no one source or determinant is likely to manifest itself consistently as *the* single explanation of a particular decision or set of decisions in foreign policy. As Smith and Smith note, the foreign policy agenda is multidimensional and fluctuating, and so too, it might be argued, is causality. It is rare that either single decisions or longer-term policies have monocausal roots. Explaining foreign policy, whether it be contemporary issues or historical decisions, requires a persistent attachment to the possibility that more than one factor is at play.

CONCLUSION:
THE PAST IN FOREIGN POLICY ANALYSIS

That a country's foreign policy invariably demonstrates both change and continuity over the course of its history is a truism worth repeating, for there is a tendency to ignore the impact that history has on the direction of a state's foreign policy. Despite the massive changes that have occurred since Confederation both within Canada (in society, technology, the economy, the state, political ideas and attitudes) and internationally (the distribution of power in the international system, the advent of nuclear weapons, the emergence of a global economy), there are a number of facets of Canada's external relations that have remained remarkably constant over a period of time, in some cases for generations. Canada's need for a great power protector, and the constraints that this places on autonomy, has always been a source of concern. There is in the 1980s no less ambivalence about the relationship with the United States than there was about the relationship with Britain before its decline. Canadians still exhibit a reluctance to spend on national defence during peacetime as did their predecessors in the decades between the world wars or before the Boer War.

This continuity is particularly evident in how Canada has managed its relationship with the United States. The neighbourly quarrels over fish, environmental pollution, boundaries, and trade irritants have kept prime ministers and presidents occupied for more than a century. The Canadian response to both American protectionism and domestic economic travails has also been consistent. The search for that most holy of Canadian grails—an economic arrangement with the Americans that will provide Canada unfettered access to their huge markets, permanent immunity from the predations of a periodically protectionist Congress, and ironclad guarantees that nothing will change on the Canadian side save an increase in prosperity—has been a feature of Canadian politics before there was a Canadian polity. It is one issue that, as J.L. Granatstein has so aptly put it, will not go away.[21] They called it by different names, but the initiatives in the 1980s of the governments of Pierre Trudeau and Brian Mulroney were firmly in this historical tradition.

Evidence of both change and continuity prompts the observation that a nation's history will always play an important part in shaping policy. Its presence may not always be completely self-conscious in the minds of the policy-makers themselves, nor easy for the analyst of foreign policy to see. But the weight of historical experience will hang, even if not heavily, in the determination of foreign policy, for there can be no denying or forgetting what has gone before. It is one of the givens (or relative invariants), like geographical location or geostrategic alignment, impossible to change except over the course of generations. As Christopher Hill would have it, "A state's past successes and failures, friendships and emnities, live on in the minds of present-day decision-makers both at home and abroad."[22] Thus the historical continuity in Canadian-American relations, John W. Holmes reminds us, is hardly surprising, for no nation can escape the inexorable consequences of its history: "Coping with the fact of the USA is and always has been an essential ingredient of being Canadian. It has formed us just as being an island formed Britain."[23]

It is because a country's foreign policy is affected by its past that this book's analysis does not proceed as though there were an obvious starting point to Canada's foreign relations. No government in Ottawa ever started with a clean slate in its external policies, not even the government of the new self-governing dominion created by the British North America Act in 1867. Sir John A. Macdonald had to deal with the remnants of the past that imposed themselves on his present, as has every prime minister since. It is with the importance of the past in mind that the analysis here, while by no means a history of Canadian foreign policy, nonetheless attempts to take a somewhat broader view of the Canadian experience in international politics, in order to tease out of historical examples, determinants and causes that have continuing relevance for understanding Canada's external policies today.

NOTES

1 Models of foreign policy-making can be found in: Richard C. Snyder, H.W. Bruck and Burton Sapin, eds., *Foreign Policy Decision-Making: An Approach to the Study of International Politics* (New York: Free Press, 1962), 14-185; Michael Brecher, Blema Steinberg and Janice Stein, "A framework for research on foreign policy behaviour," *Journal of Conflict Resolution* 13 (1969), 75-101; Graham T. Allison, *Essence of Decision: Explaining the Cuban Missile Crisis* (Boston: Little, Brown, 1971). A "pre-theory" of foreign policy that is still widely used as a guide for foreign policy analysis was developed by James N. Rosenau, "Pre-theories and theories of foreign policy," in Rosenau, *The Scientific Study of Foreign Policy* (New York: Free Press, 1971), 95-149.

2 Don Munton, "Comparative foreign policy: fads, fantasies, orthodoxies, perversities," in James Rosenau, ed., *In Search of Global Patterns* (New York: The Free Press, 1976), 258.

3 Foreign policy is not a thing in itself, Canada's foreign minister declared in 1969, but an external dimension of domestic policy. See D.C. Thomson and R.F. Swanson, *Canadian Foreign Policy: Options and Prospects* (Toronto: McGraw-Hill Ryerson, 1971), 9. Such a sentiment, as we shall see in chapter 2, has enjoyed a venerable history in Canada's foreign relations.

4 Hans J. Morgenthau, *Politics Among Nations: The Struggle for Power and Peace*, 5th ed. (New York: Alfred A. Knopf, 1948, 1973), 27-28.

5 Kenneth N. Waltz, *Theory of International Politics* (Reading, MA: Addison-Wesley, 1979), ch. 9.

6 Hedley Bull, *The Anarchical Society: A Study of Order in World Politics* (New York: Columbia University Press, 1977).

7 Such is the view of James N. Rosenau, "Introduction: new directions and recurrent questions in the comparative study of foreign policy," in Charles F. Hermann, Charles W. Kegley, Jr., and James N. Rosenau, eds., *New Directions in the Study of Foreign Policy* (Boston: Allen and Unwin, 1987), 2.

8 For two critiques of the realist perspective, see E.L. Morse, "The transformation of foreign policies: modernization, interdependence and externalization," *World Politics* 22 (April 1970), 371-92; Robert O. Keohane and Joseph S. Nye, *Power and Interdependence* (Boston: Little, Brown, 1977).

9 Steve Smith and Michael Smith, "The analytical background: approaches to the study of British foreign policy," in Michael Smith, Steve Smith, and Brian

White, *British Foreign Policy: Tradition, Change and Transformation* (London: Unwin Hyman, 1988), 15.

10 The following is a suggestive, rather than exhaustive, list of works on these aspects of Canadian foreign policy. On culture, see Andrew Fenton Cooper, ed., *Canadian Culture: International Dimensions* (Waterloo: Centre on Foreign Policy and Federalism, 1985). On immigration and refugees, Gerald E. Dirks, *Canada's Refugee Policy: Indifference or Opportunism?* (Montreal: McGill-Queen's University Press, 1977); also David B. Dewitt and John J. Kirton, *Canada as a Principal Power* (Toronto: John Wiley and Sons, 1983), ch. 7. Keith Spicer, *A Samaritan State? External Aid in Canada's Foreign Policy* (Toronto: University of Toronto Press, 1966), is a dated but nonetheless useful examination of early efforts in development assistance. A.F.W. Plumptre, *Three Decades of Decision: Canada and the World Monetary System, 1944-1975* (Toronto: McClelland and Stewart, 1977) is an analysis of international economic policy during the operation of the now-defunct Bretton Woods system. Finally, for often contending discussions of trade policy, see: Glen Williams, *Not For Export: Towards a Political Economy of Canada's Arrested Industrialization* (Toronto: McClelland and Stewart, 1983); Richard G. Lipsey and Murray G. Smith, *Taking the Initiative: Canada's Trade Options* (Montreal: C.D. Howe Institute, 1985); Michael D. Henderson, *The Future on the Table: Canada and the Free Trade Issue* (Toronto: Masterpress, 1987), and the voluminous work done by the Royal Commission on the Economic Union and Development Prospects for Canada, particularly vols. 9-14 on international trade and vols. 28-30 on Canada and the international political economy.

11 Rosenau, "New directions," 1.

12 Waltz, *Theory of International Politics*, esp. 89-91.

13 Normative democratic theory focusses on how the state ought to behave on such matters as equality, consent, sovereignty, and constitutionalism; the focus of empirical democratic theory, by contrast, attempts to explain the actual relationship between society and democratic government.

14 A classic formulation of pluralist theory would be Robert A. Dahl, *Who Governs?* (New Haven: Yale University Press, 1961).

15 For a discussion of different Marxist approaches which concludes by eschewing the search for a general theory, see Bob Jessop, *The Capitalist State: Marxist Theories and Methods* (New York: New York University Press, 1982).

16 A good formulation of statist theory is to be found in Eric A. Nordlinger, *On the Autonomy of the Democratic State* (Cambridge: Harvard University Press, 1981); also Stephan D. Krasner, *Defending the National Interest: Raw Materials Investment and U.S. Foreign Policy* (Princeton: Princeton University Press, 1978).

17 Kim Richard Nossal, "Analyzing the domestic sources of Canadian foreign policy," and Cranford Pratt, "Dominant class theory and Canadian foreign policy: the case of the counter-consensus," both in *International Journal* 39 (Winter 1983-4), 1-22 and 99-135.

18 For the seminal work on the governmental politics approach to foreign policy making, see Allison, *Essence of Decision*, esp. ch. 5-6; also Morton H. Halperin

and Arnold Kanter, eds., *Readings in Foreign Policy: A Bureaucratic Perspective* (Boston: Little, Brown, 1973), 2-40. For an application to the Canadian system, see Kim Richard Nossal, "Allison through the (Ottawa) looking glass: bureaucratic politics and foreign policy in a parliamentary system," *Canadian Public Administration* 22 (Winter 1979), 610-26.

19 It should be noted that Allison originally termed it the governmental (bureaucratic) politics model; the approach has come to be commonly known as the "bureaucratic politics" model. The term "governmental politics" is preferable, because the politics occurs within the governmental structure more widely than within the bureaucracy.

20 Rosenau, "Pre-theories and theories of foreign policy," 149. It might be noted that for a country like Canada, which Rosenau would classify as small, with a developed economy and an open polity, but which was penetrated, Rosenau hypothesized that the dominant explanatory variable would be the external.

21 J.L. Granatstein, "Free trade between Canada and the United States: the issue that will not go away," in Canada, Royal Commission on the Economic Union and Development Prospects for Canada, *The Collected Research Studies*, vol. 29: *The Politics of Canada's Economic Relationship with the United States*, Denis Stairs and Gilbert R. Winham, eds. (Toronto: University of Toronto Press, 1985), 11-54.

22 Christopher Hill, "The historical background: past and present in British foreign policy," in Smith, Smith, and White, eds., *British Foreign Policy*, 33.

23 John W. Holmes, *Life with Uncle: The Canadian-American Relationship* (Toronto: University of Toronto Press, 1981), 107-108.

PART ONE

THE INTERNATIONAL SETTING

CHAPTER TWO

The External Parameters

INTRODUCTION

Canada's foreign policy, the government of Prime Minister Pierre Trudeau informed Canadians in 1970, was "the extension abroad of national policies."[1] Although the 1970 white paper on foreign policy touted this as a "new" direction for Canada's external relations, the idea of linkage between domestic and foreign policy has in fact had a venerable history in Canada. In January 1948, Lester B. Pearson, then the senior civil servant in the Department of External Affairs, had had similar thoughts:

> Foreign policy, after all, is merely "domestic policy with its hat on." The donning of some head-gear, and going outside, doesn't itself alter our nature, our strength, and our quality very much.... Canada's foreign policy, in so far as it is Canadian policy at all, is, in fact, largely the consequences of domestic factors, some of which remain constant and others which are not easily altered.[2]

In turn, Pearson was echoing the thoughts of O.D. Skelton, one of his predecessors, who had said much the same thing a generation earlier. "An excellent address," Prime Minister W.L. Mackenzie King noted to his diary after listening to the man he would later recruit to head the External Affairs department, "pointing out that foreign policy was the extension of domestic policy."[3]

But if left unqualified, the assertion that foreign policy is merely the extension of domestic policy makes little sense. Governments cannot simply go outside and pursue their policy objectives in the way they can domestically. Within Canada, governments can achieve their policy objectives by the exercise of authority and, when authority alone is insufficient, by using the coercive power of the state to exact compliance. In foreign policy, by contrast, such conditions do not prevail. The authority of the Canadian government stops abruptly at the border: one can no longer simply command obedience to Canadian policy preferences. The reason for this, of course, is the essentially anarchical nature of international politics. Internationally, numerous independent states are all seeking to achieve their own political objectives; but they must do so without one superordinate sovereign political authority to regulate political relations between them. To be sure, this is not the raw and brutal state of nature outlined by Thomas Hobbes in *Leviathan*. As the late Hedley Bull so cogently reminded us, while the Hobbesian analogy is popular in theorizing about international relations, there is an order of sorts in what he characterized as the "anarchical society" of nation-states.[4] But, in the final analysis, each state in the international system is the ultimate arbiter of its own interests. That is, after all, what makes a state sovereign.

It is one thing to decide one's own interests and formulate one's own objectives—as all sovereign states have the ability to do. It is another thing entirely to be able to actually achieve these objectives. No state is able to avoid the difficulties of operating in an environment where one's ability to achieve political objectives is severely limited by the existence of other sovereigns. Canadian foreign policy-makers, like their counterparts elsewhere, cannot simply fashion a world to their liking by wishing away the grim realities of politics among states. Canadian objectives must always be crafted to fit what is attainable. The means adopted to achieve these goals must be appropriate to a political environment where success depends on power and influence, not authority. Thus, the purpose of this chapter is to explore the complex of constraints and imperatives imposed on Canadian foreign policy-makers by the international system.

RELATIVE INVARIANTS IN THE EXTERNAL ENVIRONMENT

There are a number of conditions with which Canada's foreign policy-makers must always work in operating in the international system. R.J. Sutherland has termed them "invariants"—unchanging conditions, usually beyond the capacities of governments to mold to their own liking.[5] However, such factors might more properly be thought of as *relatively* invariant: although in the short term they are impervious to change, over the course of a number of generations, these invariant conditions may well shift.

Geographical Location

One of the most important factors that gives shape to the environment in which a foreign policy decision-maker must operate is an exceedingly obvious one: the country's geographic location. Geography determines a country's distance or proximity to great power rivalry and its "neighbourhood." Both will have a bearing on that country's foreign policy.

Strategic importance. For the first eight decades after Confederation, Canada's geographic location meant that it was physically remote from the centre of great power rivalry—the European continent. This geographic distance meant that until the end of the Second World War, Canadian governments were never confronted by the imposing security threats that constantly faced European states. Not since the War of 1812 has Canada had cause to fear a military attack by its neighbour to the south (even though it was not until 1931 that Defence Scheme No. 1, which planned for a war with the United States, was officially laid to rest[6]). It is true that Manifest Destiny[7] would keep many Americans in the nineteenth century dreaming of expansion. As Champ Clark, the Speaker-designate of the House of Representatives, maladroitly[8] put it in Congress in 1911: "I hope to see the day when the American flag will float over every square foot of the British North-American possessions clear to the North Pole."[9] No doubt many in the United States would have agreed with the *Philadelphia Public Ledger* when it asserted flamboyantly after Independence Day in 1853 that America was bounded on the "East by sunrise, West by sunset, North by Arctic Expeditions and South as Far as we darn please."[10] However, if the United States government did as it pleased to its south, it was singularly more cautious with its northern neighbour. If nothing else, an unchanging desire for good relations with Britain deterred United States administrations in the nineteenth century from pursuing the idea of trying to end the Canadian experiment by force.[11] Nor did any other major power have the capacity—or the inclination—to test the sphere of influence created by the Monroe Doctrine in 1823 by challenging the United States—or Britain, whose naval hegemony underwrote American claims to hemispheric domination throughout the nineteenth century.

Thus, when wars involving the great powers broke out, they were always physically distant affairs. They engaged Canadians emotionally, particularly when Britain was involved, and Canadians fought—and died—in these conflicts, as they did in the Boer War and the First World War. But they never threatened Canada directly. If Canada had any strategic importance to the great powers of this era, it was in the country's geographic remoteness from the European vortex of world politics. Canada's principal utility was as a supplier to Britain of men, materiel, and food secure from direct attack. "At present," Mackenzie King noted matter-of-factly in 1938, "the danger of attack upon Canada is minor in degree and second-hand in origin."[12]

The strategic importance of Canada, and the relative security afforded by its geographic isolation, would change dramatically with the outbreak of the Second World War. The end would come quickly: by the early summer of 1940, the threat that Canadians felt was palpable. The *Blitzkreig* had overrun all of western Europe in the late spring of 1940; the possibility of a successful Nazi invasion of England seemed very real; and, what was more, though President F.D. Roosevelt was openly sympathetic to the cause of Britain and its allies, the United States was committed to remaining officially neutral. One of the critical consequences of the Nazi victories in Europe for Canada was the significant shift that occurred in strategic thinking. A decade before, close military cooperation with the United States would have been unthinkable.[13] But in the year following the fall of western Europe, Canada and the United States had effected a consolidation of hemispheric defence. In August 1940, Roosevelt invited King to Ogdensburg, New York, where the two leaders issued a joint statement agreeing to the creation of a formal mechanism of joint defence between Canada and the United States, the Permanent Joint Board on Defence. This would be followed in April 1941 by the Hyde Park Declaration, which smoothed economic cooperation between Canada and the United States in war materiel.[14]

But the shifts in strategic importance would be more long-lasting, and more far-reaching. The sense of security encouraged by the distorting distances of Mercator's projection, and the relative strategic unimportance of the country would evaporate with changes in both the balance of power and military technology. With the emergence of the Soviet Union and the United States as the pre-eminent powers in the postwar international system, Canada's geostrategic position shifted dramatically—from being an ocean east (or west) of major-power confrontations to being directly sandwiched between the two superpowers. And advances in military technology—notably the invention of atomic weapons and the development of long-range delivery systems for these weapons—heralded a new-found strategic importance. Uranium, which had been just another one of Canada's many natural resources would, by 1945, be one of the most strategic of raw materials. In a world where security is dominated by uranium-based weaponry, a country with substantial uranium deposits and production is automatically strategically important. Likewise, advances in the technology of delivering these weapons would dramatically reduce the safety of distance and just as dramatically increase Canada's geostrategic importance. Long-range aircraft would be perfected during the war years, with the result that, by the 1940s, oceans afforded less military protection than they had in the past. By the late 1950s and early 1960s, physical distance would be diminished further by the invention—and subsequent deployment—of intercontinental ballistic missiles (ICBMs).

Since 1945, Canada has occupied what one military analyst has termed "the most vital air space in the world."[15] The government in Washington, not surprisingly, has regarded that air space as integral to the defence of the continental United States against a possible attack by the Soviet Union over the polar regions. In the decade following the war, Washington wanted to ensure that surveillance and interception systems against Soviet bombers were located as close to the Soviet Union (and as far away from the American industrial heartland) as possible. What the *Financial Post* referred to as an "Atomic Age Maginot Line"[16] of radar stations and jet-interceptor bases across the Canadian and American North was deemed the appropriate solution. Yet Canada had neither the resources nor the will to erect the kind of defence against the Soviet bomber threat that would satisfy American strategic planners. As Mackenzie King noted to his diary in 1946 after attending a military briefing on defence, "It became perfectly apparent, I think to all as we listened that Canada could simply not do what is necessary to protect itself. Our country would be a mere pawn in the world conflict."[17] Certainly neither King nor his successors were willing to dip very far into the Canadian treasury to finance such a project. At the same time, however, policy-makers in Ottawa were most concerned about the implications of American strategic planning for the maintenance of Canadian sovereignty in the Arctic. No one in Ottawa wanted a repetition of the kinds of problems that had been caused during the war by the stationing of American servicemen in the Canadian north.[18]

The option chosen by both Canadian and American military planners was joint cooperation in air defence. What had begun as wartime cooperation took a more institutionalized form in the years after the war as the Soviet Union rapidly developed not only the nuclear weapons that broke the American monopoly, but the means to deliver these weapons. The North American Air Defence Command (NORAD) agreement, signed in 1958, was the culmination of this evolution. NORAD continentalized air defence—in the sense that the territory of both the United States and Canada was considered one unit to be defended against an airborne attack, and the forces of each country were combined into one command to defend the continent should such an attack occur.[19] Even after the introduction of massive land-based ICBMs in the 1960s, NORAD remained integral to American conceptions of defence: land-based ICBMs are but one of three legs of the strategic triad (the other two being the so-called "air-breathing threat"[20] and submarine-launched ballistic missiles).

It is important to recognize that the argument here is not that "Geography dictates [NORAD]," as Norman Senior mistakenly put it nearly three decades ago.[21] Geography merely dictates that Canada is located physically between the two superpowers. Rather, it is politics that dictates the consequences of geographic location. First, superpower politics require Americans to consider Canadian territory important to their defence, and to seek to use this territory to create as much distance between the continental United States and the Soviet Union as possible. Second, politics—or, more correctly, the political preferences of Canadians and the decisions of their governments—explain the Canadian attachment to continental air defence. It should be remembered that most Canadians, not only after the war but also at present, either actively supported or acquiesced in the general alignment of their country with the United States in global affairs. But there can be little doubt that the vast majority of Canadians would not tolerate the kind of massive defence expenditures necessary to provide the United States with sufficient assurance of defence against attack by manned bombers. Nor would they tolerate other possible options: either doing nothing and watching as United States forces operated unilaterally in the north without Canadian permission, or specifically allowing the United States access to the north to undertake these defence tasks. In either case, Canadian sovereignty would be intolerably violated. NORAD avoids these extremes, and is thus a quintessentially *Canadian* solution. It provides Americans with the sense of security that their northern flank is being defended to their specifications and Canadians with an assurance that the United States will not violate Canadian sovereignty by undertaking American defence tasks unilaterally. It also provides an institutional bilateral mechanism for a Canadian voice in continental defence decisions, and therefore legitimizes Canadian participation in this unequal partnership. And, most importantly, it is a defence strategy that does not burden Ottawa's treasury as much as an all-Canadian detection and interception system. Because Canadians make up about one-tenth of the North American population, the United States has generally agreed that Canada should shoulder roughly that proportion of the financial costs of the system.

But what if Canadian support for continental air defence turned to opposition? The preferences of Canadians, it could be argued, would make no difference to how the United States views Canadian territory. Whether Canadians like it or not, Canada would still be perceived as important to American defence. More importantly, the American government would regard a Canadian withdrawal from continental air defence as a distinctly unfriendly act. Besides the negative strategic implications, there is also the problem that such a move could only be justified by the Canadian government in terms that would be insulting to the United States and cast what Americans would regard as aspersions on their intentions. And if the mood were to turn ugly, the United States would have little compunction about doing what would be necessary to secure the "glacis" to the north, even if it meant offending the sensibilities—and the sovereignty—of their northern neighbours. As Arnold Heeney, then Canadian ambassador in Washington, put it in August 1959, "it is inconceivable that the United States will allow its defensive arrangements to be frustrated by our refusal to co-operate...."[22] In this sense, geographic location imposes a considerable constraint on any Canadian government which wished to withdraw from continental air defence. As long as the United States government wants some form of northern air defence, Canadians have the choice of participating—or facing the unpalatable consequences of American retaliation.[23]

The best indication of the constraints that occupying strategically important territory impose on Canadian policy-makers is the case of the Strategic Defense Initiative, or, as it was quickly dubbed, Star Wars.[24] When President Ronald Reagan outlined his conception of an "astrodome defence" for the United States in March 1983, many Canadians, including government officials, were concerned about the implications for mutual deterrence and strategic stability. In 1981, the United States had pressed for—and received—permission to change the name of NORAD to the North American Aerospace Defence Command, an ominous signal to many analysts that Canada was being drawn into something more than air defence.[25] When the Progressive Conservative government of Brian Mulroney was invited to participate in Star Wars in the spring of 1985, the government was torn. The economic benefits of SDI contracts, such as jobs and the transfer of high technology, were alluring. But many officials in Ottawa feared that SDI, rather than rendering nuclear weapons obsolete, would instead heighten tensions between the two superpowers, spark a renewed arms race, and threaten the strategic balance. Moreover, large numbers of Canadians were expressing their opposition to the prospect of being associated with SDI. In the end, the government, reflecting what Sokolsky and Jockel have termed the widespread "skeptical agnosticism" of Canadians,[26] announced in September 1985 that it had chosen not to participate in the government-to-government research program.[27]

However, it can be argued that Canada's "polite no" to the Star Wars invitation in 1985 will not be the last word on this matter. The Mulroney government merely left the issue for some future cabinet to grapple with. While the more fantastic version of SDI did not survive the Reagan presidency, having been thoroughly discredited by a parade of skeptical scientists, work on a more limited version of ballistic missile defence (BMD) continues. And, as Douglas A. Ross has demonstrated, many of the ground-based BMD weapons systems under development by the United States Department of Defense would be most rationally placed on Canadian soil, a possibility explicitly admitted by Lieutenant-General (retired)

Daniel O. Graham, one of the more vocal American proponents of SDI, in 1985.[28] In short, it is unlikely that Canadian territory will decline in strategic importance with the advent of the next generation of weapons systems. Should Washington eventually ask Ottawa for permission to base systems now in development on Canadian soil, it is equally unlikely that the Canadian government would be able to get away with another "polite no."

Neighbourhood. Canada has four neighbours, but demography, culture, language, economic structure, and ideology have combined to make the United States a more important focal point of Canadian foreign policy than the Soviet Union, Greenland, or the tiny French *départements* of St. Pierre or Miquelon in the Gulf of St. Lawrence. While it is often claimed that Canada is an Arctic nation,[29] and thus has shared northern interests with Moscow and Nuuk, in fact Canadians have a distinctly southern orientation. Fully 90 per cent of the population lives in a thin and precarious band along the southern frontier of the country—as far as possible from Arctic reaches. That most live within 300 km of what Roger Swanson has called the cellophane border[30] with the United States creates an inexorably southern exposure to American culture, mass media, society, and economics. This susceptibility is encouraged by the fact that Americans and two-thirds of Canadians share a common language. More importantly, an overwhelming majority of anglophone and francophone Canadians alike share the liberal bourgeois values dominant throughout North America, a socio-political homogenization that transcends Canada's fundamental linguistic cleavage. Patterns of economic activity—in particular the degree of trade and investment flows between Canada and the United States—are other attributes which direct the attention of Canadians southward.

Such well-worn and perhaps obvious observations about the structure, nature, and location of Canadian society bear repeating if only to explain why the focus of foreign policy in Canada has always been fixed so firmly on the United States. This fixation has been a feature of British North American politics since the 1770s. But it has steadily intensified over the course of the twentieth century with the rise of the United States as the pre-eminent power in world politics, the powerful and global expansion of American culture and economic power, and the increasing integration of the North American economy since the Second World War.

These observations also underscore another attribute of Canada's neighbourhood: its essential loneliness. The other states contiguous to Canada are neighbours in name only. For most Canadians, the neighbourhood really consists of Canada and the United States alone. From a Canadian perspective, such a limited neighbourhood has both benefits and disadvantages. Unlike most other small powers located next to great powers, Canada has no other neighbours to offset the preponderance of the United States. To be sure, occasional efforts are advanced to make common cause with the southern neighbours of the United States, but while contacts with the states of Central and South America have increased dramatically since 1968, there are few significant commonalities of interest between Canadians and those living south of the Rio Grande. Likewise, efforts are frequently made to forge closer links with Canada's transpolar neighbours in Scandinavia,[31] but the demographic realities of Canadian society make such linkages both limited and symbolic. Such lonely splendour is not without its advantages, however. The limited number in the neighbourhood has meant that the United States has never had to use the same kind of divide-and-rule tactics against Canada that it employs with its southern neighbours, that the Soviet Union employs in Eastern Europe, or that China uses in Southeast Asia.

Economic Structure

Canadians have traditionally been wedded to the benefits of comparative advantage within the "North Atlantic Triangle":[32] exporting raw materials and agricultural produce, and importing manufactured goods, first from Britain directly and then from the United States via indirect investment in branch plants located in Canada. A basic feature of Canada's economic structure is that since the repeal of the Corn Laws in 1846, the Canadian colonies, and then the Canadian nation, have never been wholly self-sufficient.

Instead, Canada has been and continues to be dependent on foreign trade for its well-being. Almost a third of the country's Gross Domestic Product is generated by exports. Of the seven industrialized states which attend the Economic Summit, only the Federal Republic of Germany is more reliant on exports. "The necessity of marketing this great surplus of commodities must always be the principal concern of Canadian foreign policy," wrote F.R. Scott in 1932.[33] So it had been, and would be. For a small country heavily dependent on trade, Rodney deC. Grey declared in 1981, "foreign policy should, in major part, be trade relations policy."[34] But Canada's choice of trading partners also has important implications for foreign policy. Over the course of the twentieth century, and particularly in the postwar period, Canada's trade has become increasingly unbalanced, concentrated in but one market: the United States.[35] By the late 1930s, nearly one quarter of Canadian exports went to the United States; 40 per cent went to Britain. By the mid-1950s, fully 60 per cent of exports went to the United States; the British share had fallen dramatically to under 9 per cent. By 1970, just under 70 per cent of Canada's trade was with the United States; by 1985, that percentage had risen to over 75.[36] Thus, Canada is not only dependent on external trade for its prosperity, it has become increasingly dependent on a single market to sustain that prosperity.

What implications does this economic structure hold for the making of foreign policy in Canada? First, and most obviously, it will inexorably shape the political and security interests and objectives of the government in Ottawa. As Gerald Helleiner told a parliamentary committee on foreign policy in 1985, "The first priority for a country like Canada, so dependent on the stability and predictability of the international economic system, must surely be, overwhelmingly, the stability and order of the international system.... There can be no higher priority for Canadian foreign policy."[37] This interconnection between peace and economic growth has always been recognized by Canadian governments.[38] It is this feature of Canada's condition, perhaps more than any other, which explains why governments in Ottawa have historically been so concerned with the maintenance of global peace and the avoidance of systemic war.

Second, the increasing concentration of Canada's trade with the United States creates extreme vulnerability. The United States, like all states, will seek to defend and advance its interests and those of its citizens. But the pursuit of self-interest by that country has the capacity to inflict severe damage on the Canadian economy, as the ravages caused by the Smoot-Hawley tariff of 1930 demonstrated.[39] This American protectionism prompted both Mackenzie King and his successor, R.B. Bennett, to raise Canadian tariffs in retaliation. As a result, Canada's trade with the United States plummeted over the next three years, deepening the Depression and its effects on production, jobs, and prosperity. By 1933, Bennett's Conservative government, backed by the Liberal opposition, was responding to protectionism as previous governments had—and would again: it sought a trade agreement with the United States to blunt the effects of the border on Canadian prosperity.[40]

It is true that some American protectionist measures are not directed primarily against Canada. Although the largest trading partner of the United States, Canada accounts for merely 20 per cent of American trade flows; American policy-makers are, as a consequence, prone to subsume Canada in their efforts to encourage "fairer" trading practices by Western Europe and Japan. However, some policies embraced by the government in Washington are frequently aimed quite purposefully at Canada. In particular, Canadian policy objectives that damage American interests are likely to set in motion the processes of retaliatory action.

There are numerous examples of the willingness of the United States, and in particular the Congress, to defend their interests by imposing retaliatory, and often punitive, measures on Canadians. The case of border broadcasting in the 1970s is illustrative. In 1976, in order to promote the funding of Canadian television, the government of Pierre Trudeau introduced Bill C-58, a number of amendments to income tax legislation. One of the most controversial was a measure to make it impossible for Canadian firms advertising on American border television stations to deduct these expenses for income tax purposes. Following the enactment of this legislation, border television station owners in the United States saw their revenue from Canadian firms drop sharply. Naturally, they were quick to press their members of Congress for retaliatory action. An opportunity came in 1977, when the United States Senate was considering amendments to the United States Income Tax Act. One of the amendments was to disallow expenses incurred at foreign conventions. Because of the negative effects this would have had on the tourist industries of the Caribbean, Mexico, and Canada, a proposal was put forward to exempt these states. But senators from the states affected by the border broadcasting legislation successfully argued for retaliatory action against Canada. Between 1978 and 1980, when a solution was agreed upon, it is estimated that the ensuing loss to Canada's tourist and convention industry was $200 million; the estimated value of advertising diverted from American border stations to Canadian networks was $20 million.[41]

The softwood lumber case provides another example of American retaliation.[42] Canada's softwood lumber industry had experienced considerable success in the American market: by 1985, Canadian softwood products accounted for a third of the American market. The softwood lumber industry in the United States, hurt by Canadian imports, sought Washington's protection. It argued that Canadian competitiveness was actually the result of the stumpage fees charged by governments in Canada for timber. These fees, the industry argued, were so low that they amounted to an export subsidy; so in 1982 the industry sought relief by petitioning the United States Department of Commerce to impose a countervailing duty on softwood imports from Canada. That petition failed, but the American industry persisted. In May 1986, the U.S. Coalition for Fair Lumber Imports refiled their petition with the Commerce Department; the United States International Trade Commission subsequently found that the policies of the Canadian provinces did indeed injure the American lumber industry. The case then proceeded to the United States International Trade Administration for a determination as to whether the stumpage fees constituted a subsidy. Much to the chagrin of the government in Ottawa, ITA's interim ruling in October was that the Canadian policies amounted to an export subsidy of 15 per cent; a final determination was due on 30 December. At this juncture, the Canadian government, convinced that it was going to lose, caved in and negotiated a compromise: it offered to impose a voluntary export tax of 15 per cent if the American industry withdrew their petition asking for a 32 per cent countervailing duty.

In both these instances, and in the case of the shakes and shingles dispute that began in 1986,[43] Americans affected by Canadian trade have sought to protect their interests. Sometimes they used the protections afforded them under United States law to challenge Canadian policy and programs in American courts. In most cases, American objections hinge on the simple fact that there is such a marked divergence in social welfare programs between the two countries. Thus, the groundfish industry on the American east coast petitioned for countervailing duties on the grounds that Canada's Unemployment Insurance program constituted a subsidy. (In this case, the ITA declared that a total of fifty-four federal and provincial programs—but not unemployment insurance—constituted a subsidy, and slapped a countervailing duty on Canadian fish imports.[44]) On other occasions, as in the border broadcasting dispute or the Trudeau government's retreat on the National Energy Program in 1980 and 1981,[45] the United States will simply use its power to assert and protect American interests against what are commonly regarded as the "unfair" trading practices of others.

The acceleration of protectionism in the United States in the late 1970s and throughout the 1980s both limited Ottawa's freedom of action and created new imperatives for Canadian foreign policy-makers in dealing with Canada's only important market. Much of the impetus for the free trade agreement negotiated by the Mulroney government in 1986 and 1987 came from the willingness of Congress and the administration to impose the kind of penalties on Canada that, cumulatively at least, the Canadian economy could not sustain for long. Thus, the principal Canadian argument for the free trade agreement was necessity: the need to negotiate an arrangement with the United States that would provide secure access to the American market and bypass the kind of disruptive and punitive measures so willingly imposed on Canadian producers by protectionist-minded Americans.

The third consequence of Canada's economic sensitivity and vulnerability is that virtually all foreign policy issues become linked to Canadian-American relations. Decisions tend to be based on a calculation of the degree to which the issue—and the options being discussed—will impinge on the relationship with the United States. Policies on such diverse issues as human rights violations by the government of Indonesia, the acquisition of nuclear-powered submarines, the restoration of diplomatic relations with Iran, the renegotiation of Canadian loans to Sudan, or the Canadian position on truce supervision in Afghanistan, tend to be filtered through this Canadian-American lens. Such a calculus is hardly unique: all states must engage in it because the interests, power, and reach, of the United States are pervasive. As the Canadian ambassador to Washington, Charles Ritchie, noted of the American government to his diary in July 1963, "They are *everywhere*, into *everything*—a wedding in Nepal, a strike in British Guinea, the remotest Greek island, the farthest outpost of

Donegal, the banks of the Limpopo. All countries' private and domestic affairs are of interest to the Americans...."[46] But for Canada, the consequences of insensitivity to American concerns are greater than for any other state. As Prime Minister Lester Pearson stated in *Maclean's* magazine in July 1967, when explaining the Canadian position on the war in Vietnam:

> This is not the over-riding consideration in determining our own policy, of course, but we can't ignore the fact that a first result of any open breach with the United States over Vietnam, which their Government considered to be unfair or unfriendly, would be more critical examination by Washington of certain special aspects of our relationship from which we, as well as they, get benefit.... It is not a very comforting thought, but, in the economic sphere, when you have 60 per cent or so of your trade with one country, you are in a position of considerable economic dependence.[47]

Pearson's concern was not that a wrong move by Ottawa would bring about instant American retaliatory measures, crippling the Canadian economy. John W. Holmes has argued that the result would be more subtle: "Whether [Canadians] like it or not—and they do not—they are vulnerable to American displeasure. This displeasure is not likely to take the form of punitive action or crude reprisal; Canadians would feel it rather in the drying up of the good will which restrains the United States from exploiting the economic and military power it has to do Canada damage."[48]

It is little wonder, then, that Canadian officials frequently demonstrate considerable sensitivity to how Canada's foreign policy reactions or initiatives will be received in Washington. On numerous occasions, Canadian policy has been determined, not directly by the American government, but by Canadian assessments that a divergent policy on an issue would not be worth the damage it would likely do to Canadian-American relations. The case of the recognition of the People's Republic of China provides a useful example. For fully nineteen years after the proclamation of the PRC on 1 October 1949, Canada refused to recognize the revolutionary Communist government of Mao Zedong, formally recognizing instead the Kuomintang (Nationalist) government of Chiang Kai-shek on Taiwan as the legal government of all China. Why? Not because the Canadian government liked the KMT: virtually all Canadian officials had little sympathy for the Nationalist government, believing it to be inefficient, corrupt, and deserving of its eventual fate. Nor because the Canadians believed that the Communist victory in China was the result of a Moscow-directed plot for world domination: the roots of the Chinese revolution, it was commonly believed, lay in indigenous social and economic conditions. Nor because the Canadian government believed in the wisdom of American policy towards the PRC: Washington's attempt to keep Beijing isolated in international affairs was seen in Ottawa as both mistaken and exceedingly short-sighted. Nor because the Americans were constantly threatening Canada with economic retaliation to keep Ottawa in line: Washington in the 1950s may have had its share of those John Holmes called the "wild men" on Asian issues,[49] but they were not constantly threatening the Canadians. They had no need to: for all that Canadians would have preferred to recognize the PRC, they calculated that the Canadian stakes in the China issue did not warrant crossing the Americans on what was in the 1950s a very high-stakes issue in Washington.[50]

It should be noted that there is nothing automatic to this kind of calculus. There have been numerous occasions when the Canadian government decided that it was in Canada's interests to cross swords with the United States in public on issues of global policy and risk the negative consequences. John Diefenbaker did so during the Cuban missile crisis of 1962; so did Pierre Trudeau—on a number of issues ranging from the bombing of Hanoi and Haiphong in December 1972 to the invasion of Grenada by American forces in October 1983. Even governments which had come to office openly determined to improve relations between Canada and the United States found reason to criticize American foreign policy. In April 1965, Pearson spoke out at Temple University on the issue of Vietnam, a case discussed in more detail in chapter 6. Likewise, from his selection as leader of the Progressive Conservative party in June 1983 to his appointment as prime minister in September 1984, Brian Mulroney consistently promised that as prime minister he would always give the United States the "benefit of the doubt," and would be far less critical of Washington's global policy initiatives than the Liberals under Trudeau. In fact, after 1984, the Mulroney government sought to distance itself from the Reagan administration on a number of foreign policy issues: Washington's policies towards the Sandinista government of Nicaragua, particularly the support of the *contras* and the economic sanctions imposed by the United States; the American interpretation of the wording of the Anti-Ballistic Missile (ABM) Treaty of 1972; the militarization of outer space; the Reagan administration's view of the Strategic Arms Limitation Treaty (SALT II); the American withdrawal from the United Nations Educational, Scientific and Cultural Organization (UNESCO); and the remnants of Reagan's policy of "constructive engagement" with South Africa still being pursued after 1985.[51]

However, on rare occasions the Canadian government has decided to support publicly an American global policy initiative with which it does not wholeheartedly agree. Perhaps the best example of this was the response of the Mulroney government to the United States bombing of a number of targets in Libya in April 1986. The American raid was carried out in response to a number of terrorist incidents in Europe which were alleged to have been supported by Libya's leader, Muammar al-Qaddafi. Despite criticism in the House of Commons from both the Liberals and the New Democrats about the impropriety of the attack, the Mulroney government came out solidly behind the American action. Both the prime minister and Erik Neilsen, the minister of national defence, argued that they had accepted the justifications offered by the Reagan administration for the raid, and considered the military attack an appropriate response.[52] The concerns apparent in official Ottawa about the use of force by one of the superpowers against a smaller power were, however, kept well hidden. For in the week that Reagan authorized the strike against Libya, the Finance Committee of the United States Senate was considering whether to approve the start of the Canada-United States free trade negotiations. On 11 April, a number of senators had quite unexpectedly indicated their willingness to deny approval for the negotiations, and indeed formalized their intention by introducing a motion vetoing the proposal on 16 April. The vote on this veto was delayed three times while frantic behind-the-scenes negotiations were conducted between the White House and Capitol Hill to secure a working majority on the committee. When the vote finally came on 23 April, the veto failed to get a majority. But it was close: the senators split 10-10 on whether to veto the negotiations, and the administration had to agree to a compromise in return for their support.[53] Given the timing of the attack on Libya, the Canadian government decided that prudence dictated overt support for the strike: not because this would gain Canada favours in Washington, but because if Canada had been critical of, or hesitant about, the attack, it might have been noticed by the senators and swayed their votes on the free trade issue.

Alignments and Alliances

Canadian foreign policy-makers are also constrained and impelled by Canada's membership in the western alliance; no government can avoid coping with the obligations that go with the benefits obtained from alliance membership.[54] At first blush, it may seem odd to consider this a relative invariant in Canadian foreign policy. The government in Ottawa could, by giving one year's notice, renounce Canadian attachment to the terms of the North Atlantic Treaty signed in April 1949, or withdraw from the North Atlantic Treaty Organization (NATO) while remaining a signatory to the Treaty itself (as the French government of Charles de Gaulle did in 1966).[55] However, while the formal language of the treaty makes the option of withdrawal appear simple, it is in fact exceedingly difficult to opt out of a functioning alliance,[56] blithe assertions to the contrary by advocates of neutrality like Gwynne Dyer notwithstanding.[57] If other members of the alliance still attach value to the institution, they will not want the overall strength of the collective to diminish by the departure of any one member, however small. Nor will they wish to encourage a bandwagon effect by doing nothing when the first one defects. Each member of the alliance has an interest in making it as costly as possible for one of their number to withdraw.

It is therefore not surprising that in 1966, the other alliance members responded negatively to the French withdrawal from NATO and the forced removal of NATO headquarters from Paris to Brussels. But France was, and remains, in a most unusual position within the western alliance, and thus protected from punitive reactions. It has considerable military power, including nuclear weapons and a large geographic reach (as persistent French intervention in west Africa amply demonstrates). And, for all of the rhetoric claiming that the *force de frappe* is designed to defend France against any and all enemies, the French nuclear arsenal is, in fact, aimed squarely at the Soviet Union. But unlike Josip Broz Tito, who pulled Yugoslavia out of the Soviet orbit in 1948 and embraced non-alignment, de Gaulle never toyed with such concepts. However much he wished to revive the past grandeur of France as a global power through a policy of *indépendentisme*, it was to be done while remaining firmly aligned as part of the North Atlantic alliance. This too helped to soften the reaction from the other NATO allies. And perhaps most importantly, because of its economic power, France is critical to the functioning of the European Communities specifically and the western coalition generally, and therefore limits both the capacity and the willingness of other western Europeans to inflict punishment.

States in a less powerful position than France should draw lessons from the French withdrawal from NATO with care. A more sobering case is that of New Zealand in the mid-1980s. The Labour Party under David Lange had promised to make New Zealand nuclear-free: after winning the general elections of July 1984, Lange modestly reoriented the country's foreign and defence policy by refusing ships armed with nuclear weapons entry into its ports, including those of its ANZUS (Australia-New Zealand-United States) ally, the United States. The reaction from Washington was harsh and punitive: the United States has formally withdrawn all intelligence and military cooperation, no longer consults with Wellington on defence matters, has suspended its security guarantee to New Zealand, and has symbolically demoted the country from an ally to merely a friend.[58] New Zealand's fate is more indicative of what a state smaller than France may expect. Moreover, if such was the reaction to a country with virtually no intrinsic strategic value, one can easily imagine what costs would be imposed on another defecting ally of greater strategic importance. Indeed, it was for this reason that the United States reacted so strongly: to deter other American allies from catching the "Kiwi disease," as officials in Washington quickly dubbed it. Other states engaging in behaviour that is perceived as damaging to the security of the alliance can generally expect no kinder treatment. Because breaking with a functioning alliance is always made costly by the other members, membership becomes a relative invariant, particularly for a smaller and less powerful member of the group.

Thus, for Canada, the NATO alliance acts as an invariant in much the same way as the aerospace defence agreement with the United States. At present, the vast majority of Canadians firmly support membership in NATO,[59] just as they support involvement in NORAD. Given this, we cannot conclude that Canada is a member of NATO as a result of coercion. But were Canadians to change their minds and seek to withdraw, the dynamics of compulsion would inevitably emerge. As long as other, more powerful, states see Canada as strategically important and wish Canadian participation, the preferences of Canadians themselves will matter little. If the Canadian government tried to alter radically its involvement in the alliance, such as withdrawing Canadian troops stationed in Europe, much less Canada's overall alignment in international politics, it is highly likely that Canada's alliance partners would make sure that neutrality was an exceedingly costly option. They would be less than rational to do otherwise. First, as Denis Brogan put it flatly in 1953, "A uranium producing country cannot be neutral."[60] Second, Canada's territory, its airspace, and its territorial waters are integral to Atlantic security, and therefore as important to Europeans as to Americans. Losing this geography to the uncertainties of neutralism would be far too costly for allies on either side of the Atlantic to embrace such an option with equanimity. Third, allowing Canada to withdraw without cost would inexorably encourage other defections among other small states in the alliance. Finally, the European members of the alliance have an interest in encouraging the maintenance of the Atlantic conception of defence by keeping both North American states within NATO's bosom. Of course, if the United States did decide to retreat from Europe into a "Fortress America" defence posture, that decision would not in any way depend on Canada's stance, but there is a symbolic importance in maintaining the involvement of all North America.

How does this relative invariant affect Canadian foreign policy? One must begin with the recognition that an alliance is essentially a bargain struck between states. In return for the security the collective provides that would be too costly or simply impossible to attain on its own, each state agrees to forego the kind of independence of action that is possible outside the strictures of alignment. Each state also agrees to contribute an appropriate portion of its wealth and energies to the collective enterprise.[61] The general contours of this bargain have two broad effects on an alliance member's foreign policy.

First, it means that on numerous international issues, an ally is deprived of the luxury of independence of action, but must coordinate its policy with the other members of the alliance. While NATO does not gag its members and force them to speak with a single voice, there is nonetheless a high premium placed on alliance unity, particularly on issues deemed to be of central importance to the allies as a collective. That "unity" is achieved by consultation, through bilateral negotiations and by using the numerous organs and institutions of the alliance. In this respect, it must be noted that policy "coordination" will always be a function of a state's power and status within an alliance. The United States, as alliance leader, has occasionally demonstrated its willingness to define alliance policy by acting unilaterally, and then using the issue of unity to prod its NATO partners to follow its lead. By contrast, smaller states, such as Canada or Belgium, could not expect to "set" policy for the alliance in such a manner.

Second, all members of the alliance will be expected to contribute in some concrete manner to the collective enterprise, usually in the form of armed forces, military bases, and weapons systems. This creates an imperative that no government can ignore, and drives much of Canadian policy on the maintenance of an inventory of weapons systems, such as main battle tanks or artillery systems, that would make little sense for the defence of Canada alone, outside the alliance context. To be sure, the standard that is commonly used to measure these contributions to the alliance—an aggregate of the percentage of Gross National Product allocated to defence—is a kind of "fun with numbers" approach to defence spending. For example, to say that a state spends four per cent of its GNP on defence is to say very little about whether the defence that can be bought with that amount (as opposed to six, nine, or two per cent) will be "enough" to defend that state. In times of peace, one never really knows how much is enough; only by fighting a war can a state ever know whether what it devotes to defence spending is sufficient to achieve its objectives. But for all the arbitrariness of the measure itself in peacetime, it *is* an important standard in an alliance context, if only because its use is so pervasive. Thus, when Canada is shown to be spending 2.1 per cent of its GNP on defence, and perennially ranking second-last in the alliance (the usual rhetorical device of critics is to remind Canadians that only the tiny principality of Luxembourg spends less of its wealth on national defence[62]), it is an important issue because of its impact on allied perceptions of Canada, and therefore on Ottawa's influence and status in alliance circles.

Capability

Finally, Canada's foreign policy-makers are bounded by the parameters of limited capability. They are ultimately constrained by the relative weakness of Canada's capabilities compared to others in the international system. Capabilities usually embrace a variety of attributes. Hans Morgenthau, whose realist theory has informed a generation of students of international politics in the postwar period, posits the following: natural resources (including food and raw materials), industrial capacity, military preparedness, and population, among others.[63] Klaus Knorr focusses on both the military and the economic bases of national power.[64] Michael Handel's measurement of a state's capabilities include population, area, Gross National Product (both absolute and per capita), size of armed forces, military expenditures, and reserves of petroleum, gas, coal, and uranium.[65]

Although it occupies more land than any other state in the international system except the Soviet Union, Canada has less capability in other areas than many states. While it is bounteously endowed with natural resources, Canada's population is, at 26 million, comparatively small. Its industrial capacity is limited and specialized. The economy as a whole is highly dependent on international intercourse and highly sensitive to economic changes outside Canada's borders. The Canadian Armed Forces are small—80,000—both relatively and absolutely, and, for all of the major acquisitions of the last decade, are not well equipped. As we will see below, this relative weakness narrows the range of choice and limits the scope of action. Not only does lack of capacity shape the Canadian government's foreign (and domestic) objectives; it also limits the tools of statecraft available to policy-makers to achieve their objectives—or to rebuff the importunities of other states in the international system.

CONCLUSION: INVARIANTS AND PARAMETER-SETTING

The conditions outlined above can be considered invariants in the sense that they are impervious to short-term change by even the most determined or ambitious government in Ottawa. No one can change Canada's geographic location, and hence no Canadian government can avoid the geostrategic consequences of geography. Only when the balance of power shifts, and global rivalry between the United States and the Soviet Union is replaced by the rivalry of another set of units may Canadian territory cease to have such strategic significance. Similarly, governments in Ottawa may tinker with Canada's economic structure, but the constraints of Canadian federalism, the pervasiveness of Canadian-American economic linkages, and the nature of representative government all preclude ambitious restructuring that would alleviate Canadian dependence on and sensitivity to the global economy. Likewise, no government in Ottawa is able to change the fundaments of Canada's national capabilities: what changes there will be in the "elements of national power" will come marginally, incrementally, and over the span of generations.

Thus, Canada's foreign policy objectives, and the means used to attain these goals, will inexorably be shaped by the unyielding constraints and imperatives imposed by geography, economic structure, alignment, and the capabilities of the country. Such conditions set stringent limits of what the government can do in foreign policy; they will frequently define what it must do; and more often than not they dictate how it may or must be done. However, these invariants serve as the parameters of decision—constraints, imperatives, and opportunities to be grappled with; the invariants themselves do not explain the government's ability or inability to achieve foreign policy goals, or its capacity or incapacity to defend Canadian interests. Such ability is determined not by Canada's attributes, but by its power. It is to the contentious issue of Canada's power in international politics that we now turn.

NOTES

1   Canada, Secretary of State for External Affairs, *Foreign Policy for Canadians* (Ottawa: Information Canada, 1970), main booklet, 9.

2   "Some principles of Canadian foreign policy," in Lester B. Pearson, *Words and Occasions* (Toronto: University of Toronto Press, 1970), 68.

3   Quoted in James Eayrs, *The Art of the Possible: Government and Foreign Policy in Canada* (Toronto: University of Toronto Press, 1961), 40*fn*.

4   Hedley Bull, *The Anarchical Society: A Study of Order in World Politics* (New York: Columbia University Press, 1977).

5   R.J. Sutherland, "Canada's long term strategic situation," *International Journal* 17 (Summer 1962), 199-201.

6   The story of Defence Scheme No. 1, formulated by the Director of Military Operations and Intelligence in the Department of National Defence in 1921, is recounted in James Eayrs, *In Defence of Canada*, vol. 1: *From the Great War to the Great Depression* (Toronto: University of Toronto Press, 1964), 70-78. "Its central assumption, on which all military planning was based," wrote Eayrs, "held that the principal external threat to the security of Canada lay in the possibility of armed invasion by the forces of the United States." Such an assumption, it should be noted, was not at all shared by senior officers in DND, and the Scheme was, Eayrs estimates, probably never read by a Canadian prime minister. It was officially cancelled in May 1931; in October 1933, for good measure, commanding officers were ordered to burn their copies of the Scheme and all documentation related to it.

7   It was America's manifest destiny, John O'Sullivan wrote in 1844, "to overspread the continent allotted by Providence for the free development of our multiplying millions." Quoted in Lawrence Martin, *The Presidents and the Prime Ministers—Washington and Ottawa Face to Face: The Myth of Bilateral Bliss, 1867-1982* (Markham, Ont.: Paperjacks, 1983), 24.

8 With the election campaign that was underway in Canada at the time over reciprocity with the United States, it was hardly an ideal or politic time to remind Canadian voters of this penchant for expansionism.

9 Quoted in J.L. Granatstein, "Free trade between Canada and the United States: the issue that will not go away," in Royal Commission on the Economic Union and Development Prospects for Canada (Macdonald Commission), *Collected Research Studies*, vol. 29: *The Politics of Canada's Economic Relationship with the United States*, Denis Stairs and Gilbert R. Winham, eds. (Toronto: University of Toronto Press, 1985), 24.

10 Quoted in Charles W. Kegley and Eugene R. Wittkopf, *American Foreign Policy: Pattern and Process* (New York: St. Martin's Press, 1979), 32.

11 To be sure, such a desire for good relations was reciprocated by the government in London, and on occasion this led to a willingness on the part of the British government to subordinate local Canadian concerns to the broader interest in the maintenance of good relations with the United States. The Alaska Boundary dispute, and the award of 1903, was one such case; it is discussed in chapter 3.

12 Quoted in James Eayrs, "The foreign policy of Canada," in Joseph E. Black and Kenneth W. Thompson, eds., *Foreign Policies in a World of Change* (New York: Harper and Row, 1963), 675.

13 When it had been proposed in 1927 that Canada increase its defence cooperation with the United States by dispatching a military attaché to Washington, Prime Minister Mackenzie King had dismissed it as "damn nonsense." C.P. Stacey, *Canada and the Age of Conflict*, vol. 2: *1921-1948: The Mackenzie King Era* (Toronto: University of Toronto Press, 1981), vol. 2, 226.

14 For a survey of these important agreements, see *ibid.*, 311-17.

15 Quoted in Stephen Clarkson, *Canada and the Reagan Challenge* (Toronto: Canadian Institute for Economic Policy, 1982), 251.

16 Joseph T. Jockel, *No Boundaries Upstairs: Canada, the United States and the Origins of North American Air Defence, 1945-1958* (Vancouver: University of British Columbia Press, 1987), 24.

17 Quoted in *ibid.*, 25.

18 For a discussion, see J.L. Granatstein, "A fit of absence of mind: Canada's national interest in the north to 1968," in E.J. Dosman, ed., *The Arctic in Question* (Toronto: Oxford University Press, 1976), 20-22.

19 For an account of NORAD's evolution, see Jockel, *No Boundaries Upstairs*; also Jon B. McLin, *Canada's Changing Defense Policy, 1957-1963: The Problems of a Middle Power in Alliance* (Toronto: Copp Clark Publishing Co., 1967), ch. 3.

20 Before the development of the cruise missile in the 1970s, manned bombers constituted one of the three legs of the triad. Now, however, one must include not only long-range bombers, which will still try to penetrate enemy territory and drop bombs, but also aircraft which will "stand off" at a distance, and release air-launched cruise missiles against the enemy. Both bombers and cruise missiles are propelled by "air-breathing" jet engines.

21 C. Norman Senior, "Some political and economic aspects of the unequal partnership between Canada and the U.S. in matters of defence," *Western*

Political Quarterly 13 (September 1960), supplement, 72, quoted in John W. Warnock, *Partner to Behemoth: The Military Policy of a Satellite Canada* (Toronto: New Press, 1970), 136.

22 Quoted in David Cox, "Canada and NORAD, 1958-1978: a cautionary retrospective," *Aurora Papers* 1 (Winter 1985), 43.

23 Michael Tucker, *Canadian Foreign Policy: Contemporary Issues and Themes* (Toronto: McGraw-Hill Ryerson, 1980), 149-50; Clarkson, *Canada and the Reagan Challenge*, 251-58.

24 In its most lavish, if totally unbelievable, version, the Strategic Defense Initiative was a space-based and ground-based defence system which was intended to provide an absolute defence against nuclear attack. SDI components would identify ICBMs as they left their silos; computers would then direct the fire of high-technology weapons systems such as hunter-killer satellites, kinetic kill vehicles, particle beam accelerators, lasers, and electromagnetic rail guns to destroy ICBMs and their nuclear warheads as they passed through the various phases of their flight to their target. In the minds of the proponents of this scheme, it was theoretically possible to track and destroy every independently-targeted warhead in every bus of every ballistic missile launched in a strike against the United States, together with every manned bomber, every cruise missile launched from land, sea, and air, and every depressed-trajectory missile fired from submarines offshore. President Reagan believed that such a fantastic scheme would render nuclear weapons obsolete.

25 Douglas A. Ross, "American nuclear revisionism, Canadian strategic interests and the renewal of NORAD," *Behind the Headlines* 39 (April 1982).

26 J.J. Sokolsky and J.T. Jockel, "Canada and the future of strategic defense," in Steven W. Guerrier and Wayne C. Thompson, eds., *Perspectives on Strategic Defense* (Boulder: Westview Press, 1987), 187.

27 Joel J. Sokolsky, "Changing strategies, technologies and organization: the continuing debate on NORAD and the Strategic Defense Initiative," *Canadian Journal of Political Science* 19 (December 1986), 751-74; also see G.R. Lindsey et al., *Aerospace Defence: Canada's Future Role*, Wellesley Papers 9 (Toronto: Canadian Institute of International Affairs, 1985).

28 SDI was in large part based on Graham's "high frontier" defence scheme of space-based weapons systems. It should be noted that General Robert Herres, the commander-in-chief of NORAD, when he testified before a House of Commons committee, was at pains to stress that Canadian participation in NORAD posed no special risks of involvement in SDI in the future. Douglas A. Ross, "SDI and Canadian-American relations: managing strategic doctrinal incompatabilities," in Lauren McKinsey and Kim Richard Nossal, eds., *America's Alliances and Canadian-American Relations* (Toronto: Summerhill Press, 1988).

29 As the Mulroney government's green paper on foreign policy in 1985 put it, "we are an Arctic nation. The North holds a distinct place in our nationhood and sense of identity. We view it as special, and ourselves as special because of it." Secretary of State for External Affairs, *Competitiveness and Security: Directions for Canada's International Relations* (Ottawa: Supply and Services Canada, 1985), 1.

30 Quoted in James Eayrs, "The cellophane border: reflections on our two realities," *The Canadian*, 22 May 1976, 4.

31 See, for example, the proposals in Franklyn Griffiths, "A northern foreign policy," *Wellesley Papers* 7 (1979).

32 For a full discussion of Canada's early economic relationships with Britain and the United States, see John Bartlet Brebner, *North Atlantic Triangle: The Interplay of Canada, the United States and Great Britain* (New York: Columbia University Press, 1945; reprinted Toronto: McClelland and Stewart, 1966).

33 F.R. Scott, "The permanent bases of Canadian foreign policy," *Foreign Affairs* 10 (1932), 627.

34 Quoted in Richard G. Lipsey, "Canada and the United States: the economic dimension," in Charles F. Doran and John H. Sigler, eds., *Canada and the United States: Enduring Friendship, Persistent Stress* (Englewood Cliffs, NJ: Prentice-Hall, 1985), 81.

35 Granatstein, "Free trade," 43.

36 *Ibid.*; also Brian W. Tomlin and Maureen Appel Molot, "Talking trade: perils of the North American option," in Tomlin and Molot, eds., *Canada Among Nations—1986: Talking Trade* (Toronto: Lorimer, 1987), 11.

37 Cited in Canada, Parliament, Special Joint Committee of the Senate and of the House of Commons on Canada's International Relations, *Independence and Internationalism* (Ottawa: June 1986), 12.

38 More recently, it was to be underscored by the Mulroney government in its Green Paper on foreign policy, tellingly entitled *Competitiveness and Security* to highlight the interconnection between the economic and political spheres.

39 The measure, introduced into the United States Congress by Senator Reed Smoot and Representative Willis Hawley even before the stock market crash on 1929, had been signed into law by President Herbert Hoover in June 1930. It provided for massive increases in the tariffs imposed by the United States on imported goods. Stacey, *Age of Conflict*, vol. 2, 126-29; also Peter Kasurak, "American foreign policy officials and Canada, 1927-1941: a look through bureaucratic glasses," *International Journal* 32 (Summer 1977), 544-58.

40 In the 1880s, for example, the idea of a customs union was debated in Canada, but it was coldly received by the Secretary of State in Washington, who bluntly declared: "But I am opposed, teetotally opposed, to giving Canadians the sentimental satisfaction of waving the British flag, paying British taxes, and enjoying the actual cash remuneration of American markets. They cannot have both at the same time." Quoted in Granatstein, "Free trade," 18.

41 Donald K. Alper and Robert L. Monahan, "Bill C-58 and the American Congress: the politics of retaliation," *Canadian Public Policy* 4 (Spring 1979), 184-95; and Isaiah A. Litvak and Christopher J. Maule, "Bill C-58 and the regulation of periodicals in Canada," *International Journal* 36 (Winter 1980-81), esp. 89.

42 The following discussion is drawn from David Leyton-Brown, "The political economy of Canada-U.S. relations," in Tomlin and Molot, eds., *Canada Among Nations—1986*, 158-61.

43 Canadian red cedar shakes and shingles, used in roofs and siding, dominated the American market. In this case, producers in the United States used section 201 of the United States Trade Act for relief. Section 201 allows the United States to impose retaliatory duties on imports which show disruptive or injurious increases. This case is surveyed by Leyton-Brown, "Canada-U.S. relations," 161-62.

44 *Ibid.*, 162-63.

45 The often heavy-handed, if eventually successful, efforts of the Reagan administration to prod the Trudeau government into abandoning many of its plans to "Canadianize" the oil industry are traced in Clarkson, *Canada and the Reagan Challenge*, 23-49.

46 Charles Ritchie, *Storm Signals: More Undiplomatic Diaries, 1962-1971* (Toronto: Macmillan, 1983), 53.

47 Quoted in John W. Holmes, *The Better Part of Valour: Essays on Canadian Diplomacy* (Toronto: McClelland and Stewart, 1970), 175.

48 *Ibid.*, 177-78.

49 John W. Holmes, *The Shaping of Peace: Canada and the Search for World Order, 1943-1957*, vol. 2 (Toronto: University of Toronto Press, 1982), 202.

50 For discussions of the China issue, see *ibid.*; also John W. Holmes, "Canada and China: the dilemmas of a minor power," in A.M. Halpern, ed., *Policies Towards China: Views from Six Continents* (New York: McGraw-Hill, 1965).

51 Adam Bromke and Kim Richard Nossal, "A turning point in U.S.-Canadian relations," *Foreign Affairs* 66 (Fall 1987), 164-67.

52 *International Canada* (April and May 1986), 7-9.

53 Thus, for example, Senator Robert Packwood of Oregon, the chairman of the committee, noted that after the administration's promises to expand the list of items open to negotiation, "There is not a fish that swims, a crop grown, or a widget that is made that is not going to be subject to negotiations." Quoted in Michael D. Henderson, "The negotiations: power, will and progress," in Michael D. Henderson, ed., *The Future on the Table: Canada and the Free Trade Issue* (Toronto: Masterpress, 1987), 154.

54 Sutherland termed this invariant "natural alliances and alignments," suggesting that "Canada's strongest natural alignment is with the United States," and that the "second natural affinity" is with western Europe, particularly Britain and France.

55 Thus, what is usually discussed as "Canada's membership in NATO" in fact involves two rather different issues. Technically, withdrawing from NATO only would mean that Canadians would no longer participate in the work of the various institutions of the alliance; and Canadian troops and military equipment would no longer be stationed in Europe under NATO auspices. However, if one of the states signatory to the North Atlantic Treaty were to be attacked, the legal obligation to aid in the collective defence of that member would still remain. By contrast, withdrawing as a signatory to the Treaty itself would mean a renunciation of that legal obligation as well as an end to all military cooperation.

56 As opposed to an alliance whose members, and the alliance leader in particular, are generally disposed to disband. Thus the Central Treaty Organization

(CENTO) quietly slid into moribundity in the early 1960s after a revolution in Iraq. Likewise, following the American withdrawal from Vietnam, the Southeast Asia Treaty Organization (SEATO) was disbanded without much rancor in the late 1970s.

57 In the mid-1980s, Gwynne Dyer presented the case for neutrality in a three- part television series, *In Defence of Canada*, and in a film directed by Tina Viljoen and narrated by Dyer, *Harder Than It Looks*.

58 Henry S. Albinski, "The ANZUS alliance under stress: regional and transregional implications," in McKinsey and Nossal, eds., *America's Alliances*, for a discussion of the New Zealand case.

59 Public opinion polls consistently show high support for membership in NATO: 85 per cent in 1986, 90 per cent in 1987. David Cox and Mary Taylor, eds., *A Guide to Canadian Policies on Arms Control, Disarmament, Defence and Conflict Resolution, 1985-86* (Ottawa: Canadian Institute for International Peace and Security, 1986), 281, and the *Guide* for 1986- 87, 262.

60 Quoted in John W. Holmes, "Most safely in the middle," *International Journal* 39 (Spring 1984), 386.

61 For discussions of alliance dynamics, see Ole Holsti, P. Terrence Hopmann and John D. Sullivan, eds., *Unity and Disintegration in International Alliances* (New York: Wiley, 1973); and Stephen M. Walt, *The Origins of Alliances* (Ithaca: Cornell University Press, 1987), ch. 1-2.

62 See, for example, the acerbic comments of Joseph J. Jockel and Joel J. Sokolsky, *Canada and Collective Security: Odd Man Out*, The Washington Papers 121 (New York: Praeger, 1986), 4.

63 Hans Morgenthau, *Politics Among Nations: The Struggle for Power and Peace*, 5th ed. (New York: Alfred A. Knopf, 1973), ch. 9.

64 Klaus Knorr, *The Power of Nations: The Political Economy of International Relations* (New York: Basic Books, 1975).

65 Michael Handel, *Weak States in the International System* (London: Frank Cass, 1981), 25; compare the approach of Ray S. Cline, *World Power Assessment 1977* (Boulder: Westview Press, 1977), 34.

CHAPTER THREE

Power and Foreign Policy

INTRODUCTION

Power occupies a central place in theorizing about foreign policy, if only because no state in the international community can avoid dealing with power—its own, and that of others. Power, as Hans J. Morgenthau succinctly put it, is the means to a nation's end, for with power comes control, and with control comes the capacity to achieve political goals.[1]

Power has been no less a preoccupation in the practice of Canadian statecraft, and the literature on Canadian foreign policy. However, as I will argue in this chapter, there has been a particularly political bent to the debate that has obscured the linkage between means and ends identified by Morgenthau. This chapter examines the contending images of Canada's power as they have developed over the course of this century, and concludes that these images do not in fact tell us much about Canadian power in international politics. It then suggests a more fruitful approach. Drawing on the writings of power analysts like David A. Baldwin,[2] it re-examines Canada's power and the techniques that the Canadian government can usefully use to advance and maintain its interests in the international sphere.

IMAGES OF CANADA'S POWER

Three contending conceptions of Canadian power in the international system compete for dominance in the literature—and the public debate—on foreign policy in Canada. For the last four decades, the dominant image has been of Canada as a "middle power." However, the primacy of the middle-power tradition has not been unchallenged. Alternative notions of

Canada as a penetrated satellite, and as a great or "principal" power, have developed largely in response to the middle-power image.

Canada as Middle Power

In the interwar years, the emphasis of Canadian foreign policy tended to be on securing recognition from the international community of what was commonly referred to as Canada's "independent personality" in world politics—a sovereign state independent of Britain and the Empire of which it had at one point been so integral a part. This manifested itself primarily in demands for separate representation at the Paris peace conference after the First World War, for separate admission to the League of Nations, and for the ability to send Canadian diplomatic representatives abroad. As a result of this focus on recognition of independence, little sustained thought was given to the question of Canada's power in the international system. Judging from the historical evidence, at least, Canadian officials in the interwar period implicitly accepted the division of the international system into a simple dichotomous hierarchy. On top were the "great powers"; on the bottom were all other states, lumped together into what German scholars in the 1930s referred to as the *Nichtgrossmachten*—the non-great powers. For example, Loring Christie, an official in the Department of External Affairs, had no delusions about Canada's power. During the Ethiopian crisis of 1935, he wrote bluntly that "if the Great Powers start, you start; if they don't, you don't; where they go, you go; when they stop, you stop.... The theory of our having a voice and control is eyewash."[3]

To be sure, Canadian officials were not indifferent or insensitive to the question of relative status *within* the ranks of the smaller powers. For example, in the discussions leading up to the peace conference in 1918, there was strong opposition, particularly in the United States, to having Canada and the other dominions given separate representation from Britain. It was argued that since they were British dominions, this would be like giving Britain additional votes. The proposed exclusion did not sit well with any of the prime ministers, provoking inevitable, if infelicitous, comparisons between their dominions and powers they considered distinctly dimmer lights in the interstate firmament. W.M. Hughes of Australia was indignant at the prospect that despite all of the men and treasure devoted to four years of fighting the war in western Europe, his country was not to be given representation in the peace negotiations, while Sweden and Belgium were. W.F. Massey complained bitterly about New Zealand being placed in the same class of states as "Cuba, Honduras, Guatemala, Hayti, &c." Prime Minister Robert Borden noted that "It is hardly to be anticipated that Canadians will consider that their country is suitably recognized by being placed on an equality with Siam and Hedjaz."[4]

Concerns also manifested themselves in the issue of the status of Canada's diplomatic representatives abroad. In September 1919, for example, Christie objected to the proposal to accord Canada's newly-appointed representative to Washington with a diplomatic rank below that of ambassador.[5] "To rank him as Minister Resident or Chargé d'Affaires," he wrote, "would be to rank him below the agents of many comparatively insignificant Powers."[6]

Canada's role in the Second World War served to catalyze Canadian thinking about the country's position in the international hierarchy. The concerns brought about by participation in that war were similar to those engendered by the First World War. The Canadian government was no longer concerned about international recognition as an independent sovereign state; rather, Ottawa wanted the great powers to recognize its war effort—a sizeable one for a state with a small population and limited resources—by giving Canada a seat in the decision-making councils of the alliance. In an eerie replay of Borden's complaints a generation earlier, King pressed the Canadian case: "You will, I am sure, appreciate how difficult it would be for Canada," he wrote to Winston Churchill, the British prime minister, "after enlisting nearly one million persons in her armed forces and trebling her national debt in order to assist in restoring peace, to accept a position of parity ... with the Dominican Republic or El Salvador."[7]

Britain and the United States initially rebuffed the Canadians with the same arguments that the French had used at the peace conference after the First World War: if countries like Canada were given a seat at the table, other allies would also claim representation, thereby making decision-making for the war effort cumbersome. In response, officials in Ottawa formulated the so-called "functional" principle of representation. Functionalism asserted that in those areas where a smaller state had both interest and expertise (in Canada's case, food or raw materials), it should be regarded as a major power, and given the right to be represented on the decision-making bodies in those areas. The limited acceptance of this principle by the United States and Britain during the war led to enhanced Canadian activity in such areas as civil aviation, atomic energy, and international trade.[8]

Increased activity in international affairs during the war by Canada and countries of similar size and stature like Australia spilled over into the planning for the postwar international system. In addition, it prompted many Canadians, both inside and outside government, to project a conception of Canada's place that was consistent with the country's contribution to the war effort. The contribution had been sizeable enough, many Canadians felt, to demand a revision of the country's status in international politics. Lionel Gelber, writing in 1944, put it in these terms:

> Under the impact of war, Canada has moved up from her old status to a new stature. With her smaller population and lack of colonial possessions, she is not a major or world power like Britain, the United States or Russia. But with her natural wealth and human capacity she is not a minor power like Mexico or Sweden. She stands in between as a Britannic Power of medium rank. Henceforth in world politics, Canada must figure as a Middle Power.[9]

The thinking among government officials was running along a similar track. Over the course of the war, the easy acceptance of the two-fold division of the world into the great and the non-great would be abandoned in favour of a more discriminating division of states. As King told the House of Commons in 1944, "The simple division of the world between great powers and the rest is unreal and even dangerous. The great powers are called by that name simply because they possess great power. The other states in the world possess power and therefore, the capacity to use it for the maintenance of peace...."[10] By May 1944, King was propounding the idea that Canada was a "power of middle size," or a "medium power," and thus should enjoy a status different from that of minor powers. In the same month, Lester Pearson was writing of Canada's membership

> among a group of States which are important enough to be necessary to the Big Four [the United States, the Soviet Union, Britain and China] but not important enough to be accepted as one of that quartet. As a matter of fact, the position of a "big little Power," or "little Big Power" is a very difficult one.... The big fellows have power and responsibility, but they also have control. We "in-between States" sometimes get, it seems, the worst of both worlds.[11]

It was not until early 1945 that the term middle power was adopted by the government in Ottawa to describe Canada's rank (and even then, it was used tentatively: the prefix "so-called" was frequently added). Its emergence can be ascribed not to some abstract intellectual exercise on the part of officials in the East Block of the Parliament Buildings where the Department of External Affairs was housed; rather, it had a specific political purpose. It was used primarily in the context of Canadian objections to proposals for a new international organization that had emerged out of the Dumbarton Oaks meetings. Of considerable concern to Canada—as well as other powers of medium size like Australia—was the planned dominance of the new United Nations by the great powers, typified by the exclusion of all but the Big Five (as the Four had by then become with the addition of France) from permanent representation on the Security Council, and the arrogation by these permanent members of a veto power in voting.

In its official comments on the Dumbarton Oaks proposals, circulated in January 1945, the Canadian government argued that while the great powers had to bear the primary responsibility for maintaining peace in the international system, the draft plan for the United Nations did not take into account the variations in strength of the smaller states. Ottawa argued that the power of the non-great powers, "and their capacity to use it for the maintenance of peace range from almost zero upwards to a point not very far behind the great powers."[12] These arguments were not persuasive enough to overcome the lingering memories of how the League of Nations had been structured without regard to the might of the great powers; so, although the British were not unsympathetic to the concerns of the middle powers, the great powers could not be moved to relinquish their oligopolistic hold on the Security Council.

Canada's quest for greater recognition of the middle powers was not abandoned, however. In a public speech in June 1945, in the middle of the San Francisco conference, Lester Pearson, by then Canada's ambassador to the United States, pressed the case of the middle powers. "We do not see," he said, "why the sovereign equality of states, a principle which must be accepted in theory, should be modified in practice only by giving special rights and privileges to great powers." He suggested, however, that

> power and responsibility should be related, that absolute equality in any world organization would mean absolute futility. No country will be able to play its proper part in international affairs if its influence bears no adequate relation to its obligations and its power. This, however, means not only abandoning the fiction that [El] Salvador and Russia are equal on the World Security Council, but also abandoning the fiction that outside the group of four or five great powers, all other states must have an exactly equal position.[13]

That stance was also being taken at the conference itself, where Australia and Canada fought hard for recognition of an appropriate role for the middle powers in the new world organization.[14] And although this middle-power crusade did not achieve all it had sought, the terminology had become fixed as an appropriate description of Canada's place in the hierarchy of powers.

But what exactly was a middle power? Carsten Holbraad has demonstrated that although this concept has been recognized for centuries,[15] it remains a most slippery and elusive one. For some, the definitional key was relative ranking in a number of national attributes. Classification could either be a rough and intuitive placement of those states in medium categories on the basis of attributes such as population, economic and military power, and status within the international community, or it could involve a more scientific attempt to place states in relation to one another. However these calculations were made, it remained evident that states such as Australia, Belgium, Brazil, and Canada were not great powers; but given their population base, level of development, and their international status, neither were they minor powers.

For others, however, middling power meant not simply an in-between *rank* in the hierarchy of states, but rather a particular *style* of foreign policy.

For example, a number of German writers in the nineteenth century put forward the idea that a *Mittelmacht* referred not merely to comparatively medium size and military power, but also to the geographic and strategic location of such states. Such states of medium size were geostrategically in the middle—geographically located between adversarial great powers, and strategically seeking to maintain a balance of power between them.[16]

The kind of thinking about middle powers that appeared after the Second World War tended to be a loose and often unconscious amalgam of these historical lines of thought. Middle powers were those of medium attributes of national capability. They were also in the geographic middle: Canadians, for example, were prone to consider themselves "sandwiched" between the USSR and the United States, while some Australians have characterized their country as occupying a position between the interests of the Northern industrialized states and those of the underdeveloped South.[17] Finally, these middle powers were also in a geostrategic middle, not unlike the *Mittelmacht* of old. They wished to maximize their own contributions to world order, minimize the ability of the great powers to exert overweening control of the institutions of international order, and contribute to preventing the great powers from plunging the system into war.

For Canadian governments in the 1950s and 1960s, middle power came to connote a style in foreign policy.[18] As John W. Holmes put it, being a middle power gave rise to a particular brand of diplomacy—what he called, tongue firmly if sardonically in cheek, "middlepowermanship."[19] It was the overriding fear that the world would again be plunged into war that helped spawn this particular kind of statecraft—predicated on the primacy of systemic peace as Canada's dominant foreign policy objective. Canada's foreign policy was marked by active attempts to mitigate political tensions and military conflicts that Ottawa feared would spark a Third World War.

Some of these attempts centred on reducing tensions between the two blocs of the tight bipolar postwar world, such as Lester Pearson's visit to Moscow in October 1955.[20] The essential modesty of these efforts at inter-bloc diplomacy has tended to fade with time; instead, there has been a tendency to overemphasize Canada's role as a "bridge" or a "linchpin"[21] between East and West during these years. It has even been suggested that Canada occupies a middle position between the opposing blocs, mediating in disinterested fashion between the two superpowers.[22] This is a pleasing, but fundamentally erroneous image of middle-power diplomacy as practiced by Canada. Never have Canadian policy-makers seen Canada as an ideological neutral. Canada was always an interested and firmly aligned member of the Western bloc. The inter-bloc diplomacy Canada engaged in was prompted by the recognition that Canada was a middle power in more ways than one. In one very real sense it was physically in the middle—situated directly between the Soviet Union and the United States. More importantly, however, decision-makers in Ottawa saw Canada as being caught in the middle of international tensions and disputes, and hence had a practical desire to work to defuse them.

On balance, it is clear that if the Canadian government during this period was active in mediation, it was more *intra*-bloc than *inter*-bloc diplomacy. These efforts at mediation within the various coalitions of which Canada is a member included specific mediatory attempts made by Ottawa to defuse disputes within the western bloc (such as the negotiated compromise over the Suez crisis in 1956); various (and mostly unsuccessful) attempts to restrain those foreign policy initiatives of the United States that policy-makers in Ottawa feared might precipitate a third systemic war this century (such as the Korean War,[23] the struggle in Vietnam,[24] or the offshore islands crises of 1955[25]); and the periodic divisions within the Commonwealth over racial domination in southern Africa.[26]

Finally, the most important aspect of Canada's middle-power diplomacy during this period was its approach to regional conflict. Policy-makers in Ottawa were quite fearful that "brushfire wars" could provide the spark that would precipitate global war, and were eager to participate in the institutionalized methods for resolving these conflicts that were evolving in the postwar period. As an outgrowth of its attachment to the United Nations as an institution for the preservation of a more general systemic peace, the government in Ottawa became a firm devotee of international peacekeeping and truce supervision, and a committed contributor to these international forces throughout the postwar period.[27]

The conception of Canada as middle power enjoyed considerable durability. Thirty years after government officials in Ottawa had tentatively suggested that Canada was a "so-called middle power," the image of Canada's rank held by many analysts and practitioners had not changed. In 1975, for example, a study of the Canadian foreign policy elite and a selected sample of foreign observers revealed that a majority of the respondents adhered to the notion of Canada as a middle power.[28]

But the pervasiveness of the middle-power image did not go unchallenged. The firmest revisionist statement came from Pierre Elliott Trudeau when he became prime minister in 1968. He made it clear that the notion of Canada as a middle power, and the style of middlepowermanship, did not sit well with him. Canadians had to remind themselves, he said in April 1968, "that we're perhaps more the largest of the small powers than the smallest of the large powers. And this is a complete change, I think, from our mentality of 20 years ago."[29] Indeed, Dobell was of the view that the new prime minister's comments on world power and Canada's place in the hierarchy of states suggested a return to the pre-1939 era when the division of the world into the great powers and all others was implicitly accepted.[30] Not surprisingly, Trudeau's rejection of middle power status also meant a concomitant rejection of middlepowermanship and the various diplomatic roles associated with it. Trudeau's emphasis in the late 1960s was on modesty and realism, which demanded that "we should not exaggerate our influence upon the course of world events."[31] It was little coincidence that his government's white paper on foreign policy, published in 1970, should predict that "Canada's 'traditional' middle-power role in the world seemed doomed to disappear."[32] It was a prediction notably lacking in prescience. As we will see in chapter 6, Trudeau would maintain Canada's middle-power role throughout his long tenure. During the 1970s, and from 1980 to 1984, Trudeau pursued many of the diplomatic roles that he had so disparagingly dismissed in the late 1960s. Despite his considerable skepticism about peacekeeping, the Canadian commitment to such roles continued.[33] Likewise, his peace initiative of 1983-84 was firmly in the middle-power tradition of his predecessors. Indeed, by 1984, Trudeau had even slipped back into the durable terminology of middle power. Reporting on his peace mission to Parliament in February 1984, he referred to the need for a middle-power role in defusing the tensions between the superpowers.[34]

After 1984, the government of Brian Mulroney was careful to eschew the use of the term middle power to describe either Canada or its foreign policy;[35] yet it remained no less committed to the pursuit of middle-power diplomacy. The attempts of both Mulroney and his secretary of state for external affairs, Joe Clark, to solve differences within the Commonwealth on the issue of *apartheid* in South Africa were firmly in the tradition of Pierre Trudeau, Lester Pearson, John Diefenbaker, and Louis St. Laurent. Similarly, in the area of peacekeeping, Canadians served with the United Nations groups overseeing the Soviet withdrawal from Afghanistan and the Iran-Iraq ceasefire; and Canada contributed its expertise in truce supervision to the peace process in Central America, and has indicated its willingness in principle to contribute Canadian forces should an international commission be established for the region.[36]

Canada as Satellite

In the late 1960s, the middle-power image of Canada was greeted with skepticism by some and complete rejection by others.[37] There is a perspective on Canada's role in international politics that goes much further than Trudeau's skepticism, embracing none of the assumptions about the capacity for independent action implicit in his early revisionism. Instead, the "satellite thesis" begins with the assumption that Canada's capacity for independent and autonomous action in international politics has been all but eliminated by its successive membership in the British and American empires. In this view, Canada's colonial status was never in its essence affected by either the British North America Act of 1867 or the Statute of Westminster of 1931. Rather, the shifting nexus of global hegemony from Britain to the United States in the first four decades of the twentieth century inexorably drew Canada, as a subordinate state, with it. Because of the economic, ideological, and cultural linkages between Canada and the United States which had been a consistent feature of life on the North American continent, the country was pulled into an emerging, even if informal, American empire.[38] In circular fashion, it was argued, Canada had gone from colony to nation to colony by the end of the Second World War. In short, what for some marked the emergence of a middle power in world politics was, for others, merely a transfer of satellitic orbit.

This view of the diminuitive power of the Canadian polity has deep historical roots. As early as 1920, well before the full impact of the shift in Canada's economic dependence from Britain to the United States had been felt, Archibald MacMechan lamented that Canada was becoming too Americanized, and was, as a consequence, little more than an American "vassal state."[39] This theme was repeated in 1946 by Professor A.R.M. Lower, who described Canada as a "subordinate state," and declared that it was a "complete satellite of the United States."[40] Such a perspective informed a succession of writers in the postwar period.

Concern over Canada's capacity for independent action in international politics reached its apogee in the 1960s. Writing in 1960, James M. Minifie rejected outright the notion of Canada as middle-power peacemaker. Rather, the country's

> [c]lose association with policies of military and economic imperialism ... makes Canada the glacis for the defence of the continental United States, makes Canada the choreboy of the Western world, [and] returns Canada from colony to satellite in three generations....[41]

Likewise, Ottawa's continued non-recognition of the government in Beijing and its policies towards the war in Vietnam came to symbolize Canada's subservient status and its domination by the United States, as did the Pearson government propensity to air its differences with Washington using "quiet diplomacy" rather than by loud and public declarations.[42] To be sure, the concerns that some Canadians had about the reach of the American empire were exacerbated, if not exaggerated, by what Canadians were seeing south of the border during this period: the racial unrest that flared across numerous American cities, student protests, and the frequent and widespread violence that seemed to be endemic to American society. Moreover, while concern over the exceedingly high levels of American ownership of Canadian industry had begun to emerge in Canadian politics in the 1950s, a decade later, the public was becoming more conscious of this issue. There was a growing fear that such a degree of foreign ownership would lead to the complete Americanization of Canada, bringing with it all of the negative aspects of American life. These concerns manifested themselves in an often strident literature which tended to dominate the foreign policy debate.[43]

Much of the literature of the late 1960s and early 1970s was not specifically concerned with establishing Canada's place in the hierarchy of world power; with but few exceptions,[44] there was little explicit and overt consideration of such matters. Indeed, it would appear that Canada's subordinate status in the American imperium was simply taken for granted, a self-evident given from which all other analysis would proceed. Many authors took their cues from George Grant's analysis of the cultural, technological, socio-economic, and hence the political, homogenization of North America, which led him to predict gloomily that "Canada's disappearance as a nation is a matter of necessity."[45] They were concerned mainly with demonstrating the nature and extent of imperial domination that was calling into question the very existence of the Canadian nation itself. As George Martell, writing in 1970, put it:

> As a country, I believe, we have had it. Our culture, our politics, our economy are almost entirely packaged in the US... It's not so much we're a colony, we're an integral part of the empire. We're Americans now, and I think we have to begin dealing with that fact....[46]

However, not all of the literature took such an unsophisticated, emotional, and polemical approach. As Michael Hawes has argued,[47] the more unsophisticated polemics of the late 1960s gave way to the kind of serious scholarship of students like Wallace Clement, Jean Kirk Laux, and Stephen Clarkson.[48] But the increase in sophistication did not lessen the conviction that the scope for independent action is minimal at best. As a major article by Clarkson in *The Globe and Mail* in May 1985 asked rhetorically: "Why bother to debate Canada's foreign policy?"[49]

Canada as Great Power

There is a third perspective of Canada's power that rejects both the ultranationalist arguments about Canada's satellitic status, and the fuzzy, if comfortable, notion of Canada as middle power. This perspective is more unselfconsciously assertive of the country's great power in the international system.

James Eayrs, for example, writing in 1975, argued that three changes after 1970 had altered Canadian power: the rise to prominence of the oil-producing states, particularly after the first oil shock of 1973-74; the growing importance of natural resources—particularly food and fuel—in international politics; and, finally, the decline of the United States as a hegemonic power in world affairs, symbolized by its ignomious withdrawal from Vietnam in 1973. These changes, in Eayrs's view, warranted a reconsideration of just how powerful Canada was. For Canada, he noted, had resources aplenty:

> Canada has almost sinfully bestowed upon it the sources of power, both traditional and new... The technology is there, or waiting... The manpower is there, or waiting... The resources are there, or waiting too—animal, vegetable *and* mineral.... (We need only decide how fast to develop them, how much to charge for them.)

Such bounteousness, he argued, endowed Canada with the capability to become a "foremost power ... foremost in the dictionary sense of 'most notable or prominent.'"[50]

Eayrs's terminology was adopted, if not endorsed, by the editors of a 1977 collection of essays on Canadian foreign policy, who entitled their work *Foremost Nation*. Norman Hillmer and Garth Stevenson argued that the term "illustrates graphically the rapid changes which the world in general and Canadian foreign policy in particular have recently undergone. Certainly most of the contributors to this volume would agree that, at the very least, Canada is not a small and fragile nation, the 'modest power' of which Prime Minister Trudeau spoke in 1968."[51]

Likewise, writing two years later, Peyton Lyon and Brian Tomlin came to a similar conclusion, but based on more empirical grounds. They constructed a series of indices of relative national power focussing on the military, economic, resource, and diplomatic capabilities of Australia, Britain, Canada, China, France, Germany, Japan, the Soviet Union, Sweden, and the United States. Not surprisingly, in each of their indices, the two superpowers ranked far above all others. But Canada placed not with the states usually thought of as middle powers—Australia and Sweden—but with those usually considered major powers: China, Britain, France, Germany, and Japan. In the overall index, Canada was ranked sixth in the international system, ahead of both Japan and France. (It is noteworthy that Cline's assessment also ranked Canada sixth, though ahead of France and Britain.[52]) As a result of these findings, Lyon and Tomlin confidently asserted, "Canada should now be regarded as a major power."[53]

The most unabashed perspective of Canada as a great power has been developed by David Dewitt and John Kirton. However, they hesitate to use the term "great power"; instead they call states such as Canada *principal powers* (the same terminology, it might be noted, that was used in the aftermath of the First World War to distinguish the victorious great powers from the vanquished great powers—and, of course, from all the rest).

Principal powers, they argue, are principal in three ways. First, they are states "that stand at the top of the international status ranking." Second, they "act as principals" in the international system, and not as the "agents" of other states. Finally, principal powers have "a principal role in establishing, specifying, and enforcing international order."[54]

Such a resurrection of the principal power category in the international hierarchy is made possible by what Dewitt and Kirton identify as a central feature of international politics in the 1980s: the decline of superpower hegemony and the consequent diffusion of power at the apex of the international system. Reflecting a popular, if peculiar, propensity in American scholarship to deny American power,[55] they argue that since the late 1960s, the United States has been rapidly declining in power. As a result, the hegemony of the American imperium has been increasingly replaced by other states. It is thus no longer appropriate to think merely in dichotomous terms about power in international politics, dividing the world into the superpowers and "the rest." In these shifting heavens, Canada's star is seen as rising. Since 1968, Dewitt and Kirton declare, Canada has been "an ascending principal power in an increasingly diffuse, non-hegemonic international system."[56]

To support this contention, they point to the global scope of Canada's various international activities, the global reach of Canadian diplomacy, the active presence of the Canadian government in a wide range of international organizations, and Ottawa's persistent commitment to modifying global order through development assistance and a continuing interest in the North-South dialogue.

Much of the principal power perspective developed by Dewitt and Kirton owes a heavy intellectual debt to Allan Gotlieb, a senior diplomat in the Department of External Affairs who has been both bureaucratic head of the department and ambassador in its most important posting. In 1979, while he was the undersecretary of state for external affairs, Gotlieb outlined a perspective of Canada as more than the modest middle power of the postwar tradition.[57] Gotlieb was to press that case again eight years later while Canada's ambassador to Washington. Writing in *The Globe and Mail* in October 1987—in the midst of the national debate on the free trade agreement then being negotiated by the Mulroney government—he argued that Canadians should recognize their power in the contemporary international system and their capacity to embrace the free trade agreement without fear of domination or absorption by the United States. Gotlieb suggested that the comfortable idea of Canada as a middle power should be critically re-examined, and that Canadians should begin to see their country in the way others, including the United States, see it: as a "major power with the international interests and capabilities such a term implies." Surveying a variety of statistical measures of performance and capability,

Gotlieb demonstrated that Canada ranked ahead of more than 150 countries. "Some middle power!" he concluded.[58]

Assessing Images of Canadian Power

Attempts to locate Canada in the international hierarchy offer a diffracted image of Canada's power. At one end of the spectrum, Canada is cast as a mere vassal state in international politics, inexorably tied to empire by economic linkages and military incapacity, forever the victim of foreign domination, forever unable to experience the joys of sovereign nationhood—complete autonomy. At the other, Canada is cast either as an emergent great power (albeit clothed in nomenclature demure enough to disguise such greatness), or as a great power simply overlooked by the rest of the international community blinded to the obvious conclusions of scientifically-verifiable statistical measures of capability. Between these extremes are conceptions of Canada as the largest of the small or the smallest of the large—or simply "in the middle."

Such contending images of power are, however, inescapable. The labours of analysts such as Cline or Lyon and Tomlin notwithstanding, it is impossible to demonstrate a country's power objectively or scientifically. Any assessment of a state's power will always be subjective, and thus variable. Part of the subjectivity stems from the fact that assessing a nation's power is a fundamentally *political* enterprise: how one views a state's power has inexorable political implications. More importantly, the perspectives on Canada's power reviewed above are, properly speaking, not assessments of power, but of status. When we describe Canada as a great power, a middle power, or a satellite, we are speaking of how others see Canada (and how Canadians see themselves) within the international hierarchy. Both, I will argue, serve to blur and distort the assessment of Canadian power in international politics.

Power and politics. Attempts to locate a nation in a hierarchy will inexorably be a political exercise. The political overtones, external and internal, are particularly evident when a state's leaders engage in assessing power. Mackenzie King's denigration of Canada's influence in the 1920s and 1930s can be seen as the careful calculation of a politician afraid of the electoral consequences of a more activist foreign policy. By the same token, the promotion of middle-power status was politically useful for foreign policy-makers in the 1940s. It provided them with status—and, as importantly, a voice and a role—in international politics that they would not otherwise have had.

Don Munton has suggested that the concept of middle power may have had domestic purposes as well. He has argued that middlepowermanship served the politicians of that era well.[59] As we will see in chapter 4, the pursuit of a middle-power role was not only good diplomacy for a state of Canada's size; it was also good politics. The idea being promulgated by the government that Canada was "in the middle" seemed to sit well with Canadians.[60] After all, there was a comforting side to being of medium power, as Botero had observed in 1589: "Middle-sized states ... are exposed neither to violence by their weakness nor to envy by their greatness, and their wealth and power being moderate, passions are less violent, ambition finds less support and licence less provocation than in large States."[61]

Just as the promotion of middle-power status will have its political purpose, so too will denigration of middle power. Trudeau's *mauvaise honte* in the late 1960s had its own political purposes. Since the foreign policy—and the formidable reputation—of his predecessor had been built largely on concepts of middle power that Trudeau thought atavistic, persistent modesty was a useful means not only of distancing the new prime minister from Lester Pearson, but also of preparing Canadians, and Canada's allies, for the policy shift that Trudeau tried to initiate. Nor can the political purposes of great-power advocacy be ignored. One may have little difficulty in agreeing with Gotlieb's claims that Canadians "would be foolish to allow myths about our vulnerability to obscure our vision, to discount our prospects," or that "We could make an error of historic proportions, as we judge one of the most consequential negotiations in our nationhood, if we fail to see ourselves as others see us." But such assertions about Canadian power must be seen principally as forensic rhetoric— inextricably tied to the free trade debate in which he, as Brian Mulroney's ambassador to the United States, was so intimately involved.

Political considerations also affect assessments by foreign nationals of another nation's rank. It is not coincidental that the most lavish assessments of Canada's power come from foreigners. Soviet leaders may assure a visiting Canadian politician that children in the USSR are taught in school that Canada is a major power.[62] Or the director of an Asian institute of international affairs may assure enquiring Canadian academics that Canada is indeed on the road to becoming a superpower.[63] But these assessments tell us more about the politeness of the assessor than about Canadian power. After all, in a world where the dominant ideology of nationalism assigns to each nation its own greatness, to suggest a more modest ranking may appear offensive.

Power and status. Determining a state's ranking in the international hierarchy is useful as a general guide to its status, or standing, in international politics. Of the three images of Canada's power we have examined, there can be little doubt that Canada enjoys the status of a middle power in contemporary international politics. Certainly it does not enjoy the status of a great, major, or even principal power. The diplomatic activities of the government in Ottawa may have a global reach; Canadian officials may enjoy regular invitations to an array of summit meetings attended by the great and near-great; and Canada may rank ahead of 150 of the 160 or so members of the international system on certain statistical criteria. However, Canada lacks the most important attribute needed for great-power status: the subjective recognition of other states. But neither is the government in Ottawa regarded as a puppet regime. Canada may be tightly aligned militarily and diplomatically with the western bloc and it may be heavily dependent on the United States economically. But, again, it lacks a critical element necessary for classification as a satellite: the dismissal by other states as a country of no global consequence. This is why, in the eyes of others and of Canadians themselves, Canada sits somewhere (however fuzzily) in the middle. Here, it might be noted, Canada keeps company with a number of other states, many distinctly unhappy with their middling location.[64]

But even if one could establish definitively an appropriate status-ranking for Canada, what would locating the country in the hierarchy tell us about Canadian power? It is suggested here that for all of the utility of rankings in establishing status, they are virtually useless in establishing a state's power. One of the difficulties of using the terminology of status ranking—great power, middle power, minor power—is that it tends to distort not only the concept of power itself, but also a clear consideration of how power—or lack of it—affects the making of a state's foreign policy.

To get a sense of a state's power in international politics, we have to move beyond status and look to a complementary method of analyzing a state's power in the international system. The power analysis approach directs our attention not to generalized inducation of status ranking, but to the possession and exercise of power.

RETHINKING CANADA'S POWER: A POWER ANALYSIS APPROACH

The Nature of Power

Power analysis attempts to eliminate what Stanley Hoffman has called the elusiveness of power.[65] It begins by trying to move closer to a definition of the term itself, usually phrased in terms of actor *A*, actor *B* and action *X*. The exercise and possession of power is thus defined in very discrete terms: the ability of A to get B to do (or not to do) X. As Robert Dahl put it, "A has power over B to the extent that he can get B to do something that B would not otherwise do."[66] Steven Lukes, by contrast, alerts us to the importance of the interests of the actors, and the essential negativity of power: "A exercises power over B when A affects B in a manner contrary to B's interests."[67]

An assessment of Canada's power in international politics would thus begin by recognizing that the issue is not where Canada ranks in the community of states, but the degree to which the government in Ottawa is able to achieve its objectives and secure Canada's interests as they are defined by officials. Power is the ability to change the behaviour of others in ways that are conducive to Canadian interests (getting the United States to enact legislation reducing the emissions that cause acid rain; getting the Japanese government to agree to voluntarily restrict automobile exports to Canada; getting the Soviet Union to pay compensation to Canadians who had relatives aboard Korean Air Lines flight 007; getting the British government to back away from a plan to label Canadian fur products). Power is also the ability to secure one's own policy objectives while deterring others from acting in a manner contrary to Canadian interests (moving the Canadian embassy from Tel Aviv to Jerusalem without the Arab states invoking economic sanctions in retaliation; enacting domestic legislation on border broadcasting without incurring economically damaging measures from the United States Congress; expelling diplomats caught in espionage operations without having Canadian diplomats expelled in retaliation). And power is the ability to rebuff the importunities of other states to act in a manner judged to be inconsistent with Canadian interests (being able to refuse an American request to participate in the Strategic Defense Initiative; refusing to invoke economic sanctions against the Sandinista government in Nicaragua). In short, power analysis focusses on the ability—or lack of it—to prevail in conflicts of interest with other states.

The Properties of Power

Power analysis begins by positing two key assumptions about the properties of power. First, power is relational: it can only be possessed or exercised within the context of a specified relationship. Second, power analysis stresses the importance of identifying the matters on which power is exercised. In the argot of power analysis, these are known as *domain* and *scope* respectively. Without specifying domain and scope, Dahl rightly asserts, any statement about power "verges on being meaningless."[68] Thus we cannot conclude that State A is powerful without specifying over whom A is powerful, and in what matters.[69] Likewise, to specify one without the other obscures the multifaceted[70] and frequently paradoxical nature of the exercise of power in international politics that allows State A to exercise power over State B in matters of civil aviation, but State B to exercise power over State A in matters of trade.

Specifying scope and domain is critical for a clear assessment of Canada's power in international politics. Because of geographic location and the other attributes surveyed in chapter 2, and because of the role of the United States in contemporary international politics, it is inevitable that Canada's foreign policy behaviour will be largely directed at the United States. The dominant domain, therefore, of both the possession and exercise of Canadian power will be *vis-à-vis* the government in Washington. Likewise, the scope of the Canadian government's foreign policy objectives is dominated by security and economic matters. For example, of the 77 foreign policy objectives identified by Canadian policy-makers in the study by Lyon and Tomlin, 38 were economic, 23 dealt with security concerns, and the remainder involved environmental issues and human rights.[71] Virtually all these foreign policy objectives involved the United States and its interests in some way. Thus, because the predominant domain and scope of Canadian foreign policy will be matters which heavily involve the United States, an assessment of Canadian power must inevitably focus on the exercise of power in the Canadian-American context.

If the interests over which one seeks to prevail are American, then one cannot but be concerned with the capabilities—or power resources—that Canada can bring to bear to ensure that its interests prevail. Discussions of power resources are usually bedevilled by two common misconceptions. First, a common assumption is that power resources are synonymous with power (and the obverse axiom: the lack of power resources means a lack of power). Thus, Lyon and Tomlin profess to be baffled: "We are left with a major mystery," they conclude after showing that, according to their statistical calculations, Canada should be a great power.[72] But there is no mystery to the "paradox of ùnrealized power"[73] if we remember that having or exercising power, and having capabilities, are not inexorably related. Capabilities do not automatically confer power. Likewise, the relative lack of power resources does not relegate one, *ipso facto*, to powerlessness. Both of the superpowers—and their adversaries—discovered this: the United States in Vietnam and the Soviet Union in Afghanistan. Indeed, the ability to prevail while working with limited capabilities is itself a power resource.

A second misconception is that power resources are fungible—in other words, that capabilities can be easily "converted" into the ability to have one's interests prevail. Although some authors glibly speak of power as being the currency of politics, it is not, as David Baldwin so cogently points out,[74] at all like currency. Currency is highly fungible: indeed, its very purpose is to provide a highly effective means for exchange. Power resources in international politics, by contrast, are highly infungible. What State A uses to exercise power over State B in one area cannot simply be converted (as currency is) to exercise comparably successful power in another area—or against other actors. For example, a naval task force may be an eminently useful and effective resource against State B after it has invaded one's territory; it may prove entirely useless as a means of getting State B to lower its tariffs on shoe imports, or getting State C to vote against a resolution in the United Nations General Assembly.

The relative infungibility of power resources helps explain why Canada's various statistical measures of strength in international politics are not necessarily an asset in achieving its international objectives. While Canada may indeed be endowed with an abundance of natural resources, as Eayrs has noted, it does not follow that the government in Ottawa will be able to convert that capability into a meaningful power resource. For example, Canada's food surplus was entirely useless when Prime Minister Joe Clark tried to ensure that Canada's interests in moving the Canadian embassy from Tel Aviv to Jerusalem prevailed over the contrary interests of numerous Arab states ranged against Canada. In that contest, the threat of Arab-led economic sanctions—together with stiff domestic criticism of the initiative—prompted Canada to back down.[75] And while Canada can be statistically ranked well ahead of 150 nations in economic capability, as Gotlieb suggests, such capability did not deter the Soviet Union from engaging in a tit-for-tat strategy of diplomatic retaliation in July 1988 when the Mulroney government declared a number of Soviet diplomats *persona non grata* for spying. Finally, all of Canada's natural resources put together would be an entirely inappropriate and ineffective power resource to use in an attempt to get the United States to abandon the protectionist measures it imposed against a range of Canadian products in the mid-1980s. Toting up a nation's capabilities provides few clues to whether it can, or will, be successful in defending or advancing its interests *vis-à-vis* other states in the international system. We must examine how these resources are used.

THE TECHNIQUES OF POWER

Kal J. Holsti reminds us that enumerating methods for exercising power in international politics has a long history: for example, the Indian theorist Kautilya, writing in 300 B.C., noted four techniques for obtaining results from other states: *sama* (conciliation), *dana* (gifts), *bheda* (dissension), and *danda* (punishment).[76] Our list of techniques is somewhat longer, but not because the means states use to prevail over others has changed considerably in the last 2200 years. Power in international politics is exercised by tools of statecraft that can be usefully thought of as being ranged on a continuum from essentially violent and costly techniques at one end to peaceful and costless techniques at the other. This range would include: persuasion (A's use of argument or entreaty to move B to a belief, position, or course of action); inducement (the offer and/or granting of rewards); coercion (the threat of deprivation of things of value); nonviolent sanctions (the actual deprivation of things of value, but not by the use of force); and force.[77] These are the overt techniques; to them must be added those instances where A is able to prevail over B's interests not by *exercising* power, but simply by *having* power. B is prompted to shape "his behaviour to conform to what he believes are the desires of ... A, without having received explicit messages about A's wants or intentions."[78] This "rule of anticipated reaction" clouds the assessment of power considerably, for A's possession, rather than intention or overt use, of power causes B's actions.

The range of techniques used by the Canadian government to exercise power in the international system will of necessity be limited. This stems from four interconnected factors: the lack of capacity; the lack of desire; the dominant domain and scope of Canada's foreign policy behaviour; and the nature of the foreign policy objectives traditionally evinced by decision-makers in Ottawa.

The Relative Irrelevance of Force

In the settlement of human conflict, force remains the *ultima ratio*—the last resort. Because of this, the ability to apply force is often confused with power. It is true that over the long sweep of history, a state's ability to prevail in a conflict has in the final analysis depended on its capacity to use military might. But force is a useful instrument of statecraft in only a few of the power relationships in international politics, and for only a few states. The superpowers, or those states with acute and imminent threats to their security, cannot ignore the consequences of relative military capabilities. In those circumstances, it will be useful—indeed necessary—to count soldiers, to enumerate the weapons of war (be they spears, muskets or ballistic missiles), to assess those military intangibles such as will and morale, and to estimate what demographic, economic, and natural resources are available to sustain the application of force. For most other states, however, the ability to employ force as an instrument of foreign policy will be, quite simply, irrelevant.

Such is the case with Canada—in all but a few, and not insignificant, instances. Canada is, as historians have been wont to put it, an "unmilitary community," a "peaceable kingdom" which devotes little of its attention and even less of its wealth to its military forces.[79] Desmond Morton has argued that "This is no accident. Canadians have come by their attitudes through the weight of historical experience. Prophets of military preparedness have lacked credibility because military neglect has not led to armed invasion or military disaster."[80] To be sure, the government in Ottawa has frequently used the armed forces in pursuit of its foreign policy objectives—at the cost of well over 100,000 Canadian soldiers killed and thousands more wounded. Four times this century the Canadian government has gone to war. In one instance, it has used force to intervene in the affairs of another country. And on numerous occasions the Canadian Armed Forces (CAF) have been used in peacekeeping operations, though only very rarely has deadly force been used.

But Canada has never used force unilaterally. The Boer War, the First and Second World Wars, and the Korean War were all fought in concert with other powers. Likewise, Canada's participation in the armed intervention in Russia following the Bolshevik revolution was as part of a multilateral force. As Stacey argues, it was originally based on the assumption that what Winston Churchill termed "this righteous crusade" to defeat the Communist revolution was part of the larger war effort against the Central Powers, Germany and Austro-Hungary. (Indeed, shortly after Canadian troops had been dispatched to Murmansk, Archangel, and Vladivostok, the armistice with the Central Powers prompted Prime Minister Robert Borden to press for their withdrawal, much to Churchill's chagrin.[81]) And all peacekeeping operations have been conducted under the auspices of either the United Nations or some other internationally-legitimized institution.

The consistently multilateral context in which Canada has used force is important, for it underscores the essential purpose of the CAF as an instrument of Canadian statecraft. The country does not maintain armed forces to be used as a direct instrument of external policy. Rather, the sole purpose of these forces is to make relatively small contributions to various international institutions to which Canada attaches value: the Atlantic alliance, the continental air defence arrangements with the United States, the United Nations, the Commonwealth, and more ad hoc institutions such as the Geneva or Paris conferences that oversaw the two peace agreements for Indochina.

It is true that there are ancillary purposes for the CAF. Aid to the civil power is one function of all armed forces, and the Canadian government has resorted to employing the CAF for this purpose, most notably during the "crisis" of October 1970 when the War Measures Act was invoked by the Trudeau government. Another is the protection of Canadian sovereignty, particularly in the Arctic. It was ostensibly for this reason that the Trudeau government purchased a small but not inexpensive fleet of long-range patrol aircraft in the mid-1970s,[82] and the Mulroney government proposed in 1987 to purchase a small but not inexpensive fleet of nuclear-propelled submarines.[83]

But the utility of the CAF as a direct instrument of Canadian statecraft is exceedingly limited. Although Canadians have historically demonstrated a willingness to wage war collectively with others, there are no states against which Canada would be willing to use force unilaterally to achieve foreign policy objectives. The conflict with France in 1988 over fishing in the Gulf of St. Lawrence demonstrates well Canada's tendency to back off before deadly force is used to press contending claims (although France also backed down, officials in Ottawa must have been mindful of the fact that the government in Paris seems to have no qualms about using deadly force against an ally, as the bombing of the Greenpeace ship *Rainbow Warrior* in New Zealand clearly demonstrated). And while the Canadian government may spend more than $10 billion on nuclear-propelled submarines, these will be highly ineffective instruments for keeping the Canadian Arctic free of the submarines of the superpowers. No government in Ottawa would actually countenance firing on either a Soviet or an American submarine discovered in waters claimed by Canada.

But if force is irrelevant as a means of prevailing in a conflict of interests with other states, possession of the capability to use force is not irrelevant to Canadian influence. There is little doubt that the historical tendency of Canadians to burden their treasury only in times of war carries a price in terms of influence within the western alliance. Canada's standing in alliance circles is greatly diminished by the widespread—even if not entirely accurate—perception that Ottawa is not spending enough on defence. Thus, Canada is accused of "moral failings" for "shirking its fair share in the defense of the West," and "taking almost a free ride on the backs of its U.S. and European allies."[84] The critical perspective of Jockel and Sokolsky is somewhat shrill, but it nicely captures the mood of many of the other allies when the defence spending figures come out each year. Diminished influence and stature in NATO, however, is a price that the vast majority of Canadians, not to mention a succession of leaders, from Pearson in the 1960s to Mulroney in the 1980s, have been more than willing to pay.

Nonviolent Sanctions

Canada has only a limited capacity for applying nonviolent sanctions against other states and has shown little willingness to do so. Until the late 1970s, governments in Ottawa historically demonstrated a marked reluctance to employ economic sanctions. In October 1935, Mackenzie King was shocked when the Canadian representative to the League of Nations, W.A. Riddell, took the initiative in proposing sanctions against Italy following the invasion of Ethiopia, and that the proposed measure on oil was being widely referred to as "the Canadian sanction." Riddell had acted without instructions from the government and King, fearing both the domestic and external consequences of League sanctions against Italy, disavowed his initiative.[85] Postwar governments have shown a similar disinclination to employ sanctions. Ottawa refused, for example, to participate in American-led economic sanctions against the People's Republic of China in the 1950s or Cuba in the 1960s and 1970s. (On the Cuban matter, Canada would be criticized in the United States: as one Cuban emigré put it, Canadians were the "Phoenicians of America. Their ships and their cargoes go where there is business to be done."[86])

Canada's historical reluctance to invoke economic sanctions cannot, however, be attributed merely to greed. In part, this reluctance was driven by a generalized preference in Ottawa for trying to keep the international trading environment from becoming intermeshed with the international political environment. As a trading country, Canada had an interest in keeping trade as open and free from restrictions as possible (except, of course, when it was in Ottawa's interests to engage in economic protectionism of its own; then it has shown no reluctance at all to impose tariffs on a wide variety of goods). In part, Ottawa's reluctance to impose sanctions was motivated by a feeling that these simply were inappropriate measures under the circumstances. Certainly, it felt that the continued exclusion of China was a mistake—this long before the immensely profitable wheat sales that began in the early 1960s. And finally, the reluctance was driven by a widespread perception that economic sanctions, as an instrument of statecraft, did not work.

However reluctant the government might have been in general, it did not eschew economic sanctions altogether. But its preference has always been to move multilaterally, in tandem with other states imposing comparable measures. Thus, in the late 1940s Ottawa embraced an embargo on strategic goods to the Soviet Union being coordinated by the western alliance; it imposed United Nations sanctions against Rhodesia after the Unilateral Declaration of Independence by the Ian Smith regime in 1965; and it joined in a variety of UN sanctions against South Africa in the 1960s. However, the government in Ottawa has occasionally imposed sanctions unilaterally: the Trudeau government did so after India detonated a nuclear device in 1974; and the Clark government sanctioned Argentina in 1979 for the human rights abuses being committed by the military junta there.

The late 1970s marked a watershed in Ottawa's approach to sanctions. Beginning in 1979, the government imposed economic and other sanctions against a variety of states in rapid succession: against Vietnam after its invasion of Kampuchea in early 1979; against the Soviet Union after its invasion of Afghanistan in December of that year; against Iran following the seizure of the United States embassy in Tehran; against Poland and the Soviet Union after the imposition of martial law in Poland in December

1981; against Argentina following its invasion of the Falkland Islands in the spring of 1982; and against the Soviet Union after Soviet fighters shot down a Korean Air Lines airliner in September 1983. Since 1984, a sustained effort at using sanctions has been directed at South Africa. Following the outbreak of renewed unrest in the black townships in the fall of 1984, the Mulroney government, in a sharp break from practice under the Trudeau government, began in July 1985 to impose a steadily mounting series of economic and other sanctions against South Africa.[87] Most of these, however, have also been imposed in the wider multilateral context of the Commonwealth.

Because economic sanctions are primarily measures imposed for acts of wrong-doing, they have limited utility against one's friends (even when they engage in behaviour that is substantially similar). Thus, for example, Canadian sanctions against the United States after it invaded Grenada and overthrew the legitimate government there in October 1983, or flew air strikes against Libya in April 1986, or shot down an Iranian airliner in the Persian Gulf in July 1988, were, quite simply, well outside the bounds of acceptable or viable policy options.

Coercion

Using threats (or negative sanctions) as a tool of statecraft is not unknown to Canadian foreign policy-makers, but its application tends to be very limited. In cases where the targets of Canadian threats are highly dependent on Canada, this instrument tends to achieve its desired effect. As we will see in chapter 9, the federal government successfully coerced francophone African states in the late 1960s to halt a bid by the provincial government in Quebec for a greater degree of international recognition. None too subtly, Ottawa reminded these states that Quebec City could hardly match the development assistance programs administered by the federal government.

But because of Canada's geographic location and economic structure, foreign policy will for the most part be directed not at states dependent on Canada, but at the United States. The calculus will be very different. If a government in Ottawa were inclined to use threats against the United States to achieve its objectives, it would have to reckon with the consequences should the threats of damage fail to deter or move the administration in Washington. When a threat fails, one has a choice: either back down or impose the threatened deprivation. Either way, in the context of the Canadian-American relationship, it is a mug's game. If the administration in Washington is not deterred or moved, and Canada fails to invoke the threatened damage, Ottawa loses whatever negotiating credibility it might possess. And if the Canadian government were actually to go ahead and impose the damage, it cannot ignore the consequences of the asymmetries of dependence on the North American continent. Despite the rhetoric of interdependence that tends to flow at official Canadian-American functions, Canada and the United States are *not* interdependent in the sense of being mutually dependent on each other. In the final analysis, Canada depends on the United States—heavily—for its security and its economic well-being; the United States is not at all comparably dependent.

Thus, governments in Ottawa have to assess the costs of engaging in coercive tactics against a state whose capabilities clearly outmatch Canada's. They know that the United States has a huge capacity to absorb what deprivations Canada could visit on it; and more importantly, it has a huge capacity to administer even more damaging blows in retaliation should a dispute intensify and escalate. They know too that the higher the stakes are for American interests, the more likely it will be that the government in Washington will use its substantial capabilities to protect those interests. As the case of the Trudeau government's National Energy Program of 1980 clearly demonstrates, a willingness to "play hardball," as policy-makers in Washington fondly call it, can easily—and quickly— replace the otherwise leavening condition of friendship between the two countries. The choice of instruments to secure Canadian objectives and interests in the Canadian-American relationship is thus inevitably conditioned by the rule of anticipated reaction. The instruments that have the probability of provoking damaging retaliation, like coercion, do not commend themselves when dealing with a state with such huge power resources.

Inducement

Offering rewards (or positive sanctions) to change the behaviour of other states has a limited utility in the Canadian case. It is true that inducement has been practical in some domains: for example, it was used to secure an economic agreement with the European Communities in 1976. As part of its "Third Option" policy of economic diversification adopted in 1972, the Trudeau government set out to negotiate a "contractual link" with the EC. The *quid pro quo* extracted from the Canadians by the Europeans was increased spending on defence and a clear commitment to NATO. The most concrete form of the inducement was a Canadian decision to purchase German Leopard main battle tanks for the CAF.[88] Nonetheless, inducement has limited uses in the premier domain—the Canada-United States relationship. Just as it takes more resources to induce a wealthy person than a poor one, so too does it require more resources than Canada has to induce a state with the capabilities and resources of the United States. In the course of the negotiations in 1986 and 1987 on the free trade agreement, there was a certain give-and-take on both sides, but as Michael Henderson has succinctly argued, given the capabilities and objectives on both sides,

Canada's ability to induce the United States into actions beneficial to Canadian interests was very limited.[89] Henderson notes that there was an asymmetry in desires at work that created an imbalance in bargaining strength: the Mulroney government wanted guaranteed and secure access to the American market more than the United States wanted whatever Canada could offer in return for an exemption from protectionist trade legislation. Indeed, when in the course of the negotiations the Reagan administration continued to impose protectionist measures on Canadian products, the Canadian side gave away a significant bargaining chip by citing these measures as proof that a free trade deal was needed.

There is a further problem with inducement: actions designed to induce may simply not be recognized as such. For example, one of the reasons why the Trudeau government agreed as early as 1982 to test the air-launched cruise missile was to induce the Reagan administration to abandon its antipathy to the measures introduced by Ottawa after the 1980 general elections. Cruise testing represented a major symbolic cost to the Trudeau government, given its long-standing antipathy towards the growth in the nuclear arsenals of the superpowers, and given the range and intensity of domestic opposition to testing. But judging from the subsequent behaviour of the government in Washington, there is little to indicate that American policy-makers regarded this as an inducement, to be met with reciprocal concessionary behaviour.

Persuasion

Because of its limited capacities, its vulnerabilities, and its dominant relationship with the United States, the Canadian government's most potent technique in achieving its objectives is the use of influence. For a state with limited ability to use the other techniques of statecraft—force, sanctions, coercion, or inducement—persuasion is the only technique left. In the context of international politics, the art of persuading an adversary to move to a position more congenial to one's interests is known as diplomacy. Canadian diplomacy is, not surprisingly, aimed at a wide variety of players on an array of issues: getting the British government to adopt economic sanctions against South Africa while at the same time trying to persuade London to abandon a plan to label Canadian furs to discourage buyers; convincing the United States Congress to amend a piece of trade legislation damaging to Canadian producers; rallying support among delegations at the United Nations General Assembly for changes in the wording of a resolution on non-proliferation; moving the Chinese to moderate their support for Pol Pot and the Khmer Rouge; urging a human rights violator to release a particular political prisoner; persuading the Australian government to accept new rules for trans-Pacific air links.

For a state in Canada's position, a *corps diplomatique* with standing and reputation is not only an essential part of the apparatus of state, but also potentially one of the state's most useful assets in its dealings with the outside world.[90] It is a power resource of considerable potency, as the record of Canadian diplomacy in the decade after the Second World War demonstrates. That era in Canada's foreign relations has come to be known as the "golden age of Canadian diplomacy." Of course, such a lavish assessment reflects in large part the mythologizing that is an inevitable part of a nation's history-making, but the hyperbole is not entirely unwarranted. During this period, the government was generally successful in achieving its foreign policy objectives and securing Canadian interests, particularly *vis-à-vis* the United States. There are a number of reasons for this. In part, it is because officials in this period recognized Canada's limitations internationally and framed their foreign policy objectives accordingly. But Canada's success during this period can also be attributed to the diplomatic skills of the secretary of state for external affairs, Lester Pearson, his diplomats in the Department of External Affairs, and the general support for diplomacy as a tool of Canadian statecraft provided by the political leadership.

By contrast, the 1970s have been characterized as an era of "frustrated designs" in Canadian foreign policy.[91] While the international context had changed somewhat from the 1950s, one can only conclude that many of the initiatives undertaken by the Trudeau government failed not only because foreign policy objectives were often cast without regard to the constraints of power, but also because the craft of Canadian diplomacy suffered considerably after 1968. Diplomacy was publicly disparaged by the prime minister and his senior advisers throughout the 1970s and never nurtured as it was in the 1950s. Trudeau underestimated the extent to which a diplomatic corps figures in the calculus of a state's power resources, and how those resources may be used to bring others closer to one's own interests.

POWER AND CANADIAN-AMERICAN RELATIONS

I have argued to this point that if one examines the pattern of Canada's international interactions, the dominant target of Canadian foreign policy will inexorably be the United States. I have also argued that the techniques of exercising power available to Canada in its relations with that country are limited. Force is not viable; nor are economic sanctions. Coercion is a dangerous game to play with a state which has a great capacity for inflicting damage, and a willingness to do so if pushed. Inducement has inherently more possibilities, but again Canadian governments are caught by the great disparities between the two countries. Persuasion, it has been suggested, is the most effective instrument, both generally in Canada's relations with other states, and specifically in the context of Canadian-American relations.

This is not to suggest that there are no limits to the art of diplomacy *vis-à-vis* the United States. On some issues, not even the finest diplomacy will prompt a change in Washington. The best contemporary example of this is the acid rain issue, which has bedevilled Canadian-American relations since it first made an appearance on the political agenda in 1977. Over the course of a decade, four Canadian prime ministers have grappled with the intractable: a United States government that resolutely refuses to move, and indeed has no incentive to do so, given the entrenched regional, political, and economic interests at stake. In the early 1980s, the Trudeau government tried persuasion in a variety of forms: rational scientific argument, quiet diplomacy, stiff diplomatic notes of protest, impassioned entreaty. The Liberals became so frustrated that they even went so far as to try overt propaganda techniques, passing out leaflets to hapless American tourists accusing their country of fouling the Canadian environment, and urging them to press for change when they got home. When Brian Mulroney and the Progressive Conservatives came to power in 1984, the tone and mood in the Canadian-American relationship changed considerably—and produced some initial success. Mulroney managed to achieve what Trudeau had not: an admission from Ronald Reagan at the Quebec summit in 1985 that both Canada and the United States had a shared responsibility to preserve the environment. But that was as far as it went. Neither the president nor Congress subsequently moved to tackle the sources of acid rain with any seriousness. The frustration of the Conservative government mounted as it rediscovered the wheel, resorting as its Liberal predecessor had done to the public diplomacy of vitriolic speeches and stiff notes of protest.[92] By the summer of 1988, American tourists were again being hit with Canadian propaganda, and it is likely that the cycle will repeat itself. But there is little more that can be done, short of embracing options that are either unthinkable or immensely costly.[93]

But Canada is not completely without levers in its relationship with the United States. First, Ottawa can take advantage of Canada's relative insignificance in the eyes of policy-makers in Washington. Canadian-American issues must compete for priority on the American foreign policy agenda with more important global questions. The attention of American foreign policy-makers is necessarily diverted and dissipated. This, of course, is a double-edged sword. It is advantageous to Canada when Ottawa acts and manages to avert a negative reaction from Washington because of relative inattention. It is, by contrast, a distinct disadvantage when Ottawa is seeking some form of action from Washington, and finds it difficult to secure a place on an always crowded presidential agenda.

Second, there are considerable constraints that act on American foreign-policy makers in their dealings with Canada. Most notably, there has been a general unwillingness in Washington to bring the huge resources of the United States to bear against its northern neighbour. To be sure, there have been several significant exceptions to this. For example, on 15 August 1971, President Richard Nixon unilaterally imposed the various elements of his new economic policy.[94] These far-ranging measures, including a special 10 per cent surcharge on imports, a proposal to foster American exports by the establishment of Domestic International Sales Corporations (DISCs), and an end to the convertibility of the dollar, were intended to reverse the dramatic slump in the United States balance of payments and ease the growing deficit. All of these measures, when enacted, would have a dramatic effect on Canada. The Canadian government of Pierre Trudeau simply assumed that the Nixon administration had formulated these measures without taking into account Canada and its close economic links with the United States, as Washington had done in 1963, 1966, and 1968, when it had introduced comparable measures to aid balance of payments. On those occasions, Canadian officials had flown to Washington to press the United States to exempt Canada from the effects of these measures. In August 1971, however, Canadian officials were surprised to discover first that there would be no exemption, and second, that these measures were actually aimed at Canada. As the United States Secretary of the Treasury, John Connolly, stated bluntly to Jean-Luc Pepin, the Canadian minister of industry, trade and commerce, the Nixon measures were intended "to shake the world. And that, brother, includes you!"[95]

A comparable assertion of American power occurred after Ronald Reagan's inauguration in January 1981. In 1980, the Trudeau government had introduced a number of new economic policies, including the National Energy Program, intended to strengthen the role of the state in the Canadian economy. Ottawa had not bothered to inform Washington beforehand and the reaction of the Carter administration to these measures, many of which adversely affected American interests, was one of "bitterness and outrage." This, however, was mild compared to the reaction of the officials Reagan brought with him to Washington. Throughout 1981 and well into 1982, the "California cowboys," as they were known in Ottawa, used a variety of tactics—Raymond Waldmann, assistant secretary of commerce in Washington called them "finger-twisting"—to press the Trudeau government to back down on numerous aspects of its economic program. As Stephen Clarkson so ably demonstrates,[96] the pressure was relentless, frequently rude, at times astounding,[97] and, not surprisingly, ultimately successful.

But, as significant as these cases are, when viewed in the historical perspective of Canadian-American relations, they represent temporary aberrations. Generally, the United States has avoided damaging the essential condition of friendship that pervades the relationship. That friendship is shaped in part by basic convergences of interest, ideology, and security; in part by the extensive economic, cultural, and personal linkages between the two societies. But it is to some extent a function of a hard calculation of national interest. The United States has little interest in upsetting what has become a very predictable relationship with a northern neighbour unlikely to take actions to undermine vital American interests. There is, therefore, generally little desire by the United States government to provoke a crisis in Canadian-American relations by using the more nasty tools of statecraft available to it. Given this constraint, the latitude for Canadian initiative, and the protection of Canadian interests, expands somewhat.

Finally, Canadians can take advantage of the amorphous structure of American government and the essentially pluralistic features of American politics. Certainly, there are disadvantages inherent in the purposeful division of powers that gives Congress so much authority over so many aspects of American foreign relations. The world is still living with the legacies of the defeat of the Versailles treaty by the United States Senate. All the contemporary trading partners of the United States have discovered what it means to have a government in Washington that is in favour of freer trade and in favour of protectionism—at the same time. For their part, Canadians were to receive a particularly forceful refresher course in American politics when in 1979, Ottawa negotiated east-coast treaties on fisheries and boundaries with the Carter administration only to have them founder in the Senate. (They were subsequently withdrawn from consideration by the incoming Reagan administration when it appeared that the treaties would fail a ratification vote in the Senate.[98])

On the other hand, this amorphousness also presents Canada with opportunities for creative statecraft. The pluralism mitigates concerted and united efforts by the United States to pursue a consistently hard line against Canada. While some Americans, both within and outside government, may be pressing for tougher measures against Canada on some issue, one will doubtless find other groups or bureaucratic/political actors to enlist as allies of Canadian interests within the policy process. For example, during the lumber disputes of the mid-1980s, while the lumber industry and their Congressional spokesmen complained loudly about the low price of Canadian lumber products, the Mulroney government was able to enlist support from the housing industry (and their Congressional supporters) for lower lumber prices. The Trudeau government had trod essentially the same path over the Garrison Diversion Unit in North Dakota a decade before.

Faced with the prospect of considerable environmental damage to Canada as a result of a massive irrigation scheme in North Dakota designed to pump waters from the Mississippi River basin over the continental divide into the Hudson Bay basin, the Canadian government worked closely with a variety of allies on the American side, including President Jimmy Carter, to have the project stopped. These groups had a variety of reasons (few having to do with a desire to protect the Canadian environment) for opposing the Garrison Diversion, but since their interests were complementary, they aided the pursuit of Canadian objectives.[99]

But in the management of the Canadian-American relationship, a correct calculation of power and the resources that can be brought to bear is critical for outcomes favourable to Canada's interests. The Alaska Boundary award of 1903 demonstrates the pitfalls of making an incorrect judgement about Canada's power *vis-à-vis* the United States. This hoary case is usually summoned out of the historical closet to demonstrate the willingness with which the imperial government in London so perfidiously sacrificed Canadian interests, an interpretation that, it can be argued, is open to some doubt. Here, however, the boundary award provides a useful illustration of the importance of power and the limits of diplomacy as a means of protecting and advancing one's interests when confronted by great power determined to prevail. The roots of the controversy go back to the late 1890s, and hinged on the interpretation of the words of an Anglo-Russian treaty of 1825 defining the Alaskan boundary. This document, which the United States inherited when Alaska was ceded by Russia in 1867, defined the boundary as a line not to exceed ten marine leagues inland from a line "parallel to the sinuosities of the coast." The problem lay in the fjord-like geography of what eventually came to be known as the Panhandle, and in particular a deep inlet called Lynn Canal, at the head of which were two well-established American communities, Skagway and Dyea. The Canadian contention was that the line should run ten leagues from the *mouth* of Lynn Canal, thus assuring Canada of access to the sea from the Yukon territory where gold had just been discovered; the Americans claimed that the line should be measured from the *heads* of the inlets, thus ensuring not only that Skagway would remain American but also that Canada would have no access to the sea north of the Dixon Entrance.

A sustained attempt to negotiate a settlement in the fall and winter of 1898-99 was made by American, British, and Canadian negotiators; included on the Canadian side was the prime minister, Sir Wilfrid Laurier. At the outset, the American negotiators tried to find a compromise that would keep Skagway American but give Canada access to the sea. However, in what Stacey describes as "a mood of rather extravagant self-confidence,"[100] the Canadians decided to refuse anything less than the original claim. Nor did they accept any proposals being made to them by the British for arbitration or settlement, believing that time, and British imperial power, was on their side.

It was a bad miscalculation. With the passage of time would come Theodore Roosevelt, who became president after William McKinley was assassinated in September 1901. Teddy Roosevelt was at his most jingoistic in the Alaskan affair. Although it was eventually agreed in early 1903 to appoint a tribunal consisting of three "impartial jurists of repute" from each side to decide on the matters in contention, Roosevelt appointed Elihu Root, a lawyer who also happened to be his Secretary of War, and two politicians, both of whom had spoken out against the Canadian claim, and neither of whom were jurists. To ensure that there would be no misunderstanding, Roosevelt's letter of instruction to his "impartial jurists" dictated that "there will of course be no compromise." Finally, for good measure, he warned the British that if London raised any "captious objections" to the American claim, "I am going to send a brigade of American regulars up to Skagway ... and hold it by all the power and force of the United States." The British government had little stomach for the prospect of a fight with Roosevelt: in the end, the British prime minister urged Lord Alverstone, the British chairman of the Canadian side, to find for the United States. He did, much to the chagrin of the two Canadian members, the government, the press, and Canadian public opinion.[101]

CONCLUSIONS:
THE LIMITATIONS OF LIMITED CAPACITY

Some states in the international system may ignore the constraints of power. For many years, for example, the People's Republic of Albania evinced a total disregard for the pragmatist's dictum that policy is the art of the possible. But Albania is an autarky, cut off by choice from intercourse with the international community. Other states, engaged in a complex web of relationships beyond their borders, do not enjoy the luxury of autarky: in seeking to achieve their objectives beyond their borders, they must confront the realities of power and its exercise. In the international system, no state is autonomous in the sense that no state, not even the most powerful, is able to ensure that its actions will accord with its preferences. And so it is with Canada: the Canadian government cannot do exactly as it pleases, either in domestic policy (if that domestic policy has external ramifications) or in external policy. If it is to be effective—in other words, able to achieve its objectives—a state's foreign policy must be crafted with careful attention to what is attainable. "Discretion in diplomacy," John W. Holmes has written, "is in the calculation of the issues at stake and the forces which can be mustered,"[102] and, of course, the forces that are likely to be mustered against one by other states.

Because of this, the question of capabilities assumes considerable importance. The principal domain of Canada's international "power relationships" is the United States, not only because of the imperatives of neighbourhood and of economic structure, but also because the United States is one of the two superpowers engaged in a struggle for dominance at the apex of the international system. It is when the focus of an assessment of Canada's power is fixed on its dominant relationship that the utility of a "power analysis" approach rather than a "power image" approach becomes evident. The picture that emerges of Canadian power is not that of a foremost nation. Rather, it is of a state which must always be sensitive to the preponderance of power on the North American continent. Power analysis also directs our attention to the importance of disparities in capability, of the importance of strategy and calculation of how to derive maximum advantage by a judicious use of the resources and techniques of power. Although there is a clear asymmetry of capabilities between Canada and the United States, Canada does not lack what power-analysts term power resources. It is not relegated inexorably to the ranks of the weak by this disparity, forever destined to succumb to finger-twisting and hardball politics. But it cannot avoid the necessity of showing "how wit with small means may accomplish wonders where great force availeth not."[103]

NOTES

1 Hans J. Morgenthau, *Politics Among Nations: The Struggle for Power and Peace*, 5th ed. (New York: Alfred A. Knopf, 1948, 1973), 27.

2 For example, David A. Baldwin, *Economic Statecraft* (Princeton: Princeton University Press, 1985).

3 Quoted in J.L. Granatstein, *The Ottawa Men: The Civil Service Mandarins, 1935-1957* (Toronto: Oxford University Press, 1982), 73.

4 Dominion prime ministers quoted in C.P. Stacey, *Canada and the Age of Conflict*, vol. 1: *1867-1921* (Toronto: Macmillan, 1977), 244-48.

5 Four diplomatic ranks were agreed to at the Congress of Vienna in 1815: Ambassador (their missions being known as embassies); Ministers Plenipotentiary rank second, their missions termed legations; followed by Minister Resident and Chargé d'affaires.

6 Canada, Department of External Affairs, *Documents on Canadian External Relations*, vol. 3: *1919-1925*, Lovell C. Clark, ed. (Ottawa, 1970), 7.

7 Quoted in James Eayrs, "Defining a new place for Canada in the hierarchy of world powers," *International Perspectives* (May/June 1975, reprinted November/December 1981), 7.

8 For discussions of the functional principle, see John W. Holmes, *The Shaping of Peace: Canada and the Search for World Order*, vol. 1 (Toronto: University of Toronto Press, 1979), 29-73; Michael Tucker, *Canadian Foreign Policy: Contemporary Issues and Themes* (Toronto: McGraw-Hill Ryerson, 1980), 6-7.

9 Lionel Gelber, "A greater Canada among the nations," *Behind the Headlines* (1944), quoted in Peter C. Dobell, *Canada's Search for New Roles: Foreign Policy in the Trudeau Era* (Toronto: Oxford University Press, 1972), 2.

10 Quoted in R.A. MacKay, "The Canadian doctrine of the middle powers," in Harvey L. Dyck and H. Peter Krosby, eds., *Empire and Nations: Essays in Honour of Frederic H. Soward* (Toronto: University of Toronto Press, 1969), 134.

11 Quoted in Eayrs, "Defining a new place for Canada," 6.

12 Quoted in C.P. Stacey, *Age of Conflict*, vol. 2: *1921-1948 — The Mackenzie King Era* (Toronto: University of Toronto Press, 1981), 380.

13 Lester B. Pearson, *Words and Occasions* (Toronto: University of Toronto Press, 1970), 63.

14 See Holmes, *Shaping of Peace*, vol. 1, 247-59, for a discussion of Canadian diplomacy at San Fransisco; for the Australian view, see Norman Harper, *A Great and Powerful Friend: A Study of Australian American Relations Between 1900 and 1975* (St. Lucia and New York: University of Queensland Press, 1987), 136-48. The leader of the Australian delegation, H.V. Evatt, did not always endear himself to others in his crusade. The Americans likened him to a "bull in a china shop," while Lester Pearson noted later that frequently Evatt had to be "saved from the snares of his courage (or if you like, pig-headedness and vanity) by other delegations including our own."

15 Carsten Holbraad, *Middle Powers in International Politics* (London: Macmillan Press, 1984), esp. ch. 1. Among the early writers on the gradation of states were Thomas Aquinas, and Giovanni Botero, a sixteenth-century professor of rhetoric who was eventually to become archbishop of Milan.

16 It is interesting to note that a century and a half later, a study of middle powers by the Research Institute of the German Society for Foreign Policy would reflect this geostrategic concern by defining a middle power as a state which played an influential role in its region. Holbraad, *Middle Powers*, 72.

17 *Ibid.* See also the discussion of distance in Annette Baker Fox, *The Politics of Attraction: Four Middle Powers and the United States* (New York: Columbia University Press, 1977), 88-91.

18 Paul Painchaud made this observation, though he termed it an "ideology of foreign policy": "Middlepowermanship as an ideology," in J. King Gordon, ed., *Canada's Role as a Middle Power* (Toronto: Canadian Institute of International Affairs, 1966), 29-35.

19 John W. Holmes, "Is there a future for middlepowermanship?" in *ibid.*, 13-28; Holmes coined the term as a spoof on the tendency of American officials to glowingly describe their diplomacy *vis-à-vis* the Soviet Union and China in the late 1950s and early 1960s as "brinkmanship."

20 For Pearson's own account, see *Mike: The Memoirs of the Rt. Hon. Lester B. Pearson*, vol. 2: *1948-1957*, John A. Munro and Alex I. Inglis, eds. (Toronto: University of Toronto Press, 1973), ch. 9.

21 The notion that Canada, because of its historical links to both Britain and the United States, could act as a "linchpin" between London and Washington, was popular during the Second World War. "The idea," John W. Holmes has written, "must have been conceived by Canadians groping for some rationalization of their frustrating position in the world, and by Britons and Americans as a post-prandial sop to a friend." *The Better Part of Valour: Essays on Canadian Diplomacy* (Toronto: McClelland and Stewart, 1970), 156. It should be noted that Mackenzie King, who was supposed to be the "linchpin," never was called on to act as such. As the Quebec Conferences in August 1943 and September 1944 amply demonstrated, F.D. Roosevelt and Winston Churchill needed no mid-Atlantic interpreter. Mackenzie King was cast instead into the unhappy role of hosting both conferences, but participating in neither. However, he was content to be frequently photographed with the two leaders, hoping to be identified with them in the minds of Canadians. Stacey, *Age of Conflict*, vol. 2, 334; also 324-26.

22 See, for example, Peyton V. Lyon and Brian W. Tomlin, *Canada as an International Actor* (Toronto: Macmillan, 1979), 13.

23 The most comprehensive account of Canadian diplomacy during this conflict is Denis Stairs, *The Diplomacy of Constraint: Canada, the Korean War and the United States* (Toronto: University of Toronto Press, 1974), esp. ch. 4.

24 Indeed, Douglas A. Ross concludes from his examination of Canada's role in Vietnam that Ottawa's diplomacy helped to forestall the possibility that the United States government would employ nuclear weapons in Vietnam. *In the Interests of Peace: Canada and Vietnam, 1954-1973* (Toronto: University of Toronto Press, 1984).

25 Quemoy and Matsu, two groups of islands located just off the coast of the Chinese mainland, were occupied by Nationalist Chinese troops when the Korean War broke out in June 1950, and were thus protected by the United States. Throughout the 1950s, the offshore islands remained an area of high tension, with both the People's Republic of China and the Nationalist forces bombarding one another with periodic artillery attacks and, more frequently, propaganda barrages. See the discussion in Holmes, *Shaping of Peace*, vol. 2 (Toronto: University of Toronto Press, 1982), 195-97.

26 Frank R. Hayes, "South Africa's departure from the Commonwealth, 1960-61," *International History Review* 2 (July 1980), 453-84; and Hayes, "Canada, the Commonwealth and the Rhodesia issue," in Kim Richard Nossal, ed., *An Acceptance of Paradox: Essays on Canadian Diplomacy in Honour of John W. Holmes* (Toronto: Canadian Institute of International Affairs, 1982).

27 R.B. Tackaberry, "Keeping the peace," *Behind the Headlines* 26 (September 1966); Lyon and Tomlin, *Canada as an International Actor*, 14-17.

28 The Canadian International Image Study was conducted by R.B. Byers, David Leyton-Brown, and Peyton Lyon; see *International Journal* 32 (Summer 1977), 605-71. Results on Canada's power reported in Lyon and Tomlin, *Canada as an International Actor*, 57, 79-93.

29 Quoted in Bruce Thordarson, *Trudeau and Foreign Policy: A Study in Decision-Making* (Toronto: Oxford University Press, 1972), 69.

30 Dobell, *Canada's Search for New Roles*, 4.

31 Quoted in Eayrs, "Defining a new place for Canada," 7.

32 Canada, Secretary of State for External Affairs, *Foreign Policy for Canadians* (Ottawa: Information Canada, 1970), main booklet, 6. For a cogent critique of Trudeau's initial statements on foreign affairs, see Peyton V. Lyon, "The Trudeau Doctrine," *International Journal* 26 (Winter 1970-1), 19-43.

33 Akira Ichikawa, "The 'helpful fixer': Canada's persistent international image," *Behind the Headlines* 37 (March 1979).

34 Canada, Parliament, House of Commons, *Debates*, unrev. vol. 127:30, 1983-84, 1211-16, 9 February 1984. Reprinted in C. David Crenna, ed., *Pierre Elliott Trudeau: Lifting the Shadow of War* (Edmonton: Hurtig Publishers, 1987), 106-110.

35 See the government's green paper on foreign policy: Joe Clark, *Competitiveness and Security: Directions for Canada's International Relations* (Ottawa: Supply and Services Canada, 1985), and the government's reaction to a parliamentary report on foreign policy: Joe Clark, *Canada's International Relations: Response of the Government of Canada to the Report of the Special Joint Committee of the Senate and the House of Commons* (Ottawa: Supply and Services Canada, 1986).

36 Canada, Parliament, House of Commons, Special Committee on the Peace Process in Central America, *Supporting the Five: Canada and the Central American Peace Process* (Ottawa: July 1988), 27-29.

37 See J.L. Granatstein, ed., *Canadian Foreign Policy Since 1945: Middle Power or Satellite?*, 3rd ed. (Toronto: Copp Clark, 1973).

38 See, for example, the argument in John Hutcheson, *Dominance and Dependency: Liberalism and National Policies in the North Atlantic Triangle* (Toronto: McClelland and Stewart, 1978), 44-45.

39 Archibald MacMechan, "Canada as a vassal state," *Canadian Historical Review* 1 (December 1920), 347-53; MacMechan particularly lamented the propensity of Canadians to flock to the "new" American cinemas, a concern that would persist over the course of the twentieth century.

40 Quoted in Philip Resnick, "Canadian defence policy and the American empire," in Ian Lumsden, ed., *Close the 49th Parallel Etc: The Americanization of Canada* (Toronto: University of Toronto Press, 1970), 99.

41 James M. Minifie, *Peacemaker or Powdermonkey: Canada's Role in a Revolutionary World* (Toronto: McClelland and Stewart, 1960), 52.

42 Michael K. Hawes, *Principal Power, Middle Power, or Satellite? Competing Perspectives in the Study of Canadian Foreign Policy* (North York: York Research Programme in Strategic Studies, 1984), 22.

43 Indicative would be: Walter Gordon, *A Choice for Canada: Independence or Colonial Status* (Toronto: McClelland and Stewart, 1966); Stephen Clarkson, ed., *An Independent Foreign Policy for Canada?* (Toronto: McClelland and Stewart, 1968); Dave Godfrey with Mel Watkins, eds., *Gordon to Watkins to You, A Documentary: The Battle for Control of our Economy* (Toronto: New Press, 1970); also Lumsden, ed., *Close the 49th Parallel*.

44 John W. Warnock, *Partner to Behemoth: The Military Policy of a Satellite Canada* (Toronto: New Press, 1970); Kenneth McNaught, "From colony to satellite," in Clarkson, ed., *An Independent Foreign Policy*, 177-78.

45   George Grant, *Lament for a Nation: The Defeat of Canadian Nationalism* (Toronto: McClelland and Stewart, 1965), *passim.*

46   George Martell, "What can I do right now? Notes from Point Blank School on the Canadian dilemma," in Lumsden, ed., *Close the 49th Parallel,* 291.

47   Hawes, *Principal Power, Middle Power, or Satellite?,* 25.

48   Wallace Clement, "Continental political economy: an assessment of the relations between Canada and the United States," *Canadian Review of American Studies* 10 (Spring 1979), 77-88; Jean Kirk Laux, "Global interdependence and state intervention," in B. Tomlin, ed., *Canada's Foreign Policy: Analysis and Trends* (Toronto: Methuen, 1978), 110-35; Stephen Clarkson, *Canada and the Reagan Challenge: Crisis and Adjustment, 1981-85,* rev. ed. (Toronto: James Lorimer, 1985).

49   *The Globe and Mail,* 24 May 1985, 7.

50   Eayrs, "Defining a new place for Canada."

51   Norman Hillmer and Garth Stevenson, eds., *Foremost Nation: Canadian Foreign Policy and a Changing World* (Toronto: McClelland and Stewart, 1977), 2. It should be noted that the editors were so impressed by the profundity of the changes in the international system in the mid-1970s that they declared that much of the existing literature on Canadian foreign policy had been rendered obsolete.

52   Cline, *World Power Assessment 1977,* 78.

53   Lyon and Tomlin, *Canada as an International Actor,* 72. Their indices are discussed on 58-71; also *fn* 3-7 and 13, on 73-75.

54   David B. Dewitt and John J. Kirton, *Canada as a Principal Power: A Study of Foreign Policy and International Relations* (Toronto: John Wiley and Sons, 1983), 38.

55   It is noteworthy that many American scholars appear to be attracted to theoretical perspectives on international politics that deny American power—and repelled by those approaches that are fundamentally accepting of the inexorable nastiness that comes with being a great power. The assertions commonly found in the international relations literature about the increasing "complex interdependence" of the contemporary international system, or the rapid decline of American hegemony, are basically power-denying, and thus, for those scholars uncomfortable with the projection of power, psychologically satisfying.

56   *Ibid.,* 40.

57   Allan Gotlieb, *Canadian Diplomacy in the 1980s: Leadership and Service* (Toronto: Centre for International Studies, University of Toronto, 1979).

58   Allan Gotlieb, "Canada: a nation comes of age," *The Globe and Mail,* 29 October 1987, A7.

59   Don Munton, "Middle power and Canadian foreign policy," paper presented to the Canadian Political Science Association, Montreal, June 1980.

60   Indeed, Holbraad, *Middle Powers,* 214, *fn* 5, suggests that preferences for "middleness" international politics may have been driven by the same kind of belief that James Mill had in the "middle" class as the "most virtuous part of the community."

61 Quoted in *ibid.*, 12.

62 So Lester Pearson was informed by his hosts during his visit to the Soviet Union in 1955: quoted in Eayrs, "Defining a new place," 7.

63 Lyon and Tomlin were told this during their "image" study: *Canada as an International Actor*, 80.

64 Based on a combination of GNP and population, Holbraad suggests 18 middle powers. In descending order of "middleness," they are: Japan, West Germany, China, France, Britain, Canada, Italy, Brazil, Spain, Poland, India, Australia, Mexico, Iran, Argentina, South Africa, Indonesia, and Nigeria. As Holbraad notes, not all of this group would feel comfortable in the middle. Some are frustrated would-be great powers; others are ex-great powers with some of the trappings of great-power status such as permanent membership on the Security Council; while others still are self-consciously middle powers. The heterogeneity and differing self-perceptions of this group demonstrates nicely the pitfalls of trying to establish middle power by statistical means. Holbraad, *Middle Powers*, 90; also 221-23: *fn* 29.

65 Stanley Hoffmann, "Notes on the elusiveness of modern power," *International Journal* 30 (Spring 1975), 184-87.

66 Robert A. Dahl, "The concept of power," in Roderick Bell, David V. Edwards and R. Harrison Wagner, eds., *Political Power: A Reader in Theory and Research* (New York: Free Press, 1969), 80; see also Hoffmann, "Elusiveness of modern power," 188.

67 Steven Lukes, *Power: A Radical View* (London: Macmillan, 1974), 27. See also Felix E. Oppenheim, "Power and causation," in Brian Barry, ed., *Power and Political Theory: Some European Perspectives* (Toronto: John Wiley, 1976), 103-108.

68 Robert A. Dahl, *Modern Political Analysis*, 4th ed. (Englewood Cliffs: Prentice-Hall Inc., 1984), 27.

69 Harold and Margaret Sprout, *Foundations of International Politics* (New York: D. Van Nostrand, 1962), 136-77.

70 David A. Baldwin, "Interdependence and power: a conceptual analysis," *International Organization* 34 (Autumn 1980), 497.

71 See Lyon and Tomlin, *Canada as an International Actor*, ch. 3, 35-55.

72 *Ibid.*, 71.

73 This paradox is discussed at length in David A. Baldwin, "Power analysis and world politics: new trends versus old tendencies," *World Politics* 31 (January 1979), 163*ff*.

74 David A. Baldwin, "Money and power," *Journal of Politics* 33 (August 1971), 578-614.

75 For an account, see Jeffrey Simpson, *Discipline of Power: The Conservative Interlude and the Liberal Restoration* (Toronto: Personal Library, 1980), 145-59.

76 Kal J. Holsti, *International Politics: A Framework for Analysis*, 4th ed. (Englewood Cliffs: Prentice-Hall Inc., 1983), 155-57.

77 Lukes, *Power*, 17-18, 32.

78 Jack H. Nagel, *The Descriptive Analysis of Power* (New Haven: Yale University Press, 1975), 16. Lukes also adds manipulation to his techniques of power: A.

by structuring B's decision-making environment, manipulates B into thinking that his interests are identical to, or coincident with, A's. Indeed, manipulation is integral to his three-dimensional view of power: see *Power*, *passim*.

79 R.B. Byers, "The Canadian military and the use of force: end of an era?" *International Journal* 30 (Spring 1975), 289-90.

80 Desmond Morton, "Defending the indefensible: some historical perspectives on Canadian defence, 1867-1987," *International Journal* 42 (Autumn 1987), 628.

81 For a good account of this odd, and largely unremembered, episode in Canadian military history, see Stacey, *Age of Conflict*, vol. 1, 276-84.

82 For an account of this procurement, see Michael Tucker, *Canadian Foreign Policy: Contemporary Issues and Themes* (Toronto: McGraw-Hill Ryerson, 1980), ch. 5, 143-74.

83 See the rationale in the government's white paper on defence: Canada, Department of National Defence, *Challenge and Commitment: A Defence Policy for Canada* (Ottawa: June 1987), 23-24, 52-55.

84 For one such critique, see Joseph T. Jockel and Joel J. Sokolsky, *Canada and Collective Security: Odd Man Out*, The Washington Papers 121 (New York: Praeger, 1986).

85 See Stacey, *Age of Conflict*, vol. 1, 180-88, for details of the "Riddell incident."

86 Quoted in Denis Stairs, "Confronting Uncle Sam: Cuba and Korea," in Clarkson, ed., *An Independent Foreign Policy for Canada?*, 61.

87 Clarence G. Redekop, "The Mulroney government and South Africa: constructive disengagement," *Behind the Headlines* 44 (December 1986); for South African policy during the Trudeau period, see Linda Freeman, "Canada and Africa in the 1970s," *International Journal* 35 (Autumn 1980); T.A. Keenleyside, "Canada-South Africa commercial relations, 1977-1982: business as usual?" *Canadian Journal of African Studies* 17 (1983); and Clarence G. Redekop, "Commerce over conscience: the Trudeau government and South Africa, 1968-1984," *Journal of Canadian Studies* 19 (Winter 1984-85).

88 See accounts in Tucker, *Canadian Foreign Policy*, 126-33; and Robert Bothwell, "'The Canadian connection': Canada and Europe," in Hillmer and Stevenson, eds., *Foremost Nation*, 24-36.

89 Michael D. Henderson, "The negotiations: power, will and progress," in Henderson, ed., *The Future on the Table: Canada and the Free Trade Issue* (Toronto: Masterpress, 1987), esp. 165-66.

90 For an extended discussion on this theme, see John W. Holmes, *Canada: A Middle-Aged Power* (Toronto: McClelland and Stewart, 1976), 44-53.

91 Tucker, *Canadian Foreign Policy*, ix.

92 For a good account, see Don Munton, "Conflict over common property: Canada-U.S. environmental issues," in Maureen Appel Molot and Brian W. Tomlin, ed., *Canada Among Nations—1987: A World of Conflict* (Toronto: James Lorimer, 1988), 178-97.

93 One possible strategem for Canadian diplomacy on acid rain that has not been tried is suggested by the Coase theorem from economics. Applying this theorem, Robert Keohane supposed that soot from a paint factory was deposited onto clothing drying in the yard of an old-fashioned commercial laundry. He assumed

that the damage was greater than the $20,000 it would cost the laundry to close the yard and install indoor dryers; he also assumed that it would cost the paint factory $10,000 to install scrubbers to eliminate the pollution. In the absence of a sovereign authority to impose a conception of the "common good" and legal liability, the owner of the paint factory would have no incentive to spend any money to eliminate the negative externalities of his operations. In the absence of law and legal liability, the laundry owner has three choices—all unpleasant (but not equally so). He can continue to lose more than $20,000 in soiled laundry; he can pay at least $20,000 to install dryers; or he can pay the owner of the paint factory anywhere from $10,000 to $20,000 to stop the pollution. (We are also assuming here a peaceable laundry owner, for a resort to violence against the paint factory or its owner is also a possibility.) The Coase theorem suggests that it is rational for the laundry owner in these circumstances to pay the $10,000 to stop the negative externalities. The similarities to Canada's dilemma on acid rain are both interesting and suggestive. See the discussion in Robert O. Keohane, *After Hegemony: Cooperation and Discord in the World Political Economy* (Princeton: Princeton University Press, 1984), 85*ff.*

94   The following discussion depends heavily on the excellent account of the Nixon "shocks" and Canada's reaction in Peter C. Dobell, *Canada in World Affairs*, vol. 17: *1971-1973* (Toronto: Canadian Institute of International Affairs, 1985), 13-29.

95   Quoted in *ibid.*, 23. Dobell notes that a great deal of Canadian resentment was directed towards the former governor of Texas, who, it seems, knew little and cared less about Canada. A man with little sensitivity to the finer points of international politics, he had little time for those in the State Department in Washington who tended to be "soft" on foreigners.

96   Clarkson, *Canada and the Reagan Challenge*, 23-49. It should be noted that this chapter was based on confidential documents leaked to Clarkson, and provides a fascinating view of the application of power.

97   One American official outlined a plan to destabilize the Liberal Party's Ontario and Quebec strongholds by "pass[ing] the word to Wall Street that Canada is not a good place to invest." The dollar would fall; inflation would rise; the standard of living in Canada would decline. As Clarkson notes, "The fine line separating brainstorming from fantasizing was easy to cross." *Ibid.*, 35.

98   The failure of the 1979 treaties prompted John W. Holmes to note testily: "The United States, we fear, is increasingly incapable of conducting rational relations with any foreign country as the federal administration ... is bound and overruled by the captious actions of a Congress that is a law unto itself, disdainful even of international commitments." *Life with Uncle: The Canadian-American Relationship* (Toronto: University of Toronto Press, 1981), 61.

99   See Kim Richard Nossal, "The unmaking of Garrison: United States politics and the management of Canadian-American boundary waters," *Behind the Headlines* 37 (December 1978).

100 Stacey, *Age of Conflict*, vol. 1, 89.

101 For accounts, see *ibid.*, 86-99; also Donald Creighton, *Canada's First Century* (Toronto: Macmillan, 1970), 96-97.

102 John W. Holmes, *The Better Part of Valour: Essays on Canadian Diplomacy* (Toronto: McClelland and Stewart, 1970), vii.

103 Quoted in Annette Baker Fox and William T.R. Fox, "Domestic capabilities and Canadian foreign policy," *International Journal* 39 (Winter 1983-4), 25.

PART TWO

THE DOMESTIC SETTING

CHAPTER FOUR

Society and Foreign Policy

INTRODUCTION

Just as a state's foreign policy decisions are shaped by the external environment and the power it exercises in pursuit of its foreign policy objectives, so too is the behaviour of policy-makers shaped by their domestic environment. Such an observation is hardly new. Over two thousand years ago, Sun Tzu suggested that the successful pursuit of a state's external relations depended on the existence of "harmony" between the people and their sovereign. In the same era, the Athenian general Pericles was compelled to address the domestic political consequences of discontent over the conduct of the Peloponnesian war. Sun Tzu's Taoist prescriptions for the successful general and Thucydides's account of the great war of the ancient Greeks share a commonality that goes well beyond their contemporaneousness. Both recognized that the relationship between the governed and their governors will affect the craft of state.[1]

This truism applies with special force in a democratic political system like Canada's. In such a system, relations between governors and the governed are conditioned by the normative considerations of liberal democratic theory. These include the equality of all citizens; individual consent to be governed; the supremacy or sovereignty of "the people"; representative institutions of governance that provide for the public accountability of the governors; and the paramountcy of constitutionalism and the rule of law. In short, the precepts of democratic liberalism suggest that the behaviour of democratic governments *should* be affected and conditioned by the preferences of groups and citizens in society.

As we saw in the introductory chapter, most theories of the democratic state tend to reflect this normative orientation. They argue that policy is best explained by reference to the interests, preferences, and political demands of individuals and groups in society—classes, interest associations of every kind, mass movements, unions, churches, firms, the media, and citizens' groups. The groups which dot society's landscape communicate their interests, preferences, and political demands to the state in a variety of ways: through public opinion that is tapped by frequent poll-taking, mass demonstrations and personal communications, lobbying of different sorts, formal representation on public committees or boards, and, of course, through voting. However, as we have seen, there is little agreement about the relative potency of these groups on the outcomes of the policy-making process. Theorists employing Marxist assumptions will stress the importance of the interests of the dominant class in determining decisions. Liberal theorists will contend that government policy is the outcome of the interplay of many, and often divergent, interests within society. Those employing statist assumptions about the relationship between state and society will fix their focus on the interests and preferences of state officials and will tend to deprecate the importance of societal actors and their preferences.[2]

The purpose of this chapter is to assess to what extent, and how, individuals and groups in society, or "societal actors," as they will be termed here, shape Canadian foreign policy. It surveys the various foreign policy interests of Canadians and their political activity. We then examine how societal actors bring their interests to bear on the making of policy.

SOCIETAL INTERESTS

Political Interests and Political Action

We must preface an examination of the societal sources of foreign policy in Canada by making explicit the assumptions about individuals, their interests, and political action that underlie the analysis below. To help organize this examination, we employ some, but not all, of the assumptions of liberal-pluralist theory.

Interests and the value-maximizing axiom. Liberal-pluralist theory assumes that all individuals within a political community have a variety of values and interests that they cherish and want to see maximized. But value-maximization hypothesis does not mean that every member of the polity will engage in political activity. Many members of a community will engage in only minimal political involvement. For some, this is because they feel their interests are more or less well served by the political system. Others, however, may feel that their interests are *not* being maximized but may not become actively engaged in political action to try to change this. Some would argue that not being involved in fact maximizes the values of these individuals, but such a dogmatic view masks the reality that often such minimal involvement is the result not of the lack of desire, but the lack of capacity and the consequent feelings of political inefficacy ("what difference will it make if I become involved?"). Still others feel their interests are not being maximized and will be prompted into political action—either to advance their interests or to protect them from the predations of others with conflicting interests.[3]

How will they do this? Since individuals, acting alone, are unlikely to be able to advance or protect their interests, they will tend to identify, associate, and organize with others who have identical or complementary interests and values. These groups of individuals with associated interests will then seek to mobilize support, both within society at large, and particularly within the state, using a number of means to express their interests.[4]

Interests: concrete and symbolic. Interests and values can be grouped into two broad categories—concrete and symbolic. Interests that directly affect an individual's welfare or well-being (usually defined in material terms, though this is not a necessary condition) are concrete interests, while those interests or values that an individual may still seek to maximize, but will not materially affect him or her, are symbolic interests. For example, the owner of a firm which imports South African fruit into Canada, an individual whose parents live in Cape Town, a sprinter who has been invited to participate in a track and field event in Durban, and a member of a campus anti-*apartheid* group will all have an interest in Canada's relations with South Africa. But their interests will differ considerably. It will affect the concrete, and material, interests of the fruit importer if the Canadian government imposes a ban on the importation of South African produce. It will affect the concrete interests of the individual with parents in South Africa if the Canadian government restricts travel between the two countries, though these concrete interests are not material. And the sprinter's concrete interests will be affected (in both material and non-material ways) by a ban on Canadian participation in South African sporting events. However, whether Canada imposes a ban on fruit imports, travel, or sporting events, the concrete interests of the member of the anti-*apartheid* group will not be directly affected (assuming that the individual is not a fruit-importing athlete with family in South Africa). Of course, this individual's symbolic interests will be much affected by the outcome of policy, for to draw the distinction is not to deprecate the emotional intensity which symbolic interests generate. The distinction is important, however, because whether an individual's interest in foreign policy is concrete or symbolic will have a marked bearing not only on the level and nature of political activity, but also on the impact of this activity on policy-makers.

Liberal pluralism: a caveat. The use here of an orthodox set of liberal and pluralist assumptions is intended to be strictly limited to understanding the interests of individuals and their political activity. It is *not* intended to suggest that liberal-pluralist theory should also be used to analyze the *effects* of this activity on policy. The theory makes the misleading assumption that all citizens have an equal opportunity to influence policy. William D. Coleman has nicely (if a little sardonically) described what is supposed to happen according to the precepts of liberal-pluralist theory: "Everyone is consulted, everyone is listened to. Then the politicians stir up this big pot of opinions until it wafts forth the vapours of the general, public interest, which are translated into law for the good of everyone."[5] But, as Coleman hastens to add, this is simply not what happens in reality: not all citizens have an equal impact on policy-making.

However, not all of the precepts of liberal-pluralist theory are equally misleading. Certainly the assumptions the theory makes about interests and political activity equip us with the capacity to organize our analysis by posing two distinct questions. First, what are the foreign policy interests of Canadians? Second, how do they go about advancing or protecting these interests? It is only then that we can assess how effective they are in shaping both the process and the environment of foreign policy decision-making.

The Range of Interests

It is appropriate to begin by asking how interested Canadians as a whole are in foreign policy. Some clearly are, but it is difficult to know what percentage simply have no interest in their country's international policies. On the one hand, there is a widespread assumption, based more on intuition than systematic evidence, that Canadians as a whole are not very interested in international affairs. They are, in this view, insular and inward-looking, more concerned with domestic interests. "The public have been mildly interested in the dispute—from the sidelines," a Department of External Affairs memorandum advised Prime Minister W.L. Mackenzie King in October 1935 during the conflict over Italy's invasion of Ethiopia (or, as it was also known then, Abyssinia). "People are immensely more interested in Alberta than Abyssinia."[6] Forty-one years later, the assumptions had not changed: Claude Wagner, the Progressive Conservative opposition critic for external affairs, told the House of Commons in 1976 that "The people of Canada care more about bread and butter issues, inflation and unemployment, than they do about foreign policy."[7]

On the other hand, public opinion polls suggest the opposite. When asked about their interest in Canada's role in world affairs in October 1987, 34.1 per cent of the 1,210 respondents were very interested, 44.7 per cent somewhat interested, 16.5 per cent not very interested, 3.8 per cent not at all interested, while eleven respondents (0.9 per cent) didn't know whether they were interested or not. Of the sample, 54.1 per cent claimed that their interest had "increased" over the previous five years, while only 5.4 per cent said that their interest had decreased over the same period.[8] Comparable results in polls done for the Department of External Affairs in 1984 and 1985 led a senior official in the Policy Development Bureau to conclude that "The picture that emerged was one of a society in which the vast majority express an interest in international events ... and expect their government to be actively engaged in finding solutions to international problems."[9] (Of course, what picture one sees in these Rorschach tests of the nation's opinion will heavily depend on one's theology: worshippers of what has become a twentieth-century political idol will draw all manner of meaningful conclusions from polls; the impious among us are likely to be less impressed.)

While we may not have a clear picture of the level of interest Canadians in general have in international politics, we cannot deny that numerous Canadians do have interests in foreign policy which they express in myriad ways. The range of these interests is rich and diverse, and it would take a larger canvas than we have here to do them justice. However, we can identify three key areas: the interests of individuals in their ethnicity, in their egoistic material and physical well-being, and in giving expression to their empathy with the well-being, both material and physical, of others.[10]

Ethnic Interests

Unlike many communities composed of ethnically homogenous groups whose genealogical forebears occupied the same territory for millenia, but like Australia, New Zealand, South Africa, and the United States, Canada is the relatively recent political creation of emigrés who fashioned their new polity after their own image (rather than integrating into the existing political communities of the aboriginal inhabitants). Immigration has thus always played a fundamental role in the shaping of Canadian society.[11] The process began with the first tenuous settlements of British, French, Dutch, and Swedes established in the late sixteenth and early seventeenth centuries. From 1600 to 1763, when perforce all North Americans east of the Mississippi (save those on the islands of St. Pierre and Miquelon) became subjects of the British Crown, the other European sponsors of North American settlements would gradually be eliminated as large-scale sources of immigrants. This was the result of successive British military victories—first against the Netherlands and Sweden, and then against France. Of course, by the time of the Conquest, the size of the French Canadian community was significant—but it would thenceforth grow primarily by a natural rate of increase. By contrast, the waves of immigrants from the British Isles would continue, swelling the size of the English Canadian community considerably.

If at the time of Confederation the ethnic composition of the nation was fairly homogenous,[12] patterns of immigration over the next century would alter the mix of the population, but not the continued dominance of the two so-called "founding" groups. The continuous flow of immigrants from Britain would be augmented by Asians brought to work the transcontinental railroad; by immigrants from northern, central, and eastern Europe who would contribute to the expansion of the prairies in the first decades of the century; and by some Americans. The diversity increased after the Second World War and the huge dislocation caused by that conflict: from Mediterranean Europe, and particularly Eastern Europe. In the late 1960s, with the liberalization of the rules governing immigration, Canada's ethnicity diversified further with increased immigration from the Caribbean, Africa, the Middle East, the Indian subcontinent, and east Asia. Crises in international politics during the postwar period also had an effect. There were marked increases in immigration to Canada after the Hungarian revolt was crushed by the intervention of the Soviet Union in 1956; after the Soviet intervention in Czechoslovakia in 1968; after Uganda's self-styled President-for-Life Idi Amin Dada expelled Ugandans of Asian extraction in 1972; and after Vietnam expelled the Hoa—Vietnamese of Chinese extraction—in 1978 and 1979. Likewise, areas of instability—or potential instability—have prompted movement: from the states of Central America wracked by oppression and war; and from Hong Kong following the negotiations between China and Britain that will see the Crown Colony revert to Chinese sovereignty on 1 July 1997.

The fundamental cleavage in Canadian politics between English Canadians and French Canadians, and the ethnic diversity of subsequent waves of immigrants, have both had an impact on Canadian foreign policy—but in different ways.

Historical duality. As we will see in more detail in the next chapter, historically both French and English Canadians had very different worldviews and very different conceptions about the appropriate role for their nation in world politics. And each group projected their foreign policy interests largely according to ethnicity. Canadians of English extraction manifested an often jingoistic concern for the British Empire of which they were a part, and for Britain, from whence they had come. One measure of this sentiment was the tendency to refer to Britain as "the Mother Country" in political discourse.[13] French Canadians, by contrast, had little such emotional attachment to Britain, even less attachment to the Empire, and virtually no comparable emotional attachment to the idea that France was Canada's other "Mother Country." Having long before been abandoned by that "mother," French Canadians tended to define their foreign policy interests primarily as unhyphenated Canadians.

Importantly, neither side could accept the other's *Weltanschauung* as legitimate in the context of Canadian politics.[14] There was, as a consequence, constant uneasiness between the two groups. The chagrin of each with the other's view on world politics was reflected, often most virulently, in foreign affairs throughout the first fifty years after Confederation, culminating in the Conscription Crisis of 1917 and its aftermath. For thirty years thereafter, the lessons of 1917 would weigh heavily in the foreign policy decision-making of the man who was also prime minister for most of that period, Mackenzie King.

The more politically divisive effects of this cleavage on foreign policy were to fade with the end of the Second World War. Indeed, they had disappeared almost completely by the time the Korean War broke out in June 1950—a month before King, by this time no longer prime minister, died. However, the bicultural, bilingual—and binational—character of the Canadian polity would continue to manifest itself in Canada's external relations. As we will see in the discussions of both the decision-makers and the role of the provincial governments in foreign policy, governments in both Ottawa and Quebec City have over the course of the postwar period sought to project the dual nature of Canada's ethnicity.

Contemporary plurality. The original ethnic duality of Canadian society has of course been overlayed by the consequences of immigration—a multi-ethnic component that has found its domestic political expression in such policies as the symbolic enshrinement of multiculturalism in law, state funding for ethnic groups and for the teaching of "heritage languages," and equity for "visible minorities." Canada's multi-ethnicity has also been reflected in foreign policy, as many recent immigrants, no less than the newly-arrived English in decades gone by, have been prone to define their foreign policy interests in ethnic terms. These interests are diverse. More often than not, ethnic groups are most concerned with the maintenance of good relations between their adopted nation and their original homeland, seeking such functional goals as the negotiation of trade agreements or direct flights between Canada and their countries.

Sometimes, however, their interests are directly political. For example, one of the prime objectives of the Canada-Israel Committee, an umbrella group established by the Canadian Jewish Congress, B'nai B'rith and the Canadian Zionist Federation, is to achieve a sympathetic "tilt" in Canada's policies towards Israel and the conflict in the Middle East. Groups like the Canadian Arab Federation and the Arab Palestine Association seek to achieve a rather different end.[15] Frequently, ethnic communities in Canada will be internally divided, reflecting the political divisions in the country of origin. Thus, for example, in December 1982, when President Zia ul-Haq of Pakistan paid a visit to Ottawa, he was greeted by very different messages from Canadians of Pakistani origin. Some took out advertisements welcoming Zia; while others, such as the Council of Concerned Pakistanis Abroad, loudly protested the human rights violations by his regime.[16] In other cases, these interests will reflect long-standing desires for independence for their homelands: for example, many members of the Armenian, Baltic, Palestinian, Sikh, and Ukrainian[17] communities in Canada have been active in pressing on the government in Ottawa to incorporate these concerns in Canada's relations with the "occupying" states. In rare cases, such advocacy takes a violent form. Indeed, the only major acts of terrorism and political assassination in Canada since the terrorist campaigns of the Front de libération du Québec (FLQ) in the 1960s have been committed by those associated with the quest for independence for Armenia and Khalistan,[18] acts of a tiny minority which unhappily but inexorably affected both communities as a whole.

On occasion, ethnic groups prompted (or forced) to leave their homelands because of political upheavals will try to ensure that relations between Canada and their homeland do not improve. For example, for well over 50 years, many Ukrainians and Ukrainian interest groups have persistently sought to maintain a hard anti-Soviet stance in Canadian policy. Although, as Samuel Nesdoly has noted, there has been a slow change over the forty years since 1945, improved relations between Ottawa and Moscow were frequently seen as evidence of a Canadian acknowledgement of the legitimacy of the Soviet "occupation" of Eastern Europe, and thus bitterly opposed.[19] Likewise, some Vietnamese Canadians who were forcibly thrown out of Vietnam in the late 1970s have been wont to convey to the Canadian government their satisfaction with the policy of punishing Hanoi that was imposed following Vietnam's invasion of Kampuchea in December 1978.[20]

Egoistic Interests

Egoistic interests are those that individuals have concerning their own material and physical well-being. In the context of foreign policy, such interests would include economic well-being and individual security—the relative freedom of the individual, as part of the political community, from the fear of physical or economic threats to personal values emanating from outside the state.[21]

Material or economic interests. As we have noted in chapter 2, much of Canada's wealth derives from the production and export of a wide range of raw materials, processed and manufactured goods. The interest of individuals in their material well-being will prompt them at minimum to protect, and at most to expand, the sources of their wealth (through the ownership of financial, industrial, or agricultural capital, or through employment). In foreign relations, this interest is persistently in evidence as Canadians seek to maximize their individual, corporate, organizational, class, and occupational well-being. The range of these economic interests is wide and varied, as can be seen by the following suggestive examples from each of Canada's major producer groups—business, organized labour, and agriculture.[22]

The interests of those who own or control the wide range of business enterprises in Canada[23] will always have an external dimension. This is particularly true of the many subsidiaries of multinational corporations with head offices in the United States, Western Europe, Japan, and Hong Kong which operate in Canada; and the many Canadian multinationals which have subsidiary operations abroad.[24] The protection and advancement of these interests occur both at the level of the individual firm and at the associational level. Obviously, individual firms (and individual owners and managers of firms) which are affected by international developments, or by government policy, will seek to maximize their parochial economic interests through political demands made directly to the state. Such interests will range from macro concerns, such as a firm's advocacy of a free trade agreement with the United States as a "good idea" in principle, to micro concerns, such as the same firm's advocacy of securing a negotiated exemption for its products under the agreement. But businesses also organize to collectively press the interests of their particular industries.[25] Canadian business is no less active collectively in foreign policy, pressing the government about its concerns on international trade policies, tariffs on imports, export promotion of the wide range of natural resources and manufactured goods produced in Canada, and on such related matters as international industrial standards, Canada's labour policies, environmental protection, and international development assistance.

Of considerable importance are the umbrella groups which press not the interests of a particular industry or sector, but the interests of business as a whole. These would include the Business Council on National Issues—a group which none too modestly has called itself "the senior voice of business in Canada"[26]—and the Canadian Business and Industry International Advisory Committee (CBI IAC). Established in 1977 to coordinate the presentation of the international views of the business community to government, CBI IAC includes among its members a number of other powerful umbrella business groups.[27] These associations are all well-endowed by their members, highly institutionalized, and permanently embedded fixtures on the policy-making scene in Ottawa.[28]

But the collective efforts of business are occasionally more ad hoc. For example, in the national debate over the free trade agreement in 1987 and 1988, a number of businesses and business groups formed an advocacy group for free trade—the Canadian Alliance for Trade and Job Opportunities—and recruited two prominent public figures, Peter Lougheed and Donald Macdonald, as co-chairmen.[29] Lougheed, a Progressive Conservative, was until November 1985 the premier of Alberta, and a persistent supporter of free trade. Macdonald was a former Liberal cabinet minister and the chairman of a royal commission that had recommended free trade.[30] Macdonald, who had broken with the Liberal Party on the free trade issue after its leader, John Turner, promised that he would rip up the agreement if elected, spent 18 months touring the country giving speeches in support of the pact (for which yeoman service Prime Minister Brian Mulroney was to reward him in August 1988 with a diplomatic posting to London[31]).

Organized labour in Canada also has foreign policy interests, but tends to define them primarily in the context of the well-being of union members.[32] In their foreign policy activities, Canadian unions are not as feisty as are, for example, Australian unions, who are prone to be highly active on foreign policy issues that do not directly affect the economic well-being of their members.[33] But they do have interests they wish to see advanced in Canadian foreign policy, both parochial (protection of jobs and industries, access to foreign markets) and international (promotion of free trade unionism in other jurisdictions, entrenchment of international labour standards, and advancement of peace, disarmament, and social justice). But occasionally, broader international goals will conflict with the economic interests of their membership. For example, in the summer of 1985, while the Mulroney government was deciding whether to participate in the Strategic Defense Initiative, the Canadian Labour Congress came out in opposition to Canadian participation. On this occasion, however, it indicated that it was unwilling to have its members involved in jobs resulting from SDI. "More jobs in a world made more dangerous," Richard Martin, the vice-president of the CLC, claimed, "is not a goal for the CLC, nor should it be for Canada."[34] On other occasions, by contrast, the concern with economic interests has prevailed. While the CLC supports "balanced, fair trade" in the international system, it is caught in a bind when freer trade poses a threat to the jobs of its members. Thus, the CLC has been a long-standing advocate of the maintenance of duties and quotas designed to minimize the flow of textiles and shoes from the Third World, though it has tried to mitigate the overtly protectionist nature of this position by arguing that because these products are produced by low-paid labour, importing them encourages exploitation of workers in the Third World. Likewise, fearing that one of the significant results of freer trade would be large-scale unemployment,[35] particularly in branch-plant secondary manufacturing industries, the CLC was also strongly opposed to the free trade initiative from its inception.[36] Following the signing of the agreement on 3 October 1987, Shirley Carr, president of the CLC, called it "a dark day for Canada." Claiming that one million jobs would be lost, she called the agreement "a national disgrace."[37]

The final producer group with economic interests in foreign policy is agriculture.[38] It should be recognized that this group includes the large corporations of agribusiness, individuals working family farms, and agricultural workers hired by both agribusiness and individual farmers. Given the importance to the well-being of Canadian agriculture of both a highly regulated domestic market and an orderly export market, agricultural producers will have an ongoing interest in both macro and micro aspects of Canada's trade policy—particularly as it relates to the promotion of exports and protection against imports. But the diversity of production means that rarely will the interests of agriculture be uniform. For example, the free trade agreement drew mixed reviews from agricultural groups.[39] It was greeted with enthusiastic support from the Canadian Cattlemen's Association and western grain growers at the prospect of export expansion, relief from poultry producers whose monopolistic marketing arrangements were protected, skepticism from fruit and vegetable farmers in British Columbia and Ontario that they would be able to survive as profitably with increased flows of produce from the American market, and outright opposition from the grape-growing and wine industry and such groups as l'Union des producteurs agricoles in Quebec.[40]

But some agricultural producers, notably grain growers on the prairies, cannot ignore the high politics of Canadian foreign policy and the impact on their interests of the ebb and flow of relations between the great powers. Since the early 1960s, a great deal of Canadian grain has been exported to Communist countries, and Canada's dominance in these markets was unrivalled by the world's other major grain exporters—Argentina, Australia, and the United States. The major shifts in grain exports were initiated by the Progressive Conservative government of John Diefenbaker. Despite his propensity for anti-Communist rhetoric,[41] and his advocacy earlier in the 1950s against selling food to Communist countries,[42] Diefenbaker presided over a radical transformation in the pattern of grain exports. In May 1961, his government had signed a credit agreement for the purchase of grain with the People's Republic of China, which was beset not only with the difficulties of the unsuccessful Great Leap Forward, but also by three successive crop failures. As a result, Canadian exports to the PRC jumped from $8.7 million in 1960 to $125.4 million in 1961 and

$147.4 million in 1962.[43] The Soviet Union and Eastern Europe had also become an important, if unsteady, market for Canadian grains during this period.[44] However, shifts in international politics have occasionally interrupted the grain flow or reduced Canada's position in the market. The Canadian dominance of the China market in the 1960s was helped by the enmity between Beijing and Washington and by strong fears of the PRC in Canberra. But with the marked shift in relations between China and the West that occurred over the course of the 1970s, the United States no longer sought to stay out of the Chinese market for grains, leading to increased competitiveness for prairie farmers. Likewise, the deterioration of East-West relations in the late 1970s culminated in an attempt to use grain exports as a technique of western statecraft. This time another Progressive Conservative prime minister, Joe Clark, sought to stop any increase in grain exports to the Soviet Union by joining the partial grain embargo proposed by President Jimmy Carter in January 1980 following the Soviet invasion of Afghanistan. (It might be noted that the embargo quickly fell apart as Americans, Australians, and Canadians watched Argentina expand its shipments to the USSR ten-fold, and as Canadians watched Americans try to divert grains originally destined for the USSR to China. By the end of 1980, Australia and Canada had backed out and Ronald Reagan, who had promised American farmers that he would terminate the ban, had been elected president. Both countries quickly signed even larger grain deals with the Soviet Union.[45])

Interests in security. To this point, we have been discussing the egoistical interests of Canadians in terms of their economic or material well-being, and the manner in which they will seek to project those interests into the external environment, or protect them from external threats. However, an individual will also be interested in security, which, in the context of international affairs, means safety from the threats of harm emanating from other states. The wording here is cautious and as precise as possible, for an interest in security is not necessarily the same as an interest in "peace," or the absence of war. Embracing a preference for war over peace as the most appropriate means of ensuring safety against harm involves, of course, a paradoxical calculus: individuals put themselves—and their community—directly in harm's way, risking injury, pain, and death, in order to protect themselves and their community from harm. But when the alternative—peace or the absence of war—is domination, enslavement, or extermination at the hands of others, individuals have historically been prone to make that calculation.

Historically, there have been circumstances under which Canadians have shown a preference for putting themselves in harm's way as a means of ensuring their security. We can see evidence of this during the interwar period. There was a sizeable "peace movement" in Canada in the late 1920s and early 1930s, which enjoyed considerable public support for its efforts.[46] From the House of Commons, J.S. Woodsworth and Agnes Macphail pressed the pacifist point of view, calling for the abolition of the Department of National Defence, and attacking cadet training for creating, as Macphail put it, "a bombastic military spirit of toy soldierism."[47] The League of Nations Society in Canada pressed the cause of peace by a wide variety of public education activities, sponsoring speakers, distributing pamphlets and posters, even ensuring that high school instruction about the League was made compulsory in every province but Ontario and Quebec (where local school boards had to approve the use of Society materials).[48] The government was pressed to attach itself to the Kellogg Peace Pact signed at Paris in August 1928,[49] and to support the World Disarmament Conferences of the early 1930s. Students at debates at McGill University and the University of Toronto were no less prone than their confrères at Oxford to find for pacifism and against war.[50] But by September 1939, these feelings were to give way to widespread support for the war that broke out in response to Adolf Hitler's drive for hegemony in Europe.

Of course, the paradoxical calculation of these preferences has been vastly complicated by the advent of nuclear weapons. No sane human in the late twentieth century has an interest in the outbreak of a full-scale nuclear war between the superpowers, given the awesome consequences for the species of a strategic exchange. But not all will have an interest in seeking either to eliminate nuclear weapons or to avoid the use of force under any and all circumstances. Thus, it is not very helpful to state that all Canadians have an interest in peace without thinking carefully about what peace is, and of equal importance, the different means of achieving it.[51]

What we can with more assurance assert is that all Canadians will have a generalized interest in (i) being or feeling secure, and (ii) avoiding the outbreak of full-scale nuclear war. However, the way in which these interests are manifested in political terms will differ considerably. For example, some will feel that both interests are adequately satisfied by the existence of two large opposing arsenals of highly destructive warheads impermeable to complete elimination in a suprise attack (or first strike). Similarly, the existence of a second-strike capability (mutual assured destruction, or MAD), combined with a trust in the essential rationality of the highly institutionalized and bureaucratized structures of governance in Washington and Moscow, are considered sufficient to ensure the maximization of both values. A belief in the logic of deterrence that underwrites present policy provides a sense of individual security.[52]

But for others, nuclear weapons offer no such assurances of safety—only the nightmarish images from popular fiction, whether it be *On the Beach* in the 1950s, or *The Day After*, *Testament*, and *Threads* in the

1980s. The logic of deterrence provides little comfort, for by its very nature, deterrence cannot be demonstrated, or guaranteed, to work.[53] And there is the conundrum that comes with the mistaken belief that the purpose of nuclear weapons is to deter nuclear war itself (rather than to deter an adversary). If one takes that view, MAD is assuredly mad: nuclear war, being unthinkable, makes the use of nuclear weapons impossible, which, in circular fashion, makes their possession seemingly illogical. As the editor of *Maclean's* argued in 1960, since "nothing can justify nuclear war.... the first step toward preventing it is to stop planning to wage it."[54] Or, as Margaret Laurence was to put it a generation later, "Why, then, the continuing buildup of nuclear weapons? These have long since ceased to be a 'deterrent,' if, indeed, they were ever so, and have become, by their very existence a monstrous threat."[55] For others still, there is the fear that the system will break down and that nuclear war will "accidentally" break out as the result of either a technical malfunction or a local or regional crisis that becomes unmanageable and escalates. And finally, for some there is simply the nagging feeling that deterrence cannot last forever. The conclusion in the face of such insecurity (that is, lack of safety) seems obvious: security can only be assured by the elimination of such weaponry.

Over the last 35 years, this sense of insecurity has led numerous people, both in Canada and elsewhere, to press for a fundamental change in the way in which their safety is assured. There have been two identifiable waves of public concern about nuclear weapons in Canada—and in other parts of the western world—in the late 1950s and early 1960s, and in the early and mid-1980s. In the earlier period, there were four leading activist "peace" organizations: the Canadian Committee for the Control of Radiation Hazards—later to become the Canadian Committee for Nuclear Disarmament—and the Combined Universities Campaign for Nuclear Disarmament, both formed in 1959 and modelled after the Campaign for Nuclear Disarmament in Britain; the Voice of Women, created in 1960; and the Canadian Peace Research Institute, formed in 1961. While these groups were generally concerned about nuclear weapons, they focussed much of their efforts on pressing the Diefenbaker government to abandon its plan to arm three weapons systems that Canada had purchased from the United States (Honest John surface-to-surface missiles, Bomarc surface-to-air missiles, and CF-104 Starfihters) with nuclear weapons. Mass demonstrations, petitions, and a vocal public debate gave rise, however, to wider expressions of concern about Canada's membership in both the Atlantic alliance and the North American Air Defence (NORAD) agreement with the United States.[56]

In the early 1980s, the weapons systems had changed, but the concerns remained the same. At issue in 1982 and 1983 was the air-launched cruise missile (ALCM) and its inertial guidance system, which the United States

Air Force wanted to test over territory comparable to the Soviet Union. In March 1983, concern over the cruise was eclipsed by President Ronald Reagan's embrace of the Strategic Defense Initiative, and the high-tech, "high frontier" gadgetry that accompanied it. This period was marked by vigorous debate, demonstrations and peace marches more massive than in the early 1960s, and the considerable mobilization of a large number of advocacy and citizens' groups concerned with "peace."[57]

However, closer examination of these two periods suggests that it is not the weapons systems themselves that give rise to these manifestations of public concern. New nuclear weapons systems are constantly being invented, developed, built in prototype, tested, funded, put in production, deployed, and kept at the ready before being mothballed, dismantled, or blown up to make way for a new generation. Yet public concern shows no such constancy. Rather, we have to look to three other factors, all interrelated, that better explain why the Canadian public felt sufficiently unsafe at these two junctures in postwar history that it was moved to express its interests in this fashion.

The first was the rise in the level of superpower tension and hostility in both periods and the concomitant fear that this hostility would result in war. In the late 1950s and early 1960s, the "brinkmanship" of Nikita Khrushchev and the administrations of Dwight D. Eisenhower and John F. Kennedy, the U-2 incident, and the erection of the Berlin Wall—all seemed to indicate the unwillingness of both superpowers to manage their rivalry peacefully. In the early 1980s, the adventurism of the Soviet government in the late 1970s had given rise to a president in Washington determined to be just as adventuristic. Reagan supported new weapons systems, such as the B-1 strategic bomber, or the MX "Peacekeeper" missiles; he took a rhetorical hard line, such as labelling the Soviet Union as the "evil empire"; and he strongly opposed Soviet interests everywhere. (Moreover, those who were openly urging the limited use of nuclear weapons for tactical purposes—the so-called NUTS doctrine[58]—seemed to be more prominent in the Washington firmament.) For their part, the Soviet leadership during this period—aging, ill, and constantly dying—seemed unrepentant and more than willing to stand up to American pressure. In short, the superpower relationship again seemed to be sliding towards the possibility of war.

The second cause of increased insecurity was the nature of the military technology being developed at the time. Canadian concerns in the late 1950s were not directed against the intercontinental ballistic missiles that were frantically being developed by both the United States and the Soviet Union, but there is little doubt that the ICBM represented a very different kind of threat to the manned bomber. Moreover, both of the superpowers were testing larger and more powerful nuclear devices during this era. Likewise, in the early 1980s, the cruise missile, and then Star Wars, became the focus of a broader concern over a new generation of weapons technology that seemed capable of upsetting the existing MAD balance. Again, neither side was interested in limiting the expansion of their arsenals.

Third, the Canadian manifestations in both eras were part of a broader movement that had its origins not in Canada but in other western societies. If one examines the chronology, it is clear that in each period the Canadian movements emerged only after comparable movements in Western Europe, such as the "Ban the Bomb" campaign in the late 1950s or the campaign against Euromissiles in the early 1980s, were well-entrenched.[59] Copycat behaviour between societies is both inevitable and widespread, and to note that it occurred in these two cases is to cast no aspersions on the copycat. But it does alert us to the element of safety (or lack thereof) as a catalyst for these interests: it should not be surprising that in both cases the anti-nuclear trend should drift westerly across the Atlantic—given the fact that the Europeans are rather closer to the Central Front than North Americans.

Empathetic Interests

Canadians have historically demonstrated that their definition of interests extends beyond egoistic concerns to the physical, material, and spiritual condition of the peoples of other nations. We have already examined one manifestation of this—the tendency of ethnic groups to feel empathy towards their homelands. Here we focus on empathy involving no such ties of ethnicity or material gain. Empathetic interests, like egoistic ones, can be divided into two general sets: those dealing with the material well-being of other individuals, and those dealing with their security. These most commonly manifest themselves as interests in international development and human rights.

Development. The concern of Canadians for international development springs most basically from a recognition of "the fat cat status which Canada occupies in the community of nations," as John W. Holmes once put it.[60] Confronted with evidence of human suffering in other parts—from hunger, malnutrition, or disease—the traditional inclination of Canadians, who in the main are well-fed and healthy compared to most of humankind, has been to attempt in some fashion to ameliorate the human condition elsewhere. Much of this inclination is, as the North-South Institute has said, the result of

> the intangible pressures of ethical values. However hard-pressed or insecure they feel economically, and however skeptical they may be of past efforts to alleviate

the lot of the world's poor, most citizens of the rich countries are still unable to deny some basic humanitarian impulse, some motive of "human solidarity" or "international social justice" for wanting to end deprivation and suffering.[61]

To be sure, one should not overstate the nature of this interest: it is neither saintly nor truly altruistic. For the vast majority of Canadians, like other humans, are not altruistic in the true sense of that word towards anyone but kin. Most will respond to evidence of human suffering elsewhere with genuine empathy, but will not be moved to take concrete action. All too easily, the images of bloated stomachs and fly-covered eyes fade or are tuned out, the troubled feelings are suppressed, and concern passes into either token action—or inaction.

However, numerous Canadians are interested in giving expression to their empathetic feelings. Often this takes a passive form, such as the high levels of support for the government's international development assistance programs in response to a pollster's question.[62] But more frequently it takes an active form, as indicated by the large number of organizations and groups which exist to press the concerns of international development, and the many individuals who donate their time, money, and energies in attempts to alleviate suffering elsewhere. These include organizations specifically devoted to development, mostly voluntary agencies.[63] But they also include numerous other groups which are involved in development assistance. Almost all of Canada's major religious groups, for example, are active in this area. Each of the major Christian churches have organizations specifically for the promotion of development.[64] Likewise, a number of women's groups have development programs: the Young Women's Christian Association of Canada, the National Council of Women, and the Canadian Federation of Business and Professional Women's Clubs, and Match, which is exclusively devoted to development.[65] This institutional proliferation has also given rise to a number of umbrella groups, including the Protestant Canadian Council of Churches and the Canadian Conference of Catholic Bishops. The key umbrella groups for voluntary agencies, the Canadian Council for International Cooperation, and its Quebec wing, l'Association québécois des organismes de coopération internationale, attempt to coordinate the efforts of their 90 members.

On occasion, the expression of empathetic interests will take a different form. Such was the case with the Ethiopian famine in the fall of 1984. After television crews "discovered" the famine for their audiences and relayed pictures of its nature and extent, the public response to these images, in Canada as elsewhere, was massive. Some private initiatives, such as the song "Tears are not Enough," which would join "We are the World" on the charts, were high-profile. But most of the response was at the local, grass roots level as hastily-organized groups sprung up to receive donations of food and money. The flow was so unprecedented and sustained that both non-governmental organizations and the government in Ottawa were hard-pressed to keep pace. In early November, Joe Clark, the secretary of state for external affairs, allocated $50 million to a special fund for Africa, some of which he promised would be used to match private donations; by 13 February 1985, Clark had to add $15 million to the original. By April, Africa Emergency Aid, a special agency created to administer the government's matching funds, announced that private donations had exceeded the original allocation by 300 per cent.[66]

Human rights. Canadians have also been prone to take an interest in the purposeful mistreatment of those outside Canada's borders. Like the interest in international development, it is neither sustained nor widespread, but there has been an historical empathy with those whose human rights have been violated, and a desire to give expression to these symbolic interests. For example, there were protests in Canada at the treatment of the Boers by the British during the South African War;[67] at the Turkish atrocities against the Armenians after 1915;[68] and at the Japanese repression of Korean nationalists in 1919.[69] Likewise, Canadians did not remain silent in the face of the expansionism of the Axis powers in the 1930s: there were protests at the slaughter of Ethiopians by the invading Italian armies and at the treatment of Jews in Nazi Germany in the 1930s. The case of the reactions of Canadians to Japanese expansion into China in the 1930s provides a good illustration of these interests at work in the prewar period.

In the early 1930s, Japan expanded into China, launching a full-scale invasion of Manchuria in September 1931 and establishing a puppet state, Manchukuo, headed by the last emperor of China. It had also attacked the port of Shanghai in December 1931, in retaliation for a widespread Chinese boycott. With the other great powers in disagreement about the most appropriate response to this aggression, the League of Nations could do little to resolve the dispute.[70] From 1933 to 1937, an uneasy peace prevailed, but in the summer of 1937, war broke out again as the Japanese pushed into China's centre, in the process committing numerous barbarities, including what continues to be known as the rape of Nanking. The widespread reaction in Canada in the fall of 1937 was one of outrage.[71] Japan was Canada's fourth largest market for exports, primarily strategic metals, the most important of which (in both dollar terms and militarily) were aluminum, lead, nickel, and zinc. As a result, much of the reaction focussed on instituting private and government bans on trade with Japan, since, as the Ottawa *Citizen* put it on 5 August 1937, "Canada is a commercial partner with Japan in the present crime against civilization." Numerous meetings were held in the fall to promote boycotts and press the government to impose an embargo on metal exports. City councils debated official boycott measures as did church congregations. Various groups, including many "patriotic associations" of Chinese Canadians, organized demonstrations, distributing pamphlets and the paraphernalia of protest like "boycott buttons." The voluntary boycott of Japanese goods, and even of stores owned or run by Japanese Canadians, proved popular, though it is difficult to ascertain how widespread it was. The enthusiasm for it, however, was by no means universal: the opposition to both private boycotts and official embargos was strong, particularly among business interests. The following excerpt from the Windsor *Star* suggests the tone of the debate in the fall of 1937:

> Horse sense is still available in Parliament Hill. Plagued by the Communist party, the C.C.F. [Cooperative Commonwealth Federation, precursor of the New Democratic Party], the Trades and Labour Congress, the League of Nations Society and other organizations which purblindly clamour for a boycott on Japanese goods, Canadian statesmen prefer to consider the consequences domestic as well as foreign. Chief of these consequences would be ... a suicidal blow to Canada's export trade....[72]

If the campaign had little effect on policy—Canada continued to sell even larger quantities of strategic materials to Japan in the late 1930s and well into 1941[73]—it is nonetheless illustrative of the empathetic interest at work.

It should be noted that prior to 1945, this interest in the welfare of others tended to be sparked not when citizens had their human rights violated by their own government, but when they were victims of a foreign power's aggression. (Members of ethnic groups were prone to raise concerns about the treatment of their fellow citizens by their own government, as both the Jews did about pogroms in Russia in the last part of the nineteenth century,[74] or as Ukrainians did in the late 1930s.[75] However, the focus here is on interests not linked to ethnicity.) More often than not, the public seemed to accept implicitly what governments in this era embraced explicitly: that what happened inside a sovereign state, including how a government treated its citizens, was simply no one else's business.

The Second World War changed this. In 1945, the United Nations legitimized the conception of universal human rights, enshrining the idea in the Universal Declaration that was adopted in 1948. That, and the revelations of the full extent of the treatment of both the Jews and other Europeans in Nazi death camps, served to change how Canadians regarded human rights violations. Since then, how other governments treat their citizens has been a constant, if not widespread, focus of Canadian interests. At different times over the postwar period, human rights violations by a large number of countries have caught the attention of the Canadian public at large.[76]

However, the public's interest tends to be both episodic and unsystematic. Some violations seem to drift in and out of the public consciousness. The case of South Africa is a good example of this: the interest of the general public in *apartheid* has shown a habit of peaking at crisis points, most recently in 1977-78 and in 1984-86, but of dying out in between, even though the institutionalized racism that provoked their concern has not in its fundaments changed over the last four decades. Likewise, some massive violations draw attention, while others go completely unremarked by the public at the time—the genocide in Kampuchea in the mid-1970s, for example. Usually, attention is focussed tightly only when some event involving the violator—like a visit by a leader or the outbreak of violence—jogs the collective memory and provides a focus, and a forum, for criticism. For example, the relatively infrequent visits by Canadian and Soviet leaders between the two countries have provoked protests that died quickly after the fact. Indeed, sometimes a visit will provoke criticism that had not been there previously. There had been virtual silence in Canada on the human rights record of the government of General Suharto in Indonesia in the mid- and late 1970s, even though Amnesty International and the United States Congress had cited Djakarta as one of the most persistent violators, and even though Indonesia was engaged in an alleged campaign of repression in East Timor, which it had invaded in December 1975. However, when it was announced that Prime Minister Pierre Trudeau was to visit Indonesia in January 1983, a great deal of public criticism of both the Indonesian record and Canadian policy suddenly emerged.[77]

If the interest of the public as a whole is episodic, there are numerous Canadian interest groups which have maintained a steady pressure not only on the Canadian government to bring Ottawa's influence to bear to alleviate violations, but on the human rights violator itself, and those associated with it. The interdenominational Taskforce on Churches and Corporate Responsibility maintains a steady watching brief on Canadian corporate behaviour in areas like South Africa, Latin America, and Central America. The Canadian section of Amnesty International, which is based in England, "adopts" political prisoners (but only those who have not used or advocated the use of violence) and works to have them released—usually with considerable success.

Conclusion

The picture painted here is of necessity limited. We have not examined the full range of interests that Canadians have been prone to express, nor all of the organizations and groups that exist to press collectively the concerns of Canadians. For example, we have not looked at those interests that fall into a number of the categories outlined above, such as the strong interests that Canadians have in environmental protection.[78] However incomplete, the picture demonstrates that Canadians not only have a range of interests in international politics but also a willingness to express them in a variety of political contexts. It is to a consideration of how the expression of these interests actually affects Canadian foreign policy that we now turn.

SOCIETAL INFLUENCE

Two Levels of Societal Influence

There are two ways in which individuals and groups in Canadian society will affect foreign policy-making. Societal actors will have an impact on the *decision-making process*: the specific decisions, or policy choices, that the Canadian government takes in international affairs. And they may affect the broader *decision-making environment* in which those choices are made—by determining the bounds within which the government has to operate. This more diffuse environment determines not which specific choices are to be made, but which issues must be dealt with, and sets the bounds of acceptable policy choices. Such a distinction between the process and the environment of decision-making is, of course, somewhat artificial. In the real world of policy-making, neither decision-makers themselves, nor those societal actors who are pressing their demands on government, think in these terms. However, drawing this analytical distinction allows us to probe the various ways in which the influences of societal actors are brought to bear on foreign policy in Canada, and to assess with greater accuracy society's impact on policy outcomes.

Within the framework of these two environments, we can explore the four possible ways Denis Stairs suggests that public opinion may affect (or "set") foreign policy. Two of these—administration-setting and policy-setting—focus on the decision-making process; the others—agenda-setting and parameter-setting—concern the decision-making environment.[79]

The Decision-Making Process

Administration-setting. In principle, the administration—or implementation—of foreign policy could be shaped by societal actors and interests. In some areas of domestic policy, groups are invited by the state to participate in the implementation of government policies and programs. The self-management of doctors and lawyers is one example of the private administration of public policy; agricultural marketing boards would be another. In foreign policy, there are instances of this kind of administration-setting—the case of Africa Emergency Aid, for example—but they are few. In most areas of foreign policy, Canadian governments have zealously excluded participation by societal actors in the actual administration of policies and programs. Instead, that task is carried out by a professional bureaucracy that is generally unpenetrated by societal actors.

In international or multilateral negotiations, the tendency to exclude domestic groups is more pronounced in some issue areas than in others. In low policy areas, the government will frequently invite representatives of the industry affected to sit as members of Canadian delegations to these negotiations. In the 1970s, the delegations to international negotiations on fisheries, deep-sea mining, and tariffs featured regular participation by those whose concrete interests were going to be affected by the outcome of the talks. For example, Stairs notes that the advisers to the Canadian negotiators on the East Coast maritime boundary with the United States were the president of the Nova Scotia Fishermen's Association, a fleet captain with National Sea Products, a skipper, a union representative, and a member of the Atlantic Fishing Vessel Owners' Association.[80]

In matters of high policy, by contrast, the tendency is to exclude societal groups from the process of policy implementation. For example, when Pierre Trudeau undertook his peace initiative in the winter of 1983-84, a few societal actors were consulted but they were not included in the actual process of trying to reduce East-West tensions. "Administering" the initiative—deciding which leaders Trudeau was to visit, what issues were to be raised, and actually doing the talking—was the exclusive prerogative of state actors alone—the prime minister and his officials. Likewise, when prime ministers or secretaries of state for external affairs "implement" policy by their attendance at summit meetings, it is without the participation of those not inside the government.

It is true that on occasion, experts from outside the state apparatus may be brought in on a temporary basis to implement or administer policy—high and low. Simon Reisman was recruited from the private sector by Brian Mulroney in 1985 to negotiate the free trade agreement with the United States. Reisman was no stranger to Ottawa: he had been a deputy minister of finance and indeed it was he who had negotiated sectoral free trade in automobiles, the Auto Pact of 1965. But he was there temporarily. By 1988, with the deal negotiated and signed, he had returned to the private sector. Likewise, Mulroney appointed Bernard Wood, executive director of the North-South Institute in Ottawa, to be his personal emissary to the black southern African states in June 1986. Wood's task was to meet with leaders of the Front Line states, in preparation for a mini-summit of the Commonwealth to be held in London that August, to discuss the responses to the report of the Group of Eminent Persons that had attempted to negotiate with the South African government on behalf of the Commonwealth. But again, this was a limited job. And limited involvement is the rule rather than the exception.

This is, as Stairs notes, partly due to the traditional secrecy surrounding the actual implementation of external policy. The shroud of secrecy that covers the deliberations of cabinet, and the privileged status of communications from other governments, make it difficult to delegate the tasks of administration to domestic groups. Then there is the nature of statecraft itself. The processes of diplomacy and negotiation, which lie at the core of a state's international activities, do not allow policy-making and policy-implementation to be easily compartmentalized. In foreign affairs, the administration and the making of policy are, in a real sense, one and the same.

Policy-setting. At a more general level, societal preferences may determine what specific policies are to be pursued by the state. The pressure of public opinion and specific interest groups may, in theory at least, dictate the government's policy objectives.

There are a number of specific instances where it is evident that the preferences of domestic groups prevailed over those of the state. For example, in 1975, the United Nations planned to hold a congress on the prevention of crime in Toronto. Because the Palestine Liberation Organization had been granted observer status in the UN in 1974, PLO representatives were invited to attend. This raised a furor, particularly in the host city. Many regarded the PLO as a terrorist organization: the memories of the attacks linked to the PLO in the early 1970s, particularly the massacre of twelve athletes at the 1972 Olympic Games in Munich, had not dimmed much in the intervening two and a half years. They pressed the federal government to deny PLO representatives the right to enter Canada. While Jewish groups took the lead, they were joined by numerous other individuals for whom the idea of representatives of a self-confessed terrorist organization attending a conference devoted to the prevention of crime was too absurd. Also opposing the admission of the PLO was the provincial Progressive Conservative government of William Davis. Although the Davis government had plumped for the congress to be held in Toronto in the early 1970s, by 1975 it wanted no part of it for the simple and expedient reason that Ontario was on the verge of a provincial election campaign. For its part, the federal Liberal cabinet was caught in a bind. On the one hand, as a member of the United Nations and a signatory of international agreements designed specifically to allow diplomats free access to meetings of international organizations, Canada was obliged to allow representatives of all groups which had been granted international recognition into the country to attend this meeting. On the other hand, it was interested in mollifying the mounting and insistent opposition in Toronto. Fearing that public anger over the issue would manifest itself in electoral losses for the provincial Liberal party in Ontario, the federal government tacitly acceded to these pressures by requesting that the UN postpone the crime congress. The United Nations refused, and moved the congress to Switzerland.[81]

But the juxtaposition of interests in this case was unusual, if not unique. The emergence of the issue coincided with an election campaign; it was an issue of intense interest to Canada's Jewish community, which happens to be concentrated in both of Canada's most populous urban centres, Toronto and Montreal; there were those in the federal cabinet from Toronto who argued strongly against admission; there was the party factor—pressure on the federal Liberals from their provincial brethren concerned about spillover in the provincial elections; finally, the subject matter of the conference itself did not make for an easy defence of the rights of the PLO. In short, the pressure on the federal cabinet would have been distinctly less severe had either an election not been in the offing or had the conference been held in another city (and perhaps had it not been focussed on the prevention of crime.) A useful contrast is provided by a UN conference on habitation, held in Vancouver a year later: there was no comparable political conflict over the admission of PLO representatives at that meeting.

More commonly, attempts by domestic groups to "set" policy against the government's preferences fail. This was the case with the protests against Japan in the fall of 1937 mentioned earlier. The government of Mackenzie King had numerous reasons not to involve Canada in the Far Eastern conflict—or in any international conflict for that matter—as we will see in the next chapter. Nor did King have any interest in crossing the various groups in Canada with a concrete interest in continuing the trade with Japan. As a result, he resolutely resisted public pressures for any form of action, arguing that Canada should take no action that would put it on one side or the other in the Sino-Japanese conflict. Moreover, he said, while his government was interested in human welfare in "the Orient, Spain, or in any part of the world, it was particularly concerned with the welfare of the Canadian people."[82]

The issue of cruise missile testing in the early 1980s provides a more contemporary illustration of this process at work. When it became known in 1982 that the Canadian government was planning to allow the United States Air Force to test the inertial guidance system of the air-launched cruise missile over Canada, a wave of public protest erupted. In the fall of 1982 and the spring of 1983, huge rallies were held across the country pressing the government to refuse to test the cruise. In Vancouver alone, over 65,000 people joined the city's mayor in a march through the streets. Petitions and letters flooded into Ottawa. A makeshift "Peace Camp" was erected on Parliament Hill (much to the chagrin of one Conservative MP, Erik Neilsen, who termed it an "eyesore.") While various peace groups were spear-heading the opposition, they were joined by numerous others, gaining the support of scientists, church leaders, labour leaders, academics, and a variety of literary figures. The Canadian Conference of Catholic Bishops and the moderator of the United Church added their voices to the protest. After ALCMs tested in the United States crashed, the premier of Saskatchewan, Grant Devine, asked the minister of national defence for assurances that the tests would not be held at the Primrose Air Weapons Range on the Saskatchewan-Alberta border until concerns about technical problems had been cleared up. Operation Dismantle threatened that if the cabinet approved the request, it and sixteen other groups would take the federal government to court, on the grounds that cruise testing constituted a threat to their right to life guaranteed under section 7 of the new Charter of Rights and Freedoms. Public opinion polls revealed that most Canadians were opposed to cruise testing.[83] One member of Parliament, Paul McRae (Lib: Thunder Bay-Atikokan), openly worried about the political consequences of all of this pressure. Speaking to the House of Commons on 2 May 1983, he explicitly linked his anti-cruise position to poll results. He noted that 60 per cent of polled Canadians opposed the cruise, and that there was a strong anti-cruise sentiment in the United States. "In 1984 Canadians and Americans will be expressing themselves at the polls. Can anyone doubt," he wondered aloud, "that the majority on both sides of the border will deal harshly with politicians who are not serious about arms control?"[84]

For all the clamour, however, the government held firm, refusing to alter its course. On 9 May 1983, Prime Minister Trudeau wrote an "open letter" to Canadians, published in all newspapers, defending the decision.[85] On 14 June the government used its majority in the House of Commons (with an assist from the Progressive Conservatives, all but four of whom voted with the government) to vote down a motion by the New Democratic Party opposing the cruise, 213-34.[86] The government chose to announce its decision when it was least likely to draw parliamentary criticism or media attention: on the evening of 15 July, after Parliament had recessed for the summer. (It also happened to be a Friday night, which prompted Pauline Jewett, the NDP external affairs critic, to term the timing "a sleazy Liberal trick."[87]) The first tests began in March 1984.

The cruise missile issue demonstrates how and why the government can avert attempts by societal actors to set policy. To begin with, the state is rarely confronted with united preferences on policy issues. In the case of the cruise, it is true that the opposition to testing was considerable and vocal, but there were many Canadians who were either indifferent or supported the government's decision, a split borne out by the polls. As long as there is division within society, as there was on the cruise issue, the state can with relative ease rationalize *its* choice. Such a calculus was admitted candidly by deMontigny Marchand, a deputy minister in the Department of External Affairs in the summer of 1983:

> We can listen and we can accommodate, to some extent we can even manage certain contradictions, but we cannot avoid the overriding need for a policy which is a coherent synthesis of national interests and priorities.... There will be times when government exercises its leadership somewhat ahead of public opinion.[88]

Nor does the government tend to worry about the kind of electoral retribution over which McRae was fretting. As Ivan Head, Trudeau's adviser on foreign policy in the Prime Minister's Office, admitted in 1977, "I very seldom give much thought to what we'll look like in the next election" when offering advice, though, as the unusual case of the crime congress suggests, there will be exceptions to this general rule.[89] There are two reasons for such confidence. First, specific foreign policy issues do not lend themselves well to electoral retribution. Opposition to specific issues of high policy will likely be diffused among the electorate and lack geographic concentration. Conversely, opposition to specific low policy issues, such as fisheries, or environmental threats, is likely to be so geographically concentrated that it will create regional, rather than national, electoral problems. The same Burkean principles invoked by deMontigny Marchand would apply no less to such cleavages.

Second, at election time voters do not behave as though they were participating in a referendum, with but one single issue, much less one single foreign policy issue, at stake. While the incidence of single-issue voting is not unknown, Canadians, as Clarke and his colleagues have demonstrated so clearly,[90] are influenced by myriad factors that frequently shift in importance from one election to the next. Voting choices seem to depend on a highly unpredictable mix of policy preferences, some of which may be national in scope, some local. To complicate the matter further, Clarke et al. demonstrate that voting is not always based on policy issues alone. Numerous other factors may affect the calculus (such as it is): perceptions of the qualities of the parties, their leaders, and the local candidates will enter the mix.[91]

Thus, as Clarke et al. point out,[92] we cannot meaningfully conclude from the results of an election that a particular outcome was the result of the collective preference on a single policy issue. This is truer still of foreign policy issues—even though opposition parties are sometimes wont to cast the results of elections in such terms.[93] But in historical memory, this is precisely how such elections tend to be remembered. For example, the common interpretation, prevalent in much of the free trade debate in the 1980s, is that the 1911 general elections represented a repudiation of a single policy—free trade, or reciprocity as it was termed then. Likewise, the defeat of the Progressive Conservative government in 1963 is frequently explained as the defeat of Diefenbaker's nuclear weapons policy. But the historical shorthand, however convenient it may be, ascribes to the Canadian people a unity of purpose that stretches credulity. It surely overlooks the multiplicity of factors at work. The vote in 1911 has to be seen as something more than simply a rejection of the reciprocity treaty that the Liberal government of Sir Wilfrid Laurier had negotiated with the United States, and an embrace of the Conservative rallying cry "No Truck or Trade with the Yankees." Also at issue was Laurier's policy on Canada's contribution to the Royal Navy. One can certainly interpret the outcome in 1911 as a simple combination of these issues, as Mackenzie King did, claiming that the defeat was the result of an "unholy alliance between the [Quebec] Nationalists ... and the Tories of the other provinces."[94] But if we can assume that Canadians in 1911 were no less wont to predicate their votes on a variety of factors than their progeny three generations later, then we also have to assume that a more complicated mix of issues was at work. In 1963, Diefenbaker's defeat was not simply a rejection of his refusal to arm Honest Johns, Bomarcs, and Starfighters with nuclear weapons. Numerous other factors, including the collapse of support within the cabinet itself, the state of the economy, and the deterioration of Diefenbaker's leadership qualities, contributed to his downfall.[95] Indeed, as one of Canada's foremost historians, Ramsay Cook, has noted, "To many electors in times past these foreign policy problems doubtless loomed less large than they have to later textbook writers."[96]

The Decision-Making Environment

Agenda-setting. This is the process of establishing which foreign policy issues are deemed important enough by societal actors to warrant government attention and action. The state, to paraphrase Marx, may make its own agenda but it cannot make it entirely as it pleases. There is little doubt that external events play a critical role in determining what Ottawa's foreign policy agenda will be. Some will be entirely expected and predictable, for Canada's involvement in foreign affairs has its own seasonal rhythm. All of the major summits that the prime minister attends are set on a regular basis: the annual Economic Summit and meeting with the president; the biennial Commonwealth, and the irregular francophone summits. In the spring there are the annual NATO ministerial meetings and the appearance of the external affairs minister at the annual meeting of the foreign ministers of the Association of Southeast Asian Nations (ASEAN); in the autumn, the secretary of state for external affairs normally goes to New York for the annual session of the General Assembly; while the minister of finance will be in Washington for the annual meeting of the International Monetary Fund. (Some of these meetings even allow for extremely long-term planning, notably the septennial turn that Canada takes in hosting the Economic Summit.) But some external occurrences will be entirely unforeseen: the declaration of a war, the assassination of a foreign leader, the shooting down of a civilian airliner, the outbreak of rioting that leads to repression or revolution, the sudden imposition of a tariff—such events will thrust themselves rudely and unexpectedly onto a government's agenda.

But that agenda may be equally affected by societal actors. Generally, the capacity of societal actors to put an issue on the agenda is dependent on the degree of societal support for that issue. When it came to power, the Mulroney government was not seeking thorny foreign policy issues to deal with, given its concern with the issue of Canadian-American trade. But, given the range and intensity of public concern, there was little that could be done to avoid the various issues that were pushed onto the agenda after September 1984: the deteriorating situation in South Africa; the famine in Ethiopia; the request to participate in the Strategic Defense Initiative; the hardening policy of the Reagan administration towards Nicaragua; the passage of an American icebreaker, the *Polar Sea*, through the Northwest Passage; the American bombing of Libya; and the continuing problem of acid rain.

To be sure, there are issues that because of a lack of widespread public interest do not become intensely political. The concerns of some Canadians over the shooting down of Iran Air 655 by a United States cruiser, the *U.S.S. Vincennes*, in July 1988 were never widely enough shared for the incident to become a political issue—in marked contrast to the public concern over the downing of Korean Airlines 007 by a Soviet fighter in September 1983. Likewise, despite the continuing interests of some Canadians, such issues as the ongoing testing of the cruise missile did not make it onto the agenda in anything more than a cursory way.

And then there are all of those issues that the government does not have to deal with—for the simple reason that Canadians showed no demonstrable interest in them. Consider, for example, Canadian reactions to the use of poisonous gas by Iraq against its own Kurdish population in the spring of 1988. Iraq had broken what is probably the most durable and widely-kept rules in the behaviour of states in the twentieth century. (Even the Nazis, who were capable of massive evil, did not resort to the use of poisonous gas to reverse their military fortunes in 1944 and 1945.) But the Iraqi use of gas was simply a non-issue for most Canadians: there were no protests, marches, or organized campaigns. It was left to the government in Ottawa to put it on its own agenda. Likewise, the continued indifference in Canada to the little wars which took numerous lives in gruesome ways—in Chad, in eastern Africa, in the western Sahara, in Timor, or in Kampuchea—were issues of government, not public, concern.

Why are some issues of such concern to Canadians that they are thrust onto the agenda, while others produce little or no reaction? A good part of the explanation for this phenomenon can be found in the discussion of interests in the first part of the chapter, and the recognition that many issues will not arouse concern because they do not touch the concrete interests of Canadians. Thus, for example, because they viewed the Iran-Iraq war that began in 1980 as essentially self-contained and posing little or no danger to their security, Canadians in the main proved to be little interested in the hundreds of thousands of casualties inflicted by both sides over the eight years of fighting.

But another part of the explanation lies in how the issues are structured for the public. The media, both print and electronic, play a critical role in structuring and shaping society's perceptions of issues and their relative importance. The choices made by editors and producers about which stories are important involve a dynamic process of trying to reflect on the one hand a judgement about what is "important" and, on the other, an educated guess about what they think their readers or viewers will want to see. This calculus will inexorably have political effects, for individuals will respond to cues about international affairs that they receive from the mass media. As we will see in the next chapter, newspapers historically have played an important role in both the reflection and the maintenance of dominant ideas about Canada's role in foreign affairs.

But while the media itself has changed considerably over the last 50 years—for example, there has been a growth of professionalism, a wider sense of public responsibility, and a concomitant decline in the number of "rags" that dot the face of Canadian journalism—the media plays no less an important role today in agenda-setting. For example, the famine in Ethiopia in the fall and winter of 1984-85 would not have provoked the same public response without the involvement of the media; nor, it could be suggested, would there have been such fluctuations of interest in South Africa had the media continued to have unrestricted access. As it was, the government in Pretoria came to understand that much of the West's opposition to *apartheid* was being fuelled by the continuous televised images of South African security forces indiscriminately beating people with whips and attacking them with guard dogs. The censorship imposed in the summer of 1985 had precisely the effect intended: the concern that had been widespread lessened considerably.[97]

The media's role in shaping the news, in turn, has an impact on foreign policy. As Denis Stairs has noted, while the media may not have an important influence on the substance of foreign policy, they have "a very significant impact on the day-to-day activities of the men who make it."[98] Politicians are sensitive to the foreign policy issues reported on the front pages of *Le Devoir* and *The Globe and Mail*, Canada's premier newspapers, or broadcast on the variety of electronic media, for any issue may be raised in the House of Commons during Question Period or at a press conference. This, in turn, makes the bureaucracy sensitive to the media's treatment of foreign issues, for it will be to the bureaucrat that the politician will turn, not only in search of the appropriate response, but also to anticipate which issues will be raised. Of equal importance is the possibility that the issues raised in the media will catch the interest of the public, and again, the politicians do not want to be caught unawares. For example, Trudeau's reactions to questions put to him about Canada's assistance to the victims of the Nigerian civil war of the late 1960s is indicative of his surprise that such an issue was of any interest: "You have the funniest questions. We haven't considered this as a government."[99]

However, it should be noted that while the state may not be able to determine its own agenda, it still has considerable latitude in choosing how to deal with issues on that agenda. As we have seen, the state remains relatively impervious to policy-setting by societal actors. A government may be compelled to act, but not in a specific manner.

CONCLUSIONS:
SOCIETAL INFLUENCE AND PARAMETER-SETTING

To this point, I have argued that we can see an ascending scale of influence of societal actors on Canada's foreign policy behaviour. At the level of administration-setting, we see relatively little influence or involvement by societal actors. When policy is to be implemented, that political task is performed by the bureaucracy or, when summit diplomacy is involved, by elected officials. Only rarely are private citizens or groups involved. At the level of policy-setting, we have seen that individuals, groups, and organized interests in society will all be exceedingly active in their attempts to set policy by pressing the state to adopt foreign policy positions that accord with their interests. However, *activity* should not be mistaken for *influence*. While numerous groups are active, generally they enjoy little influence over the exact policy behaviour of the state. In short, at the level of the decision-making *process*, the state in Canada is, to borrow a term from structural Marxism, "relatively autonomous" in foreign policy. Foreign policy outcomes have generally been the reflection and expression of the state's own interests, defined by state officials as the "national interest," rather than the reflection of the interests of any one group or class in society.

However, this impermeability shifts somewhat once one moves into the decision-making *environment*. As we have noted with the agenda-setting function, societal actors can and do determine what issues the government must deal with. They do so, it was suggested, in a basically pluralist fashion: when there are numerous individuals and groups interested in an issue, it will become an "agenda" issue. This is, of course, to say nothing about how "politically weighty" these groups will be. As we have seen above, and as critiques of liberal pluralism remind us, numerousness by itself is no guarantee of success in setting policy.

The final level of possible societal influence on foreign policy in Canada is the level of parameter-setting. At this most general level, society can in theory define the bounds of acceptable policy actions. Parameter-setting establishes "certain limits on what the policy-makers are actually able to do—able, that is, within the range of what they regard as acceptable, or tolerable, political and other costs. Such opinions [of societal actors] can serve, in short, to confine the policy community's range of politically workable choices."[100] At this level, Stairs argues, the state is considerably constrained by societal preferences. These are essentially negative in nature: they serve to rule out certain options rather than insist on particular courses of action. Also, the parameters of "acceptable behaviour" established by society will be exceedingly broad. Because of this latitude, it is unlikely that government officials will be *unanimously* agreed on a course of action that falls outside the range of acceptable behaviour.

It is at this level, I will argue, that society has the most potent influence on the state's foreign policy behaviour. The next chapter is devoted to an elaboration of parameter-setting in practice: demonstrating how societal actors set the boundaries of acceptable policy behaviour and what their impact has been on Canadian foreign policy over the last century.

NOTES

1   Sun Tzu, *The Art of War*, James Clavell, ed. (New York: Delacorte Press, 1983), 9, 13-14, 30, 77; Thucydides, *The Peloponnesian Wars*, Rex Warner, trans. (Harmondsworth: Penguin, 1954, rev. ed., 1972), 158-63.

2   For a fuller discussion of these approaches, see Kim Richard Nossal, "Analyzing the domestic sources of Canadian foreign policy," *International Journal* 39 (Winter 1983-4), 1-22.

3   William Mishler, *Political Participation in Canada: Prospects for Democratic Citizenship* (Toronto: Macmillan, 1979); in the American context, see Sidney Verba and Norman H. Nie, *Participation in America: Political Democracy and Social Equality* (New York: Harper and Row, 1972).

4 Robert V. Presthus, *Elite Accommodation in Canadian Politics* (Toronto: Macmillan, 1973).

5 William D. Coleman, *Business and Politics: A Study of Collective Action* (Kingston and Montreal: McGill-Queen's University Press, 1988), 4.

6 Quoted in Donald Page, "The Institute's 'popular arm': the League of Nations Society in Canada," *International Journal* 33 (Winter 1977- 8), 59.

7 Canada, Parliament, House of Commons, *Debates*, 30th parl., 2nd sess., vol. 1, 21 October 1976, 303.

8 North-South Institute, *Review '87/Outlook '88* (Ottawa: North-South Institute, 1988), 2.

9 P.H. Chapman, "The Canadian public and foreign policy," *International Perspectives* (January/February 1986), 14.

10 Elizabeth Riddell-Dixon breaks down foreign policy interests, and the groups that exist to protect and advance them, rather differently. She makes a fundamental distinction between economic and non-economic interests, and subdivides groups on essentially functional, rather than purely "interest" lines. Thus, five economic subcategories are identified: business (including natural resources), agriculture, labour, professional, and consumer. Under non-economic, she identifies veteran/military; women's; religious; ethnic; citizens; and "special foreign policy." See *The Domestic Mosaic: Domestic Groups and Canadian Foreign Policy* (Toronto: Canadian Institute of International Affairs, 1985).

11 For one discussion of these origins, see G.P. deT. Glazebrook, *A History of Canadian External Relations*, vol. 1: *The Formative Years to 1914* (Toronto: McClelland and Stewart, 1966), ch. 1.

12 C.P. Stacey, *Canada and the Age of Conflict*, vol. 1: *1867-1921* (Toronto: Macmillan, 1977), 4-5: as of the first census in 1871, exactly 60 per cent of the new Dominion's 3,485,761 citizens reported their origin as the United Kingdom (the largest group being from Ireland); 31 per cent as French Canadian. The next largest ethnic group were Germans, who comprised 6 per cent.

13 See, for example, the debate in the House of Commons in September 1919 on a resolution by the prime minister, Sir Robert Borden, to approve the Treaty of Versailles. This debate is discussed in Stacey, *Age of Conflict*, vol. 1, 288-294.

14 For example, it was not uncommon for English Canadians to brand French Canadian opposition to wars that did not involve Canadian interests directly as "treason." See below, ch. 5.

15 For a good discussion of the Middle East conflict in Canadian politics, see David Taras and David Goldberg, eds., *The Domestic Battleground: Canada and the Arab-Israeli Conflict* (Montreal: McGill-Queen's University Press, 1989).

16 Riddell-Dixon, *Domestic Mosaic*, 3.

17 For one account of the long and completely unsuccessful efforts of the Ukrainian community to budge Ottawa from its position that the Ukraine is a Republic of the Soviet Union, see Samuel J. Nesdoly, "Changing perspectives: the Ukrainian-Canadians' role in Canadian-Soviet relations," in Aloysius Balawyder, ed., *Canadian-Soviet Relations, 1939-1980* (Oakville: Mosaic Press, 1981), 107-27.

18 On 8 April 1982, a Turkish diplomat was shot and seriously wounded by a group calling itself the Armenian Secret Army for the Liberation of Armenia; on 27 August 1982, a group calling itself the Justice Commandos for the Armenian Genocide assassinated the Turkish military attaché; on 12 March 1985, a group calling itself the Armenian Revolutionary Army attacked the Turkish embassy, killing a Canadian guard. On 23 June 1985, a bomb in baggage en route to Bombay that had been put aboard a CP Air flight from Vancouver to Tokyo exploded at Narita airport killing two Japanese baggage handlers; almost simultaneously, an Air India flight from Toronto to London—which had connected with a flight from Vancouver—exploded over the north Atlantic, killing all 329 aboard. Although the Air India explosion left no evidence, in 1988 the Canadian government extradited Inderjit Reyat Singh, who lived in Duncan, B.C. at the time, from Britain to face charges in connection with the Narita killings.

19 See Nesdoly, "Changing perspectives," 116: "Confronted with a thawing Cold War they [Ukrainian Canadians] urgently warned their unappreciative government not to be taken in by the so-called peaceful co-existence policy..."

20 Kim Richard Nossal, "Les sanctions économiques et les petits états: le cas de la 'punition' du Vietnam par le Canada," *Etudes internationales* 18 (septembre 1987), 523-44.

21 For a cogent discussion of the problems of thinking about what it means to be "secure" in international politics, see Barry Buzan, *People, States and Fear: The National Security Problem in International Relations* (Brighton: Wheatsheaf Books, 1983), esp. ch. 9.

22 Riddell-Dixon, *Domestic Mosaic*, 6-21.

23 Here "business" is defined very widely to include any enterprise that operates in order to make a private profit: it would thus include primary producers in the fisheries, mining, forestry, and crude energy sectors; secondary manufacturing and processing; construction; wholesale and retail trade; communications; and financial services. The agricultural sector constitutes a special case and so is treated separately.

24 On multinationals and the projection of their interests generally, see Robert Gilpin, *The Political Economy of International Relations* (Princeton: Princeton University Press, 1987), ch. 6; in a Canadian context, see Isaiah A. Litvak and Christopher J. Maule, "Canadian-United States corporate interface and transnational relations," and David Leyton-Brown, "The multinational enterprise and conflict in Canadian-American relations," both in *International Organization* 28 (Autumn 1974); and David Leyton-Brown, "The nation-state and multinational enterprise: erosion or assertion," *Behind the Headlines* 40 (September 1982).

25 For a comprehensive survey of business associations, see Coleman, *Business and Politics*.

26 *Ibid.*, 83, 86. With four of the leading multinational oil companies on its membership list, the BCNI coordinated discussions between the oil companies, federal officials, and the government of Alberta that eventually led to the downscaling of the National Energy Program.

27 Notably, the Canadian Chamber of Commerce; the Canadian Council of the International Chamber of Commerce; the Canadian Manufacturers' Association; the Canadian Association—Latin America and the Caribbean; the Canadian Committee of the Pacific Basin Economic Council; the Canadian Export Association; and the Canadian Importers Association. See Riddell-Dixon, *Domestic Mosaic*, 8.

28 John Kirton and Blair Dimock, "Domestic access to government in the Canadian foreign policy process, 1968-1982," *International Journal* 39 (Winter 1983-4), 95.

29 It might be noted that a comparable initiative was also undertaken in the United States. More than 175 companies and trade associations formed the American Coalition for Trade Expansion with Canada. *The Globe and Mail*, 9 June 1987.

30 Macdonald had been a member of Trudeau's cabinet in the late 1970s. In 1978, he resigned to return to his law practice, but when Trudeau announced in 1979 that he was retiring, Macdonald decided to run for the Liberal leadership. However, when Trudeau decided to lead the Liberals into the general election campaign over the winter of 1979-80, Macdonald withdrew. In 1982, Trudeau appointed him the chairman of the Royal Commission on the Economic Union and Development Prospects for Canada. As commissioner, he became convinced of the need for a free trade agreement with the United States: the commission's final report recommended that option. However, the report did not appear until September 1985—well after the 1984 election that brought Brian Mulroney to power, and after Mulroney had already embraced the idea.

31 *The Globe and Mail*, 6 August 1988, A1, B1. Charles Ritchie, a professional diplomat appointed as Canada's High Commissioner to Britain in 1967, opined that since Anglo-Canadian relations were by then so untroubled, the appointment was "a rest cure." "The attractions are obvious: to reside in London in a fine house, to be given entry to the varied English social and political worlds. I had reason to be delighted with my good fortune." *Storm Signals: More Undiplomatic Diaries, 1962-1971* (Toronto: Macmillan, 1983), 87, 90.

32 For a survey of labour groups and their interests in foreign policy, see Riddell-Dixon, *Domestic Mosaic*, 24-28.

33 For example, on different occasions in the 1970s, the labour movement in Australia engaged in industrial action against goods coming either to or from Chile, France, the United States, and Indonesia. Henry S. Albinski, *Australian External Policy Under Labor* (Vancouver: University of British Columbia Press, 1977), 309-11.

34 *International Canada* (June and July 1985), 3.

35 For a sensitive discussion of the psychic and social consequences of free trade, see J. Paul Grayson, "Free trade, unemployment and social adjustment, in Michael D. Henderson, ed., *The Future on the Table: Canada and the Free Trade Issue* (Toronto: Masterpress, 1987), 121-39. It should be noted, however, that Grayson's analysis is predicated on an assumption that a free trade agreement will inexorably bring unemployment with it.

36 For example, in October 1985, the then-president of the CLC, Dennis McDermott, rejected an offer from the Mulroney government to participate in

an advisory panel on free trade on the grounds that the government had already made up its mind to pursue the initiative.

37   *Toronto Star*, 5 October 1987.

38   On this policy area, see Grace Skogstad, *The Politics of Agricultural Policy-Making in Canada* (Toronto: University of Toronto Press, 1987).

39   The implications of a free trade agreement for agriculture are discussed in Bruce W. Wilkinson and M. Shabany Ghazvini, "Agriculture in a free trade agreement," in Maureen Appel Molot and Brian W. Tomlin, eds., *Canada Among Nations—1985: The Conservative Agenda* (Toronto: James Lorimer, 1986), 196-214.

40   *The Globe and Mail*, 6 October 1987.

41   For Diefenbaker's own account of his record of speaking out against the "diabolical cruelties perpetrated by the USSR against captive peoples," see *One Canada: Memoirs of the Right Honourable John G. Diefenbaker*, vol. 2: *The Years of Achievement, 1956 to 1962* (Toronto: Macmillan, 1976), 108-10.

42   In March 1954, Diefenbaker had admonished the Liberal government of Louis St. Laurent not to be lured by the attractiveness of trading with the other side, particularly in such a strategic commodity as food. Peter C. Newman, *Renegade in Power: The Diefenbaker Years* (Toronto: McClelland and Stewart, 1963), 263.

43   Peyton V. Lyon, *Canada in World Affairs*, vol. 12: *1961-1963* (Toronto: Oxford University Press, 1968), 420-28; also Peter Stursberg, *Diefenbaker: Leadership Gained* (Toronto: University of Toronto Press, 1965), 134-39.

44   Over the period 1963 to 1979, an average of 20 per cent of Canada's annual grain exports went to the Soviet Union and Eastern Europe. However, the year-to-year percentages tended to fluctuate considerably. In 1963-64, 27.7 per cent of grain exports went to the Soviet Union (41.2 per cent to the USSR and Eastern Europe combined); the following year, by contrast, only 2.2 per cent went to the Soviet Union (17.9 per cent to the USSR and Eastern Europe). Carl H. McMillan, "Canada's postwar economic relations with the USSR—an appraisal," in Balawyder, ed., *Canadian-Soviet Relations*, 145, table 4.

45   Robert L. Paarlberg, "The 1980-81 US grain embargo: consequences for the participants," and John Kirton, "Economic sanctions and alliance consultations: Canada, the United States and the strains of 1979-82," both in David Leyton-Brown, ed., *The Utility of International Economic Sanctions* (London: Croom Helm, 1987).

46   A good account of anti-militarism in this period can be found in James Eayrs, *In Defence of Canada*, vol. 1: *From the Great War to the Great Depression* (Toronto: University of Toronto Press, 1964), 104-119.

47   Quoted in *ibid.*, 306. One of Canada's more colourful orators, Macphail once denounced Empire Day as "the occasion for nothing but a strutty, silly, pompous, bombastic performance by military men and those who are backing them." *Ibid.*, 105.

48   Donald Page, "The Institute's 'popular arm': the League of Nations Society in Canada," *International Journal* 33 (Winter 1977-8), 49.

49 Calvin Coolidge's secretary of state, Frank B. Kellogg, proposed a pact, to be subscribed to by all nations, renouncing war as an instrument of foreign policy. For an account of the Canadian involvement, see Stacey, *Age of Conflict*, vol. 2: *1921-1948: The Mackenzie King Era* (Toronto: University of Toronto Press, 1981), 97-103.

50 Student activity is described in Eayrs, *In Defence of Canada*, vol 1, 110-11.

51 A cogent critique of the Canadian "peace" movement's propensity to ignore these and other issues can be found in James Keeley, "Myth and magic in disarmament," *International Perspectives* (September/October 1983), 11-14.

52 For one sensitive discussion of nuclear weapons that lives up to the claim in the subtitle, see Leon Wieseltier, *Nuclear War, Nuclear Peace: The Sensible Argument about the Greatest Peril of Our Age* (New York: Holt, Rinehart and Winston, 1983).

53 Gwynne Dyer likens the logic of the belief that the North Atlantic alliance has deterred a Soviet attack on Western Europe to the story of the man travelling on a train through Belgium with his umbrella open. A fellow passenger asks why he has his umbrella up inside the train. "To keep the elephants away," he replies. "But there are no elephants in Belgium," remonstrates the other passenger. "See?" says the first, "It's working..."

54 Quoted in Lyon, *Canada in World Affairs*, 87.

55 Margaret Laurence, "Foreword," in Ernie Regehr and Simon Rosenblum, eds., *Canada and the Nuclear Arms Race* (Toronto: James Lorimer, 1983), xi.

56 For accounts of the "nuclear weapons" issue in the early 1960s, see Jon B. McLin, *Canada's Changing Defense Policy, 1957-1963: The Problems of a Middle Power in Alliance* (Baltimore: Johns Hopkins University Press, 1967), ch. 4 and 6; Lyon, *Canada in World Affairs*, 76-222.

57 The following list provides some indication of the range and diversity of "peace" groups that existed by the mid-1980s: Alberta Nurses for Nuclear Disarmament; Canadian Association of Municipal Nuclear Weapons Free Zones; Canadian Coalition for Nuclear Responsibility; Canadian Disarmament Information Service; Canadian and International Physicians for the Prevention of Nuclear War; Canadian Peace Alliance; Canadian Peace Educators' Network; la Coalition québécoise pour le disarmement et la paix; Edmonton Peace Council; Gabriola Island Peace Association; Niagara Peace Movement; International Youth for Peace and Justice Tour; Lawyers for Social Responsibility; Mouvement option paix québec; Nanoose Conversion Project; Operation Dismantle; PEACEFUND Canada; Peace Parties Network; Project Ploughshares; Ponoka Peace CAPP Gang; Psychologists for Peace; Science for Peace; Students against Global Extermination; Toronto Disarmament Network; Union des pacifistes du Québec; World Without War Research and Education Network. Most of this list is from John D. Young, "Canada and the neutrality issue in the context of a 'widening Atlantic,'" paper presented to a Conference on Canada-US Security, Queen's University, Kingston, 17 June 1988. Riddell-Dixon, *Domestic Mosaic*, 59, estimates that in Toronto and Vancouver alone there were 250 active peace groups.

58   The acronym NUT (for nuclear utilization theory) was used by Howard Margolis and Jack Ruina in a 1979 article; Spurgeon M. Keeney Jr. and Wolfgang K.H. Panofsky adapted this to NUTS—nuclear utilization target selection—to derive a synonym for MAD. See their "MAD versus NUTS," *Foreign Affairs* 60 (Winter 1981-82), esp. 289.

59   Robert J. Jackson, "Consensus, compromise and crusades: the domestic politics of European security," *International Journal* 40 (Winter 1984-5), 145-59.

60   John W. Holmes, *Canada: A Middle-Aged Power* (Toronto: McClelland and Stewart, 1976), 293.

61   North-South Institute, *In the Canadian Interest? Third World Development in the 1980s* (Ottawa: North-South Institute, 1980), 27.

62   Peyton V. Lyon, "Introduction," in Lyon and Tareq Y. Ismael, eds., *Canada and the Third World* (Toronto: Macmillan, 1976), xliii, *fn* 48, reports a 72 per cent level of support in 1975; the North-South Institute's poll of October 1987 also reported a level of 72 per cent, which it noted were "broadly consistent" with polls conducted in 1980, 1985, and 1986. *Review '87/Outlook '88* (Ottawa: North-South Institute, 1988), 8.

63   Examples would be: the Canadian University Service Overseas (CUSO) and its francophone branch, Service universitaire canadien outre-mer (SUCO); Inter Pares; Match, a women's group which directly funds development projects initiated and implemented by Third World women; Oxfam-Canada and Oxfam-Québec; the Canadian branch of the United Nations International Children's Emergency Fund—UNICEF Canada; the World University Service of Canada; World Vision Canada; and the Young Men's Christian Association of Canada.

64   For example, the Catholic Organization for Development and Peace; the Primate's World Relief and Development Fund of the Anglican church; the Committee on the Church and International Affairs of the United Church; Presbyterian World Service and Development; Lutheran World Relief; and the Mennonite Central Committee. Riddell-Dixon, *Domestic Mosaic*, 37-42; also Robert Matthews, "The churches and foreign policy," *International Perspectives* (January/February 1983), 18-21.

65   Riddell-Dixon, *Domestic Mosaic*, 35-37.

66   *International Canada*, October and November 1984, 5-7, and April and May 1985, 15.

67   Robert J.D. Page, ed., *Imperialism and Canada, 1895-1903* (Toronto: Holt, Rinehart and Winston of Canada, 1972), 61-91; Joseph Levitt, ed., *Henri Bourassa on Imperialism and Biculturalism, 1900-1918* (Toronto: Copp Clark Publishing, 1970), 35-43.

68   Stacey, *Age of Conflict*, vol. 1, 258.

69   In 1919, Canadian missionaries in Korea, which in 1910 had been colonized by Japan, launched a campaign to draw Canadian attention to the violent and bloody repression carried out by the Japanese authorities there following a nationalist uprising in May. An account of this episode is contained in a forthcoming work by James Eayrs: *Canada and Northeast Asia*, vol. 1: *Japan Expands and Explodes: 1895-1945*, ch. 1.

70 The best account of Bennett's policies on this crisis and of the speech given by Canada's representative to the League, C.H. Cahan, is to be found in Donald C. Story, "The Cahan speech and Bennett's policy towards the Far Eastern conflict 1931-3," in Kim Richard Nossal, ed., *An Acceptance of Paradox: Essays on Canadian Diplomacy in Honour of John W. Holmes* (Toronto: Canadian Institute of International Affairs, 1982), 17-38.

71 The following is based on the account in A.R.M. Lower, *Canada and the Far East—1940* (New York: Institute of Pacific Relations, 1941), 23-28.

72 Quoted in *ibid.*, 39.

73 H.F. Angus, *Canada and the Far East, 1940-1953* (Toronto: University of Toronto Press, 1953), 12.

74 See Taras's essay on the history of the Jewish community in Canada in Taras and Goldberg, eds., *Domestic Battleground*.

75 Nesdoly, "Changing perspectives," 109-112.

76 Margaret Doxey, "Human rights and Canadian foreign policy," *Behind the Headlines* 37 (June 1979); T.A. Keenleyside and Patricia Taylor, "The impact of human rights violations on the conduct of Canadian bilateral relations: a contemporary dilemma," *Behind the Headlines* 42 (November 1984); and Robert O. Matthews and Cranford Pratt, eds., *Human Rights in Canadian Foreign Policy* (Montreal and Kingston: McGill-Queen's University Press, 1988).

77 *International Canada* (December 1982 and January 1983), 15, and Sheldon E. Gordon, "The Canadian government and human rights abroad," *International Perspectives* (November/December 1983), 9. The irony in this case was that in the intervening years, the Indonesian government had actually improved its human rights record.

78 For a discussion of interest groups in the environmental issue area, see Riddell-Dixon, *Domestic Mosaic*, 54-58.

79 Denis Stairs, "Public opinion and external affairs: reflections on the domestication of Canadian foreign policy," *International Journal* 33 (Winter 1977-8), 130-38. It should be noted that Stairs orders these categories differently.

80 *Ibid.*, 149. On the boundary question, Erik B. Wang, "Canada-United States fisheries and maritime boundary negotiations: diplomacy in deep water," *Behind the Headlines* 38/39 (April 1981). On fisheries, Stephen Greene and Thomas Keating, "Domestic factors and Canada-United States fisheries relations," *Canadian Journal of Political Science* 13 (December 1980), 731-50. On deep-sea mining, Elizabeth Riddell-Dixon, "State autonomy and Canadian foreign policy: the case of deep seabed mining," *Canadian Journal of Political Science* 21 (June 1988), 297- 318. On trade, Gilbert R. Winham, "Bureaucratic politics and Canadian trade negotiation," *International Journal* 34 (Winter 1978-9), 64-89.

81 *International Canada* (May 1975), 165-66.

82 King to the House of Commons, 11 February 1938, quoted in Lower, *Canada and the Far East*, 31.

83   Adam Bromke and Kim Richard Nossal, "Tensions in Canada's foreign policy," *Foreign Affairs* 62 (Winter 1983-84), 341-42; also *International Canada* (April/May and June/July 1983).

84   Canada, Parliament, House of Commons, *Debates* 1983, vol. 22, 25043, 2 May 1983. McRae, it might be noted, did not run in the next election; the Liberal candidate in Thunder Bay-Atikokan ran third.

85   The text of the letter is reproduced in C. David Crenna, ed., *Pierre Elliott Trudeau: Lifting the Shadow of War* (Edmonton: Hurtig Publishers, 1987), 50-52.

86   For the cruise debate, see House of Commons, *Debates*, 1983, vol. 23, 26315-29 and 26343-62, 14 June 1983.

87   *The Globe and Mail*, 16 July 1983; on the importance of making political announcements on a Friday, see David Taras, "Prime ministers and the media," in Leslie A. Pal and David Taras, eds., *Prime Ministers and Premiers: Political Leadership and Public Policy in Canada* (Scarborough: Prentice-Hall Canada, 1988), 39.

88   deMontigny Marchand, "Foreign policy and public interest," *International Perspectives* (July/August 1983), 9.

89   Quoted in Don Munton and Dale H. Poel, "Electoral accountability and Canadian foreign policy: the case of foreign investment," *International Journal* 33 (Winter 1977-8), 219, *fn* 6; in an interview in May 1983, Trudeau indicated that he predicated policy on what he thought was right and hoped that at the next election the voters would see "some value" in his government's policies: *Toronto Star*, 14 May 1983, B7.

90   Harold D. Clarke, Jane Jenson, Lawrence LeDuc and Jon H. Pammett, *Absent Mandate: The Politics of Discontent in Canada* (Toronto: Gage Publishing, 1984). See also John C. Courtney, ed., *Voting in Canada* (Scarborough: Prentice-Hall Canada, 1967); Harold D. Clarke et al., *Political Choice in Canada* (Toronto: McGraw-Hill Ryerson, 1979); Robert J. Jackson, Doreen Jackson, and Nicolas Baxter-Moore, *Politics in Canada: Culture, Institutions, Behaviour and Public Policy* (Scarborough: Prentice-Hall Canada Inc., 1986), ch. 11.

91   Clarke et al., *Absent Mandate*, 135-38.

92   *Ibid.*, ch. 7.

93   For example, in 1963, the leader of the NDP, Tommy Douglas, described the election as a referendum on nuclear arms. Lyon, *Canada in World Affairs*, 199. Likewise, in 1988, the leader of the opposition, John Turner, called on the Mulroney government to "let the people decide" the free trade agreement by calling an election on the issue.

94   Quoted in Stacey, *Age of Conflict*, vol. 1, 147.

95   The fullest account of the fall of the government on 4 February 1963 and the ensuing election campaign from a foreign policy perspective is Lyon, *Canada in World Affairs*, 176-222.

96   Ramsay Cook, "Foreign policy and the election," *International Journal* 18 (Summer 1963), 374.

97   "Awareness" of *apartheid* followed this pattern: in July 1985, a full 52 per cent of Canadians polled claimed that they had not heard about South Africa's racial policies. By September, that had dropped to 34 per cent. In June 1986, the number of "unaware" Canadians had risen to 39 per cent. It is interesting, however, that over this period, the policy preferences of "aware" Canadians hardened. In June 1985, 19 per cent favoured cutting all ties with South Africa. This figure climbed to 26 per cent in September and 35 per cent by June 1986. Don Munton and Timothy M. Shaw, "*Apartheid* and Canadian public opinion," *International Perspectives* (September/October 1987), 11.

98   Denis Stairs, "The press and foreign policy in Canada," *International Journal* 33 (Spring 1976), 238.

99   Stairs, "Public opinion and external affairs," 131, *fn* 6.

100 *Ibid.*

CHAPTER FIVE

Dominant Ideas

INTRODUCTION

In the previous chapter, it was suggested that societal interests exert only a marginal impact on the foreign policy decision-making process. Greater influence was seen at the more general level of the decision-making environment. It was suggested that societal interests have the most capacity to influence policy at the level of parameter-setting—by establishing the bounds of acceptable policy options. This chapter seeks to explore the parameter-setting role of "dominant ideas" in Canadian foreign policy. It examines the notion of dominant ideas and then explores the three ideas that have been dominant since 1867—imperialism, isolationism, and internationalism.

CULTURE, IDEOLOGY, AND DOMINANT IDEAS

Policy-makers in any society are most markedly affected by the patchwork of ideas, attitudes, and beliefs dominant in their society at any given time, and it is in this way that society leaves its most profound mark on the environment in which decisions are made. This is as true for foreign policy as it is for purely domestic decisions. As the historian Robert Dalleck puts it, those who decide on a country's course in world politics cannot divorce themselves from the interplay of "undercurrents, of mood, tone or milieu, of a climate of feeling that almost imperceptibly insinuates itself into concrete ideas and actions."[1] These ideas form the parameters of decision, or the bounds of acceptable policy behaviour.

The complex of political ideas, beliefs, and attitudes of a society forms its *political culture*.[2] Within a political culture there may exist a number of *ideologies*—more or less systematic ways of thinking, both normatively and empirically, about social, economic, and political relationships between humans in society, although one ideology usually predominates.[3] In the context of policy-making, Bruce Doern and Richard Phidd suggest an additional level of descending generality: *dominant ideas*, related to ideologies, but carrying "a separate force of their own."[4]

The purpose of this chapter is not to discuss the national political culture in Canada writ large.[5] Nor is its purpose to examine, as Denis Stairs has so eloquently done,[6] how this broader notion of culture affects the country's external behaviour. Nor does it seek to demonstrate the attachment of Canadians to the dominant ideologies of democratic liberalism[7] or nationalism,[8] and what impact these ideologies have had on Canada's economic structure, its political institutions, or the policy behaviour of successive Canadian governments. Rather, the focus is on those ideas, attitudes, and beliefs held by Canadians about their country's proper place in world affairs.

Characterizing these beliefs and ideas presents a taxonomical problem. On the one hand, they clearly comprise a subset of the larger political culture but they are not "subcultures" as that term is usually understood and used in the literature.[9] And while they are of course linked to ideas about political action, beliefs about Canada in world affairs are too narrowly conceived to qualify as "ideologies" in their own right.[10]

On the other hand, one could use another notion common in the analysis of international politics—"national character." This approach suggests, in brief, that each country, like each individual, has a particular "personality," the traits of which will be reflected in its foreign policy. As Hans Morgenthau put it: "National character cannot fail to influence national power; for those who act for the nation ... all bear to a greater or lesser degree the imprint of those intellectual and moral qualities which make up the national character."[11] We can trace this approach as far back as Thucydides and the contrast of Spartan and Athenian "character" portrayed in Pericles's funeral oration.[12] But it is still commonly used in foreign policy discourse. For example, American rhetoric following the downing of Korean Airlines 007 by the Soviet Union had a distinctly Periclean tone, frequently attributing the incident to the nature of Soviet society.[13] As Seymour M. Hersh put it, with all of this rhetoric, "the shootdown of Flight 007 had become, for most Americans, an example of the intrinsic differences between the Soviet society and their's [sic]: the Soviets had done what no American fighting force would do—they had deliberately shot down an innocent airliner...."[14] Nor has the use of "national character" been absent from discussions of Canadian foreign policy. For example, when it was announced in August 1988 that Canada had agreed to contribute to a United Nations peacekeeping force to oversee the ceasefire between Iran and Iraq, one historian denounced the plan as "absolute insanity" on the grounds that Iran and Iraq were "lunatic countries" which were unlikely to keep the peace.[15] However, for all of its continued popularity as a means of characterizing other societies, "national character" has fallen into disuse as an analytical tool, and deservedly so: its precepts are both simplistic and prone to stereotyping, prejudice, and racism.[16]

Closely related to national character are such concepts as "national ethos" and "national style." None of these serves as well as the Doern-Phidd notion of dominant ideas in capturing the intermediate position of beliefs, values, and attitudes in the realm of foreign affairs. Before examining the dominant ideas of imperialism, isolationism, and internationalism, three attributes of this concept need some expansion.

The Latency of Dominant Ideas

Well might Denis Stairs, Canada's keenest student of opinion and foreign policy, describe his subject as "maddeningly elusive."[17] The dominant ideas of foreign policy are by their very nature less than tangible. Indeed, more often than not dominant ideas remain latent: although we assume they exist, we cannot with ease demonstrate their existence for the simple reason that they are not expressed. And they are infrequently expressed because they are rarely challenged.

For example, opinion polls show that there is widespread public support for Canadian membership in the Commonwealth, an outgrowth, as we will see, of dominant ideas about Canada's attachment to Britain and commitment to internationalism.[18] But this support is rarely expressed actively, without the prompting of a pollster's question. To test the depth of support for this facet of Canadian foreign policy, a government would need to propose that Canada withdraw from that association. But no government has ever sought to do so. Thus, one of the serious and unresolved problems of assumptions about dominant ideas—a shortcoming that cannot but condition consideration of the following discussion—is their latent quality.

The Context of Dominant Ideas

Ideas about a country's place in the world do not develop in a social, economic, and political vacuum. They are inextricably tied not only to the dominant ideology of the polity but also to specific economic and political realities at a given time in a nation-state's history. The three dominant ideas examined in this chapter must be seen as emerging within a nexus of political, social, and economic structures—not only in Canada, but worldwide.

The roots of imperialist sentiment in Canada thus evolved within the context of the social linkages between the "Mother Country" and its North American offspring; the economic ties between the new dominion and British economic interests; and the political location of Canada as part of a global and hegemonic empire with its base in London. Similarly, isolationism in the interwar period must be seen in the context of the aftermath of Canada's participation in a ruinous war in Europe that had altered Canadians' perceptions of themselves and their relations with Britain; a decline in both British wealth and hegemonic power; a new trend towards institutionalization within the international system, notably the rise of the League of Nations; and a global economic crisis marked by extreme self-interest on the part of both the public and governments alike. Internationalism emerged within the context of a new international order following the Second World War. This order was marked by the emergence of new great powers, and a new great-power rivalry. But the United States was the international system's preponderant power, with massive economic and military capabilities relative to all other states in the system, including the Soviet Union. The order was also marked by the continuation of efforts begun in 1919 to create the institutional structures of order. In addition, the economic context would be very different for Canada. With a massive war production linked closely to the United States, the economic ties with Britain would decrease in importance. In short, it must be remembered that these dominant ideas evolved in the context of larger trends in the shifts in the military and economic power of the great powers that are, as Paul Kennedy reminds us, constantly taking place in the international system as the great powers travel what Otto von Bismarck called the "streams of Time."[19] As the military and economic power of Britain declined, and the American power rose over the first half of the twentieth century, Canada, tied so closely to both, could not help being caught in the current.

The Transience of Dominance

Like the power of great powers, the dominance of ideas tends to change over time, shifting with changes in the socio-economic context of the Canadian state. The evanescence of dominance means that decision-makers in Ottawa may be confronted with similar situations at different times in history, but the interplay of dominant ideas at the time will incline them to very different behaviour. The South African War of 1899 and the South Atlantic War of 1982 offer a number of interesting parallels to demonstrate this.[20] Both involved the defence of the interests of British subjects but neither conflict involved a threat to Britain's vital interests; both were fought in the antipodes (and thus physically distant from Canada); and on both occasions Britain fought against a smaller power in a conflict that did not directly involve any of the great powers.

But for all these parallels, the reactions in Canada, of both the government and the public, differed considerably. In 1899, the government of a reluctant Sir Wilfrid Laurier authorized the dispatch of troops to South Africa in response to an implicit request for military support from the imperial government in London. The public mood was intense. In English Canada, it was feverishly jingoistic, with young men flocking to recruiting centres to volunteer their services for the British cause. The English-language press was enthusiastic and bombastic, riddled with inflammatory exhortations for military action. Privately, the scions of Canadian journalism were no less insistent: one editor told Laurier that the government's choice was simple: send troops or "get out of office." A government MP who ventured to criticize the British government for its war policies in South Africa would be hissed in Parliament and called a traitor in the press. In French Canada, emotions ran no less high, with violent street demonstrations and symbolic desecrations of the Union Jack.[21]

The mood in 1982, by contrast, was calm, unemotional, and unconcerned. No one volunteered to fight, for there was nothing to volunteer for. No troops were sent—or requested. The Canadian government's response was to criticize Argentina for using force and to impose limited economic sanctions but in the main Ottawa continued to do business with Argentina. Likewise, there was no comparable domestic political conflict over the Falklands incident (and the only desecration suffered by the Union Jack was its appearance on tongue-in-cheek T-shirts sold by British-style pubs).[22]

In short, radical differences can be seen in these two cases. But without reference to the public attitudes, beliefs, and values at the turn of the century, we cannot understand why Laurier should at first have been reluctant to involve Canada in the South African war; why his cabinet was so bitterly divided; why the prime minister was branded disloyal for his initial hesitation; and why, surely, his government would have fallen had he not agreed to authorize the dispatch of troops to the British cause; in short, why the issue was so emotion-laden. Conversely, to get some measure of how little currency, much less dominance, the idea of imperialism enjoyed in Canada after the passage of eight decades, consider what the public response would have been had the government of Margaret Thatcher requested that Ottawa contribute a Canadian contingent to the Falklands conflict. What had been clearly necessary for a government's survival in 1899 would surely have led to a government's demise in 1982.

The ideas dominant in society would not have tolerated non-involvement in 1899 nor active involvement in 1982.

The transience of dominant ideas tends to be slow and at times almost imperceptible. Ideas do not appear and disappear in a stroke; instead, they are in a constant state of flux, some in decline, some ascending. Thus there will be periods when an idea in decline coexists with one that is ascending. Indeed, politicians and bureaucrats often find it difficult to assess the degree to which an idea will linger in the population. As we will see, the government of Louis St. Laurent would discover in the aftermath of the Suez crisis in 1956 that the remnants of sentimental attachment to Britain remained strong in much of English Canada well into the 1950s.

What causes the transience in dominance from one idea to another? The changing context of social, political, and economic relationships inevitably plays a part in shaping long-term shifts. But transience also tends to be catalyzed and accelerated by profound upheavals in the human condition: plagues, natural disasters, economic collapse, civil or global war. It is no coincidence that we see rapid shifts in dominant ideas during two periods of great stress for the Canadian polity: during the First World War, when imperialism lost much of its appeal, and during the Second World War, when isolationism gave way very rapidly to internationalism. Indeed, it could be argued that the durability of attachment to the dominant idea of internationalism in Canada can largely be explained by the absence of a comparable cataclysm since 1945.

A CENTURY OF DOMINANT IDEAS

The often contending ideas about Canada's foreign policy focus on the broad question of how the government should fashion Canada's relations with the outside world. We can identify three dominant ideas that have been embraced in the last century in response to this question. *Imperialism*, dominant in the years prior to the First World War, was an admixture of sentimental, economic, and legal attachment to the British Empire. Imperialism regarded empire as a normative good and suggested that Canada's interests in the international system be defined exclusively in terms of the Empire. *Isolationism*, particularly in an historical context, is usually associated with the policies pursued by the United States in the interwar period. It suggests that national interests can be best advanced by a policy of non-involvement in world affairs and by avoiding obligations to the states-system. As we will see, Canada embraced a particular kind of isolationism in the interwar period. *Internationalism* is the antithesis of isolationism. It suggests that the interests of the state are best served when it plays an active role in international politics and particularly when it contributes to the establishment and maintenance of international order. This invariably involves an acceptance of more, not less, responsibility in the international community. The idea of internationalism has been dominant since the end of the Second World War, and though challenged from time to time, has demonstrated considerable durability since then.

Three caveats must be offered at this juncture. First, the focus here is proximate, not precise. The portraiture of these three ideas is, of necessity, done in the broadest of brushstrokes. In particular, the era of dominance of each idea must be approximate, for the transition from one idea to another is neither neat nor instantaneous. Second, attachment to these ideas is assumed to be pervasive, not unanimous: not every member of Canadian society robotically moved according to the precepts of these dominant ideas. Indeed, each of these ideas spawned its own antithesis, and it is this clash of the dominant idea with its antithesis that makes them inexorably political. Third, we are looking for dominance, not exclusivity. Imperialism, isolationism, and internationalism do not comprise the exhaustive list of ideas concerning foreign affairs that Canadians have embraced over the last century.

Imperialism

Because empire as a form of political organization entails the denial of the right of a people to determine their own affairs, it should not be surprising that the idea of empire as a normative good finds little favour in the latter part of the twentieth century, when the global states-system is organized explicitly on the principle that is the very antithesis of empire: national self-determination. Yet a century ago, before the rise of the national state throughout the international community, empire was the dominant form of political organization in international politics. And it was felt by many in this era that the imperial form of government could encompass both the principles of self-determination *and* the maintenance of a centralized political unit spanning both continents and nations, acting as a unified and monolithic political and economic force in the relations of states.

The idea of imperialism was central to how all Canadians in the latter quarter of the nineteenth century were obliged to conceive of their nation's relations with Britain. Canada was but one unit within a larger political and economic organization, the British Empire. While Canada might be self-governing in matters of domestic policy, on matters of foreign policy it was in theory, though not always in practice, subject to the authority of the imperial government in London. Formal political allegiance was therefore always dual: loyalty to Crown and Canada as a separate political community went hand-in-hand with loyalty to Crown and Empire.

For many Canadians, as we have seen in chapter 4, loyalty to Empire went well beyond such a legal-formal allegiance to the Crown. It was also a matter of sentiment—the emotionalism of attachment to *patria*—fatherland, or native land—though Canadians from Britain seemed to prefer the more maternal appellation, "Mother Country." But the pride in, and love for, Britain and things British so evident in English Canadians was not simply patriotism. Nor, it is important to recognize, can we regard such sentiments as nationalism, for those imbued with an attachment to Empire also tended to be strong Canadian nationalists.[23] Rather, imperialism was "love of Empire" (with a capital E). This emotional attachment took different forms. In some guises it was marked by the same evangelical spirit of Kipling's "white man's burden". In others, it took the form of loyalty to the people, often expressed in overtly racist terms[24] and frequently with an anti-French Canadian flavour. It was also an attachment to the political ideology and institutions of British governance. It was often militaristic and bellicose in the populist tradition of British jingoism. In others still the attachment was an outgrowth of the deep religious schisms that cleaved the dominion. But in the main, it was none of these: "More common was the imperialism of those bound to the old country by less clearly formulated sentiments [of] a natural affection for their Motherland."[25]

Imperialism as a dominant idea in Canadian foreign policy enjoyed a remarkably speedy rise, reaching its apogee at the time of the South African war. Even as late as 1885, it did not enjoy sufficient popularity to force decision-makers to bend to its dictates. When an uprising in the Sudan prompted British military intervention, the Australian colonies offered to assist with their own contingents. But Sir John A. Macdonald did not feel impelled to join in the emotionalism triggered by the death of General Charles "Chinese" Gordon at Khartoum. Instead, he wrote to the Canadian high commissioner in London that no Canadian troops were going to be offered. "Our men and money would ... be sacrificed to get Gladstone and Co. out of the hole they have plunged themselves into by their own imbecillity [sic]."[26]

Fourteen years later, as we have seen, Laurier could not have taken such an attitude. By this time, sentiment in English Canada had hardened. It had been whipped up by what Henri Bourassa, one of Canada's foremost nationalists and a fervent opponent of imperialism during this period, was fond of calling the "reptile press," and opiated into what John W. Holmes has termed the "hallucinations of Jubilee imperialism."[27]

The highest stage of Canadian imperialism was to be found in the advocacy of the institutionalization of the Empire. This form of imperialism, widespread after the surge of imperial sentiment occasioned by Queen Victoria's diamond jubilee in 1897, favoured a federative Empire. In the minds of the Imperial Federation League, and its successors—the British Empire League and the Round Table movement— the Empire could be fashioned into a multinational federation underwritten by liberal-democratic principles and the institutions of responsible government. They proposed the establishment of a representative government, elected by the many subjects of the Sovereign beyond the seas, with the authority to make decisions for the Empire as a whole, but responsible to the Empire as a whole.[28] Such an idea, however, always foundered on the rocks of the contradictions implicit in the imperial arrangement: the British had little desire to share political authority over *their* affairs with either the self-governing "colonials," or with those peoples commonly regarded as incapable of governing themselves, much less Britons.

Imperialist sentiment raised two other related problems in this era. First, imperialism in any guise was basically incompatible with the dualistic nature of the Canadian polity. The paradoxical demands of dual loyalty to Canada and Empire were relatively easy for those Canadians of British extraction to manage. But such divided loyalty sat uneasily with the duality of Canadian society, cleaved by linguistic, racial, and religious schisms. Certainly imperialist sentiment found little favour amongst French Canadians. As Bourassa put it in 1917:

> French-Canadians are loyal to Great Britain and friendly to France; but they do not acknowledge to either country what, in every land, is considered the most exclusively national duty: the obligations to bear arms and fight... The only trouble with the French-Canadians is that they remain the only true "unhyphenated" Canadians. Under the sway of British Imperialism, Canadians of British origin have become quite unsettled as to their allegiance... The French-Canadians have remained, and want to remain, exclusively Canadian....[29]

It should be noted that such sentiments did not signify a lack of commitment among the dominant elites of French Canadian society to membership in the Empire and the formal fealties this required. Indeed, it is clear that these local elites were instrumental in maintaining such allegiance. In this respect, the hierarchy of the Roman Catholic church played an important role in legitimizing the imperial connection. "Loyalty for the children of the Church of Christ is not a matter of sentiment," the archbishop of Quebec wrote to the faithful in Montreal in 1900, "it is a serious and strict duty of conscience, derived from a sacred principle." Indeed, Archbishop Bégin felt compelled to add (for this was written during the South African war), "it would be impossible to find ... a succession of men, who have been more loyal than the bishops, the clergy of Quebec."[30] But such sentiments as Bourassa expressed did represent a very different emotional response to Britain and Empire.

The second incompatability was that membership in empire was inconsistent with a desire, shared by English and French Canadians alike, for self-government. Neither the government nor the people, even the most imperialistic, had any formal say in the most important decision a community faces—the waging of war. As Bourassa reminded a Canadian Club audience in 1912, "the seven millions of people in Canada have less voice, in law and in fact, in the ruling of that Empire, than one single sweeper in the streets of Liverpool... [H]e at least has one vote to give for or against the administration of that Empire."[31]

However, as long as the Empire—and therefore Canada—were at peace, these incompatabilities could remain largely latent. It was when the Empire was at war that the second incompatability seriously exacerbated the first and the contradictions broke into the open. The Boer War, and the political controversy and conflict it engendered in Canada, proved to be merely a rehearsal for the Great War.

The sentimental attachment to the British Empire underlay the willingness with which many Canadians went to war in August 1914. It is true that the declaration of war on Germany was issued by the King on the advice of his ministers in London, not in Ottawa. They had, as Bourassa had said, no voice: when Britain was at war, all of the Empire was, *ipso facto*, at war. But for the vast majority of English Canadians, such legalities were quite irrelevant. The result would have been the same—willing participation on the side of the Mother Country. For French Canadians, by contrast, there was no such automaticity of identifying their interests with the European war.

But the actual process of fighting this war fully exposed the internal contradictions within the Empire—and within Canada. This was a war unlike any other in human experience. Within months, the two opposing armies had entrenched themselves in a vast front that stretched from Switzerland to the English Channel, lobbing artillery shells as fast as they could be produced and engaging in numerous and bloody attempts to break through the opposing lines. Much of the fighting that resulted from this immobility achieved little; but the human and material costs were massive. And therein lay the problem for the dominions: the government in London expected members of the empire to contribute their young men and their wealth for the successful prosecution of the war, but the various dominions had no control over the conduct of the war.[32] Increasingly, as the number of casualties grew, the enthusiasm that had been so marked in the fall of 1914 waned. The Unionist coalition government under Sir Robert Borden was to discover this in the elections that were held in December 1917. While the Unionists won a clear majority, the popular vote, particularly among civilians, demonstrated significant areas of dissension in Ontario, Quebec, and the Maritimes.

The length and nature of the war had another effect. By the end of 1916, the insatiable appetite of the trenches had largely exhausted the supply of those willing to volunteer for overseas duty. Borden had to decide whether to limit Canada's contribution to the war to those who volunteered or to maintain a high level of military activity by conscription. For French Canadians, who in the main shared little of the emotional commitment to the war that had spurred voluntary recruitments in English Canada, the prospect of being forced to fight what many regarded as an "English" war posed a major threat to their interests, and they visited their wrath on the Conservatives in the elections of December 1917—and in many elections thereafter. Of course, for many English Canadians, the reaction of French Canada to the Military Service Act was merely more evidence of perfidy, treason, and abandonment of the Mother Country in its hour of need. Sectarian violence, particularly in Quebec over the Easter weekend of 1918, and constant rancour, gave vent to these divergent interests. The war, in short, not only placed considerable strain on the relationship between the imperial and dominion government; it also exposed the fundamental cleavages within the country.

Given the stresses that the war produced in Canada, the enthusiasms of imperialism began to give way to two other ideas about Canada's foreign relations. The first was "autonomism." Few called it "independence," for that was what Americans had sought, and that was unseemly. Rather, autonomism was the desire to control *all* elements of policy, domestic and external. It was a logical outgrowth of the autonomy in domestic policy achieved with Confederation in 1867, and while many Canadians had advocated autonomism before 1914, its acceptance was greatly catalyzed by the Great War. This was felt primarily within the government itself, and was manifested in Borden's insistence on more effective consultation in the conduct of the war; separate representation for Canada at the peace conference; and separate Canadian membership in the new international organization, the League of Nations. That such independent initiatives did not bring down on his head the vitriol of imperialists is indicative of the shifts occurring in the public mood at the time.

Indeed, it was the outgrowth of the wartime and postwar demands by the dominion governments, particularly the Canadians and South Africans, that lead to the transformation of the Empire into the Commonwealth. For the *de facto* rights of sovereign statehood sat uneasily with the continued *de jure* constitutional subordination of their governments to the government in London. At a succession of conferences in the 1920s, the Empire was negotiated out of existence. In 1926, the Imperial Conference agreed with the report of the inter-imperial relations committee, chaired by the Earl of Balfour, that the dominions

> are autonomous communities within the British Empire, equal in status, and in no way subordinate one to another in any aspect of their domestic or external affairs, though united by a common allegiance to the Crown, and freely associated as members of the British Commonwealth of Nations.[33]

The essence of the Balfour committee's statement of 1926 was enshrined in the Statute of Westminster, 1931, which put a formal end to Empire.

But, it should be noted, the growing autonomism of the 1920s did not suddenly extinguish those sentiments that had fuelled the enthusiasm for war in 1914. Imperialist sentiment lingered, particularly in British Columbia, southern Ontario, and the Maritimes. The daily press both reflected—but also kept alive—such ideas. The *Evening Telegram* of Toronto was by far the most notorious torch-bearer, opposing anything that smacked of anti-imperial sentiment. In 1921, it launched a series of attacks on the new League of Nations Society, which was trying to build support in Canada for the new international institution: "Don't be uncharitable to a minority who will not enthuse over your League of Nations Society. They are not all cynics and jeerers and sneerers. They are just British with good stout, honest British doubts."[34] Likewise, when Canadian policy diverged slightly from Britain over sanctions against Italy in 1935, the *Telegram* published a cartoon entitled "His Master's Voice," showing a French Canadian cabinet minister restraining the Canadian representative to the League on the whispered instructions of a priest.[35]

Indeed, sentiments of attachment to Britain were clearly evident in the late 1930s, the legal and constitutional freedom won in the Statute of Westminster notwithstanding. Supporting Britain in the Second World War was never in question for the majority of Canadians. As J.L. Granatstein and Robert Bothwell have so succinctly put it, throughout the interwar period, "support for Britain was first a moral duty, and a political duty, if it was at all, a long way after.... Canadian autonomy once achieved turned out to be like free will: it existed to enhance the righteous choice."[36]

The degree to which this attachment to Britain lingered, though in somewhat different form than the jingoism of the turn of the century, can be seen in the case of the Suez crisis of 1956.[37] At the United Nations, Lester Pearson, the external affairs minister, tried to negotiate a compromise solution and managed to secure agreement to a number of resolutions that would put a United Nations Emergency Force between the combatants. But in the process, the Canadians found themselves voting on a number of occasions against Britain and France. Moreover, in an emergency debate in the House of Commons, St. Laurent claimed to be "scandalized" by what he sarcastically referred to as "the supermen of Europe." Pearson, for his part, claimed that Canada was not "a colonial chore-boy running around shouting 'Ready, aye, ready'."[38] The phrase "ready, aye, ready" has had a long history in Canadian politics as signifying support for Empire, but made most famous by Arthur Meighen in 1922.[39] By using it in such a disparaging manner, Pearson was taking a dig not only at the Progressive Conservatives but indeed at all those who still thought in terms of defining Canadian policy according to British interests.

The failure of the St. Laurent government to support Britain—as Australia and New Zealand were doing—did not sit well with many English Canadians. *The Globe and Mail* ran a series of editorials denouncing the government. Howard Green, a Conservative MP who was to become foreign minister under John Diefenbaker in 1959, attacked St. Laurent for criticizing "our two mother countries," and "knifing our best friends in the back."[40] Even Meighen emerged briefly from retirement to give an updated version of his celebrated speech 34 years earlier. Canada, he said, "should have sought without delay alignment unmistakably and strongly with Britain."[41] The issue was raised in the election campaign of 1957: on a number of occasions, Diefenbaker discovered that he could draw a favourable response, particularly in Ontario and the Maritimes, by calling attention to Canadian policy on Suez.[42]

Just as Suez demonstrated to both the English and French the shifts in international power that had taken place in the international system, so too it represents the last time that "support for Britain" would be a major issue in Canadian foreign policy. Sentiment for Britain continues, of course, but by the 1960s, Britain had, in terms of foreign relations, ceased to hold special importance.[43] Thus, when Brian Mulroney crossed swords with Margaret Thatcher over sanctions against South Africa in the mid-1980s, there was no bluster about support for Britain. The imperialist idea had died away, long before the demise of the *Telegram* in 1971.

Isolationism

The second dominant idea to which the First World War gave rise was isolationism. In the interwar period, Canadians borrowed this concept from the United States and bent it to their own purposes. Isolationism had been firmly embedded in the conduct of American foreign policy since 1789, and by the end of the First World War was well defined as doctrine.

The two most important elements of the isolationist credo were avoidance of European politics, and of alliances as a tool of statecraft. Both had deep roots in American thought. Even before the Revolution, Thomas Paine had argued that America should "steer clear of European contentions"; John Adams claimed that the United States should "separate ourselves, as far as possible and as long as possible, from all European politics and European wars."[44] Isolationism put into practice George Washington's admonition to Americans in his farewell address in 1796 to avoid what Thomas Jefferson had called "entangling alliances" that would surely suck the new republic into the vortex of world politics and rob it of its newly-won independence.[45] Thus, although the United States had entered the Great War in 1917, the return to traditional diplomacy was "an almost unconscious reflex."[46] The most visible manifestation of the resurgence of traditionalism was the refusal of the Senate to ratify the Treaty of Versailles, thereby keeping the United States out of the League of Nations.

There was, by contrast, no such tradition in Canada. It is true that prior to the war, a comparable view of European power politics was not unfashionable. Such political opposites as Sir Wilfrid Laurier and Henri Bourassa were both wont to refer to Europe as the "vortex of militarism."[47] Indeed, at the Imperial Conference of 1911, Laurier would opine that "All the nations of Europe today, in my humble estimation have gone, if I may say so, quite mad."[48]

But if after the First World War Americans were wont to embrace isolationism again *despite* their brief participation in the European conflict, Canadians were inclined to embrace isolationism *because* of their long war. The human costs of four years of mindlessly trading swatches of mud along the Western Front were gruesome for all participants. But for Canada, with its small population, the toll was particularly grim. The depressing rota of what Desmond Morton has called the "human wreckage" provides some slim indication. In 1916, Canada's population was roughly eight million. Over 619,000 served with the forces, of which 446,000 were volunteers; 425,000 served in Europe. The percentage of casualties was high: 230,000, or a quarter of all men of military age. A total of 60,661 Canadians, nearly one per cent of the entire population, were killed. Of those who survived, 34,000 needed artificial limbs, and 60,000 received disability pensions.[49]

The "richer dust" of 60,000 of their compatriots in "some corner of a foreign field" impelled Canadians not into a more active diplomacy but into withdrawal from world politics. Canadians began to express more widely that basic tenet of American isolationism: a deep resentment of European politics. The historical connection was made explicitly during a debate on the Treaty of Versailles in September 1919 by C.G. "Chubby" Power, a Liberal MP from Quebec: "Our policy for the next hundred years should be that laid down by George Washington ... absolute renunciation of interference in European affairs... I believe the people of Canada will approve of this policy, namely, to let Europe be the arbiter of its own destiny while we in Canada [turn] our energies to our own affairs...."[50] At times the tone was savage: "It was European policy, European statesmanship, European ambition, that drenched the world with blood," N.W. Rowell, the Canadian representative, fulminated at the first meeting of the League of Nations in 1920. "Fifty thousand Canadians under the soil of France and Flanders is what Canada has paid for European statesmanship trying to settle European problems."[51] Such acidic sentiments were not the monopoly of government spokesmen. A citizen wrote to the prime minister in 1923 that Canadians should remove themselves "from the horrors and paralyzing burdens of further European wars. Surely *we* at least who have got nothing out of the war except graves, pension lists, and grinding debt and taxation, should have learned our lesson once and for all time?"[52]

Much of the discontent focussed on the League of Nations in Geneva. At issue was article X of the League's Covenant,[53] the nub of the collective security provisions. Article X carried with it the ultimate obligation (if collective security was to work) to declare war on an aggressor. This was seen as a means by which Canada could be drawn back into the vortex. Few Canadians were as blunt (or as rude) as William E. Borah, the leading isolationist in Congress, who dismissed the League on the floor of the Senate as "the gathered scum of the nations organized into a conglomerate international police force."[54] But the fear that League membership would drag North America into another European war was shared by Canadians. The view of C.A. Gauvreau (Lib: Témiscouata) was indicative: "I see in the League of Nations a source of trouble, of entanglements and international dangers the more to be apprehended because there are in Europe so many sore and bleeding wounds not yet healed up."[55] More than one speaker in the debate on the Versailles treaty sounded the theme raised by Lucien Cannon: "I am not in favour of England ruling this country, but I would rather be ruled by England than by Geneva."[56]

Such sentiments came more easily because of the physical distance between Canada and the vortex. From the fastness of North America, where interstate aggression was *infra dig*, the collective security arrangements of the League appeared distinctly one-sided. The classic position was put by Raoul Dandurand, leader of Mackenzie King's Liberal government in the Senate. Representing Canada at the League Assembly in 1924, he said that "in this association of Mutual Insurance against fire, the risks assumed by the different States are not equal. We live in a fire-proof house, far from inflammable materials."[57]

Likewise, isolationist sentiment came more easily in Quebec for reasons connected with the traditional lack of appeal of imperialism. P.B. Waite has argued that emotional remoteness from France led to a Québécois definition of themselves as a North American, not a European, people. "Laissons l'Europe à ses heurts d'idées, à ses chocs de régimes, à ses querelles racistes," *Le Devoir* editorialized in 1938. "Enracinons-nous au sol d'Amerique."[58] "French Canadians are in favour of isolation in one form or another," Léon Mercier Gouin, a Quebec lawyer wrote in 1937. "From this it follows that we do not intend to have Canada become one of the policemen of the world. 'Charity begins at home,' and our internal problems are quite enough for us."[59] The durability of French Canadian isolationism can be seen in attitudes towards the prospect of a European war. "Notre mot d'ordre est net," asserted *l'Action Nationale*, a nationalist paper, after Italy's invasion of Ethiopia in 1935. "Pas un homme, pas un sou, pas un fusil, pas une cartouche pour les guerres de l'Angleterre."[60]

However, Canadian isolationism did differ from American isolation in one important respect. There was no sentiment, within the government or the public, for a rejection of membership in the League. For example, when a Conservative senator introduced a motion for Canadian withdrawal from the League in 1934, he was disavowed by his leader, Prime Minister R.B. Bennett; no one else spoke in favour of the proposal; and the motion was handily voted down.[61] The reason for this apparent inconsistency was that Canadians, but particularly their leaders, looked at League membership as a valuable symbol of Canadian autonomy and were disinclined to sacrifice it for the sake of consistency. In short, autonomism demanded membership in the League, but isolationism demanded that every effort be made to avoid entangling Canada in obligations that might again draw the community into a foreign war, exposing anew the deep divisions on this most important question.

By the late 1930s, with the rise of the Nazis, German rearmament, and Adolph Hitler's eastern expansion, the prospect of war loomed considerably larger. Frank Underhill of the University of Toronto might continue to preach isolationism, writing that in response to the rumblings of a European war, Canadians should "like Ulysses and his men, sail past the European siren, our ears stuffed with tax-bills."[62] But increasingly fewer Canadians, in both English and French Canada, were inclined to view the rise of Nazi Germany with such indifference. Instead, public opinion seemed torn between the demands of isolationism, the fear of Germany, and sentiment for Britain. O.D. Skelton, the under-secretary of state for external affairs, put forward the following analysis of public opinion in early 1939:

> It is unquestionable, looking back over the past twenty years, that nationalist and peace feeling have grown rapidly in Canada and imperialist and war feeling have rapidly declined. It is probable that those opposed to participation in British wars now constitute a majority of the people in Canada. But it is also clear that the imperialist minority have a weight beyond their numbers because of their greater share of wealth, influence, assurance and public position; the greater number of men now in high positions, business or governmental, formed their opinions at a time when imperial or colonial views were dominant.[63]

He was to be proved wrong about "majority opinion." When Germany invaded Poland on 1 September 1939, Canada's interwar isolationism came to an end with majority support. The Canadian Parliament went through the ritual of approving a separate Canadian declaration of war—which King George VI dutifully announced on 10 September, a week after Britain's declaration. That the country went relatively united into this war can be seen from the proceedings in Parliament. The pacifist leader of the Cooperative Commonwealth Federation, J.S. Woodsworth, voiced his objections, but the rest of his party had decided not to oppose the war. Only three Quebec nationalists expressed dissent; the government's promise on 9 September that there would be no conscription no doubt helped quell what concerns there might have been among Quebec MPs. To be sure, there would be no enthusiasm in Quebec for this war, but there would be little of the fractious conflict that had marked Canada's involvement in the First World War (even when in 1944 the government reneged and introduced conscription). It is important to note, however, that there was similarly little enthusiasm in English Canada for war. Memories of the last war were still too fresh to prompt the kind of jingoist zeal that had greeted the outbreak of war in 1914.[64]

Internationalism

Isolationism holds to a belief in the rightness of acting unilaterally in international politics, of avoiding prior commitments to use national resources for the maintenance of order in the states-system. It is marked by indifference or outright hostility to international institutions as a means of regulating, managing, or tempering conflict between states. Internationalism is predicated on a markedly different set of values, beliefs, and ideas about the proper role of a state in world politics.

Internationalism embraces the same goal as isolationism—the avoidance of war—but seeks to achieve that end by different means. Internationalism begins by accepting the validity of the argument that peace is indivisible. In other words, internationalists hold that the fate of any one state and the peace of the international system as a whole are inexorably interconnected. The outbreak of war in a seemingly distant part of the globe has every potential for plunging the whole system into conflict. And physical distance from the vortex of great power rivalry is not necessarily a guarantee of non-involvement. Moreover, the advances of technology render notions of "fire-proof houses" obsolete. In the internationalist view, such interconnectedness and vulnerability demand engagement in world politics, not withdrawal.

Internationalist engagement is marked by four related elements. First, the notion of responsibility is the hallmark of internationalist statecraft: each state which has an interest in wishing to avoid war has a responsibility for playing a constructive part in the management of conflict that will inevitably arise in the interstate system. Second, multilateralism is seen as critical for defusing the clash of interests that can lead to war. States should be prepared to forego the advantages of acting unilaterally in international politics in the larger interests of establishing and maintaining order within the community of states. Third, a commitment to international institutions follows naturally, for institutionalization promotes multilateralism and dampens the unilateral impulse. Finally, support for institutions must be given concrete expression by a willingness to enter into prior commitments to use national resources for the system as a whole.[65] But it should be noted that this definition of internationalism cast Canada as an *aligned* member of the international community. Canadian internationalism was, and is, framed within the context of the rivalries at the apex of the international system that emerged before the Second World War was even over. Military alignment with the United States and Western Europe against the Soviet Union, and participation in the multilateral and institutional manifestation of that alignment are inexorably tied to this dominant idea.

The cataclysm of a six-year war that came less than a generation after the "war to end all wars" transformed public ideas in Canada about the proper posture of Canadian statecraft. Over 42,000 Canadians died between 1939 and 1945 but there was no repetition of the mood after the Great War. One can discern little sentiment for a disengagement from world affairs. Instead, there was a widespread willingness to embrace the ideals of internationalism being pursued by the government in Ottawa.

As Donald Creighton has put it, the war had brought about a "diplomatic revolution" within the government.[66] There were many "revolutionists"—in the Department of External Affairs and in Mackenzie King's cabinet. But the key figures were Louis St. Laurent, who was appointed secretary of state for external affairs in 1946 and who would have the mantle of the Liberal leadership passed to him in 1948, and Lester B. Pearson, who in 1946 was appointed the under-secretary of state for external affairs and who would join St. Laurent's cabinet as foreign minister in 1948.

Both were avowed internationalists. Pearson had served in London and Geneva in the late 1930s, where he had watched with "impatience" King's cautious interwar policies.[67] As early as January 1942, he was urging the abandonment of isolationism: "in 1919 we were only interested in the road back. We know where that led. We must now keep our eyes on the road ahead... This time we must maintain, for the organization and application of the peace, the spirit and forms of international cooperation which we are forging in the heat and flames of war."[68] Pearson's precepts of internationalism—responsibility, multilateralism, commitment, and international institutions—sprang from "his preoccupation with peaceful methods of resolving conflict."[69] As he wrote in his memoirs, "Everything I learned during the war confirmed and strengthened my view as a Canadian that our foreign policy must not be timid or fearful of commitments but activist in accepting international responsibilities."[70]

St. Laurent's attachment to such ideas was just as strong. In October 1945, in the debate on the United Nations Charter, he argued that "Canada is prepared to take whatever risk may be involved in joining this organization, because the other risk, that of not having an international organization, is something of such consequence that one dare hardly envisage it."[71] Four months after King appointed him to the external affairs portfolio, St. Laurent delivered what has come to be regarded as the classic statement of postwar Canadian internationalism. In the Gray Lecture at the University of Toronto in January 1947, he outlined the five principles on which Canadian foreign policy was to be based: national unity, political liberty, the rule of law in international affairs, the values of a Christian civilization, and the acceptance of international responsibility.[72] Importantly, two of these principles—the rule of law and the acceptance of responsibility—broke sharply with Canada's prewar diplomacy.

John W. Holmes has cautioned that "The 'revolution' ... can be over-dramatized. It was a change more of will than of policy."[73] Yet the changes in Canadian policy in the five years after the war were no less significant than the changes in attitude. Internationalism in practice would bring policies unthinkable a generation earlier: a strong and durable commitment to the United Nations,[74] one concrete measure of which was the dispatch of troops to fight in the Korean War;[75] support for a multiracial Commonwealth after the independence of India, Pakistan, and Ceylon after 1947;[76] and, most importantly, strong support for the creation of a peace-time alliance, which was by 1951 to involve the unprecedented stationing of Canadian troops on active service abroad.[77]

The internationalism of the immediate postwar period, it should be stressed, was not the result of the pressure of public opinion. St. Laurent was not compelled to seek an activist role for Canada in the United Nations in the way that Laurier was compelled to join the South African war or that King was deterred from an activist role in the League. Rather, internationalism was urged upon a receptive public by government officials. Having decided that an Atlantic alliance would be beneficial for Canadian interests, St. Laurent and his colleagues and their bureaucrats set about to convince the public, in numerous speeches given throughout 1948, that Canada should be counted among the founding members. It was called a "crusade" by the media; it was not a title of which St. Laurent was ashamed.[78]

Government officials were so effective in spreading the international creed that their radical departures in foreign policy provoked only the slightest opposition domestically, mostly from Quebec. Five MPs from that province voted against the United Nations Charter in 1945, the only members of Parliament to do so. Only two negative votes—again both from Quebec—were cast against the North Atlantic Treaty. In 1950, the outbreak of the Korean War brought not bitter division but a measure of consensus. English-language papers were fully behind participation; indeed, the government was criticized for not doing enough. Initially the French-language press was in the main noncommittal, caught in what Denis

Stairs has called the cross-pressures arising from "a conflict between a traditional commitment to isolationism on the one hand, and a hostility to communism on the other."[79] But by the time St. Laurent announced in August the government's intention to send ground forces, only *Le Devoir*, the newspaper established by Henri Bourassa, carried on the founder's tradition by opposing participation. Another measure of this consensus can be seen in parliamentary debates. There was bipartisan support for Canadian participation and only one dissenting vote. In 1919, the member for Témiscouata, C.A. Gavreau, had opposed a commitment to the League; a generation later, his successor, Jean-François Pouliot, would raise a lone voice against the commitment in Korea. He would, however, be disavowed by fellow Liberals from Quebec; and in the press, he would be accused of talking "nonsense" and "living in a world which died when an atomic bomb fell on Hiroshima." The irony was not lost on the *Ottawa Journal*:

> It would have seemed a strange debate to Laurier and Borden and Meighen... There was the Canadian Parliament begging its executive ministers to send ships or troops or planes to fight in a far-off mountainous land where no Canadians are and whose economic interest to Canada is less than that of Smiths Falls.[80]

Internationalism, John Holmes has written, "was almost a religion in the decade after the Second World War."[81] The hold of its orthodoxy would prove exceedingly durable. For many years, the idea of Canadian activism on behalf of the larger community of states as a normative good would underwrite Canadian participation in every major UN peacekeeping operation;[82] service on two truce supervisory commissions in Indochina;[83] and personal initiatives by Canadian leaders to resolve interstate conflict, such as Pearson's diplomacy over the Suez crisis in 1956, for which he was awarded the Nobel Prize for Peace.

Times changed, however. The fervour of that first decade waned as the opportunities for Canada to put its internationalist ideals into practice diminished. There was less scope for the kind of "middlepowermanship" examined in chapter 3. The world of the 1960s had been transformed by a number of developments. The process of decolonization reduced the possibilities for UN-sponsored peacekeeping operations. Europe and Japan had recovered from their wartime devastation, which placed strains on the western alliance over which Canada had neither control nor influence. The rise of China as an autonomous major power threatened to alter the global balance. Detente between the two superpowers eased the tight bipolarity which had prompted Canadian diplomatists into such activity in the postwar decade. If religiosity is measured only by activism in peacekeeping and mediatory diplomacy, by the late 1960s, Canadians were lapsed internationalists.

The fervour of the early years may have been diminished, but the institutional manifestations of Canadian internationalism—attachment to the United Nations, the Commonwealth, and the North Atlantic alliance—would remain ritualistic "cornerstones" (as they are often described) of Canadian policy. The public's attachment to these multilateral institutions would remain consistent for well over a generation, from Pearsonian internationalism of the 1950s to the embrace of "constructive internationalism" by the government of Brian Mulroney in the 1980s.[84]

This attachment to internationalism has not gone unchallenged or unquestioned, however. In the late 1960s, for example, Pierre Trudeau would challenge the orthodoxy after he was selected leader of the Liberal party. "There comes a time for renewal," the white paper on foreign policy published by his government in 1970 declared boldly, "and in 1968 the Government saw that for Canada's foreign policy the time had arrived."[85] The white paper called into question many of the traditional manifestations of internationalism, including the relevance of United Nations peacekeeping, Canada's role in international affairs, and even the commitment to the North Atlantic Treaty Organization. Likewise, both the New Democratic Party and the Parti québécois rejected the internationalist manifestations of postwar policy and embraced neutralist foreign policies in the late 1960s, both promising to withdraw from NATO and the North American Air Defence agreement if elected.[86]

But it is indicative of the persistence and dominance of the internationalist idea that such challenges were ultimately unsuccessful. The NDP has not, since 1969, been able to surmount the fundamental difficulty of embracing a policy option that 85 per cent of Canadians oppose. Its parliamentary leadership tried over the course of the 1970s and 1980s to distance itself from the neutralist plank, but without success. The rank and file have insisted on keeping it as part of the party's program. For its part, the Parti québécois learned more quickly. By the time the PQ government published its white paper on sovereignty-association in 1979 as part of its campaign to negotiate a withdrawal from Confederation, it had abandoned its earlier commitment to neutralism. Indeed, the PQ's blueprint for a foreign policy for an independent Quebec was ironically Pearsonian to the core: military alignment with the west, including membership in NATO and NORAD; membership in the UN, *la francophonie*, and even the Commonwealth; and an activist role for Quebec in interstate diplomacy.[87]

And for all the cavalier criticisms of the late 1960s, Trudeau never did abandon those fundamentals he had challenged so ardently.[88] In particular, his government remained committed to peacekeeping, to the UN, and to international mediation, as his peace mission in 1983-84 demonstrated. Indeed, the role of public opinion in defining the range of acceptability of policy options regarding NATO was nicely captured in the summer of 1983, by Trudeau's external affairs minister. "I don't think this Government will ever lead Canada out of the North Atlantic Treaty Organization," Allan MacEachen stated explicitly, "I think that is an issue ... far beyond the realm of possibility unless there is a dramatic change in Canadian public opinion."[89]

CONCLUSION

Ideas and Other "Isms"

It should be stressed that the focus of this chapter has been on sets of broad ideas about foreign policy. It has not attempted to provide a survey of the many other sets of attitudes or beliefs Canadians hold that will bear on foreign policy. These are the bundles of beliefs, attitudes, and opinions on a variety of matters to which we loosely tag the suffix "ism" to denote some vague coherence. In the context of Canadian foreign policy, numerous "isms" have made their appearance over the last century, some of them inexorably tied to the three dominant ideas discussed in this chapter. For example, jingoism, chauvinism, racism, and militarism are attitudes and beliefs inextricably tied to ideas about empire. Likewise, anti-militarism, pacificism, and neutralism have also featured in the politics of Canadian foreign policy.

Anti-communism has always been strong in Canada, a function of the dominant ideological mix of individualism, capitalism, and liberalism. It has, however, always been reflected in the widespread antipathy to the state first embracing communism: anti-Sovietism has been an integral part of the beliefs and attitudes of many Canadians since the October Revolution, the more so since the emergence of the Soviet Union as a superpower. Indeed, one cannot divorce the essential anti-Sovietism that has driven Canada's alignment in world politics from Canadian attachment to internationalism. However, anti-Sovietism and anti-communism should not be regarded as synonymous. Canadians have always demonstrated an antipathy to whichever state happens to be the dominant adversary of Canada's close friends and allies.[90] Thus it could be suggested that the anti-German hysteria[91] in Canada prior to and during the First World War was at bottom a function not of differences in ideology, but of the great power rivalry between Britain and Germany. So too, it might be suggested that anti-Sovietism has more to do with the USSR's rivalry with the United States than it does with the official ideology of that polity.

However, the most durable of these bundles of attitudes and beliefs is not related to any of the three ideas examined in this chapter.

Anti-Americanism is a fundamental attribute of another dominant ideology in Canada, that of nationalism,[92] but it has made a frequent appearance in Canadian politics and foreign policy. This is hardly surprising: Canada owes its beginnings to an act of anti-Americanism—by those unwilling to join other North Americans in their bold new republican experiment. Likewise, it owes its continued existence to an ongoing act of anti-Americanism—the maintenance of a separate polity on the North American continent.

While they have not been examined in detail, these "isms" frequently play an important part in shaping the moods, opinions, and attitudes of Canadians—and in shaping the decision-making environment—no less so than dominant ideas.

Dominant Ideas and Policy-Makers

This chapter has argued that imperialism, isolationism, and internationalism have dominated public discussion and debate regarding foreign policy. These ideas demonstrate how society can influence foreign policy-makers by setting the parameters of policy. Three concluding observations can be made about the impact of dominant ideas on policy-makers.

First, such ideas exert a pervasive, yet subtle, influence on the making of policy, serving to define the parameters of acceptable policy options. However, these parameters are exceedingly wide, giving the government considerable latitude in specific policy choices. For example, in the postwar period there has been such a wide consensus on Canadian membership in NATO that a withdrawal from the alliance would be outside the bounds of permissible behaviour. But within those boundaries, governments have had considerable latitude to define Canadian NATO policies as they wish.

Second, the ideas dominant in society and those dominant within the state apparatus need not coincide. While the isolationism of the early 1920s is an example of coincidence, at times the government may be ahead of public opinion as it was in the case of autonomism during the First World War and in the early 1920s. At times, it may lag behind. For example, Mackenzie King had been so affected by the issue of conscription that in March 1948, when the government decided to commit Canada to an Atlantic alliance, he was overcome with fear that this would eventually lead to yet another conscription crisis: "I found myself perspiring from sheer anxiety."[93]

Third, state officials will not hesitate to take the lead in giving impetus to dominant ideas in society, and to use their authority to legitimize some ideas over others. Such was the case with the pursuit of autonomism by Borden and King, and the pursuit of internationalism by St. Laurent and

Pearson. Similarly, officials may seek to work actively against the growth of other ideas that might challenge their preferred ideas.[94]

NOTES

1 Robert Dalleck, *The American Style of Foreign Policy: Cultural Politics and Foreign Affairs* (New York: Alfred A. Knopf, 1983), xiii.

2 Gabriel A. Almond and Sidney Verba, *The Civic Culture: Political Attitudes and Democracy in Five Nations* (Princeton: Princeton University Press, 1963); Almond and Verba, eds., *The Civic Culture Revisited* (Boston: Little, Brown, 1980). A cogent discussion of this notion applied to Canadian politics may be found in Robert J. Jackson, Doreen Jackson, and Nicolas Baxter-Moore, *Politics in Canada: Culture, Institutions, Behaviour and Public Policy* (Scarborough: Prentice-Hall Canada Inc., 1986), 75-125.

3 For one discussion, see John Plamenatz, *Ideology* (New York: Praeger, 1970).

4 G. Bruce Doern and Richard W. Phidd, *Canadian Public Policy: Ideas, Structure and Process* (Toronto: Methuen, 1983), 54-59.

5 Following Whittington, I assume that one national political culture can be identified: Michael S. Whittington, "Political culture: the attitudinal matrix of politics," in John H. Redekop, ed., *Approaches to Canadian Politics* (Scarborough: Prentice-Hall Canada Inc., 1978), 138-53; for arguments suggesting that the political culture in Canada is fragmented by the country's cultural, linguistic, regional, and other cleavages, see David Bell and Lorne Tepperman, *The Roots of Disunity: A Look at Canadian Political Culture* (Toronto: McClelland and Stewart, 1979).

6 Denis Stairs, "The political culture of Canadian foreign policy," *Canadian Journal of Political Science* 15 (December 1982), 667-90.

7 See, for example, Michael M. Atkinson and Marsha A. Chandler, "Strategies for policy analysis," in Atkinson and Chandler, eds., *The Politics of Canadian Public Policy* (Toronto: University of Toronto Press, 1983), 3-19.

8 For a dated yet still relevant discussion, see John W. Holmes, "Nationalism in Canadian foreign policy," in Peter Russell, ed., *Nationalism in Canada* (Toronto: McGraw-Hill Ryerson, 1966), 203-220.

9 Normally, this term refers to identifiable subpopulations within a society, such as the working class "subculture" or the Scottish "subculture." Dennis Kavanagh, "Political culture in Great Britain: the decline of the civic culture," in Almond and Verba, eds., *Civic Culture Revisited*, 166-67.

10 For a somewhat opposing view, see the discussion of "political culture" in Michael Tucker, *Canadian Foreign Policy: Contemporary Issues and Themes* (Toronto: McGraw-Hill Ryerson, 1980), 2-5.

11 Hans J. Morgenthau, *Politics Among Nations: The Struggle for Power and Peace*, 5th ed. (New York: Alfred A. Knopf, 1973), 132-33.

12 Thucydides, *The Peloponnesian War*, Rex Warner, trans. (Harmondsworth: Penguin, 1954), 144-49.

13   Seymour M. Hersh, *"The Target Is Destroyed": What Really Happened to Flight 007 and What America Knew About It* (New York: Vintage, 1987), 184-85, 229-230; Alexander Dallin, *Black Box: KAL 007 and the Superpowers* (Berkeley: University of California Press, 1985), 10-13.

14   *"The Target Is Destroyed"*, 337. Hersh of course was writing before the *U.S.S. Vincennes*, in July 1988, did precisely what no American fighting force would do: it downed Iran Air 655, with the loss of 290 lives. That incident demonstrated not only the fallacy of the "national character" approach, but also the dangers implicit in sanctimonious moralizing in international politics.

15   *The Globe and Mail*, 11 August 1988, A1. The historian was J.L. Granatstein. For his earlier views on peacekeeping, see "Canada and peacekeeping: image and reality," *Canadian Forum* (August 1974), 14-19, reprinted in J.L. Granatstein, ed., *Canadian Foreign Policy: Historical Readings* (Toronto: Copp Clark Pitman, 1986), 232-40.

16   Nowhere is this better seen than in historical views of Canadians about the effect of a northern climate on their own "national character." "The very atmosphere of her northern latitude, the breath of life that rose from lake and forest, prairie and mountain," wrote Isaac Brock's biographer earnestly in 1909, "was fast developing a race of men with bodies enduring as iron and minds as highly tempered as steel." In 1905, a clergyman had these thoughts on the effects of climate on character: "[L]ong winters cultivate thrift, energy and fore-thought, without which any civilization would perish, and at the same time give leisure for reading and study. So the Scottish, the Icelanders, the Swedes and the northern races generally, are much better educated than the Latin and southern races." Rudyard Kipling, concerned with promoting "hardness" in racial character and attacking the "softness" he felt was developing in the British "race," saw in Canada cause for optimism: "there is a fine, hard, bracing climate," he said in 1899, "the climate that puts iron and grit into men's bones." For these nescient gems, and many more besides, see the survey by Carl Berger, "The true north strong and free," in Russell, ed., *Nationalism in Canada*, 3-26.

17   Denis Stairs, "Public opinion and external affairs: reflections on the domestication of Canadian foreign policy," *International Journal* 33 (Winter 1977-8), 128.

18   For example, see the opinion results quoted in Mildred A. Schwartz, *Public Opinion and Canadian Identity* (Berkeley: University of California Press, 1967), 74.

19   Paul Kennedy, *The Rise and Fall of the Great Powers: Economic Change and Military Conflict from 1500 to 2000* (London: Unwin Hyman, 1988), 540.

20   During the goldrush of the 1880s, numerous British citizens had migrated to the quasi-independent South African republic of Transvaal until they outnumbered the Afrikaaners. Paul Kruger, president of the Transvaal, responded by effectively disenfranchising the Uitlanders ("outlanders," or foreigners) in the 1890s. It was ostensibly to secure their political rights that the British government escalated tensions with the Transvaal in 1898 and 1899, prodding the Afrikaaners to issue an ultimatum that led on 12 October 1899 to the outbreak of hostilities. On 2 April 1982, Argentina invaded the Falkland Islands, a British colony over which Buenos Aires claimed sovereignty. The Argentine

forces handily routed the 80-man garrison of Royal Marines and established control over the 1800 "Kelpers," as the islanders are known. The immediate response of the government of Margaret Thatcher was to dispatch a naval task force to the South Atlantic to recover the islands, which they did in June.

21 C.P. Stacey, *Canada and the Age of Conflict: A History of Canadian External Policies*, vol. 1: *1867-1921* (Toronto: Macmillan, 1977), 57-74; excerpts from the contemporary press are reproduced in Robert J.D. Page, ed., *Imperialism and Canada, 1895-1903* (Toronto: Holt, Rinehart and Winston, 1972), 61-91. The editor was John Willison of the *Globe*, a Liberal newspaper: see Stacey, *Age of Conflict*, 59-60. The "disloyal" MP was Henri Bourassa: his writings and speeches on the South African war are reproduced in Joseph Levitt, ed., *Henri Bourassa on Imperialism and Biculturalism, 1900-1918* (Toronto: Copp Clark, 1970), 35-43.

22 *International Canada*, April and May 1982, 16.

23 Carl Berger, *The Sense of Power: Studies in the Ideas of Canadian Imperialism, 1867-1914* (Toronto: University of Toronto Press, 1970), 259-65; also Holmes, "Nationalism in Canadian foreign policy," 203-206.

24 See above, the discussion on "national character," and the quotations from Berger, "True north."

25 H. Blair Neatby, "Laurier and imperialism," in Carl Berger et al., *Imperial Relations in the Age of Laurier* (Toronto: University of Toronto Press, 1969), 2.

26 Stacey, *Age of Conflict*, vol. 1, 41-44.

27 Such as the following paean penned by one Nova Scotia poet on the occasion of Victoria's jubilee in 1897: "Hail our great Queen in her regalia/One foot in Canada, the other in Australia." Cited in Holmes, "Nationalism in Canadian foreign policy," 206 and *fn* 3.

28 See the discussion in Berger, *Sense of Power*, 120-27; James Eayrs, "The Round Table Movement in Canada, 1909-1920," *Canadian Historical Review* 38 (March 1957), reprinted in Berger et al., *Imperial Relations*, 61-80.

29 Levitt, ed., *Bourassa on Imperialism*, 174.

30 Page, ed., *Imperialism and Canada*, 75.

31 Levitt, ed., *Bourassa on Imperialism*, 64.

32 As David Lloyd George, the British prime minister, noted in December 1916: "The more I think about it, the more I am convinced that we should take the Dominions into our counsel in much larger measure than we have hitherto done in our prosecution of the war. They have made enormous sacrifices, but we have held no conference with them as to either the objects of the war, or the methods of carrying it out. They hardly feel that they have been consulted. As we must receive even more substantial help from them before we can hope to pull through, it is important that they should feel that they have a share in our councils as well as in our burdens." Quoted in Donald Creighton, *Canada's First Century* (Toronto: Macmillan, 1970), 145.

33 Quoted in G.P.deT. Glazebrook, *A History of Canadian External Relations*, rev. ed., vol. 2: *In the Empire and the World, 1914-1939* (Toronto: McClelland and Stewart, 1966), 90-91.

34 Quoted in Donald Page, "The Institute's 'popular arm': the League of Nations Society in Canada," *International Journal* 33 (Winter 1977- 8), 39-40.

35 Stacey, *Age of Conflict*, vol. 2: *1921-1948: The Mackenzie King Era* (Toronto: University of Toronto Press, 1981), 186.

36 J.L. Granatstein and Robert Bothwell, "'A self-evident national duty': Canadian foreign policy, 1935-1939," *Journal of Imperial and Commonwealth History* 3 (January 1975), 212; reprinted in J.L. Granatstein, ed., *Canadian Foreign Policy: Historical Readings* (Toronto: Copp Clark Pitman, 1986), 125-44. Granatstein and Bothwell quote Stephen Leacock, writing on this subject in the summer of 1939. "If you were to ask any Canadian, 'Do you have to go to war if England does?' he'd answer at once, 'Oh, no.' If you then asked, 'Would you go to war if England does?' he'd answer 'Oh, yes.' And if you asked 'Why?' he would say, reflectively, 'Well, you see, we'd have to.'"

37 In response to the nationalization of the Suez canal by Egyptian president Gamel Abdel Nasser in July, Israel launched a military attack on Egypt on 29 October 1956. This was followed by British and French attacks beginning on 31 October, which caused a deep rift between Washington and its two major European allies. This split caused great consternation in Ottawa: "It is hard for a Canadian to think of any consideration—other than national survival or safety—as more important [than Anglo-American friendship]," Pearson wrote Sir Anthony Eden, the British prime minister, on 1 November. Accounts of Canada's role in this crisis may be found in John W. Holmes, *The Shaping of Peace: Canada and the Search for World Order, 1943-1957*, vol. 2 (Toronto: University of Toronto Press, 1982), 348-70; Pearson's own account is in *Mike: The Memoirs of the Rt. Hon. Lester B. Pearson*, vol. 2: *1948-1957* (Toronto: University of Toronto Press, 1973), ch. 10-11.

38 James Eayrs, *Canada in World Affairs*, vol. 9: *October 1955 to June 1957* (Toronto: Oxford University Press, 1959), 188.

39 As we will see in the next chapter, the Liberal government of Mackenzie King turned down a British request for military assistance to the Gallipoli peninsula. Meighen, then leader of the opposition Conservatives, gave a speech in Toronto in which he criticized King's refusal, claiming that "When Britain's message came, then Canada should have said: 'Ready, aye, ready; we stand by you.'" Stacey, *Age of Conflict*, vol. 2, 30. Although Meighen was excoriated for this speech in many quarters, and while the phrase was associated thereafter with the Conservatives, the phrase already had a long history of use in Canadian politics—by both Liberals and Conservatives. Meighen's phrasing in 1922 was virtually identical to the words that Laurier, then the leader of the opposition Liberals, had used in August 1914 in support of the Canadian declaration of war by the Conservative government of Sir Robert Borden: "When the call comes," Laurier had stated, "our answer goes at once, and it goes in the classical language of the British answer to the call to duty: 'Ready, aye, ready.'" Quoted in Stacey, *Age of Conflict*, vol. 1, 176. In turn, Laurier was but echoing Sir George E. Foster, a Conservative MP, who on 16 January 1896 had said to the House of Commons: "It is the right and duty of Britain herself and of every dependency that belongs to her to be ready, aye, ready as well as steady in its sentiments of loyalty and devotion for the Empire as a whole."

40 Peter Stursberg, *Lester Pearson and the American Dilemma* (Toronto: Doubleday Canada, 1980), 156-57.

41 Quoted in Eayrs, *Canada in World Affairs*, 188, *fn* 50.

42 *Ibid.*, 190-91.

43 See the essays in Peter Lyon, ed., *Britain and Canada: Survey of a Changing Relationship* (London: Frank Cass, 1976).

44 Thomas N. Guinsburg, *The Pursuit of Isolationism in the United States Senate from Versailles to Pearl Harbor* (New York: Garland Publishing, 1982), 1.

45 Alexander de Conde, *Entangling Alliance* (Durham: Duke University Press, 1958). Indeed, an interesting indication of American insularity is that until 1906, when Theodore Roosevelt visited Panama, presidents by tradition never left United States territory during their term of office. Woodrow Wilson's participation in the peace conference after the First World War marked the first time that an incumbent president had left the western hemisphere.

46 Robert J. Art, "America's foreign policy: in historical perspective," in Roy C. Macridis, ed., *Foreign Policy in World Politics*, 5th ed. (Englewood Cliffs: Prentice-Hall, 1976), 345.

47 Laurier quoted in Desmond Morton, *Canada and War: A Military and Political History* (Toronto: Butterworths, 1981), 50; also C.P. Stacey, *Mackenzie King and the Atlantic Triangle* (Toronto: Macmillan, 1976), 25; Bourassa quoted in Levitt, *Bourassa on Imperialism*, 48, 53.

48 Stacey, *Age of Conflict*, vol. 1, 141.

49 Figures from Morton, *Canada and War*, 82, 86; Stacey, *Age of Conflict*, vol. 1, 192, 235.

50 Canada, Parliament, House of Commons, *Debates*, 1919, vol. 1, 230, 11 September 1919.

51 Quoted in James Eayrs, "'A low dishonest decade': aspects of Canadian external policy, 1931-1939," in Hugh L. Keenleyside et al., *The Growth of Canadian Policies in External Affairs* (Durham: Duke University Press, 1960), 61.

52 Quoted in James Eayrs, *In Defence of Canada*, vol. 1: *From the Great War to the Great Depression* (Toronto: University of Toronto Press, 1964), 6.

53 Article X read: "The Members of the League undertake to respect and preserve against external aggression the territorial integrity and existing political independence of all Members of the League. In case of any such aggression or in case of any threat or danger of such aggression the Council shall advise upon the means by which this obligation shall be fulfilled."

54 Quoted in Guinsburg, *Pursuit of Isolationism*, 32.

55 House of Commons, *Debates*, 1919, vol. 1, 146-47, 9 September 1919.

56 Quoted in Richard Veatch, *Canada and the League of Nations* (Toronto: University of Toronto Press, 1975), 29. The next day, Ernest Lapointe claimed that Canada would be "governed by and from Geneva." House of Commons, *Debates*, 1919, vol. 1, 157, 10 September 1919.

57 Veatch, *Canada and the League*, 19-20.

58 Quoted in P.B. Waite, "French-Canadian isolationism and English Canada: an elliptical foreign policy, 1935-1939," *Journal of Canadian Studies* 18 (Summer 1983), 141.

59 Robert Bothwell and Norman Hillmer, eds., *The In-Between Time: Canadian External Policy in the 1930s* (Toronto: Copp Clark, 1975), 20.

60 Waite, "French-Canadian isolationism," 136.

61 Stacey, *Age of Conflict*, vol. 2, 164-65.

62 R.A. Mackay and E.B. Rogers, *Canada Looks Abroad* (Toronto: Oxford University Press, 1938), 164-65.

63 Quoted in Norman Hillmer, "The Anglo-Canadian neurosis: the case of O.D. Skelton," in Lyon, ed., *Britain and Canada*, 77-78.

64 On the declaration, see Stacey, *Age of Conflict*, vol. 2, 260-64.

65 It should be noted that internationalism is often defined simply as international activity, with or without the elements of responsibility. See, for example, Charles W. Kegley, Jr. and Eugene R. Wittkopf, *American Foreign Policy: Pattern and Process* (New York: St. Martin's Press, 1979), 29-32; also David B. Dewitt and John J. Kirton, *Canada as a Principal Power* (Toronto: John Wiley and Sons, 1983), 48-57.

66 The title of ch. 7 in Donald Creighton, *The Forked Road: Canada, 1939-1957* (Toronto: McClelland and Stewart, 1976).

67 L.B. Pearson, "Forty years on: reflections on our foreign policy," *International Journal* 22 (Summer 1967), 357.

68 Lester B. Pearson, *Words and Occasions* (Toronto: University of Toronto Press, 1970), 55.

69 Denis Stairs, "Present in moderation: Lester Pearson and the craft of diplomacy," *International Journal* 29 (Winter 1973-4), 145.

70 *Mike: The Memoirs of the Rt. Hon. Lester B. Pearson*, vol. 1: *1897-1948* (Toronto: University of Toronto Press, 1972), 283.

71 Dale C. Thomson, *Louis St. Laurent: Canadian* (Toronto: Macmillan, 1967), 176.

72 Reprinted in R.A. Mackay, ed., *Canadian Foreign Policy, 1945-1954: Selected Speeches and Documents* (Toronto: McClelland and Stewart, 1970), 388-99; also in Granatstein, ed., *Canadian Foreign Policy*, 25-33.

73 Holmes, *Shaping of Peace*, vol. 1 (Toronto: University of Toronto Press, 1979), 4.

74 For a survey of Canadian policy towards the United Nations in the immediate postwar period, see Holmes, *Shaping of Peace*, vol. 1, ch. 8-9.

75 The best source on Canada and the Korean War is Denis Stairs, *The Diplomacy of Constraint: Canada, the Korean War and the United States* (Toronto: University of Toronto Press, 1974).

76 Holmes, *Shaping of Peace*, vol. 2, ch. 8; Eayrs, *In Defence of Canada*, vol. 3: *Peacemaking and Deterrence* (Toronto: University of Toronto Press, 1972), ch. 4.

77 For the events leading up to the signing of the North Atlantic Treaty, see Eayrs, *In Defence of Canada*, vol. 4, ch. 1-2; also Holmes, *Shaping of Peace*, vol. 2, 98-122. The text of the Treaty is reprinted in Mackay, ed., *Canadian Foreign Policy, 1945-1954*, 192-95.

78 Eayrs, *In Defence of Canada*, vol. 4: *Growing Up Allied* (Toronto: University of Toronto Press, 1980), 51.

79 Stairs, *Diplomacy of Constraint*, 58.

80 *Ibid.*, 55-57.

81 Holmes, *Shaping of Peace*, vol. 2, 119.

82 Peyton V. Lyon and Brian W. Tomlin, *Canada as an International Actor* (Toronto: Macmillan, 1979), 15; Alastair Taylor et al., *Peacekeeping: International Challenge and Canadian Response* (Toronto: Canadian Institute of International Affairs, 1968).

83 The Canadian government served on the International Commissions for Supervision and Control (ICSC) in Vietnam, Laos, and Cambodia from 1954; at the conclusion of the Vietnam war in January 1973, Ottawa served for six months on the International Commission for Control and Supervision (ICCS). The most comprehensive survey of the entire period is Douglas A. Ross, *In the Interests of Peace: Canada and Vietnam, 1954-73* (Toronto: University of Toronto Press, 1984). For the early years, see James Eayrs, *In Defence of Canada*, vol. 5: *Indochina: The Roots of Complicity* (Toronto: University of Toronto Press, 1983).

84 This term, in essence a rededication to activist diplomacy within the context of multilateral institutions, was first proposed by the Special Joint Committee of the Senate and of the House of Commons on Canada's International Relations in their report *Independence and Internationalism* (Ottawa, June 1986), 137-40; their recommendation that Canada pursue a policy of constructive internationalism was endorsed by Joe Clark: see Secretary of State for External Affairs, *Canada's International Relations: Response of the Government of Canada to the Report of the Special Joint Committee of the Senate and the House of Commons* (Ottawa, December 1986), 89.

85 Canada, Secretary of State for External Affairs, *Foreign Policy for Canadians* (Ottawa: Information Canada, 1970), main booklet, 8.

86 Garth Stevenson, "Foreign policy," in Conrad Winn and John McMenemy, eds., *Political Parties in Canada* (Toronto: McGraw-Hill Ryerson, 1976), 264.

87 See below, ch. 9.

88 Harald von Riekhoff, "The impact of Prime Minister Trudeau on foreign policy," *International Journal* 33 (Spring 1978), 267-86.

89 *The Globe and Mail*, 15 August 1983, 8.

90 The case of Japan provides an interesting example of where the friendships and enmities of international politics clashed with more visceral sentiments. In the first two decades of this century Japan was allied to Britain, and therefore to Canada, and was thus supposed to be a "friend." However, to the acute embarrassment of both the government in Ottawa and the imperial government in London, many Canadians refused to cooperate. In particular, British Columbians and their provincial government persistently abused and discriminated against Japanese-Canadians on the west coast. The efforts of the federal government to disallow, or have the courts invalidate, numerous provincial laws did little to mitigate the unrestrained and pervasive racism in the province. A.R.M. Lower, *Canada and the Far East—1940* (New York: Institute of Pacific Relations, 1941), ch. 6.

91 For example, after the outbreak of the war in 1914, the provincial government and the mayor of Toronto insisted that three professors of German be fired from the University of Toronto; likewise, it was deemed unseemly to have an Ontario town named Berlin, so a more suitable British name, that of Lord Kitchener, was substituted in its place.

92 Most students of nationalism note that the existence of others against whom a common antipathy can be directed is an essential component of the nationalist ideology. Thus, while it is popular for nationalists to claim that they are pro-Canadian, not anti-American, the distinction is analytically, if not politically, specious: being "pro-Canadian" is, *ipso facto*, anti-American. Boyd C. Shafer, *Nationalism: Its Nature and Interpreters* (Washington: American Historical Association, 1976); also Kim Richard Nossal, "Economic nationalism and continental integration: assumptions, arguments and advocacies," in Royal Commission on the Economic Union and Development Prospects for Canada, *Collected Research Studies*, vol. 29: *The Politics of Canada's Economic Relationship with the United States*, Denis Stairs and Gilbert R. Winham, eds. (Toronto: University of Toronto Press, 1985), 58-62.

93 Quoted in Eayrs, *In Defence of Canada*, vol. 4, 38.

94 For example, it might be argued that one of the reasons why officials worked so hard and so diligently after the Second World War to shape public opinion was to prevent what C.P. Stacey called the "tough weed" of isolationism from taking root again. Stacey, "From Meighen to King: the reversal of Canadian external policies, 1921-1923," *Transactions of the Royal Society of Canada*, series IV, vol. 7, 1969, 246.

PART THREE

THE GOVERNMENTAL SETTING

CHAPTER SIX

The Political Executive

INTRODUCTION

The focus thus far has been on the two environments—the external and the domestic—in which Canadian foreign policy decisions are made. Beginning with this chapter, we examine the governmental setting of foreign policy decision-making. Just as a country's foreign policy will be affected by both international and domestic politics, so too will it be affected by the form of government and how authority and power are distributed within the state apparatus. A country's foreign policy will be affected if the state apparatus is highly institutionalized and bureaucratized, for the higher the degree of institutionalization, the less latitude political leaders have for dominating the process of decision. External relations will also be affected if the legislature is constitutionally separate from the executive, wielding autonomous political authority in the making of foreign policy. By contrast, if the constitutional authority for foreign affairs is delegated to the executive, the power of the decision-makers is considerably enhanced. Finally, whether a country has a unitary or a federal system of government will have an impact on foreign policy. The explicit division of sovereign authority in a federal system considerably constrains the federal government's power. And, as we will see, Canada presents a unique case in the international system. The purpose of the next four chapters is to examine the interplay of politics within the state apparatus—to look at the distribution of authority and the exercise of power among the political executive, the bureaucracy, the legislature, and the provincial and federal governments.

✕ THE SOVEREIGN AND THE LOCUS OF AUTHORITY

We begin by looking at the decision-makers themselves—those men and women who have the political authority to make the decisions that shape Canada's behaviour in the international system. The answer to the question "Who makes foreign policy for Canada?" is at once simple and complex: the conduct of foreign affairs is the responsibility of the Crown. But one cannot clearly understand the locus of authority for foreign policy decisions without referring to both the nature of the contemporary international system on the one hand and the evolution of Canadian political institutions on the other.

The Crown's responsibility for conducting this state's external relations is a consequence of the doctrine of sovereignty, which is an essential organizing feature of the contemporary international system. Formalized by the Peace of Westphalia of October 1648, the idea—and the practice—of sovereignty implies that there is one supreme political authority for each polity in the international system. In the dynastic era when the doctrine emerged, that supreme authority was vested in one individual—the sovereign.[1] In Britain, therefore, it was the Crown who conducted relations with other sovereigns, sending ambassadors, negotiating treaties, and waging war.[2] While the once-absolute power of the British sovereign continued to be eroded by the evolution of representative government in the 150 years after Westphalia, the prerogative powers of the Crown in foreign affairs remained largely unchanged and unaffected by the growing power of Parliament.

Canada inherited this formal structure of foreign policy decision-making from the United Kingdom over the six decades of slow evolution to independent statehood. Canada's head of state—Queen Elizabeth II—is vested with the constitutional authority to make all those decisions that shape the country's role in world politics. As in Britain, the powers to negotiate and ratify treaties with other sovereign powers, to conduct diplomatic relations, and to wage war are all part of the royal prerogative— those powers exercised by the sovereign that have not been limited by statute, disuse or contractual agreement.[3]

Needless to say, the formalities of the Crown's authority in Canadian politics must be interpreted in the context of what MacGregor Dawson has termed that "preposterous and illogical" institution—cabinet government.[4] Formal authority may rest with the Crown; but as Colin Campbell so aptly reminds us, "This tidy legal-formal picture bears no resemblance to reality."[5] The actual decision-making power (or "conventional authority") in foreign policy is of course no longer exercised by the British sovereign,[6] or by the Crown's representative in Canada,[7] but by the Crown's advisers in cabinet. Although their decisions are taken in the name of the Crown, ministers in cabinet thus have the ultimate authority for the decisions which define both objectives in the international system and the means to achieve them.

Locating the formal authority for the conduct of foreign policy, wrapped though it may be in the symbolic anachronisms of a long-moribund absolutism, explains why foreign policy decision-making in Canada is properly the responsibility of the political executive alone. It explains why the other institutions of governance, notably the legislature and the judiciary, have a limited legitimate role in the shaping of external policy. It also explains why the focus of a study of foreign policy must inescapably be on the cabinet, and in particular on that central core of ministers most heavily involved in foreign policy decision-making. Depending on the issue, that circle may include the minister of national defence, the minister of finance, the minister of international trade, or the minister of state for external relations. But on virtually all important issues, the prime minister and the secretary of state for external affairs will be at the centre.

THE PRIME MINISTER

The enduring traditions of the Westminster model have it that the prime minister is, as a member of a collegial collective, only *primus inter pares.* In fact the prime minister occupies a central and commanding position in Canadian politics. To be sure, a prime minister's freedom of action may be constrained by numerous factors. Statute and constitutional provisions may pose limits; convention, such as the federal principle in cabinet-making, may also restrict. But within these parameters, a prime minister's prerogative is sweeping. As a result, each prime minister has demonstrated a clear pre-eminence in policy-making, and has inevitably left a personal mark on national policy and politics.

Such pre-eminence springs in the first instance from the multiplicity of political functions a prime minister acquires when called on by the governor general to form a government. The prime minister is the head of the government, its chief spokesman and defender, in and outside Parliament; chairman of a cabinet of his own creation; and head of the parliamentary caucus and the extra-parliamentary party. On him the focus of the polity is inexorably fixed; on him the fate of his government will frequently hang. The centrality of the office itself creates the tendency for political pre-eminence. Second, the pre-eminence of the first minister has been given added impetus because of the pattern of prime ministerial tenure in Canada. All but a few of the country's first eighteen prime ministers served for periods of either forgettable brevity or cloying longevity. While three prime ministers—Sir Charles Tupper, Joe Clark, and John Turner[8]—were dispatched after less than a year in office, four men held the portfolio for 72 of the first 117 years after Confederation. Sir John A. Macdonald, Sir Wilfrid Laurier, W.L. Mackenzie King, and Pierre Elliott Trudeau were each sustained in office for more than a decade and a half. Such longevity had an inexorable impact on prime ministerial power. While these men were, as Robert Craig Brown reminds us, very much creatures of their parties,[9] they nonetheless grew to dominate cabinet, caucus, party, and, not incidentally, country.

Pre-eminence in Practice

The prime minister has been no less prone to exert similar pre-eminence in the making of external policy. It is not coincidental that the distinct eras in Canada's foreign relations identified by political scientists and historians tend to be coterminous with the tenure of prime ministers.[10] Each prime minister has left a particular mark on the country's external policy, as the following brief sketches of prime ministerial involvement in foreign policy suggest.

Borden and King.   By the time Robert Borden was elected prime minister in 1911, he had already given some indication that the dominions should have a voice in the making of policy for the Empire. "[S]hall it be that we, contributing to defence of the whole empire, shall have absolutely ... no voice whatever in the councils of the empire touching the issues of peace or war throughout the empire?" he had asked the House of Commons, none too eloquently, in November 1910. "I do not think that such would be a tolerable situation. I do not believe the people of Canada would for some moment submit to such a condition."[11]

But it was not until Britain, and therefore Canada, was at war four years later that Sir Robert (as he had become in June 1914) found cause to act on such sentiments. A succession of crises, beginning with the conflict over orders for military materiel placed by the British in the United States instead of Canada, prompted Borden to take a progressively harder line with Britain. When, for example, he went to London to secure information about the war effort, he complained that he was led "from pillar to post" by the bureaucracy. He went to Bonar Law, the colonial secretary, and threatened that unless he was given the information "which is due to me as Prime Minister of Canada, I shall not advise my countrymen to put further effort into the winning of the War."[12] David Lloyd George, the minister of munitions, was hastily called, and managed to mollify Borden.

However, the British government continued to determine war policy unilaterally, periodically calling on the dominions for more men to fill the trenches of the Western Front. For his part, Borden continued to press for a more active role in the determination of policy, only to be told by Bonar Law in late 1915 that there seemed to be no war in which "this could practically be done." The prime minister's reaction was indicative of his mood, and reminiscent of his speech to the Commons in 1910:

> It can hardly be expected that we shall put 400,000 or 500,000 men in the field and willingly accept the position of having no more voice and receiving no more consideration than if we were toy automata. Any person cherishing such an expectation harbours an unfortunate and even dangerous delusion. Is this war being waged by the United Kingdom alone or is it a war waged by the whole Empire?[13]

By 1918, Borden had been propelled by the exigencies of war into pressing for a more independent voice and adopting a more independent policy. As he confided to his diary in December 1918, "I am beginning to feel that in the end and perhaps sooner than later, Canada must assume full sovereignty."[14] Thus, as we saw in chapter 3, Borden openly crossed the British government on the issue of the western intervention in Siberia. He was to press for separate representation at the peace conference and for separate membership in the League of Nations.

William Lyon Mackenzie King assumed office in December 1921. With the exception of two interruptions—in 1926 and from 1930 to 1935—he was prime minister until November 1948. King led the Liberal party into seven electoral contests and won six of them. One of the keys to understanding the extraordinary feat of King's 7,828 days as prime minister is to recognize his essential pragmatism in politics. He always took great pains to ensure that Canada's many cleavages did not ripen into schisms that would undo his party's hold on power.

In foreign policy, this required the active pursuit of a policy of caution in all matters. First, it meant putting an end to the idea of a common foreign policy for the Empire and achieving Borden's "full sovereignty" for Canada. A common foreign policy for the Empire was tested severely during the Chanak crisis of September 1922. On 15 September, the Imperial government asked the dominions to send a military contingent to secure the Gallipoli peninsula from the "ruthless hands" of Turkish nationalists. King's response was brief. He cabled London that "public opinion in Canada would demand authorization on the part of Parliament as a necessary preliminary to the despatch of a contingent." That would be his position, even in the face of further British pleas for a statement of support from Ottawa.[15] The fate of a common policy for the Empire would be sealed at the Imperial Conference of October and November 1923. At these meetings, King claimed that each dominion had to be responsible for its own external relations. This position found favour with the British for if the Foreign Office in London could not administer a common foreign policy for the Empire, then it preferred "a system under which Britain would pursue her own foreign policy, and the Dominions would pursue theirs..."[16]

The second facet of this policy of caution involved limiting obligations to the League of Nations, particularly in the late 1930s, when King embraced the same policies of appeasement of Germany as Britain and France.[17] King's argument was consistent throughout the interwar period: before Canada could agree to any League action, the matter would have to be put to Parliament.[18] The "Parliament will decide" formula was ingenious politically. It was, of course, completely specious in formal constitutional terms for it was the executive, not Parliament, which had the authority to make such decisions. But it allowed King to avoid having to face a possible repetition of the divisions engendered by the First World War. The lessons of conscription, and the fate of the Conservatives, were always with King. Borden had been warned by his two ministers from Quebec that conscription would "kill them politically and the party for 25 years."[19] (As it turned out, the Conservatives were consigned to Quebec's political wilderness for much longer than merely one generation.) For King, the lesson was clear: avoid such a fate by avoiding the wars that would give rise to the need for conscription.[20]

C.P. Stacey, one of the foremost historians of Canada's foreign policy during the interwar period, has stressed the "overmastering importance" of the prime minister. Canadian policies in the 1920s and 1930s were, he argued, "essentially the personal policies of the man who held that office, and nowhere was this more clearly the case than in the field of external affairs."[21] One small, but telling, indication of the personalized nature of policy-making during this period was the way in which decisions were normally made. It was not unusual for the prime minister to receive a memorandum from his civil servants outlining a foreign policy problem, noting the advantages and disadvantages of alternative courses of action, and recommending a solution. King would then simply scribble his agreement (or lack of it) in the margin.[22] Stacey's assessment is supported by those who witnessed this pre-eminence exercised. Lester Pearson, who was to sit in the prime minister's chair himself, wrote to a colleague after attending meetings of the War Committee of cabinet: "it's enlightening to notice Mr King's absolute ascendency [sic] over & complete domination of his colleagues."[23]

Trudeau and Mulroney. Pierre Trudeau and Brian Mulroney provide a contemporary example of prime ministerial pre-eminence in foreign policy. Both of them brought to office a very definite set of ideas about foreign policy, and both sought to bring about a marked shift in the country's foreign policy.[24]

When Trudeau assumed the leadership of the Liberal party in April 1968, he brought with him a desire to recast Canada's role in world affairs.

A little over a month later, his government announced that a "severe reassessment" of foreign policy would take place. Trudeau's criticisms of existing policy were wide-ranging and fundamental, and fixed firmly on the policies pursued by his predecessor, Lester Pearson. First, he argued, Canadian foreign policy had not kept abreast of changes in the external environment. Policies that were designed for the tense years of tight bipolarity—the commitments to the North Atlantic Treaty Organization (NATO) and the North American Air Defence (NORAD) agreement—were no longer appropriate in an era of relaxed tensions and growing multipolarity. Foreign policy, the prime minister asserted, was being overly determined by defence policy. Second, it was argued that the stress placed on the search for peace and order in the international system—typified by attachment to the United Nations and UN-sponsored peacekeeping missions—meant that Canadian interests were being neglected by decision-makers overly concerned about the country's role in the world. In particular, the prime minister objected to the kind of middlepowermanship practiced in the 1950s and 1960s, dismissing it as "helpful fixing." In short, Trudeau held that Canadian foreign policy no longer served the national interest. He was also dissatisfied with the way in which policy was made: it tended to be dominated by the external affairs minister and his department, with little involvement by others who had a legitimate interest in the policy process.

Armed with such objections, Trudeau set about trying to remold both the process and substance of foreign policy. Foreign policy-making was subject to the same processes of rational decision-making introduced into the entire policy process.[25] More importantly, however, the substance of policy was to change, with the publication in 1970 of his white paper on foreign policy. It was, as we will see in chapter 7, very much a reflection of the prime minister's own views. Its French title, *Politique étrangère au service des Canadiens*, conveyed the essence of the change more clearly than the ambiguous *Foreign Policy for Canadians*:[26] the white paper called for a narrower definition of interest in foreign policy. Termed the "Trudeau Doctrine" by Peyton Lyon, it sought to focus Canada's foreign policy on economic growth, combatting pollution, defending sovereignty, and seeking to expand the range of international relationships to offset the dominance of the United States.[27]

Having recorded his ideas about foreign policy for posterity, Trudeau spent the rest of his long tenure as prime minister ignoring, contradicting, or reversing the main tenets of the white paper. By 1984, he would have discovered, by turns, the utility of Canada's military alignments, the usefulness of peacekeeping, and the helpfulness of helpful fixing. His government's foreign policy was to continue to manifest many of the elements of Pearsonian internationalism, and the prime minister himself was to play an active role in summit diplomacy, from his mediatory efforts at the Commonwealth meeting in Singapore in 1971 to his peace mission in the winter of 1983-84.

But for all of the changes in outlook that Trudeau had undergone between 1968 and 1984, his pre-eminence in the policy process remained undiminished. His numerous, if sporadic, personal initiatives in international politics were marked by a personal enthusiasm and commitment that allowed him to define the goals sought (even if not the outcomes desired).

Brian Mulroney came to power on 17 September 1984 determined, as Trudeau had been, to change Canada's foreign policy. His critique of foreign policy also fixed on his predecessor, in particular the state of Canadian-American relations under the Trudeau government. Between 1980 and 1984, relations between the two countries were less than harmonious. The Reagan administration's response to the National Energy Program; the heated dispute over acid rain; and divergence in views on global policy issues all contributed to the conflict between the two countries.

Mulroney was determined, as he put it after his selection as Progressive Conservative leader, to "refurbish" the relationship. To achieve this, the policy initially chosen was a closer alignment with the United States. As Leader of the Opposition, Mulroney evinced a simplistic pro-American, anti-Soviet posture that was a virtual mirror of Reagan's own view. For example, while Trudeau characterized the downing of KAL 007 as an accident, Mulroney called it an act of cold-blooded murder. Likewise, when the United States invaded Grenada in October, the Conservatives took exception to the Trudeau government's criticism of the invasion.[28] In his public speeches, Mulroney began to warm to the themes that would dominate the 1984 election campaign: Canada under the PCs would be a "better ally, a super ally" of the country's "four traditional allies" (Israel having been unsubtly added to the usual list of the United States, Britain, and France). A Conservative government, he promised, would stop being so critical of United States policy and would give Washington the benefit of the doubt. It would also spend more on defence. Finally, he promised to bring in a "new era in civility" on bilateral relations between Canada and the United States.

To be sure, much of Mulroney's rhetoric during this period must be put in the context of the electoral contest underway in 1984. Thus, the repeated references to Israel and his harsh anti-Sovietism were directed primarily at a domestic audience. For example, at a rally of Estonians in Toronto, Mulroney roundly denounced the USSR for keeping the world "half slave and half free." He reminded the rally that John Diefenbaker had also criticized the Soviet Union at the United Nations in the early 1960s, prompting Nikita Khrushchev to bang his shoe on his desk; he, Mulroney, would do no less for the cause of the Eastern Europeans.[29] In this, Mulroney was not only perpetuating a bit of Conservative mythology (for Diefenbaker was not even in New York for the shoe-banging), but also perpetuating the historical propensity of Progressive Conservative leaders to woo ethnic communities during election campaigns.[30]

As prime minister, Mulroney put his own stamp on the decision-making process.[31] But as importantly, he put a particular stamp on the substance of policy. He abandoned many of the ideas about foreign policy he had brought to the office. In practice, he was neither as pro-American or anti-Soviet as his rhetoric suggested. With the Soviet Union, he maintained a delicate balance, continuing to press the USSR on human rights concerns, but maintaining a progressively more cordial relationship with Moscow. Likewise, Mulroney proved to be somewhat less than a "super ally" of the United States. He frequently distanced his government from the Reagan administration on a variety of issues—from adherence to the Strategic Arms Limitation Treaty (SALT) to Washington's policies on Central America. Nor was Mulroney inclined to lend legitimacy to the Strategic Defense Initiative: when the Reagan administration invited its allies to participate in SDI, the Progressive Conservative government replied with a "polite no" in September 1985. And although the government embraced a long list of new weapons systems in its white paper on defence in 1987, in fact Mulroney did not increase defence spending in his first term.

Mulroney's impact on policy can best be seen in the evolution of Canadian policy towards South Africa. *Apartheid* had not been a focus of Mulroney's interest prior to the renewed outbreak of unrest in South Africa. But following Pretoria's declaration of a state of emergency in 1985, Mulroney largely abandoned the approach towards South Africa that had been pursued by the Trudeau government in the 1970s and early 1980s, embracing an increasingly sanctionist policy. In this, Canadian policy directly confronted the anti-sanctionist approach favoured not only by the Reagan administration but also by the British government of Margaret Thatcher.

By the end of the 33rd Parliament, Mulroney was demonstrating what every prime minister had before him: a desire and a capacity to dominate the process of foreign policy decision-making. Two factors afford a prime minister the ability to leave a particular mark on external policy, and propel him into the international arena.

The Power of Appointment

One of a new prime minister's first responsibilities is, in a very literal sense, to create a government. He must appoint the ministers of his cabinet. He must select a clerk of the Privy Council, the most senior civil servant and the bureaucratic head of the Privy Council Office (PCO). In consultation with the clerk, the prime minister must appoint deputy ministers for government departments; advisers in such key central agencies as the Prime Minister's Office (PMO) and the PCO;[32] members of a burgeoning number of federal agencies, boards, and commissions; and ambassadors to foreign capitals. The *duty* to appoint means that no prime minister can avoid those personnel decisions which so relentlessly shape an administration. By the same token, however, the *prerogative* to appoint gives the prime minister a potent means of imposing his policy preferences on those admitted to his government.

A prime minister's appointments are critical to the process of policy-making, domestic and foreign. In deciding who will occupy foreign policy-making positions, the prime minister determines the kind of advice on foreign affairs the government will receive; the quality of bureaucratic and ministerial talent that can be brought to bear to support successful Canadian statecraft; the nature of the interplay among the individuals in the senior reaches of the state upon whom the prime minister must ultimately depend; and the nature and quality of the representation of Canadian interests abroad. Instructive examples of how the prerogative to appoint may influence the foreign policy decision-making process span the history of the country's role in international politics.

In the early 1920s, Mackenzie King brought Professor O.D. Skelton, the dean of arts at Queen's University, to Ottawa as a member of the Department of External Affairs. In 1924, King appointed him as the undersecretary of state for external affairs, the bureaucratic head of the department. It was a position that Skelton was to retain until his premature death from a heart attack in 1941. This was one of a number of critical appointments to the civil service in the interwar years that was to reshape the nature of not only the bureaucracy but of the Canadian state itself.[33] Skelton's appointment helped influence the course of foreign policy during the interwar years, for he had isolationist and anglophobic tendencies that both balanced and complemented King's views.[34] More importantly, however, Skelton also had a significant long-term effect on the conduct of Canadian statecraft. He brought to Ottawa the view, uncommon at the time, that appointment to the civil service should be based not on an individual's loyalty to the political party in power but strictly on merit. Over his 16-year tenure, Skelton was able to realize his vision of an external affairs bureaucracy staffed by professionals. He established a foreign service examination, and filled the slowly expanding Department with a group of young professionals, in the process laying the foundation for the active role that Canada was to play in international politics after the Second World War.

Louis St. Laurent's appointment of Pearson as his foreign minister in 1948 similarly altered both the substance and process of foreign policy in the postwar era. Pearson was a senior bureaucrat in the Department of External Affairs at the time of his sudden elevation to the cabinet. As he wrote later, "It felt like being promoted from general manager to president in ... 'External Affairs Ltd.'"[35] Such a transfer from the bureaucratic to the political level meant that the minister and his departmental officials enjoyed an exceptionally close and easy relationship in the shaping of policy in the 1950s. Likewise, the minister's diplomatic skills, learned and honed during a long apprenticeship in the bureaucracy, enabled him—and thus the government—to pursue a brand of statecraft that has since become known as Canada's "golden age" in international affairs.

The case of Michael Pitfield's involvement in the reorganization of the Department of External Affairs in the early 1980s also demonstrates the power of appointment. Trudeau had been impressed with Pitfield's work in the PCO in the early 1970s and had selected him to be the clerk of the Privy Council in January 1975. He was dismissed by Joe Clark in 1979, and went to teach at Harvard University. But Trudeau quickly rescued him from exile in academe after the 1980 election to resume the duties of clerk for the new government. Pitfield's six-year tenure as Ottawa's most powerful civil servant coincided with a substantial restructuring of the machinery of government.[36] The culmination of this process—before Pitfield was called to his reward in the Senate—was the radical reorganization of External Affairs that merged the Department of Industry, Trade and Commerce and DEA into one "new" department. (The reorganization of the foreign affairs bureaucracy during the Trudeau period is discussed in detail in chapter 7). It is no coincidence that the changes in process and substance of foreign policy-making occurred under Pitfield, for the idea was his, and he was instrumental in securing political support for these changes. His organizational theories and his perspective on the nature of international politics in the late 1970s and early 1980s underwrote his views on the proper and appropriate administrative structure for the conduct of foreign relations. His personal relationship with Trudeau underwrote his ability to secure the approval of the political leadership in cabinet for his ideas. And, finally, his authority as clerk underwrote his ability to overcome the parochial vested interests of two historically distant but interrelated departments of government to shape a "new" Department of External Affairs.

After Brian Mulroney became prime minister in September 1984, he appointed a group of people to senior foreign policy-making positions who had a considerable impact on the tone and direction of Canadian external relations. Because of the views he had expressed in his year as leader of the opposition, many expected Mulroney to fill these positions with people from the right wing of his party, such as Sinclair Stevens, who had been the external affairs critic before the election, and who had hard-line views on foreign affairs. Instead, the prime minister passed over Stevens, who was given an economic portfolio. For foreign policy positions, Mulroney opted for a group whose positions on external affairs were firmly in the internationalist tradition. Clark, whom Mulroney had defeated for the leadership of the party a year earlier, was appointed the secretary of state for external affairs. Douglas Roche, a former Conservative member of Parliament, was appointed ambassador for disarmament. Roy McMurtry, a former minister in the provincial Ontario government, was appointed high commissioner in London. In a surprising move, Mulroney asked Stephen Lewis, the former leader of the New Democratic Party in Ontario, to become permanent representative to the United Nations. David Macdonald, a minister in the Clark government in 1979, was appointed to oversee relief efforts during the Ethiopian drought of 1984. Thomas Hockin, an academic who specialized in Canadian foreign policy, was appointed to co-chair a special parliamentary committee on international relations. Bernard Wood, director of the North-South Institute, was appointed as the prime minister's personal emissary to southern Africa. Even the Prime Minister's Office, traditionally the domain of "political" appointees, was eventually headed by Derek Burney, a career bureaucrat with long experience in diplomacy. The party's right wing had to content itself with the defence portfolio, which was given to Robert Coates. Even then, within two years, the hard-liners on foreign policy had resigned from cabinet.[37] With the foreign policy positions dominated by moderates, it is not surprising that in the years after 1984, foreign policy demonstrated a distinctly traditional aspect.

The Imperatives of Summitry

A prime minister's pre-eminence is reinforced by the prevalence of summit diplomacy in contemporary statecraft. While the management of a state's foreign policy can be left to the professionals in the foreign service, diplomats always remain agents for their principals—the state's leaders. On numerous occasions, however, those principals will for a variety of reasons seek to deal directly with each other, eliminating the intermediary role of diplomatic agents.

Diplomacy at the summit is hardly a new phenomenon in interstate relations. Throughout history, leaders of states have sought to negotiate directly with one another. This propensity is particularly pronounced at the end of general, or systemic, wars. The enduring general peace of nineteenth-century Europe was fashioned by the assemblage of reigning monarchs, princes, and plenipotentiaries who gathered in Vienna over the winter of 1814-1815. Statesmen, not just their diplomats, negotiated the short-lived peace at Versailles after the First World War. And the meetings of Winston Churchill, F.D. Roosevelt, and Joseph Stalin at Potsdam and Yalta not only laid the foundations for the postwar international order, but also marked the first time that "summit" was used to describe such statecraft.[38] However, if "summit diplomacy" is but a new term to describe an old phenomenon in international politics, there can be little doubt that in the years since 1945 the use of summitry in interstate relations has intensified considerably.

Canada has not been immune to this broader trend. The prime minister is involved in a number of summit meetings. Some meet only once: the 1981 meeting of the heads of selected states from north and south at Cancun, chaired by the Canadian prime minister and the Mexican president, for example. Others, like the meetings of the NATO heads of government, are irregular. Others still have become highly regularized: the economic summit of the leaders of seven western industrial states is held annually; the Commonwealth Heads of Government Meetings is held biennially. Francophone summits, a new development given particular impetus by Mulroney, were held in 1986 and 1987. In addition to these multilateral forums, a prime minister also conducts wide-ranging bilateral summitry with foreign leaders, both in Canada and abroad. Of these summits, the most important are the meetings the prime minister holds with the president of the United States. Since 1985, at the initiative of Mulroney,[39] these have been regularized annual events.

The Commonwealth summit. These are held every second year in different Commonwealth capitals. The Meetings provide a forum for talks between Commonwealth leaders on a variety of often contentious political topics. The stress, however, is on privacy and informality: there are no speeches aimed at a visitor's gallery or the media and no recorded votes. Tradition dictates that what transpires in the talks not be revealed publicly. But the leaders and their officials invariably hold press conferences both during and after the meetings that convey a sense of the meeting. Officially, however, there is only the ubiquitous final communiqué, embodying decisions taken by consensus.

The Commonwealth summit is no longer the most important of the meetings to which the prime minister is invited but it is the oldest. The Meetings had their origins in the halcyon days of Empire, and have undergone a slow evolution in name and function that reflects the changing nature of the membership over the past century. Their beginnings were desultory and inauspicious: the first Colonial Conference was called in 1887 to discuss Imperial defence, telegraphs, and postal services. This conference was, however, hardly "diplomacy at the summit." The British luminary was the colonial secretary, not the prime minister; nor was this a meeting of equals, for only Britain could claim to be sovereign and only one of the other participants was at that time self-governing. And, for its part, that lone self-governing dominion was so uninterested in the proceedings that it was represented by Sir Alexander Campbell, the lieutenant-governor of Ontario, and Sanford Fleming, the surveyor of the Canadian Pacific railway.[40]

However, the idea of gathering together representatives of different parts of the Empire persisted, particularly among those stouter imperialists in Britain who sought to create institutional mechanisms for the conduct of a united foreign policy for the Empire. Thus the 1887 conference was followed by others in 1894, 1897, 1902, and 1907. In 1907, the designation was changed: it was henceforth to be an Imperial Conference, to reflect the achievement of self-governing status by Australia in 1901 and New Zealand in 1907. It was also agreed that the British prime minister would replace the colonial secretary as the chairman of the meetings.

It is ironic that the Imperial Conferences which followed these early efforts proved to be the vehicle for the eventual transformation of Empire. At the meetings held after the First World War, dominion prime ministers sought an opportunity to address both the constitutional and policy issues of their relations with Britain. Not only were they able to rebuff continued British pressures for coordination in matters of defence, but they used the conferences to press for an end to formal British authority over their foreign policies, and bring the idea of a common Imperial foreign and defence policy to an end. Indeed, it was at the 1926 meeting, as we have seen, that the prime ministers agreed to autonomy for the dominions in external policy, laying the foundation for the passage of the Statute of Westminster in 1931—and the subsequent emergence of the modern Commonwealth.[41]

The Imperial Conferences gave way in the 1940s to "Prime Ministers Conferences" as the Commonwealth continued to grow. By the time the prime ministers gathered in January 1951, two of the seven dominions which had attended the last grand Imperial Conference in 1937—Newfoundland and Eire—were no longer participating. The remaining members had been joined by the newly independent states of the Indian subcontinent, radically transforming the association of "white" dominions.[42] But the change was not only racial; it was also constitutional. The new Indian government, seeking to break with the British Raj symbolically as well as literally, wanted to become a republic. No longer would it be with the others "united by a common allegiance to the Crown," as the Statute of Westminster had put it. But New Delhi also wanted to retain its association with the Commonwealth. This desire was accommodated by the negotiation in 1948 and 1949 of the "London formula." Under this arrangement, the other members accepted Indian membership on the understanding that while there would be no formal tie to the British Crown, the sovereign in Britain would be recognized by India "as the symbol of the free association of [the Commonwealth's] independent member nations and as such the Head of the Commonwealth."[43]

The eventual acceptability of a republican, non-white member set the stage for the rapid growth of the Commonwealth during the waves of decolonization of the 1950s and 1960s. By 1987, when the Commonwealth met in Vancouver, that number had swelled to 48, encompassing nations from every continent and with a wide variety of political systems.[44] Indeed, it was the latter feature that prompted a change of name for the Commonwealth summits. By this time, not every leader was a prime minister. While India had maintained its initial commitment to a republican variant of the Westminster model,[45] surviving even Indira Gandhi's "emergency" in the mid-1970s, the vagaries of domestic politics in other members of the Commonwealth had begotten a number of distinctly unparliamentary forms of government. At the 1975 meetings, for example, the nomenclature of Commonwealth leaders reflected this diversity. Joining the prime ministers in Kingston, Jamaica were a dozen presidents, including two presidents-for-life and the head of a "one-party participatory democracy"; two chairmen of Supreme Military Councils; and a Deputy Chief Martial Law Administrator. In the event, a more appropriate, even if less elegant, name was chosen.

Attendance at the Commonwealth Heads of Government Meetings has always afforded the prime minister an opportunity for individual diplomacy, and each one from Borden to Mulroney has had occasion to use the informality of the meetings and the authority of his office to engage in international negotiation unencumbered by the constraints of cabinet, Parliament, or the bureaucracy. This tendency was more pronounced before 1946, when the prime minister was, by statute, also the secretary of state for external affairs. At the 1921 Imperial Conference, for example, Arthur Meighen strongly opposed the renewal of the Anglo-Japanese alliance, which was favoured by Britain and the Pacific dominions but opposed by the United States. Meighen's opposition, which was being voiced without the knowledge of his cabinet,[46] provoked a split in the Commonwealth and altered the Conference's position on the question of renewal.[47] It is true that Meighen was receiving his cues from Loring Christie, the legal adviser in the Department of External Affairs;[48] but it was Meighen, not Christie, who had to take up the cudgels against the other prime ministers ranged against him.

Meighen's case is not unusual. At Commonwealth conferences thereafter, prime ministers have been prone to make policy simply by their active participation in the meetings. King's mediatory diplomacy at the 1926 Imperial Conference helped formalize the independence of Canada and the other self-governing dominions—a not insignificant step—but this had not been planned in advance. At the 1932 Imperial Economic Conference in Ottawa, R.B. Bennett's rudeness towards the British ended up effectively determining Canada's policy on trade with Britain. When King annoyed his fellow prime ministers at the 1937 Imperial Conference by picking apart the final communiqué to excise anything that might smack of a commitment to collective security under the League of Nations, he was in essence making policy.[49]

Postwar prime ministers have been as prone to make policy at Commonwealth conferences. Indeed, it has been in the context of these meetings that prime ministerial initiatives have helped give rise to Canada's reputation as a mediator in international affairs. Canadian prime ministers have, by their participation in the summits, played a significant part in preventing the cleavages inherent in the association from developing into irreparable ruptures. This has been particularly true on the issue of white minority rule in southern Africa, a question that has bedevilled the Commonwealth since the 1950s. Canadian prime ministers, reflecting a broader interest in preserving the Commonwealth as a unique international institution, have consistently sought to keep the association from breaking apart over the institutionalized racism in Rhodesia and South Africa. John Diefenbaker played such a role in 1960 and 1961, proposing a compromise on the question of South African membership in the Commonwealth that helped mitigate the split along racial lines that was developing between the Afro-Asian members on the one hand and Britain, Australia, and New Zealand on the other.[50] Pearson's diplomacy at the Prime Ministers' Meetings in the mid-1960s aimed to find acceptable middle ground between Britain and the black African states on the question of Rhodesia following Ian Smith's Unilateral Declaration of Independence in 1965.[51] Although Trudeau came to the prime ministership openly skeptical of mediatory diplomacy, he found himself playing just such a role at the Commonwealth conference in Singapore in 1971 over the issue of British arms sales to South Africa.[52] At the Lusaka meetings in 1979, the agenda was dominated by the issue of the civil war in Rhodesia/Zimbabwe; although other leaders played the dominant roles, Joe Clark, who had only been prime minister for two months, nonetheless volunteered for a mediatory role.[53]

Brian Mulroney carried forward this tradition in the 1980s. Following the renewed unrest and violence in South Africa in the fall of 1984, the issue of *apartheid* once again came to dominate the Commonwealth agenda—at Nassau in 1985 and at Vancouver in 1987. By the late 1980s, however, the British prime minister, Margaret Thatcher, had no allies in her bid to keep the Commonwealth from endorsing strong economic sanctions against South Africa. With the support of other key states, Mulroney took the lead at both meetings to try to sway Thatcher on the question of sanctions, but without success. Indeed, at the Vancouver meetings, Mulroney's efforts sparked a heated dispute with the British prime minister and efforts by British officials to discredit the Canadian position.[54]

The Commonwealth Heads of Government Meetings also provide a forum for the pursuit of prime ministerial initiatives on other international issues. At the meetings Trudeau attended in the 1980s, he used the opportunity to press two different personal diplomatic initiatives he was undertaking. At Melbourne in 1981, he attempted to rally support for his North-South diplomacy.[55] Likewise, in the autumn of 1983, Trudeau launched his "peace initiative" involving a diplomatic effort to reduce tensions in east-west relations that had grown to dangerous levels following the Soviet downing of Korean Air Lines flight 007 in September. He used the Commonwealth meetings in New Delhi to try to secure wider support from like-minded states—notably Australia and India—for his peace initiative.[56]

The Commonwealth meetings do not always deal with issues that are central to Canada's foreign policy concerns. But governments in Ottawa have traditionally regarded this unusual association of nations as of considerable importance to the maintenance of a broader international order. However, precisely because of the range of its membership, it is a most fragile institution. Because Canada is, besides Britain, the oldest member of the Commonwealth, it is perhaps not surprising that the Canadian prime minister is regarded as a key figure in Commonwealth politics. Given this, and the importance attached to the maintenance of the Commonwealth, no postwar prime minister has been prone to ignore the opportunities for activism and leadership in this summit forum.

The economic summit. The second summit meeting to which the prime minister is regularly invited cannot claim such longevity as the Commonwealth meetings. Nor can Canada claim the seniority or the status it has in the Commonwealth. The first meeting of the industrialized states of the west was held at the Chateau de Rambouillet in France in November 1975. The purpose of this meeting was to prepare the western states for the Conference on International Economic Cooperation (the North/South Conference), which was due to be held in Paris that December. To this preparatory meeting were invited the heads of government of the major industrialized countries: the United States, Japan, the Federal Republic of Germany, Britain, France, and Italy.

Canada was not invited. The French government, which was issuing the invitations, was adamantly opposed to Ottawa's participation on two grounds. First, the French argued that since Canada was merely an economic appendage of the United States, separate representation was unnecessary. Second, Paris suggested that if a minor economic power like Canada were invited, Belgium and the Netherlands would then have a claim, making the summit too large. Ottawa pointed out that if Italy, then in serious economic difficulties, had been invited, Canada should have a right to attend. While the others were not unsympathetic, they proved unwilling to insist. Long and plaintive were the protests from the Canadian government at this exclusion. "We have the economic position in the world to justify our attendance," complained the secretary of state for external affairs to the House of Commons two weeks before the summit.[57] But it was to no avail: neither protests nor diplomatic efforts to wangle an invitation succeeded in moving Giscard d'Estaing.

Following the imbroglio over the Rambouillet summit, Ottawa renewed its efforts to secure an invitation to the next summit, which was to be hosted by the United States in Puerto Rico in 1976. This time, however, it was Gerald Ford who was issuing the invitations, and he extended one to Trudeau—over continued French objections. But Canada was not yet admitted to the economic summit club as a matter of right. Ford noted that Ottawa was being invited because the meeting was being held in the western hemisphere and because of the ties between Canada and the United States. It was Trudeau's performance at the Puerto Rico summit that, according to one observer, impressed the other heads of government sufficiently that in 1977, when the economic summit was held in London, Canada was invited unadorned by attempts to rationalize its attendance.[58] Since then, Canada has been regarded as a permanent member of the "Summit Seven," and has hosted two summits, the first in Montebello, PQ in 1981, the second in Toronto in 1988.

Since the meeting at Puerto Rico, the economic summit has become increasingly institutionalized. While the summit has not yet been marked by the quintessential stamp of institutionalization—the establishment of a permanent secretariat—most aspects of the meetings have become highly regularized. Early on, for example, it was agreed that the locale of each year's meeting would be rotated among the members and that the host would chair the meetings.[59] The seven leaders each have a personal representative whose responsibility it is to plan the summit. These representatives—or "sherpas," as they are colloquially known (after the indispensable guides to another kind of summit)—engage in extensive planning and negotiation prior to each meeting, thrashing out what issues will—and will not—be on the agenda, and even working on a draft of the final communiqué months before the actual meeting.[60]

While the issues of the global economy, energy and North-South relations tend to dominate the agenda, discussion is not limited to these problems. At each meeting, the leaders have been unwilling to forego the opportunity of exchanging views on political and security questions. At the 1978 Bonn meetings, the issue of aircraft hijacking found its way onto the agenda, with the Seven agreeing that they would suspend air service to countries refusing to extradite or prosecute hijackers. At Venice in 1980, the Soviet invasion of Afghanistan prompted a discussion that revealed the extent of the split in the west over policy towards the Soviet Union. At Versailles in 1982, conflict over western economic sanctions against the USSR was again apparent. At Venice in June 1987, the issue of sanctions arose yet again, though this time the focus was South Africa.

For the leader of a smaller state like Canada, participation in this summit offers both opportunities and imperatives. It affords a prime minister an entrée to high-level discussions on a wide range of global economic and political questions. And it provides an arena in which to attempt to affect the course of great power diplomacy. Both Trudeau and Mulroney made full use of this opportunity, but with mixed results. The unanimous agreement on hijacking grew out of an idea by Trudeau, worked through with support from the Japanese prime minister. At the Montebello summit which he hosted in 1981, Trudeau tried unsuccessfully to make North-South issues the focal point of the meetings to swing support for new initiatives in that area. In 1987, at the Venice summit, Mulroney tried to ensure that the issue of *apartheid* would be included in the final communiqué—but without success.

However, summit participation imposes obligations that constrain freedom of action. While decisions agreed to by the Seven do not have the binding force of law, they have exerted considerable influence on the domestic policies of the Seven.[61] As one senior External Affairs official has noted, the "communiqués provided 'mutual reinforcement' which helped leaders resist domestic pressures in their own countries."[62]

The francophone summit. The meetings of the heads of government of the world's francophone states are a relatively recent development: the first one was not held until 1986.[63] On 17-19 February, in Paris, 41 states with a French component in their present or past, including Vietnam and Egypt, gathered for the first meeting. It is not that no one had thought of the idea. As early as the late 1950s, the idea of a summit of French-speaking countries had been bruited about. But the government in Paris, particularly under Charles de Gaulle and his Gaullist successors, had little interest in creating a French-speaking equivalent of the Commonwealth Heads of Government Meetings. Paris was content with maintaining its relations with its former colonies bilaterally or regionally, so that "French power and influence could be employed with maximum effect."[64] A second problem was posed by Canada's federal system, an issue we will examine in detail in chapter 9. As Monique Landry, the minister for external relations, said in February 1987:

> Let us be quite frank: one of the obstacles to such a meeting of Francophone countries had always been the difficulty of having the federal government and Quebec sit down at the same table in a spirit of respect for each other's legitimate powers.[65]

Not until 1983 did French President François Mitterand finally agree to a suggestion by Trudeau for a francophone summit, but the proposal ultimately foundered because the government of Quebec under René Lévesque mounted an intensive lobbying campaign in Paris for full participation. Mitterand, fearing an embarrassment to Canada-French relations over internal divisions within Canada, decided to withdraw the idea.

When Mulroney became prime minister in September 1984, he gave renewed impetus to the idea. Finding the French government receptive to the idea of a summit, he negotiated an agreement with Paris on Quebec's participation, and, just days after Lévesque resigned as leader of the Parti québécois in October 1985, an agreement with Quebec City outlining the conditions under which the provincial government could participate in a francophone summit. The first summit in Paris saw, for the first time, two provincial premiers—Robert Bourassa, whose Liberals had replaced the PQ in the Quebec elections of November 1985, and Richard Hatfield of New Brunswick—attend an international summit as virtually equal participants with the federal head of government.

The Paris summit was not, however, an unqualified success. The federal-provincial agreement specified that provincial premiers could only make interventions at the summit on some issues, and even then only with prior permission from the prime minister. Bourassa, with Mulroney's prior agreement, had made an intervention on agriculture. However, at a news conference afterwards, presumably in an effort to boost his popularity with separatists, Bourassa loudly proclaimed that he had not sought the prime minister's permission. His boast, according to Kirton, "led some of the sovereign states at the conference to wonder if this Canadian province was a sufficiently responsible international actor to be entrusted with the delicate task of hosting the next francophone summit."[66] However, Mulroney's intervention and Mitterand's support ensured that the second summit, held in September 1986, was hosted by the Quebec government.

The presidential summit. One of the enduring responsibilities of the prime minister has been to conduct diplomacy with the president of the United States. Since Mackenzie King's brief meeting with Calvin Coolidge in Washington in November 1927, prime ministers have sought to establish a personal relationship with their American counterpart. Indeed, it is notable that since 1930, all prime ministers, with but two exceptions,[67] have held a summit meeting with the president within six months of taking office. Similarly, all American presidents from Roosevelt to Reagan have met with the prime minister within four months of their inauguration.[68] Canadian-American summits have been held in a variety of contexts and settings: at multilateral summits, or at purely ceremonial affairs, including state funerals, though substantive business is not usually conducted on such occasions.[69] At times the emphasis is on informality: one summit between St. Laurent and Dwight Eisenhower was held over a game of golf. The prime minister later suggested, tongue-in-cheek, that

> a game of golf was about the best way to have an international conference because you are getting off the go-cart quite frequently for only a couple of minutes but for time enough to reflect on what has been said ... and to reflect on what is going to be said when you get back on....[70]

Until 1985, there was no planned predictability to these summits, however. They simply occurred. Beginning with the "Shamrock" summit in Quebec City on 18 March,[71] the presidential summit became an annual affair, held in March or April.

These summits are held for a number of reasons. First, prime ministers and presidents have traditionally welcomed "the opportunity [summits] offered for better acquaintanceship," as Diefenbaker put it after his first meeting with John F. Kennedy.[72] This initial summit allows the leaders to get a measure of one another and to establish a personal relationship with their opposite number. Second, summit meetings may be ceremonial in purpose. The signing of an international agreement, the opening of a park, or the dedication of a bridge all provide an opportunity to engage in the rhetoric of neighbourhood. Most Canadians and some Americans are only too familiar with the repertoire of transborder clichés. After some 85 summit meetings this century, speech-writers are hard-pressed to come up with fresh ways of saying the same thing about the friendship between the two countries. But such rhetoric, while cloying, is a necessary part of Canadian-American relations. It provides an opportunity for public assurances by those at the summit that the world's most complex international relationship continues to function smoothly. Likewise, what John Holmes has called "the blandishments of hands-across-the-border oratory"[73] also provides assurances to Canadians that the United States remains disinclined to treat its northern neighbour as great powers have traditionally dealt with small states on their borders.

Third, meetings of the president and prime minister provide a forum for negotiation to clear problems in the relationship that prove resistant to resolution at lower levels. For example, when Canada experienced a mounting balance-of-payments problem with the United States in the early years of the Second World War, Mackenzie King took up the matter with F.D. Roosevelt. They met at the president's Hyde Park estate, and after a brief chat, issued the Hyde Park Declaration. Under this agreement, the United States agreed to purchase $200 to $300 million in defence equipment from Canada to relieve the deficit.[74] None too modestly, King afterwards recorded to his diary the reaction of C.D. Howe, his minister of munitions and supply:

> Howe was overjoyed with what had taken place... Said something about [my] being the greatest negotiator the country had... Could hardly believe that so much could have been accomplished in so short a time. Said it had straightened out the most difficult of problems they had had for months.[75]

Likewise, Trudeau also used this technique successfully. After the August 1971 "shocks," he visited Richard Nixon in Washington and in just over two hours the two leaders successfully negotiated a mutually satisfactory agreement on the import surcharge.[76] He was to use it again in 1977 over the Garrison Diversion Unit,[77] which had festered on the agenda of environmental issues during the Nixon and Ford administrations. Trudeau was urged to discuss the matter with Jimmy Carter directly. It was after their February 1977 summit that Carter added the GDU to his "hit list" of water projects, settling the issue (temporarily, as it turned out: Congress was to prove most resistant to the president's plans).

However, as Swanson notes, the sword has another edge. If negotiations are carried to the summit, and an impasse is reached, "there is no higher political authority to invoke...."[78] This situation has arisen a number of times. For example, Trudeau's summit with Reagan in September 1981 was devoted to the National Energy Program, but a deadlock was quickly reached, with both leaders merely restating their positions.[79] Likewise, while Mulroney, as we saw in chapter 3, was able to move Reagan somewhat on the issue of acid rain at the 1985 summit, the two leaders were unable to reach any further agreement at their next summit meetings.

Much has been written about the importance of good personal relations between the president and the prime minister on the conduct of the broader relationship. For example, Lawrence Martin has argued that "They set the guiding tone, the leading temperament. If there is genuine warmth between them, there is usually the same between the countries."[80] On closer inspection, however, what we find is that "good chemistry" between the leaders (as it was widely called after the Reagan-Mulroney summits) has no positive effect on the relationship but that "bad chemistry" can have a negative impact.

Thus, for all of the good chemistry between leaders like Trudeau and Carter, or Mulroney and Reagan, bilateral issues between the two countries continued to irritate the relationship. No amount of good chemistry has caused the problem of acid rain to dissipate. Warm feelings between Mulroney and Reagan did not stop the president from invoking duties on various Canadian products or stop the prime minister from imposing a duty on American feed corn imports in November 1986. In short, while presidents and prime ministers may enjoy a good personal relationship, this has little impact on their roles as leaders of their respective countries, and the political imperatives that come with their respective offices. A good personal relationship merely makes the clash of interests a little less rancorous.

However, bad chemistry can have a noticeably negative impact on the relationship as a whole. In particular, bad feelings between the leaders will have a trickle-down effect on relations between Canadian and American officials at lower levels and may also have a negative impact on policy. Three prime ministers were to experience the effects of a poor personal relationship with an American president. The dislike that Kennedy and Diefenbaker had taken to one another[81] was mirrored at the official level, as Charles Ritchie, the ambassador in Washington, quickly discovered.[82] Moreover, Diefenbaker's penchant for distinctly anti-American and undiplomatic behaviour,[83] and the Kennedy administration's willingness to be equally undiplomatic,[84] brought the Canadian-American relationship to a crisis point. Pearson, who had had a good personal relationship with Kennedy, and who had gotten along well with Johnson after November 1963, managed to dissipate all good will when he gave a speech at Temple University in Philadelphia on 2 April 1965, criticizing the American bombing of North Vietnam.[85] Johnson lost his temper with Pearson the following day at Camp David, berating him loudly and loutishly for his speech.[86] From then until 1968, when both leaders retired, there would no longer be a personal relationship between them. When in January 1973 Parliament approved a resolution "deploring" the United States bombing of Hanoi and Haiphong, Nixon was extremely angry at Trudeau. Not understanding the imperatives of minority government,[87] Nixon interpreted the resolution as an unfriendly and hostile gesture. The anger of the White House was reflected in other quarters in Washington, infecting other items on the bilateral agenda well into 1973.[88]

In sum, we can note those periods in Canadian-American relations when a good personal relationship between the leaders coincides with a period of relative harmony in relations between the two countries—such as King's close relationship with Roosevelt in the 1940s or Pearson's relationship with Kennedy in 1963. But we cannot assume that there is a causal relationship between good chemistry between the leaders and absence of conflict in the relationship.

Summitry: conclusions. Summitry—with the president, with other leaders of the Seven, with Commonwealth or NATO leaders—provides the prime minister with a unique opportunity for diplomacy that is, in its essence, private. No other member of the political executive enjoys such access to the summit: that prerogative belongs to the head of government alone. Indeed, even if a prime minister were disinclined to take advantage of the opportunities offered by summitry, and few are, he could not send a subordinate "without appearing to insult other national leaders...."[89] It is also private in the sense that at the summit the prime minister is very much alone. However large an entourage of cabinet colleagues, senior bureaucrats, ambassadors, personal advisers, and "handlers" a prime minister may bring with him, however well he has been briefed or coached by his officials, much of the outcome will be determined by his own performance and his personal relations with his opposite numbers.

The Limits of Pre-eminence: Conclusions

The prime minister, by virtue of his position, is able to play a significant role in the shaping of external policy. The authority of the office itself, the power of appointment, and the imperatives of summitry will all contribute to the dominance of the policy process. To be sure, a prime minister does not—indeed he could not—take a personal hand in those many daily decisions and actions that in their totality comprise Canada's international behaviour. His pre-eminence is manifested in the general policy direction the government as a whole takes.

It should be noted in conclusion, however, that pre-eminence does not imply mastery. While each prime minister has been able to exert dominance in the policy process, none has been able to do exactly as he wishes in foreign affairs. A Carlylesque view, which reduces politics to the histories of individual "great men,"[90] is inappropriate in most contexts. It is particularly inappropriate in a Canadian context, where the prime minister, as the head of a democratic responsible government of a small state in international politics, is bound and constrained by relations with colleagues in cabinet, by the bureaucracy, Parliament, and the provinces, by the polity, and by the often unforgiving nature of the international system itself. But prime ministers are not, to use Borden's phrase, toy automata, responding in mechanistic and deterministic fashion to the forces of international, domestic, and governmental politics. Their personal qualities and idiosyncrasies, their moods and emotions, cannot be dismissed as unimportant, for in diplomacy, where words are actions, such traits invariably bear on policy outcomes.[91] Rather, assessing the prime minister's impact on foreign policy involves a balance: recognizing the importance of individual factors without losing sight of the broader structural constraints under which any prime minister operates.

THE SECRETARY OF STATE FOR EXTERNAL AFFAIRS

The minister charged with the statutory authority for the conduct of Canada's foreign relations is the secretary of state for external affairs. That Canada's foreign minister carries such a stylized title rather than the more mundane "minister of external affairs" derives more from the origins of the portfolio than a desire to bestow grandiosity on the incumbent. As we will see in the next chapter, when a separate department for external relations was created in 1909, it was given to the secretary of state's department. Until 1912, the secretary of state was responsible for both domestic and external affairs. When in 1912 responsibility for external affairs was transferred to the prime minister, the designation followed.[92] Until 1946, the prime minister was also by law the external affairs minister. But the Second World War, bringing as it did a hugely expanded role for the state in both domestic and foreign policy, changed the personal approach to policy-making in the interwar years. By 1946, it had become clear to Mackenzie King that he could no longer handle what by then had become a major portfolio in addition to the press of other prime ministerial duties, and in September he passed the external affairs portfolio to Louis St. Laurent.

The relationship between a head of government and a foreign minister is fraught with the potential for tension, largely because of the considerable overlap of their roles. The head of government, not the foreign minister, is invited to meetings at the summit; the spot is fixed on the head of government as the personification of the state in international politics. There is thus always the possibility that a foreign minister will live in a prime minister's shadow. No other portfolio carries with it this inherent disadvantage. Moreover, such tension is heightened when a prime minister has become accustomed to exercising the prerogatives of both portfolios himself. This was certainly the case with King, who spent his last years as prime minister chafing at the policies that St. Laurent was pursuing. The result, according to Eayrs, was a "difficult and unsatisfactory relationship."[93]

But with King's passing, the relationship between prime minister and foreign minister was for many years conditioned by the pattern of recruitment within the Liberal party during this era. When St. Laurent became prime minister in 1948, he recruited Pearson into Parliament from his position as deputy minister in External Affairs; Pearson became SSEA in St. Laurent's government. In 1957, Pearson succeeded St. Laurent as leader of the party, though by this time the Liberals were in opposition. However, in 1963, Pearson became prime minister. Thus from 1948 to 1957, and from 1963 to 1968, the links between the prime minister and External Affairs were unusually close.[94]

Diefenbaker's Progressive Conservative government from 1957 to 1963 interrupted this pattern. First, Diefenbaker proved unwilling to give responsibility for external policy to his cabinet colleagues. "I have followed the tradition of the United Kingdom," he claimed, "that the Prime Minister must take a particular interest in that field of national activity on which [the] safety of the state so highly depends."[95] Of King's seven successors, only Diefenbaker chose to hold the external affairs post himself—for the first twelve weeks of his ministry, and for three months after his first secretary of state for external affairs, Sidney Smith, died of a heart attack in 1959. But even when Smith was given the external affairs portfolio, Diefenbaker could not resist seeking to dominate.[96] When Howard Green, an old friend of the prime minister, was appointed to succeed Smith, the relationship was more harmonious. Certainly Green was left to pursue his special interest in disarmament while the prime minister focussed on other aspects of policy.[97]

When Pierre Trudeau came to power, the close relationship between the prime minister and External Affairs ended. None of Trudeau's four foreign ministers—Mitchell Sharp (1968-74), Allan MacEachen (1974-76 and 1982-84), Don Jamieson (1976-79), and Mark MacGuigan (1980-82)—had a comparable relationship with the foreign affairs bureaucracy. Nor did Flora MacDonald, who was Joe Clark's SSEA in 1979-80, nor Jean Chrétien, who briefly was SSEA in 1984 in John Turner's ministry. (Clark, Mulroney's SSEA, had of course been prime minister himself, and thus was well-acquainted with foreign affairs.[98])

After 1968, the pattern of the relationships between prime minister and SSEA varied considerably. The sharpest difference was between Trudeau and MacGuigan: their perspectives on global issues diverged markedly. On such issues as the imposition of martial law in Poland in December 1981; the escalation in violence in El Salvador in 1981 and 1982; or the Vietnamese occupation of Kampuchea, MacGuigan tended to mirror the more hawkish and anti-Soviet views of Alexander Haig, Reagan's first secretary of state. These troubles were invariably attributed to Soviet expansionism and imperialism. Trudeau, by contrast, shared calmer Western European perspectives on Soviet intentions and was more prone to attribute unrest to indigenous causes. As a consequence, Canadian statements on these issues were frequently contradictory.

However, it is clear that a rudimentary division of labour emerged in each case, with the prime minister assuming a particular dossier close to his interests. Thus, at different times during his tenure, Trudeau pursued his personal interest in foreign policy management, nuclear suffocation, the North-South issue, and "peace" between the superpowers. In Mulroney's case, the issues of free trade with the United States and *apartheid* in South Africa were the prime minister's "own" issues: if Clark was involved—as indeed he was in the case of South Africa—it was more as a supporting player.

According to Thordarson,[99] the external affairs portfolio has lost much of its prestige since the days of St. Laurent and Pearson, when it was seen as a stepping-stone to the leadership of the party.[100] But both in government and in opposition, it retains sufficient prestige that it is seen as a useful political tool by party leaders. For example, Trudeau used it to reward MacEachen for his role as House Leader during the 1972-74 minority government. More commonly, however, it has been used to reward supporters at leadership conventions: as his first SSEA, Trudeau appointed Sharp, whose support in Trudeau's 1968 bid for the leadership was important; in 1979, Clark made Flora MacDonald his SSEA after she threw her support to him in the February 1976 convention; in 1983, Mulroney made Sinclair Stevens, a key supporter in the bid to oust Clark, the PC external affairs critic. But it has also been used as a means of mollifying opponents for the party leadership.[101] Pearson made Paul Martin, who had run against him in 1957, external affairs critic, and then minister; Turner made Chrétien his SSEA; and Mulroney gave the External Affairs portfolio to Clark in 1984.

But despite its prestige, the portfolio has also become very onerous. The SSEA is not only technically responsible for the conduct of the full range of foreign relations, including foreign trade, but is also responsible for both the Department of External Affairs and the Canadian International Development Agency (CIDA). In addition, the foreign minister must represent Canada in numerous sub-summit meetings. Attempts have been made to lighten the burden of the portfolio, bringing other ministers into the process.

WIDENING THE CIRCLE: OTHER MINISTERS

The External Affairs Triumvirate

After 1968, the growth in the scope and range of Canada's foreign affairs would place a considerable strain on the capacity of the secretary of state for external affairs to discharge these numerous responsibilities. However, the ability to respond to these pressures by simply appointing more ministers to deal with them was constrained by a countervailing pressure exerted by the convention of cabinet structure in Canada. In Britain, a distinction is made between the "ministry" (which includes all ministers of the Crown responsible for government departments) and the "cabinet"—the ultimate decision-making body—which does not include all those in the ministry. In Canada, by contrast, convention dictates that all ministers of the Crown sit in cabinet.

This convention has had numerous effects on the machinery of government, for it limits not so much the number of state agencies that can be created, but the number of political heads that can be allocated to them. If each department or agency were assigned a separate minister, and each minister were given a seat at the cabinet table, the cabinet, already bloated at 40 members, would swell to unmanageable proportions. This convention has therefore encouraged the growth of huge and sprawling departments (such as the Ministry of Transport, responsible for a wide range of policy issue areas) or "twinned" departments (Health and Welfare, Employment and Immigration, or Energy, Mines and Resources). It has also encouraged assigning ministers responsibility for a number of departments and agencies.

However, the pressures of three areas which received increased attention in Canada's external relations during this period—international francophone affairs, development assistance, and trade—were ineluctable. Thus, despite the constraints of convention, the structure of ministerial responsibility for foreign affairs would change considerably over the 1970s and 1980s as new ministers were brought into the process.

A minister of international francophone affairs?   One of the enduring tensions in Canadian politics has been the linguistic cleavage between anglophones and francophones. Law, convention, and policy have only been partly successful in bridging the gulf between the two communities, as the persistence of the language question into the late 1980s shows. Before 1968, one of the important conventions in Canadian politics was the emergence of "lieutenants" for prime ministers and party leaders—senior members of the party who could communicate (in both a figurative and literal sense) with the "other" linguistic community. The two francophone prime ministers prior to 1968—Laurier and St. Laurent—were both fluent in English, but both had lieutenants to smooth their relations with English Canada. In the case of anglophone prime ministers, their abilities to communicate (in a literal sense) with francophone Canadians varied. Most needed a francophone in a very basic way—to overcome their inability to speak and listen to several million Canadians. Trudeau and Mulroney, completely fluent and at ease in both official languages, have effectively brought prime ministerial unilingualism to an end.

In external affairs, the problem of language arrived late. Before 1960, external relations were predominantly anglophone, with Britain and the United States, and neither Laurier nor St. Laurent had problems communicating with their British, Commonwealth, or American counterparts. So too the Department of External Affairs was a predominantly anglophone bureaucracy, where the few francophones wrote their memos and dispatches—even to one another—in English.

The anglophone dominance was to change after 1960. Externally, the rapid collapse of the French empire had led to a sudden burgeoning of francophone states in the international system. Domestically, successive governments in Ottawa, catalyzed by the assertion of the Quiet Revolution in Quebec, sought to give greater expression to the linguistic and cultural duality of the polity by strengthening Canada's ties with this group of states, known as *la francophonie*.[102] This diversification *did* pose a linguistic and cultural problem. Between 1909 and 1988, only two francophones held the position of SSEA: St. Laurent between 1946 and 1948, and Chrétien between June and September 1984. The 16 external affairs ministers in the other 77 years were all anglophones, many, though not all, unable to speak French fluently.

Before 1976, the response to the increased need for a minister who was fluent in French was strictly ad hoc. When duties in French had to be performed, a francophone minister was called on. For example, in 1971, Gérard Pelletier, the secretary of state, headed the Canadian delegation to the meetings of l'Agence de Coopération culturelle et technique; he would be called on again for this role in 1973, though by this time he was minister of communications. In 1972, he travelled to Bordeaux to open a school of international management. Jean Marchand, a minister without portfolio, headed the delegation to the fourth meeting of l'Agence in 1975. When a highway being built with CIDA funds was ready to be opened in Niger in 1976, Jean-Pierre Goyer, the minister of supply and services, did the honours.

Prodded into greater activity by the victory of the Parti québécois in November 1976, the Trudeau government sought to institutionalize what had in effect become a francophone lieutenant for the secretary of state for external affairs. In May 1977, Goyer was given the role of "special adviser" to the SSEA in the area of "international francophone affairs."[103] (The arrangement was carried on during the Clark government in 1979, when Martial Asselin was given ministerial responsibility for development assistance, discussed in the next section.) This ministerial role would be further institutionalized in 1982, when Trudeau reorganized the machinery of government.

A minister of development assistance?   At the same time that language was becoming more problematic in foreign policy, the issue of ministerial responsibility for the Canadian International Development Agency also began to assert itself. In the late 1970s, it was argued that CIDA should be given departmental status, with its own minister. The SSEA's workload would not only be considerably reduced but more importantly, it was argued, development assistance policy would receive different treatment around the cabinet table if there were a minister wholly responsible for CIDA.

The idea was tried by Joe Clark in 1979: Senator Martial Asselin, who had served in Diefenbaker's cabinet in the early 1960s, was made the minister of state responsible for CIDA (and also performed francophone duties for Flora MacDonald). However, this appointment must be seen in the context of the operation of the "federal principle" of cabinet-making in Canada, the minimum requirement of which is that each province be represented in cabinet. Clark had just two members of the House of Commons to draw on from Quebec, and so sought to increase that province's representation in cabinet by drawing on members of the Senate (a technique also used by the Liberals, which frequently lacked MPs west of Manitoba). The experiment was as short-lived as the Clark government: CIDA was returned to the SSEA after the return of the Liberals in February 1980, and there it would stay until the advent of the Mulroney government.

A minister of international trade? We have already noted the historical importance of external trade to Canadian wealth. Yet there has been no government department exclusively devoted to international trade questions, nor a minister exclusively responsible for this aspect of policy. For most of Canada's history, responsibility for trade policy concerns were shared between the Departments of External Affairs, Finance, and Trade and Commerce. The promotion of external trade fell to the Trade Commissioner Service, which was housed in a "twinned" department—Trade and Commerce—that was responsible for both the promotion of external trade and domestic commerce (and after 1969, when the Industry portfolio was merged with Trade and Commerce, industrial development). By the late 1970s, IT&C was responsible for a wide array of policy areas, such as tourism, business development, international trade policy, export promotion, international marketing, and domestic industrial design.

While throughout the 1970s the government in Ottawa struggled with attempts to create an "industrial policy" for Canada, and at the same time sought—without success—to diversify the patterns of Canada's international economic intercourse, there was little consideration given to the creation of a Canadian version of the Japanese Ministry of International Trade and Industry (MITI)—a separate bureaucratic structure with its own minister and the capacity for centralized coordination of international economic policy. In part, this was because of the nature of Canadian federalism, with jurisdiction over economic issues shared between the provinces and the central government, and in part because of the political bureaucratic strength of the existing departments in Ottawa that loosely shared responsibility for international economic policy.

The triumvirate formalized. In January 1982, Trudeau reorganized the major economic departments of government. As we will see in the next chapter, the foreign policy bureaucracy was also included in this reorganization. But there were changes at the ministerial level as well. The "new" Department of External Affairs, which encompassed the "old" External Affairs and the trade side of the abolished Department of Industry, Trade and Commerce, was to be responsible for all Canada's foreign economic relations, as well as the "political" side of foreign policy. Rather than add further responsibilities to the secretary of state for external affairs, the prime minister announced the creation of two new ministerial portfolios. A minister of international trade was appointed to promote external trade and commerce and to deal with aspects of international trade policy. Another minister for external relations was to be appointed, in the words of the legislation, to "assist the [SSEA] in carrying out his responsibilities relating to the conduct of Canada's international relations." The expected nature of this assistance can be seen from Trudeau's first two appointments to this portfolio—Charles Lapointe and Jean-Luc Pepin, suggesting that the new external relations portfolio was an institutionalized continuation of the "francophone adviser" role created in the mid-1970s.

This ministerial triumvirate was left in place by Mulroney in 1984. In the years that followed, however, both positions were to attain more importance in the policy process than during the final years of the Trudeau government, when MacEachen, before he was appointed to the Senate, dominated the ministers in what were commonly called the "junior" external affairs portfolios.

Mulroney's first minister of international trade was James Kelleher, a junior minister who was not on the powerful Priorities and Planning (P&P) Committee of cabinet. Kelleher found himself in a distinctly subordinate position to Clark. However, the portfolio assumed greater importance after Kelleher was replaced by Pat Carney in the cabinet shuffle of 30 June 1986. But once Canada and the United States began negotiating the free trade agreement, Clark sought to be relieved of the burden of managing trade. Carney, a powerful minister in her own right and a member of the P&P Committee, was given responsibility for the trade negotiations with the United States.

Joining Clark and Kelleher in 1984 as minister for external relations was Monique Vézina; she was replaced by Monique Landry in the 1986 cabinet shuffle. However, the Mulroney government, like the Clark government before it, gave some ministerial responsibility for CIDA to the minister for external relations. This arrangement was criticized by the House of Commons Standing Committee on External Affairs and International Trade under the chairmanship of William Winegard (PC: Guelph). The Winegard committee argued that the time had come to do away with the portfolio of external relations and appoint instead a minister for international development whose mandate would be exclusively the "political management" of both CIDA and Canada's development assistance programs.[104] The government came part of the way: on 3 March 1988, it announced that Landry would indeed be delegated more authority over CIDA. However, her new title, minister for external relations and international development, suggested that the portfolio would also include the role of francophone lieutenant.[105]

Cabinet Involvement in Foreign Policy

In theory, cabinet is a group of ministers which collectively decides the foreign policy decisions and actions of the Canadian state. To what extent practice mirrors theory is difficult to ascertain. On the one hand, it is clear that the "major" foreign policy decisions that have confronted Canadian governments over the last century have been put before cabinet for discussion and resolution. In such cases, cabinet ministers deliberated; to what extent the outcome of decisions was influenced by individual members is difficult to know—in part because of the shrouds of cabinet secrecy and in part because of the paucity of good memoirs by individuals of political consequence.

On the other hand, there are a number of occasions when foreign policy decisions have been arrived at without discussion by the full cabinet. For example, Diefenbaker, who at the time was also SSEA, approved the signing of the NORAD agreement on the advice of his minister of national defence alone.[106] Likewise, during the Cuban missile crisis, Diefenbaker made numerous decisions without informing his cabinet colleagues.[107] Pearson and his SSEA, Paul Martin, frequently would make foreign policy decisions on their own and inform their cabinet colleagues *ex post facto*, much to the chagrin of at least one of their number, Pierre Elliott Trudeau.[108]

It was Trudeau's experience in the Pearson cabinet that prompted him to reform the cabinet structure in the late 1960s. These reforms were designed to promote more active cabinet deliberation on all policy issues. Issues were to be dealt with by cabinet committees (in foreign policy, the Cabinet Committee on External Policy and Defence[109]) which were empowered to take autonomous decisions. Their decisions would then be circulated to all cabinet ministers. Only if there were objections would an issue be discussed in the weekly plenary cabinet meeting. Thus did the Trudeau system encourage collegial participation in foreign policy-making—in theory at least.

In practice, however, the very nature of foreign policy mitigates against collegiality exercised once a week. There are occasions when international negotiations will not wait and when decisions on tactics must be made quickly. Likewise, most external events of importance require a quick response from Ottawa, usually precluding the possibility of calling the cabinet together. Moreover, foreign policy, like public policy, is frequently marked by technical detail. Ministers, already hard-pressed with the responsibilities of their own portfolios, are unlikely to be able to master the intricacies of another minister's portfolio. Deference to the responsible minister's recommendations inexorably follows. Finally, ministers, responsible for a segmented piece of the policy spectrum, are not immune to the dynamics of regularized small group interaction involving what tend to become policy fiefdoms. A minister will discover that his collegial involvement in another minister's portfolio will quickly breed "interference" in his own department's affairs. Therefore, the prime minister or the ministers directly responsible are likely to exert the most influence in major decisions affecting Canadian foreign policy.

CONCLUSION

By the late 1980s, the foreign policy decision-making structures had evolved considerably from the days when Mackenzie King could make foreign policy by scrawling "I agree" on a memorandum from his undersecretary of state for external affairs. Inexorably, the circle of ministerial decision widened as the volume, scope, and complexity of the business of foreign policy itself widened, and as the state grew to meet these demands. However, there are limits to such expansion. The imperatives of summitry and the importance of personal involvement in diplomacy are no less important today than they were in the 1920s. For all of the increased institutionalization and bureaucratization, the importance of those men and women at the apex of the decision-making system has not diminished markedly.

NOTES

1   Alan James, *Sovereign Statehood: The Basis of International Society* (London: Allen and Unwin, 1986); for a sensitive discussion of sovereignty and the use of force, human rights, and justice, see Stanley Hoffmann, *Duties Beyond Borders: On the Limits and Possibilities of Ethical International Politics* (Syracuse: Syracuse University Press, 1981).

2   It is thus not by chance that the American constitution of 1787 gave the legislature, not the executive, the power to approve the appointment of ambassadors, to ratify international treaties, and to declare war. The American founding fathers, wishing to avoid the reproduction of British absolutism in the

governance of their new society, inevitably fixed on the power in foreign affairs implied by the doctrine of sovereignty.

3 For a discussion of the royal prerogative, see R. MacGregor Dawson, *The Government of Canada*, 5th ed., rev. by Norman Ward (Toronto: University of Toronto Press, 1970), 146-47.

4 *Ibid.*, 167.

5 Colin Campbell, SJ, "Political leadership in Canada: Pierre Elliott Trudeau and the Ottawa model," in Richard Rose and Ezra N. Suleiman, eds., *Presidents and Prime Ministers* (Washington: American Enterprise Institute, 1980), 54.

6 However, it might be noted that although all the sovereign's prerogative powers were transferred to the Crown's representative in Canada by King George VI in 1947, the sovereign still exercises some symbolic powers in foreign affairs. For example, Canada's diplomatic representatives are sent abroad under the authority of Queen Elizabeth II herself and not her representative in Ottawa. For one account of a dispute between the government in Ottawa and the Queen on these powers, see *International Canada* (December 1972), 238-39.

7 The governors general in the dominions were representatives and agents of the British government as well as representatives of the sovereign until 1926. In that year, it was agreed that, if a dominion wished it, the governor general would cease to be the representative of the British government. Instead, London would dispatch its own diplomatic representatives—styled "high commissioners"—to the dominion's capital. H. Duncan Hall, *Commonwealth: A History of the British Commonwealth of Nations* (London, 1982), 593-605. Nor does the governor general play the often substantive role in Canadian foreign policy-making that he once did: see James Eayrs, *The Art of the Possible: Government and Foreign Policy in Canada* (Toronto: University of Toronto Press, 1961), 28-31.

8 Arthur Meighen was prime minister in 1926 from 29 June to 25 September; but he had held the prime ministership for just over a year six years earlier.

9 Robert Craig Brown, "Fishwives, plutocrats, sirens and other curious creatures: some questions about political leadership in Canada," in Leslie A. Pal and David Taras, eds., *Prime Ministers and Premiers: Political Leadership and Public Policy in Canada* (Scarborough: Prentice-Hall Canada, 1988), 29.

10 Walter D. Young, "Leadership and Canadian politics," in John H. Redekop, ed., *Approaches to Canadian Politics* (Scarborough: Prentice- Hall Canada, 1978), 283. A good example of this tendency is provided by David Dewitt and John Kirton in *Canada as a Principal Power* (Toronto: John Wiley and Sons, 1983). The authors identify five "eras" of foreign policy between 1947 and 1982. They studiously avoid identifying eras by prime minister; instead they attach periphrastic labels to each era (for example, 1957 to 1963 is termed the "era of competitive fragmentation"). In fact, each era down to the 1970s corresponds exactly to the tenure of St. Laurent, Diefenbaker, Pearson, and Trudeau.

11 Quoted in C.P. Stacey, *Canada and the Age of Conflict*, vol. 1: *1867-1921* (Toronto: Macmillan, 1977), 151-52.

12 Gaddis Smith, "Canadian external affairs during World War I," in Hugh L. Keenleyside et al., *The Growth of Canadian Policies in External Affairs* (Durham: Duke University Press, 1960), 41.

13 Quoted in Stacey, *Age of Conflict*, vol. 1, 192.

14 Quoted in Smith, "External affairs during World War I," 57.

15 The story of Canada's response to the Chanak crisis is best told by Stacey, *Age of Conflict*, vol. 2: *1921-1948: The Mackenzie King Era* (Toronto: University of Toronto Press, 1981), 17-31.

16 *Ibid.*, 71.

17 For two differing assessments, see James Eayrs, "'A low dishonest decade': aspects of Canadian external policy, 1931-1939," in Keenleyside et al., *Growth of Canadian Policies*, 59-80; and J.L. Granatstein and Robert Bothwell, "Canadian foreign policy, 1935-39," in Granatstein, ed., *Canadian Foreign Policy: Historical Readings* (Toronto: Copp Clark Pitman, 1986), 125-44.

18 See Richard Veatch, *Canada and the League of Nations* (Toronto: University of Toronto Press, 1975).

19 As Borden noted to his diary in May 1917: quoted in Stacey, *Age of Conflict*, vol. 1, 218.

20 The lesson would always be there: in 1944, King was still pressing the anti-conscription case in the same electoral terms. If the government had to introduce conscription for overseas duty, he said, "the Liberal party would be completely destroyed, and not only immediately but for [an] indefinite time to come." Quoted in Stacey, *Arms, Men and Governments: The War Policies of Canada, 1939-1945* (Ottawa: Information Canada, 1970), 446.

21 Stacey, *Age of Conflict*, vol. 2, ix.

22 R. Barry Farrell, *The Making of Canadian Foreign Policy* (Scarborough: Prentice-Hall Canada, 1969), 10-11.

23 Quoted in James Eayrs, *In Defence of Canada*, vol. 3: *Peacemaking and Deterrence* (Toronto: University of Toronto Press, 1972), 7.

24 For a more detailed comparison, see Kim Richard Nossal, "Political leadership and foreign policy: Trudeau and Mulroney," in Pal and Taras, eds., *Prime Ministers and Premiers*, 117-118.

25 Bruce Thordarson, *Trudeau and Foreign Policy: A Study in Decision-Making* (Toronto: Oxford University Press, 1972); Thordarson, "Posture and policy: leadership in Canada's external affairs," *International Journal* 31 (Autumn 1976). For the introduction of "rational" decision-making, see G. Bruce Doern and Peter Aucoin, eds., *The Structures of Policy-Making in Canada* (Toronto: Macmillan, 1971), ch. 2-3.

26 Canada, Secretary of State for External Affairs, *Foreign Policy for Canadians* (Ottawa: Information Canada, 1970).

27 Peyton V. Lyon, "The Trudeau Doctrine," *International Journal* 26 (Winter 1970-1), 19-43.

28 *International Canada* (October and November 1983), 7-8, 17-18.

29 *Toronto Star*, 13 July 1984, quoted in David Taras, "Brian Mulroney's foreign policy: something for everyone," *Round Table* 293 (1985), 40.

30 For example, Diefenbaker frequently used anti-communist rhetoric during the 1962 and 1963 election campaigns; Joe Clark promised to move the Canadian embassy to Jerusalem during the 1979 elections in the hope that this would win Jewish votes; in the 1980 election, held in the immediate aftermath of the Soviet

invasion of Afghanistan, Clark and his external affairs minister, Flora MacDonald, embraced a robust anti-Sovietism.

31 For example, John Kirton, "The foreign policy decision process," in Maureen Appel Molot and Brian W. Thomlin, eds., *Canada Among Nations—1985: The Conservative Agenda* (Toronto: James Lorimer, 1986).

32 Colin Campbell and George J. Szablowski, *The Superbureaucrats: Structure and Behaviour in Central Agencies* (Toronto: Macmillan, 1979), 46- 48.

33 J.L. Granatstein, *The Ottawa Men: The Civil Service Mandarins, 1935-1957* (Toronto: Oxford University Press, 1982).

34 For an excellent survey of these tendencies, see Norman Hillmer, "The Anglo-Canadian neurosis: the case of O.D. Skelton," in Peter Lyon, ed., *Britain and Canada: Survey of a Changing Relationship* (London: Frank Cass, 1976), 61-84.

35 Lester B. Pearson, *Mike: The Memoirs of the Rt. Hon. Lester B. Pearson*, vol. 2: *1948-1957* (Toronto: University of Toronto Press, 1974), 4.

36 For one critical assessment, see Christina McCall-Newman, "Michael Pitfield and the politics of mismanagement," *Saturday Night* (October 1982), 24-44. His own views on government organization are to be found in "The shape of government in the 1980s: techniques and instruments for policy formulation at the federal level," in Thomas A. Hockin, ed., *Apex of Power: The Prime Minister and Political Leadership in Canada*, 2nd ed. (Scarborough: Prentice-Hall Canada, 1977), 54-63.

37 Coates was forced to resign within several months after it was discovered that while inspecting Canadian forces in Germany, he had visited a strip joint; Stevens had to resign over a conflict of interest involving one of his companies.

38 The communiqué at the conclusion of Churchill's meeting with Roosevelt at the Quebec Conference in 1943 noted that "it is indispensable that entire unity of aim and method should be maintained at the summit of the war direction." Quoted in Roger Frank Swanson, *Canadian-American Summit Diplomacy, 1923-1973* (Toronto: McClelland and Stewart, 1975), 2.

39 Mulroney's initiatives in establishing the francophone summit, and in regularizing the summit with the president were part of a wider pattern, according to John Kirton: the prime minister "aggressively sought to employ summit forums for a more ambitious set of purposes than ever before." "Managing global conflict: Canada and international summitry," in Maureen Appel Molot and Brian W. Tomlin, eds., *Canada Among Nations—1987: A World of Conflict* (Toronto: James Lorimer, 1988), 33.

40 Stacey, *Age of Conflict*, vol. 1, 44-46.

41 G.P. deT. Glazebrook, *A History of Canadian External Relations*, vol. 2: *In the Empire and the World, 1914-1939* (Toronto: McClelland and Stewart, 1966), ch. 16 and 17.

42 For a discussion of reactions to the idea of a multiracial Commonwealth, see John W. Holmes, *The Shaping of Peace: Canada and the Search for World Order, 1943-1957*, vol. 2 (Toronto: University of Toronto Press, 1982), 167-72.

43 For a detailed account of the negotiations which led to this compromise, and the role that Ottawa played in maintaining Indian membership, see Eayrs, *In Defence of Canada*, vol. 3, 236-56.

44 James Eayrs, "Commonwealth anxieties," in his *Northern Approaches: Canada and the Search for Peace* (Toronto: Macmillan of Canada, 1961), 74-100. A list of Commonwealth members can be found in Margaret Doxey, "Canada and the evolution of the modern Commonwealth," *Behind the Headlines* 40 (November 1982), 20, appendix.

45 Though a republic, India had in fact adopted the Westminster model in 1947, merely substituting an indigenous president to perform the symbolic functions that the Crown performs in representative systems like Britain, Canada, or Australia.

46 Eayrs, *Art of the Possible*, 8.

47 Stacey, *Age of Conflict*, vol. 1, 340-48; Eayrs, *In Defence of Canada*, vol. 1: *From the Great War to the Great Depression* (Toronto: University of Toronto Press, 1964), 18-20.

48 "Such 'foreign' policy as Canada had under Meighen," Stacey has opined, "was largely of Christie's making." *Age of Conflict*, vol. 1, 321.

49 For accounts of these meetings, see Stacey, *Age of Conflict*, vol. 2, *passim*. On the 1937 meeting, Eayrs's account differs somewhat: *In Defence of Canada*, vol. 2: *Appeasement and Rearmament* (Toronto: University of Toronto Press, 1965), 53-60.

50 Frank R. Hayes, "South Africa's departure from the Commonwealth, 1960- 61," *International History Review* 2 (July 1980), 453-84.

51 Arthur E. Blanchette, ed., *Canadian Foreign Policy, 1955-1965* (Toronto: McClelland and Stewart, 1977), 302-308; Frank R. Hayes, "Canada, the Commonwealth and the Rhodesia issue," in Kim Richard Nossal, ed., *An Acceptance of Paradox: Essays on Canadian Diplomacy in Honour of John W. Holmes* (Toronto: Canadian Institute of International Affairs, 1982), 141-73.

52 Clarence G. Redekop, "Trudeau at Singapore: the Commonwealth and arms sales to South Africa," in Nossal, ed., *Acceptance of Paradox*, 174-95.

53 The *Manchester Guardian*, 19 August 1979, noted that it was "a job that he did superbly." Quoted in Doxey, "Canada and the modern Commonwealth," *fn* 17.

54 Clarence G. Redekop, "The Mulroney government and South Africa: constructive disengagement," *Behind the Headlines* 44 (December 1986); Douglas G. Anglin, ed., *Canada and South Africa: Challenge and Response* (Ottawa: Carleton International Proceedings, summer 1986); Dan O'Meara, "Crisis of apartheid: the Canadian response," *Peace and Security* 1 (Summer 1986), 2-3.

55 For details of this initiative, see Kim Richard Nossal, "Personal diplomacy and national behaviour: Trudeau's North-South initiative," *Dalhousie Review* 62 (Summer 1982), 278-91.

56 A voluminous literature exists on the peace initiative: for a detailed account of the actual initiative, see Richard and Sandra Gwyn, "The politics of peace," *Saturday Night* (May 1984), 19-32; his speeches are reproduced in C. David Crenna, ed., *Pierre Elliott Trudeau: Lifting the Shadow of War* (Edmonton:

Hurtig Publishers, 1987), ch. 4-5; for a good assessment of the initiative and the debate that surrounded it, see Harald von Riekhoff and John Sigler, "The Trudeau peace initiative: the politics of reversing the arms race," in Brian W. Tomlin and Maureen Molot, eds., *Canada Among Nations — 1984: A Time of Transition* (Toronto: James Lorimer, 1985), 50-69.

57 Canada, Parliament, House of Commons, *Debates*, 3 November 1975.

58 Alex I. Inglis, "Economic summitry reaches time of testing in London," *International Perspectives* (September/October 1977), 33.

59 By 1988, the economic summits had gone through two rotations: Rambouillet (1975); Puerto Rico (1976); London (1977); Bonn (1978); Tokyo (1979); Venice (1980); Montebello (1981); Versailles (1982); Williamsburg (1983); London (1984); Bonn (1985); Tokyo (1986); Venice (1987); and Toronto (1988). See the regular reports in *International Perspectives*: Richard Gwyn, "Report on the Bonn summit: a need for world-management," (November/December 1977), 33-36; Michel Vastel, "Impotence of the Big Seven in the wake of Afghanistan," (July/August 1980), 3-6.

60 Sylvia Ostry, Canada's ambassador for multilateral trade negotiations, was Mulroney's personal representative for the summits in Bonn, Tokyo, Venice, and Toronto: for an account, see Stevie Cameron, "Scaling summits," *The Globe and Mail Report on Business Magazine* (June 1988), 60-66.

61 For example, much of the Bonn summit was devoted to reductions in government expenditure as a means of affecting the global economy. Following his return from Bonn, Trudeau announced an immediate cut in federal government spending. Within a month, $3.7 billion in spending cuts, ranging across the spectrum of government programs, had been announced. *International Canada* (July and August 1978), 159-62.

62 See the account of the speech given by Allan Gotlieb, then the under-secretary of state for external affairs, on the summits: *International Canada* (April 1981), 87-88.

63 The best account of the development of the francophone summit is to be found in John Kirton, "Shaping the global order: Canada and the francophone and Commonwealth summits of 1987," *Behind the Headlines* 44 (June 1987).

64 *Ibid.*, 4.

65 Canada, Department of External Affairs, *Canadian Foreign Policy Series*: Monique Landry, "The Francophone summit and the Francophones outside Quebec," 11 February 1987, 2.

66 Kirton, "Summits of 1987," 7-8.

67 The two exceptions were Trudeau, who never met with Lyndon Johnson when their terms of office overlapped in 1968, and John Turner, who did not meet with Reagan during the two and a half months in 1984 that he was prime minister.

68 Swanson, *Canadian-American Summit Diplomacy*, table 9, 22 for the meetings down to 1973. The pattern has continued since then: Trudeau met with Gerald Ford in December 1974 following Richard Nixon's resignation in August; with Jimmy Carter in February 1977; Joe Clark met with Carter at the Tokyo economic summit in June 1979; Reagan visited Trudeau in Ottawa in March

1981. Mulroney had met with Reagan in June 1984, as leader of the opposition; within a week of being sworn in as prime minister in September 1984, he visited Washington again.

69 Prime ministers and presidents have met at F.D. Roosevelt's burial in 1945, at John F. Kennedy's funeral in 1963, and Dwight D. Eisenhower's burial in 1969.

70 Quoted in Swanson, *Canadian-American Summit Diplomacy*, 161.

71 So-called not only because it was held on St. Patrick's Day, but also because both Reagan and Mulroney had made a great deal of their common Irish background. At a gala held on the evening of 18 March, for example, the president and prime minister treated the audience to a rendition of "When Irish Eyes are Smiling."

72 Swanson, *Canadian-American Summit Diplomacy*, 197.

73 John W. Holmes, *Life with Uncle: The Canadian-American Relationship* (Toronto: University of Toronto Press, 1981), 4.

74 Stacey, *Arms, Men and Governments*, 489; R.D. Cuff and J.L. Granatstein, "The Hyde Park Declaration, 1941: origins and significance," in Cuff and Granatstein, *Canadian-American Relations in Wartime* (Toronto: Hakkert, 1975); text of the declaration reprinted in Swanson, *Canadian-American Summit Diplomacy*, 78-79.

75 J.W. Pickersgill, ed., *The Mackenzie King Record*, vol. 1: *1939- 1945* (Toronto: University of Toronto Press, 1960), 202.

76 Peter C. Dobell, *Canada in World Affairs*, vol. 17: *1971-1973* (Toronto: Canadian Institute of International Affairs, 1985), 26-28.

77 See above, ch. 3.

78 Swanson, *Canadian-American Summit Diplomacy*, 14.

79 Stephen Clarkson, *Canada and the Reagan Challenge* (Toronto: Canadian Institute for Economic Policy, 1982), 23-39.

80 Lawrence Martin, *The Presidents and the Prime Ministers* (Toronto: Doubleday, 1982), 7.

81 On their first meeting in February 1961, Kennedy's biographer wrote, "Kennedy thought [Diefenbaker] insincere and did not like or trust him." Quoted in Peyton Lyon, *Canada in World Affairs*, vol. 12: *1961-1963* (Toronto: Oxford University Press, 1968), 493. For his part, the prime minister thought the president brash and arrogant. As Basil Robinson, Diefenbaker's liaison with External Affairs in the Prime Minister's Office, wrote: "It is disturbing that the Prime Minister seems to have formed some rather unfavourable early impressions. I just hope these can be erased." Quoted in Martin, *Presidents and Prime Ministers*, 183.

82 "[Kennedy's] reception of me, while perfectly civil, was, I thought, distinctly cool, and I came away with the impression that this reflected his attitude towards the Canadian government and particularly towards Mr Diefenbaker." Charles Ritchie, *Storm Signals: More Undiplomatic Diaries, 1962-1971* (Toronto: Macmillan, 1983), 6; also 23-24.

83 For example, during the election campaign in the spring of 1962, Pearson, then the leader of the Liberal opposition, was invited to a White House ceremony for Nobel prize winners, and was photographed with Kennedy. Believing that the

president was deliberately trying to bring down his government by giving Pearson publicity, Diefenbaker dressed down the United States ambassador to Ottawa for an hour and a half, and threatened to make public a somewhat embarrassing American briefing paper that Kennedy had mislaid on a visit to Ottawa in May 1961. (Instead of following standard diplomatic practice of photocopying such documents and returning them to the owner, the prime minister had kept the original.) Martin, *Presidents and Prime Ministers*, 191-99; Peter Stursburg, *Diefenbaker: Leadership Gained, 1956-62* (Toronto: University of Toronto Press, 1975), 172-73; Lyon, *Canada in World Affairs*, 496-502.

84 For example, when Diefenbaker announced publicly to the House of Commons his own interpretation of secret negotiations between Canada and the United States on the nuclear weapons question, the State Department in Washington issued a public press release challenging the prime minister's interpretation. Even Ritchie, no great fan of Diefenbaker's, thought the "heavy-handed and overbearing action of the State Department ... intolerable." Ritchie, *Storm Signals*, 32.

85 Pearson had told close friends that he thought the air strikes were "obscene," and felt compelled to make an effort to alter Johnson's policies. Accordingly, in his speech accepting a peace award from Temple University, he suggested publicly that the United States should halt the bombing and negotiate with North Vietnam. Johnson was, to put it mildly, furious. The prime minister had chosen to ignore the ethos of diplomacy which dictates that government leaders do not criticize the policies of other governments while on their soil. Moreover, bombing halts were going to be used by the United States as part of a "carrot-and-stick" approach to Vietnam. By publicly suggesting a bombing halt, Pearson was pre-empting such a move, for Johnson could not suspend the bombing, at least in the short term: it is not in the habit of American presidents to appear to be swayed by criticism from a smaller ally.

86 Martin's graphic account in *Presidents and Prime Ministers*, 1-5, 224-227, claims that during this incident, Johnson physically lifted the prime minister up. This version is denied by Ritchie, the Canadian ambassador, who was watching the two leaders on the patio through a window. See his *Storm Signals*, 80-83.

87 The Parliament that had been elected in the October 1972 elections was scheduled to meet after the new year in 1973. The Liberals were in a minority situation, with the New Democratic Party holding the balance of power. Although by the time the new Parliament met the bombing had been terminated, the NDP wanted to respond with a parliamentary resolution "condemning" the bombing. The government sought to avoid a parliamentary tangle over this issue by introducing its own motion which contained the diplomatically softer word "deploring."

88 Douglas A. Ross, *In The Interests of Peace: Canada and Vietnam, 1954- 73* (Toronto: University of Toronto Press, 1984), 342-43; also Dobell, *Canada in World Affairs*, 401-403.

89 Richard Rose, "British government: the job at the top," in Rose and Suleiman, eds., *Presidents and Prime Ministers*, 36.

90 Thomas Carlyle wrote that "Universal History, the history of what man has accomplished in this world, is at bottom the History of the Great Men who have worked here." See the discussion in David Taras and Robert Weyant, "Dreamers of the day: a guide to roles, character and performance on the political stage," in Pal and Taras, eds., *Prime Ministers and Premiers*, 3-5.

91 Such an impact can be seen with each postwar prime minister: St. Laurent's nervous depression in 1956 affected his participation in the Commonwealth meetings; Diefenbaker's paranoid behaviour in 1962 and 1963 deeply affected the course of Canadian-American relations; Pearson's propensity for compromise and moderation, which had been so important for his diplomacy over Suez, proved to be a distinct liability when he was prime minister; Trudeau's intellectual skills and his propensity for not suffering fools gladly were both an asset and a liability at summit meetings; Mulroney's penchant for grandstanding hyperbole, when carried to the Bonn summit in 1985, caused considerable embarrassment for his government.

92 Eayrs, *Art of the Possible*, 19-22.

93 *Ibid.*, 25.

94 On the close relationship between St. Laurent and Pearson, see Thordarson, "Posture and policy," 679-79. As Pearson later recounted in his memoirs, the prime minister had implicit trust in his foreign minister: "'Don't worry,' he told me. 'Do what is best. Do the right thing, and I'll back you.'" Quoted in Eayrs, *Art of the Possible*, 26.

95 Quoted in W.A. Matheson, *The Prime Minister and the Cabinet* (Toronto: Methuen, 1976), 161.

96 Eayrs recounts Smith's introduction to his portfolio: a few moments after being sworn in, Smith was asked by reporters to outline his opinions on Canadian policy over Suez. When it became apparent that Smith favoured the approach taken by the defeated St. Laurent government, Diefenbaker cut in, contradicting his new minister. "This initial reprimand," Eayrs concludes, "set the tone of their relationship..." *Art of the Possible*, 26-27.

97 For diverging views on the relationship between Diefenbaker and Green, see Thordarson, "Posture and policy," 679, and Eayrs, *Art of the Possible*, 28.

98 David Cox, "Leadership change and innovation in Canadian foreign policy: the 1979 Progressive Conservative government," *International Journal* 37 (Autumn 1982).

99 Thordarson, "Posture and policy," 681-82.

100 Indeed, Pearson himself reckoned that his work in the external affairs portfolio and his Nobel Prize in 1957 contributed heavily to his leadership victory. *Mike*, vol. 3, 28.

101 It might also be noted that by giving his chief rival the external affairs portfolio, a prime minister minimizes the threats to his leadership. Not only does the SSEA have to spend a fair amount of time outside Canada, but he or she is unlikely to garner the political spotlight, because of summitry and the relatively low profile of foreign policy in national politics.

102 Louis Sabourin, "Canada and francophone Africa," in Peyton V. Lyon and Tariq Y. Ismael, eds., *Canada and the Third World* (Toronto: Macmillan, 1976), 134-61.

103 *International Canada* (May 1977), 134.

104 Canada, Parliament, House of Commons, Standing Committee on External Affairs and International Trade, *For Whose Benefit? Report of* SCEAIT on Canada's Official Development Assistance Policies and Programs (Ottawa, May 1987), 114-17.

105 *The Globe and Mail*, 4 March 1988.

106 Jon B. McLin, *Canada's Changing Defense Policy, 1957-1963* (Toronto: Copp Clark, 1967), 43-46.

107 Diefenbaker's unilateral decision-making during this crisis is well- documented in Lyon, *Canada in World Affairs*, 32-47, esp. 37, *fn* 55.

108 Thordarson, "Posture and policy," 683.

109 It should be noted that the cabinet committee on foreign policy was eliminated by Mulroney in September 1984; it was, however, restored in the summer of 1985.

CHAPTER SEVEN

The Bureaucracy

INTRODUCTION

Cabinet ministers may be vested with the authority to make foreign policy decisions for Canada, but the process of decision-making is inexorably affected by those agencies of the state created to implement political decisions. The bureaucracy in democratic systems does more than merely implement decisions and administer programs authorized by law or by executive fiat. A bureaucracy's functions include the provision of policy information and advice to elected leaders, and therein lies a source of potent influence over the shaping of policy decisions.[1]

The "foreign policy bureaucracy" in Canada defies easy identification. Usually, one department alone can claim to be the pivotal point for advising on and implementing the government's general orientation to the international system—the foreign office. A discussion of the bureaucratic sources of foreign policy must therefore begin with the Department of External Affairs. But it should be remembered that there are few government agencies whose programs or activities do not have at least peripheral external ramifications. Over 30 federal departments, agencies, or Crown corporations have jurisdiction over policy issues which have an international focus. In addition, many provinces have developed bureaucracies for the conduct of their own external affairs.[2]

ORGANIZING FOR FOREIGN AFFAIRS

"A foreign office," James Eayrs has written, "while not necessarily a frill of government, is an optional part of the state apparatus.... [C]ritics contend that it is no longer necessary to entrust the management of external relations to an elite sector of the public service. They even contend that the foreign office is obsolete."[3] However, few states choose to try and do without. The vast majority have created an agency whose officials are responsible for six key functions: representing the state in other capitals; providing information and assessments on conditions in other states; providing advice to political leaders on issues on the foreign policy agenda; conducting negotiations with other governments; protecting the interests of their state's citizens abroad; and advancing the interests of their state in the international system. The pervasiveness of foreign ministries owes more to the immutability of the requisites of statecraft than it does to any desire for mere symbolic prestige, as Eayrs suggests.

It is true that there are those who are fond of arguing that changes in the international system have made diplomacy obsolete. For example, in 1980, Pierre Elliott Trudeau asserted that "Traditional concepts of foreign service have diminished relevance in an era of instantaneous, world-wide communications, in which there is increasing reliance on personal contacts between senior members of governments, and in which international relations are concerned with progressively more complex and technical questions."[4] However, even the most superficial survey of how autonomous political entities have, over the course of human history, conducted relations with one another would lead one to agree with John Holmes's assumption that diplomacy is a "primitive instinct."[5] Moreover, Trudeau's beliefs notwithstanding, technological developments in the present era may have changed the *modes* of diplomacy but they have not altered—indeed, they could not alter—the *purpose* of diplomacy as a tool of statecraft. Nor has widespread summiteering eliminated the need for a professional *corps diplomatique* to conduct the craft of state when the political leaders have returned to their capitals.

The primary task of diplomacy is to achieve foreign policy goals by peaceful means. Whether the objectives are parochial (securing concessions in a trade treaty) or wide-ranging (avoiding the outbreak of systemic war), diplomacy will be an indispensable tool to achieve them. A state needs negotiators and interlocutors who have the skill to move others to positions closer to its own interests by a judicious mix of coercion, inducement, and persuasion. Indeed, for states such as Canada, with limited capabilities, a dependence on persuasion means that a diplomatic service will be one of the most potent power resources to achieve its objectives. On those issues over which smaller states have little control—systemic peace or war, or relations between the great powers—diplomacy assumes a special importance. The art of facilitating dialogue between the great powers, of defusing tension, and of encouraging calm, moderation, and compromise, is all too often the only means at a small state's disposal. And such efforts are impossible without a professional organization which can act continuously to give expression to both the broad and narrow interests of a state.

This the Canadian government would discover—albeit slowly. From 1867 to the present, there has been a steady growth in the foreign policy bureaucracy. Four broad periods can be identified: from Confederation to the establishment of the Department of External Affairs in 1909; from the beginnings of a modest foreign office which underwent little growth until 1939; the rapid and continuous expansion in the two decades after the Second World War; and a period of reorganization that began with the Trudeau government.

The Early Years: 1867-1909

When the British government assented to Confederation in 1867, a foreign ministry was not considered a frill of government; it was not even contemplated. Both British and Canadians regarded the foreign policy, and hence the diplomacy, of the Empire as indivisible. Self-governing the dominion might be, but intact Imperial global policies would have to remain. Responsibility for the conduct of Canada's foreign policy rested, as a result, with the government in London. Such an arrangement was, as George Glazebrook has noted,[6] perfectly acceptable to British and Canadians alike. Wishing neither full independence nor complete colonial subordination, they were prepared to live with the ambiguity of what Sir Richard Cartwright, a prominent Liberal, once termed Canada's "tadpole sort of existence."[7]

Yet the impulse towards a separate diplomacy was ineluctable. On matters that necessitated communication with other states and a physical presence abroad (such as attracting immigrants, settling boundaries, fisheries, and trade issues with the United States, or promoting trade with Europe), the government found itself drawn into diplomatic relations. The formal process was cumbersome at best, circumscribed as it was by the punctilios demanded by Imperial unity. In order to communicate with the United States, for example, the cabinet would have to route correspondence through the British governor general in Ottawa, who would then process it through the Colonial and Foreign Offices in London, which would then send it to the British ambassador in Washington for presentation to the Department of State. There were, as Glazebrook points out, modifications to this in practice. The British, having little wish to handle the day-to-day practicalities of Canadian trade, allowed Ottawa to conduct its own commercial diplomacy.[8]

In the beginning, the government in Ottawa directed its external efforts to increasing immigration into an empty dominion. In 1868, the Dominion

Agency for Emigration was opened in London, and in the 1870s, no fewer than twelve Immigration Offices were established from Antwerp to Worcester. Likewise, the requisites of trade prompted the opening of a world-wide network of Trade Commissions, and by 1907, twelve offices were stimulating and expediting the exchange of goods abroad.[9] In 1880, a high commissioner was appointed to London, and, two years later, the federal government asked Hector Fabre, who was the Quebec government's Agent General in Paris, to act in a similar capacity for Ottawa. While these officials were agents of the Canadian state abroad, they were not diplomats in anything but the most superficial sense. They were not accorded diplomatic status; nor, importantly, were they representatives of a government with an independent international personality, capable of conducting an independent foreign policy.

The first 40 years of Canada's existence demonstrate why Eayrs's claim that "Any government could conduct its foreign affairs without a ministry created expressly for that purpose" should be viewed with some skepticism. A state's leaders, Eayrs argues, "could rely instead upon their own resources and those of their staffs to supervise and coordinate departments of trade, defence, immigration, agriculture, fisheries and any others doing the country's business abroad, resorting again to their own resources to attend to any residue that might show up as 'foreign policy' pure if not so simple."[10] Perhaps Eayrs had these formative years in mind, for this is precisely how Canada conducted its foreign relations until the First World War. The emphasis during this period was on ad hocery. Relations and negotiations with other states were carried on by different cabinet ministers and senior civil servants depending on the issue involved. Portfolios did not always determine which minister would be involved. For example, when the government in Ottawa wanted to restrict immigration from Japan, it dispatched the postmaster-general, Rodolphe Lemieux, and the under-secretary of state, Joseph Pope, to Tokyo in 1907.[11] At times foreign relations were conducted by individuals who were not even in government: George Brown, proprietor of the Toronto *Globe*, negotiated a draft treaty with the United States in 1874; Sanford Fleming, the surveyor of the Canadian Pacific Railway, represented Canada at the 1887 Colonial Conference in London.[12] Nor was there a centralized system of record-keeping. Correspondence on a variety of international subjects was scattered among different departments in Ottawa. Well might Pope, conducting emigration talks in Japan in 1907, complain that if it had not been for the records kept by the British embassy in Tokyo, the Canadian negotiating position would have been untenable.[13]

This system survived until the turn of the century. "The machinery creaked," Glazebrook observed, "but on the whole it served the purpose."[14] However, it became increasingly clear that it was a less than efficient way of conducting foreign relations. For example, the high commission in London served as a base for officials from six different departments but there was no centralized control. "You will readily recognize," the then-high commissioner complained to the prime minister, Robert Borden, in 1914, "that the situation is not conducive to good business and often produces overlapping and is very awkward."[15]

Modest Beginnings: 1909-1939

Although the system had evolved because of the imperial connection, the British, who had to carry much of the administrative load of Canada's foreign relations, came to be less than happy with the arrangement. By 1908, Earl Grey, one of the few British governors general to take an active interest in Canada's external affairs,[16] was complaining to the colonial secretary in London that negotiations with the United States were not proceeding smoothly because of the "chaotic conditions of the Administration here *qua* External Affairs. There is no Department, no official through whose hands all matters dealing with external affairs must go. Consequently there is no record, no continuity, no method, no consistency." He concluded by opining on Ottawa's bureaucratic expertise in foreign affairs at that time: "We have only three... One drinks at times, the other has a difficulty in expressing his thoughts... and the third is the Under Secretary of State, Pope—a really first-class official."[17]

Joseph Pope had been involved in external relations since the early 1880s, and was a leading proponent of a separate foreign ministry. But it was not until Grey and James Bryce, the British ambassador in Washington, had added their voices to Pope's that Sir Wilfrid Laurier agreed in 1908 to create a foreign ministry. The new Department of External Affairs (DEA) was created by statute in 1909; the word "external" was chosen because the "affairs" related as much to Britain and to the various parts of the Empire as they did to other states, and these were not "foreign" countries.[18] At first DEA was put under the authority of the secretary of state, but in 1912 it was taken over by the prime minister.[19] Pope was appointed as the department's deputy minister (his official title was the under-secretary of state for external affairs), and, with a budget of $14,950, two clerks, a secretary, and temporary offices over a barber shop, he began a 16-year superintendency over the new department.[20]

Modestly the department began, and modest it remained until the outbreak of the Second World War. With Pope's retirement in 1925, Mackenzie King appointed O.D. Skelton, whom he had recruited from Queen's University in 1924. Skelton, in turn, recruited what one historian has termed "an extraordinary crew of well-educated and well-trained young officers,"[21] among them Hugh Keenleyside, Lester Pearson, Hume Wrong and Norman Robertson. By the 1950s, these "young officers" would have transformed DEA and the diplomatic corps into what a former British diplomat would praise as "an elite organization of high quality [with] a deservedly high reputation."[22] But that was two decades in the future. In the interwar years, the department was so modestly staffed that it was not much in need of the formalities of organization charts much beloved by managers of the public service in the postwar period. There could be no organization chart for a department which assigned its few officers tasks on an ad hoc and arbitrary basis. Officials in the East Block of the Parliament buildings—whence External had moved after its adoption by the prime minister—were given "dockets" to cover as the need arose. For example, at one point early in his career, Pearson's caseload included dockets on lighthouses in the Red Sea, aviation licences in Canada and Switzerland, international tariffs on cement, and the protection of young female artists travelling abroad.[23] To such a mélange one could not with ease apply normal standards of organization.

Nor were the small department's organizational patterns challenged by the exceedingly modest growth of Canadian representation abroad during the interwar years. While the trade commissioner service continued to expand, promoting trade on all continents but one (no fewer than 50 trade offices were opened between 1907 and 1939), only three diplomatic missions were opened after the Imperial Conference of 1926 that sanctioned separate foreign policies for the dominions. In February 1927, Vincent Massey presented his credentials to the president of the United States; in 1928, the office in Paris was given diplomatic status; and in 1929, a mission was opened in Tokyo.[24] This did contribute to a modest increase in staff. But the basic size and pattern of organization remained unchanged until 1939.

Expansion: 1939-1968

The outbreak of the Second World War ended the era of modesty. When war was declared, the government in Ottawa decided to establish diplomatic posts in those states considered important to the war effort. Missions were immediately set up in Australia, New Zealand, South Africa, and Ireland. Within three years, diplomatic relations had been opened with the allied governments-in-exile in London, Newfoundland, Argentina, Brazil, Chile, China, and the Soviet Union.[25] The wartime expansion of the diplomatic service abroad was matched by a growth of staff in Ottawa, as the small contingent from the interwar years was augmented by temporary wartime appointments, drawn in the main from the universities.

The expansion continued apace after the war, a function of both the new spirit of commitment to internationalism and also the rapid pace of decolonization. In the 25 years after 1945, the number of international institutions which Canada joined—and to which the government would send representatives—grew to over 200. The number of sovereign states in the international system continued to expand and so did the number of missions abroad. In 1945, Canada maintained 22 diplomatic missions; this number had grown to 101 by 1970. While there were 67 members of the foreign service in 1946, by 1970, that number had grown to 725.[26]

Another measure of growth was the increasing complexity of the department. Its organizational response to postwar expansion was essentially protozoan. Orthodox methods of organizing a foreign office had been introduced during the war. By 1945, the internal organization of the department was marked by institutionalized "divisions" responsible for diverse aspects of DEA's work. Besides an administrative section and functional divisions (legal, treaty, economic, information), there were three "political" divisions, unimaginatively titled Political I, II, and III.[27] Over the next 25 years, those eight divisions would grow, by fission and conjugation, to 71 administrative, managerial, functional, and geographic units.[28] Indeed, by the late 1960s, External's headquarters had become so large that it had long since spilled out of the East Block of the Parliament Buildings into a dozen office buildings dotted around downtown Ottawa. (Eventually, in 1973, the department would be moved into its present home, the Lester B. Pearson Building, on Sussex Drive.)

During this period, the organization of foreign relations reflected a continuing division of bureaucratic labour. Two external concerns were as salient in the 1950s and 1960s as they had been at the time of Confederation: the promotion of external trade and the movement of people into Canada. The Department of Trade and Commerce continued to manage the first.[29] Immigration initially fell under the domain of the Department of Mines and Resources; after 1950, it was the responsibility of Citizenship and Immigration, and finally, in 1966, an expanded Manpower and Immigration.[30] No longer, however, was the mission to attract migrants to an empty country but to regulate the flow of prospective immigrants. National Defence, constricted during the interwar period, was responsible for implementing Canada's twin commitments to NATO and NORAD.[31] Finance was constantly involved, not only in the evaluation and approval of government spending on Canada's new commitments, but also in international monetary affairs.[32]

In addition, new bureaucracies evolved in this period to administer new elements of external policy. The Gouzenko affair,[33] immediately following the war, introduced Canada to statecraft's demi-monde. Catalyzed by evidence of Soviet espionage, the Royal Canadian Mounted Police rapidly developed an intelligence, countersubversion, and counterespionage capacity. Unlike the Central Intelligence Agency or the KGB (Komitet Gosudarstvennoye Bezopastnosti), the Security Service was not an "offensive" intelligence agency: it conducted no external covert operations. But its domestic operations were both an outgrowth and an integral part of Canada's external alignments, and in the postwar period it grew in organizational complexity.[34] Similarly, the development assistance program inaugurated under the Colombo Plan in 1950 spawned a new bureau. At first, the foreign aid program was administered by the International Economic and Technical Co-operation Division of the Department of Trade and Commerce, created in 1951. IETCD's growth throughout the 1950s mirrored the increasing complexity of the development assistance program. In 1960, it was taken out of Trade and Commerce and given a separate existence as the External Aid Office. Headed by an official from DEA, the EAO was a "semi-autonomous" agency reporting to the secretary of state for external affairs. In 1968, the name, but not the relatively autonomous relationship within the bureaucracy, was changed. "Aid," with its overtones of charity, was replaced with "development assistance": the EAO was rechristened the Canadian International Development Agency (CIDA).[35]

By the end of the 1960s, a complex and philoprogenitive bureaucratic apparatus for the conduct of foreign policy had developed. In a generation, the bureaucratic landscape had changed dramatically. The departments responsible for the oldest external functions of the Canadian state—trade and immigration—had expanded their overseas operations. Old bureaus with new foreign policy mandates and agencies created to administer new external policy missions crowded the field. The foreign office itself had undergone a massive transformation.

Ironically, by the late 1960s, there were curious parallels with the early years. Numerous agencies were involved in the formulation and execution of different aspects of foreign policy. Not only did External Affairs, Trade and Commerce, and Manpower and Immigration each maintain a separate foreign service, but federal programs were also being delivered by numerous other departments represented abroad.[36] While a profusion of interdepartmental committees in Ottawa tried to coordinate the efforts of these agencies, and while DEA exercised a broad leadership role, in the main each department went about its business within its own policy sphere largely resistant to central coordinative tendencies.[37]

The Trudeau Years

The system was untidy, or such was the view of the new prime minister in 1968. The next 15 years would be dominated by what Denis Stairs has called "the relentless preoccupation of our governors with refining the administrative machine,"[38] as Trudeau and his advisers tinkered with the foreign policy bureaucracy in the hopes of eliminating the untidiness.

Throughout these years, the foreign policy bureaucracy was periodically assaulted by the political leadership's attempts to bring an end to what was seen as bureaucratic disorder bred by two decades of growth and diversification.

Denigration, 1968-70. The first assault was on the special position of External Affairs. DEA had always enjoyed a close relationship with the prime minister—partly because of the statutory proprietorship enjoyed by prime ministers until 1946, and partly because of the idiosyncratic pattern of recruitment to the ministry after 1946. Louis St. Laurent moved from the external affairs portfolio to the prime ministership, and Pearson was recruited from the senior echelons of the bureaucracy to be secretary of state for external affairs, and in 1963, to the prime ministership. In addition, the department saw itself—and indeed was seen—as an elite corps within the civil service, retaining its own examinations, recruitment practices, and training.[39] Both these factors had given External a primacy of place within the federal bureaucracy in the postwar period.

By contrast, Trudeau, in word and deed, left in little doubt his distance from External Affairs. In a television interview in January 1969, he was to give expression to a theme that would recur throughout his tenure: the notion that diplomacy is atavistic and that therefore the department which is responsible for diplomacy is, if not irrelevant, then certainly of secondary importance. "I think the whole concept of diplomacy today is a little bit outmoded," he said. "I believe it all goes back to the early days of the telegraph when you needed a dispatch to know what was happening in country A, whereas now most of the time you can read it in a good newspaper."[40] Such musings might be put down to inexperience; but eleven years later, Trudeau, by then the doyen of western statesmen, was to voice similar doubts about "a concept of diplomatic practice grounded in an age which has disappeared and which, in any case, predates Canadian experience. Traditional concepts of foreign service have diminished relevance [today]... I am not sure that our approach to foreign service adequately reflects this new era."[41] In the early years, the department had to contend with the consequences of such a view, particularly the trimming of its budget.[42]

Perhaps more important was the cabinet's "contemptuous rejection of its advice"[43] on a number of important policy issues. In 1968, the Trudeau government had accepted External's recommendations on what Canada's response should be to the Nigerian civil war—that Ottawa could, and should, do nothing about the secessionist state of Biafra. While this advice was grounded in the accepted notion of non-interference in the internal affairs of other states, it did not foresee that the public would be swayed more by Biafran starvation than adherence to the cardinal dictum of interstate relations. The government was, as a consequence, subjected to considerable domestic criticism. "Biafra was our Bay of Pigs," Thordarson would be told by one External Affairs official.[44] Thereafter, External's advice would be suspect; its recommendations would no longer receive the kind of easy acceptance by ministers so common in the postwar period. Recommendations on Canada's commitment to NATO and on the question of sovereignty in the Arctic went unheeded. The department's drafts for the white paper on foreign policy were rejected by the ministers on the grounds that they were "inadequate."[45]

Desuetude may be all the more unpleasant if the political leadership relies on alternative sources of information, expertise, and advice. Countervailing expertise on international affairs appeared in the Prime Minister's Office (PMO) and the Privy Council Office (PCO). In the process, roles and functions over which External Affairs had previously exercised a monopoly were usurped. Ivan Head, a former foreign service officer himself, was installed in the PMO, first as Trudeau's legislative assistant, then as special assistant on international affairs. He played an important role in such key foreign policy issues as the Nigerian civil war, the NATO decision of 1969, and policies towards the Arctic. Head also accompanied the prime minister on foreign trips, and often acted as Trudeau's personal representative to other leaders. (This was at the time when Henry Kissinger, Richard Nixon's national security adviser, tended to exclude the State Department from a role in the formulation of foreign policy. A comparison between Kissinger and Head was inevitable, even if unwarranted.[46]) In the Privy Council Office, Michael Pitfield, a long-time personal friend of Trudeau, was deputy secretary (plans). Pitfield exercised an influence over the foreign policy process that was to increase substantially with his appointment in 1975 as clerk of the Privy Council.[47]

The more overt denigration of External Affairs did not last for long, largely because Trudeau's initial interest in foreign policy waned considerably after the publication of the white paper in 1970. By 1971, Peter Dobell notes, "greater harmony" between cabinet and the department prevailed.[48] The prime minister had stopped making off-the-cuff comments about the diplomats, the budget had been restored, the department's policy recommendations were no longer greeted with distrust by cabinet, and the influence of the PMO—though not the PCO—was in slow decline. Harmony there might have been, but External's position had been completely changed. The denigration, however brief, is important, because it altered abruptly External's dominance in foreign policy and the close relationship with the political leadership it had enjoyed from its inception in 1909. It had become an ordinary department, as an in-house study concluded: "the Department of External Affairs does not have significantly closer links to the Prime Minister than other major agencies of the Government. ...[I]t has to compete for his attention in the quality of advice it offers and the effectiveness of the services it performs."[49]

New process, new players. The descent—such as it was—tended to be reinforced by changes in the policy process introduced by Trudeau and the rise of new bureaucratic players. No longer was External Affairs able to present its minister with an issue for a decision, with *its* recommendations, and secure quick agreement after the secretary of state for external affairs telephoned the prime minister. Issues were now subject to discussion by interdepartmental committees, to ensure that the domestic ramifications of external behaviour (and external ramifications of domestic interests) received full discussion. The decisions of state were subjected to careful and institutionalized coordination to ensure that foreign policy behaviour fell within the government's policy and spending priorities.[50] This change in process brought new players into the foreign policy-making process to challenge External's dominance.

As the foreign policy-making agenda became increasingly dominated by low concerns, those departments into whose bailiwicks such issues fell were encouraged to take a more active role in foreign policy formulation. Departments which had not participated in foreign policy formulation in any significant way in the past, save when External would consult their experts, found themselves closely engaged. The development of international bureaucratic capabilities followed naturally. Expanded "international" divisions sprouted up in departments like Agriculture; Communications; Consumer and Corporate Affairs; Energy, Mines and Resources; Environment; Fisheries and Oceans; Labour; National Revenue; Regional Economic Expansion; and Supply and Services.[51] Indeed, this bureaucratic growth was one of the reasons why these domestic departments played a prominent role in the formulation of foreign policy in the early 1970s. As they developed an expanded bureaucratic capacity in foreign affairs, there was an inevitable tendency to want to use their new bureaus by asserting their expertise in this area.

Likewise, greater authority over coordination of foreign policy was given to three central agencies: the Prime Minister's Office, the Privy Council Office, and the Treasury Board Secretariat.[52] Two of these agencies, the TBS and PCO, developed an institutionalized expertise that enabled them to become involved in foreign policy decision-making. The Defence, External and Cultural Affairs division of the Program Branch of TBS and the External Policy and Defence Secretariat of PCO were both active in the coordination of foreign policy in the 1970s. Within the PMO, there was no comparable institutionalization: the key figure was the prime minister's special assistant on international affairs.

The PCO also exercised its influence in another important way: its officials in the Machinery of Government Secretariat were not idle in the 1970s, as they and the clerk of the Privy Council tinkered with what was commonly seen as a machine in need of fine tuning. Between 1970 and 1983, the foreign policy bureaucracy had undergone four reorganizations.[53] Each time the terminology used was different, but the end result was the same: to resolve the inherent untidiness of the foreign policy system.

Integration, 1970. "To meet the challenges of the coming decades," the 1970 white paper declared grandly, "the Government needs a strong and flexible organization for carrying out its reshaped foreign policy... The Government has decided that there should be maximum integration in its foreign operations that will effectively contribute to the achievement of national objectives."[54] Some interpreted this as heralding the end of the foreign office and its absorption by the trade commissioners: "So the Department of External Affairs is to go the way of the army, navy and air force," James Eayrs wrote in 1970, "not into oblivion but into homogeneity."[55] But it was not to be, at least not then. Although a task force had recommended unification of the foreign service, the government opted for "integration."

The main mechanism chosen for this was a new Interdepartmental Committee on External Relations. The membership included key members of the senior civil service: the clerk of the Privy Council; the secretary of the Treasury Board; the president of CIDA; and the deputy ministers of Manpower and Immigration, Industry, Trade and Commerce, and Public Works. The under-secretary of state for external affairs was granted the chairmanship, but External Affairs was granted no authority to manage the external operations of the different departments. ICER, as it was known, was designed as a key coordinating mechanism for the external operations of four departments with very different, and not always reconcilable, missions. Part of its problem, Ahmed Dahamni notes, was that ICER "se situait à un niveau de décision administratif et non pas politique,"[56] and that it was responsible for making decisions more properly reserved for ministers in cabinet. But even as an administrative mechanism of coordination, it failed. Without clear lines of authority, the result was perhaps predictable: "infighting ensued (reportedly sometimes over trivial concerns), and then, as the protagonists grew weary of the fray, there was a wary truce."[57] By the mid-1970s, ICER had quietly been allowed to slip into disuse.[58]

Consolidation, 1980. After his re-election in 1980, Trudeau acted on a PCO proposal that the various foreign services operating abroad be consolidated under DEA. All the senior executive foreign service officers of External Affairs, of Industry, Trade and Commerce (IT&C), and of Employment and Immigration (E&I) were to be fully integrated into External Affairs: from this common pool were drawn the heads of posts for Canada's missions around the world. Those officers at lower levels were to be left within their departments. The idea behind this scheme was to allow posts abroad to operate more efficiently by streamlining the authority of the head of post. Instead of having to coordinate the activities of officials at a mission abroad who were receiving instructions from DEA, CIDA, IT&C, and E&I in Ottawa, the head of post would have authority over all staff, regardless of their function.[59]

Reorganization, 1982. Consolidation proved to be but a prelude. On 12 January 1982, the prime minister used his prerogative and restructured the machinery of government. All departments with an economic mandate were affected. A new "central agency," the Ministry of State for Economic and Regional Development, replaced the Ministry of State for Economic Development; the Departments of Regional Economic Expansion and Industry, Trade and Commerce were replaced by a Department of Regional Industrial Expansion. It was decided that the Department of External Affairs should be part of this new emphasis on economic development. A polite fiction was maintained: DEA, like IT&C, was no more. Instead, there would be a new "Department of External Affairs," comprising the "old" DEA, the trade side of IT&C, including those parts of the Trade Commissioner Service not included in consolidation, as well as the Export Development Corporation and the Canadian Commercial Corporation. Only CIDA was left unscathed, although officials hinted that its turn would come.

The internal organization of the new department reflected the tripartite ministerial structure discussed in the previous chapter. In addition to the under-secretary of state for external affairs, there was a deputy minister (foreign policy) and a deputy minister (international trade). The deputy ministers presided over two "wings" of the department. One was the foreign policy, or "political" side, quickly dubbed the "left wing," (ostensibly because of its location on the department's new organization chart). The other was the "trade wing." In the "centre," reporting directly to the under-secretary of state for external affairs, were the policy planning, management, and personnel bureaus. However, unlike most organizational structures, where the cat's cradle of linkages converge at the apex of the organization, the lines in the "new" DEA did not converge. There were in fact three deputy ministers: the under-secretary of state, the DM (foreign policy), and the DM (international trade). How this "management team," as they were wont to describe themselves, would interact with the management team of three ministers in cabinet was not altogether clear at the time the details were announced in April 1982. Parallel structures were created on both wings of the department. There would be a division, for example, charged with Asian affairs on the foreign policy side, while an Asian affairs division would operate on the trade side. How the two sides were to operate in the bosom of one unit was also unclear.

Another reorganization, 1983.   By November 1982, it was obvious that the reorganization was not working. The small and cohesive Trade Commissioner Service was complaining publicly of being "overwhelmed" by "antediluvian" bureaucratic procedures in External, and of being "deliberately torn down." External Affairs officials, faced with a massive influx of trade officials, lost traditional perks like private offices. A large organization was made even larger, leading to complaints about morale.[60] It was, in short, "a large bureaucratic mess."[61] In the winter of 1982-83, Trudeau rotated his senior mandarins. Pitfield was rewarded with a Senate seat. Gordon Osbaldeston moved from External to be the clerk of the Privy Council. External Affairs was given to Marcel Massé, who had been Clark's clerk, but who had been shuffled to the presidency of CIDA to make room for Pitfield in 1980. Massé moved quickly to reorganize External. In July 1983, the organizational structure introduced by Pitfield was scrapped. Gone were the team management approach and the parallel wings of the department. In their place was a more traditional way of organizing a foreign ministry, with five geographic branches—Asia and the Pacific, Africa and the Middle East, Latin America and the Caribbean, Europe, and the United States—each headed by an assistant under-secretary of state for external affairs reporting to the USSEA. Each branch was subdivided into at least three operating divisions (trade development, political relations, and programs).[62]

By the end of the Trudeau era in 1984, despite 15 years of restructuring the foreign policy system, there was little evidence that the foreign affairs bureaucracy was any more finely tuned, any more rational, or any more useful. The grail-like quest for the perfect bureaucratic machine had in the main been conducted by administrative theorists like Pitfield who lacked a broader appreciation of the purposes of diplomacy. Foreign policy under Trudeau was seen as little more than an engine for domestic economic development, and the foreign service as merely a vehicle for "program delivery." It had been fashionable to mock diplomats as unimportant, and the rituals inherited from aristocratic forebears at the Congress of Vienna as arcane. The ad hocery that is statecraft's essence was frequently decried, and External Affairs as the institutional repository of diplomatic skills was often dismissed as largely irrelevant.

Changes Under Mulroney

However, many of these changes were short-lived:[63] most of the obsession with elaborate management schemes for the foreign affairs bureaucracy went with Pitfield to the Senate. Even before Mulroney was elected in September 1984, the elaborate foreign policy machinery was allowed to fall into disuse by Turner.[64] In Mulroney's first year in office, that process accelerated, leading initially to what Harald von Riekhoff described as "quasi-anarchical" foreign policy management.[65] Since 1985, however, the coordinating role of the PCO has shifted considerably, the senior reaches of DEA have been reorganized, and a new under-secretary of state, James Taylor, a career diplomat, was appointed. Taylor, more concerned with the substance of foreign policy than with merely its management, assumed the more traditional role of the under-secretary—that of the government's chief adviser on foreign policy.[66]

The key change in the foreign policy bureaucracy introduced by Mulroney was the creation of a separate agency for the negotiation of the trade agreement with the United States. Usually, international negotiations on trade would be conducted by External Affairs, but the importance of this issue was such that the government decided to create an autonomous Trade Negotiations Office under Canada's chief negotiator, Simon Reisman, who reported directly to the minister for international trade. The TNO was staffed by officials seconded from other agencies of government like Regional Industrial Expansion, Finance, External Affairs, and the PCO, with some drawn from outside the bureaucracy.[67]

THE INFLUENCE OF THE BUREAUCRACY

How potent is the bureaucracy in the making of Canada's foreign policy? The question is underwritten by a key problem of contemporary governance: the degree to which the agencies created to advise political leaders, implement their policies, and administer their programs, have come to dominate the policy process at the expense of the autonomy of the elected representatives.

Ministers and Mandarins

One should begin by making a distinction between the *influence* of permanent officials and their *power* to transform their own policy preferences into state practice. "Civil servants do not make policy, all rumour to the contrary notwithstanding," Mitchell Sharp declared in 1958, "that is the prerogative of the elected representative of the people. But in this day and age civil servants do have a profound influence on the making of policy."[68] Such was the perspective of a former deputy minister of trade and commerce who had just resigned from the civil service. In 1963, Sharp returned to the Department of Trade and Commerce, this time as its minister; in 1968, he was appointed Trudeau's first secretary of state for external affairs. But his views did not change much. In 1981, no longer in cabinet (though as northern pipeline commissioner, still in government), Sharp reiterated his view that public servants "wield great influence," attributing this to his belief that "Government is, in fact, a specialized affair which cannot be run successfully by amateurs without professional advice and professional execution. With rare exceptions, in a parliamentary system politicians are amateurs in any field of government administration..." But, he added, it depended on the minister to assert the prerogative of authority that was explicitly recognized by both senior civil servants and ministers. "I understood the functions of my departmental advisers," he asserted. "I consulted them daily... I asked them questions and listened to their answers. Sometimes I agreed; and sometimes I didn't. In the end I made my decisions and they carried them out."[69]

However, that was not the experience of one of Sharp's successors. Flora MacDonald was Clark's secretary of state for external affairs in 1979-80. Following the defeat of the Clark government, MacDonald publicly criticized the senior bureaucrats in External Affairs. In a widely-publicized account,[70] she implied that bureaucrats manipulated "a new minister, just trying to find his or her way through the labyrinth of bureaucracy ... not only vulnerable but, indeed, almost without protection." She lamented the "entrapment devices" of her officials: "The unnecessarily long and numerous memos ... the crisis corridor-decisions I was confronted with— here is the situation (breathless pause), let us have your instructions." She complained of the "one-dimensional opinions put forward in memos," and of being deprived of "the luxury of multiple-choice options on matters of major import." It is easy to note that there are, of course, ways of coping with such ploys. As Sharp reminded MacDonald none too subtly in a rejoinder, "it was our own fault for letting the system get out of hand."[71]

But ministers will sometimes be unwilling or unable to propose policy directions for officialdom to oppose. The politicians may instead abdicate responsibility for policy formulation to the civil service and become, in Douglas Hartle's words, "toothless tigers who gum the policy proposals of the senior bureaucracy."[72] Professor Hartle, one must assume, knows whereof he speaks: in an earlier incarnation he was a deputy secretary in the Treasury Board Secretariat, and well acquainted with the relationships between ministers and their mandarins. The problem of allowing civil servants to formulate policy proposals that are then passed "on the distracted nod of ministers"[73] is by no means new. Mackenzie King was no toothless tiger, to be sure, but he too discovered the extent of his dependence for advice on Skelton when the latter died suddenly in 1941. "I have been tremendously at fault," King recorded in his diary after Skelton's funeral, "in not concentrating more on work and perhaps mastering more myself, and trusting too greatly to the outside aides... I was glad to have [Skelton] as a guide, but there are times when [his influence] was almost too strongly exerted to the extent of unduly influencing Government policy."[74]

But King found it hard to take his own advice. In the immediate postwar period, he grew more dubious about the appropriateness of expanding Canada's external relations. Yet his reservations remained hidden, recorded only in his diary. In December 1947, for example, he wrote that Pearson, then the under-secretary of state for external affairs, "with his youth and inexperience and influenced by the persuasion of others around him, had been anxious to have Canada's External Affairs figure prominently in world affairs and has really directed affairs from New York when he should have been in Ottawa, and without any real control by Ministers of the Crown...."[75] John W. Holmes, who was an official in DEA at the time, concludes that on the question of general foreign policy directions in the immediate postwar period, External Affairs was "on the whole, well out in front of government." But, Holmes adds, "it would be a mistake to see this as a simple struggle between utopian officials and unimaginative politicians... In this case, [the bureaucracy] provided an appropriate kind of leadership by formulating goals and schemes to attract the support of cabinet."[76] Is this an instance of public servants "unduly influencing Government policy," as King put it, or what MacDonald (quoting, with evident approval, Anthony Wedgewood Benn) calls "civil service policy" being foisted on unwitting politicians?

There no doubt exists a "civil service policy"—a view held by senior officials of both pressing problems and optimal solutions. These bureaucratic definitions of the "national interest" are shaped by individual and bureaucratic ideas about the public good, the requisites of organizational health, and the career ambitions of individual civil servants.[77] This view of what should be done, needless to say, may—or may not—be in accord with the individual or collective views of the elected representatives, who, quite understandably, have a different set of personal, political, and organizational imperatives. When there is a gap, ministers may impose their views; civil servants may only try to persuade their political overlords of the civil service view, for theirs is not to impose.

If civil servants do engage in persuasion, they have a number of advantages over ministers, the most important of which is a virtual monopoly over information and analysis of that information. In foreign policy, this is all the more significant, for most of the intelligence that informs bureaucratic recommendations on policy is kept shrouded by the state under the veils of secrecy—a practice usually justified as being necessary either for national security or for the success of interstate negotiations. As a result, politicians rarely have alternative sources of analysis that can claim to be as authoritative as the bureaucracy's. To be sure, some have tried. Flora MacDonald, for example, sought to establish "a better equilibrium between ministers and mandarins" by seeking sources of advice from outside government. But if these outside sources do not have access to both the information and expertise of the bureaucracy, they are ill-equipped to compete. The results can be embarrassing. Clark's decision to move the Canadian embassy in Israel from Tel Aviv to Jerusalem was in large part predicated on the analysis tendered by a Toronto lawyer who confidently predicted that while the Arab states would protest the move vigorously, they would take no substantive action against Canada.[78]

However, these sources of bureaucratic power must be balanced against the perceptions of individual bureaucrats who recognize the formal structure of political authority. Not only does this leaven what would otherwise develop into undisguised abuses of authority, but it also allows effective ministers to exercise prerogatives that are properly theirs.[79] From this perspective, it is clear that the consensus in DEA on the most appropriate policy for Canada in the postwar period was an example of civil service policy. It is also clear that senior officials worked hard to secure ministerial approval for what was in essence "their" policy. Yet there is no indication that the officials who spawned those policies—men like Pearson, Norman Robertson, Hume Wrong, or Escott Reid—did not recognize explicitly that they might propose, but ministers dispose. The prime minister himself did have some doubts on this score. To his diary, King lamented "the idea which has been growing up in E.A. [External Affairs] that these advisers are the men who are to settle everything and Ministers or P.M.'s only to be second."[80] But the plaints of ministers from King to MacDonald notwithstanding, there is little direct evidence that the senior members of the foreign affairs bureaucracy have ever considered themselves "statesman in disguise."[81]

Three Levels of "Policy"

One of the problems in the debate over the influence of the public service on the making of foreign policy is that the English language treats the word "policy" with uncharacteristic imprecision. The process of setting general objectives (security from external aggression, for example, or achieving greater economic independence); the general means of realizing those ends (joining an alliance or diversifying trade); and specific and concrete actions (the allocation of military resources to an alliance or the dispatching of trade missions)—all are characterized by the word policy. But we are referring to three very different types, or levels, of policy-making. The most general level connotes the ultimate *long-range goals* of the state. The next level refers to those *strategies* chosen to achieve long-range ends. At the lowest level of generality, there are the concrete, specific *tactics* employed by a state to implement its strategies. If one differentiates between the various levels of policy in such a fashion—as the Chinese language does[82]—it is possible to come somewhat closer to assessing the problem of bureaucratic power and influence over foreign policy-making in Canada. Using these distinctions, for example, we can see that the statement of policy in the 1970 white paper was intended to lay out long-term objectives, one being an increase in economic independence. The 1972 Third Option policy, by contrast, was cast at a different level. The Third Option, which entailed decreasing reliance on trade with the United States by restructuring the economy and increasing economic interaction with the rest of the industrialized world, was a general means of achieving that goal of economic independence. The framework agreements, signed with Japan and with the European Communities in 1976, were also policy, but at the tactical level—seeking, as those agreements did, to give expression to both the Third Option and, ultimately, to the long-term goals laid out by the government in 1970.

The potential for bureaucratic influence is least at the most general level of policy-making for, in theory at least, it falls to the political leadership to decide general objectives. This is a responsibility recognized by all players in the policy game. However, political leaders have not been prone to lay out general, long-term objectives in foreign policy. To be sure, St. Laurent provided an outline of objectives in the Gray Lecture in 1947; and the Mulroney government issued a green paper on foreign policy and a detailed response to a parliamentary report on Canada's international relations in 1986.[83] But only once since Canada acquired an independent personality in world politics has a government in Ottawa felt compelled to canonize its foreign policy objectives in a white paper.

The Trudeau government's *Foreign Policy for Canadians*, published in 1970, tried to make explicit Canada's objectives in international affairs: to safeguard sovereignty; to promote economic growth; to foster social justice; to ensure a harmonious natural environment; to work for peace and security; and to achieve an improved quality of life. The bureaucracy's impact on the setting of these objectives was minimal, as Bruce Thordarson makes clear in his account of the making of the white paper.[84] The cabinet, when presented with draft statements prepared by the bureaucracy, rejected their formulations. DEA was instructed to return with a statement of priorities that more closely reflected the wishes of cabinet. So External

Affairs had an official cull from Trudeau's writings and speeches an indication of what he might want as long-term objectives for foreign policy. The final product of this exercise—the main booklet of the multi-coloured white paper—might have been drafted by the civil service but it bore the clear stamp of Trudeau's own wishes.

It is one thing for ministers to define long-term aims and priorities for the state in world politics, and to ensure that *Foreign Policy for Canadians* prominently adorned desks of diplomats from Beijing to Buenos Aires and points between. It is another thing entirely to develop an appropriate statecraft to give meaning to what otherwise remain sleek phrases, devoid of content. If the bureaucracy failed to have an impact on the priorities exercise of 1970, its influence was brought to bear on the creation of policy at lower levels. In 1972, the SSEA, Mitchell Sharp, unveiled the means by which the government was going to achieve the goals laid down in 1970. Canada would revamp its relationship with the United States, diversify its economic relations, and thus (it was hoped) lessen the dependence on the United States.[85] By all accounts, the Third Option was very much the handiwork of External Affairs, which, much chastened by cabinet's rejection of its advice and the prime minister's denigration of its role, had worked to devise a way to give effect to these long-term aims. Particularly after the Nixon "shocks" of 1971, the Department, according to one senior official, "set about in a serious and unprecedented way to rethink our relationship with the Americans."

This example is at once illustrative and unrevealing. On the one hand, it demonstrates that determined ministers may impose their views at this highest level of policy-making, and in essence force the bureaucracy to accept policy positions which are unpalatable. It also demonstrates that at the level of broad strategy, ministers must (and do) enlist the expertise of their bureaus if they wish to give concrete expression to general aims, affording the civil service considerably more influence at this level. On the other hand, the 1970 white paper and the 1972 options paper represent an aberration in the way Canadian governments normally formulate policy; one should therfore draw lessons from this case with some care. The norm has been to avoid the grand Cartesian schema as a basis for statecraft, to view clearly specified goals with a decidedly jaundiced eye. "I see policy," Charles Ritchie, a senior diplomat, confided to his diary, "as the tortuous approach to an ill-defined objective. All-out decisions, unqualified statements, irreconcilable antagonisms are foreign to my nature and to my training. In these ways I reflect my political masters, the inheritors of Mackenzie King...."[86] An inheritor of a different sort was more blunt. "As a general rule," Geoffrey Pearson wrote in 1977, "governments do not *plan* foreign policy." Lester Pearson's son had just finished a stint as director of the Policy Analysis Group, the division of External Affairs charged with developing long term policy objectives.[87] "Planning," the younger Pearson continued, "suggests clear objectives, identifiable means of reaching them, and some control of the environment in which one is operating. These conditions are not often present in world politics."[88]

That the grand designs of the early 1970s were quietly laid to rest shortly thereafter is blunt testimony to the problems inherent in trying to plan a small state's foreign policy in a thoroughly rational fashion. It also helps explain why both ministers and their civil servants are prone to concentrate on the day-to-day problems of Canadian diplomacy—"policy" at the lowest level. How will the delegation vote on a resolution before the UN General Assembly? How should a *note verbale* which will be delivered to the Soviet foreign ministry be worded? Should spare parts manufactured by a firm in Winnipeg be exempted from an arms embargo being contemplated against a state divided by civil war? What kinds of allocations should be made for a rural development scheme in the Sahel? Such are the "little" decisions of the foreign policy-maker. Put forward to ministers, and often approved on their "distracted nod," these are essentially bureaucratic decisions in the sense that officials, armed with the authority bestowed by expertise, can define tactics on behalf of political leaders who are constrained by their own human limitations. The minister who would try to personally supervise every aspect of the vast range of foreign relations, or who would try to monitor all the actions that are taken daily on Canada's behalf in the international system, would fast become swamped in a heavy sea of dispatches, telexes, interdepartmental memoranda, and cabinet briefing books. It is at this level that the bureaucracy is likely to exert the most influence on the process. Expertise, access to information, and the ability to draw on the accumulated organizational "wisdom" of the executive departments makes the bureaucrat an obvious source of advice for the minister who, having defined an end, must seek the means to achieve it. The dependence of ministers on their civil servants for advice on the essentially technical tactics of statecraft provides those who tender that advice with potent influence.

CONCLUSION

The agencies which have grown over the course of the twentieth century to provide advice to the political leadership on international affairs have also come to exert an increasing influence on the foreign policy process. But, it has been argued in this chapter, the influence of bureaucrats is least evident at the highest level of policy: the setting of general objectives for the state in international affairs. This is consistent with the image developed by Aberbach, Putnam, and Rockman of the relations between bureaucrats and politicians in Western democracies.[89] Their "energy/equilibrium image" suggests that in a division of political labour between bureaucrats and elected politicians, the setting of broad objectives and the articulating of ideals is seen by both groups as the appropriate responsibility of politicians.

It has been argued here that bureaucratic influence is most pronounced at the lowest, or tactical, level of foreign policy-making. This, however, has important ramifications for any general conclusions about the influence of the bureaucracy for Canadian foreign policy is concerned largely with short-term considerations, with the longer-term objectives only rarely considered. This considerably enhances the capacity of the bureaucracy to have its policy preferences manifested in foreign policy.

NOTES

1   See the discussion in V. Seymour Wilson, *Canadian Public Policy and Administration* (Toronto: McGraw-Hill Ryerson, 1981), ch. 4.

2   John J. Kirton, "Foreign policy decision-making in the Trudeau government: promise and performance," *International Journal* 33 (Spring 1978), 293-94.

3   James Eayrs, "Canada: the Department of External Affairs," in Zara Steiner, ed., *The Times Survey of Foreign Ministries of the World* (London: Times Books, 1982), 96.

4   Trudeau, in his letter of instruction to Pamela McDougall establishing the Royal Commission on Conditions of Foreign Service, 28 August 1980: reprinted in Canada, Royal Commission on Conditions of Foreign Service, *Report* (Ottawa, 1981), viii.

5   John W. Holmes, *Canada: A Middle-Aged Power* (Toronto: McClelland and Stewart Limited, 1976), 45.

6   G.P. de T. Glazebrook, *A History of Canadian External Relations*, rev. ed., vol. 1: *The Formative Years to 1914* (Toronto: McClelland and Stewart Limited, 1966), 85.

7   Quoted in H. Gordon Skilling, *Canadian Representation Abroad: From Agency to Embassy* (Toronto: Ryerson, 1945), 186.

8   Trade negotiations "came to be direct in all but form, and the Canadians associated in them corresponded directly with the prime minister." Glazebrook, *Canadian External Relations*, vol. 1, 201.

9   The offices of "commercial agents"—they were renamed trade commissioners in 1907—were located in Sydney, Capetown, Mexico City, Yokohama, and a number of European and American cities by the turn of the century. Royal Commission on Conditions of Foreign Service, *Report*, table FST-2, 95-105; also O. Mary Hill, *Canada's Salesman to the World: The Department of Trade and Commerce, 1892-1939* (Montreal: McGill- Queen's, 1977).

10   Eayrs, "Canada: External Affairs," 96.

11 James Eayrs, "The origins of Canada's Department of External Affairs," *Canadian Journal of Economics and Political Science* 25 (May 1959), 114-5.

12 C.P. Stacey, *Canada and the Age of Conflict: A History of Canadian External Policies*, vol. 1: *1867-1921* (Toronto: Macmillan of Canada, 1977), 30-1 and 45.

13 Eayrs, "Origins of External Affairs," 114-5, for details.

14 Glazebrook, *Canadian External Relations*, vol. 1., 84.

15 Canada, Department of External Affairs, *Documents on Canadian External Relations*, vol. 1: *1909-1918* (Ottawa, 1967), 18.

16 Much to the chagrin of officials in Ottawa: Mackenzie King, at the time a senior civil servant, confided to his diary that "The truth is His Ex. is getting into too many things"; Sir Wilfrid Laurier "wished Earl Grey would mind his own business." Eayrs, "Origins of External Affairs," 116, *fn*. 22.

17 Quoted in *ibid.*, 117.

18 Both Australia and New Zealand decided in the early 1970s to replace "External" with "Foreign" in the names of their foreign ministries. In Canada the designation stuck—long after the achievement of independence in foreign policy.

19 Eayrs, "Origins of External Affairs," 119-21; also *Documents on Canadian External Relations*, vol. 1, 12.

20 James Eayrs, *The Art of the Possible: Government and Foreign Policy in Canada* (Toronto: University of Toronto Press, 1961), 66.

21 J.L. Granatstein, *A Man of Influence: Norman A. Robertson and Canadian Statecraft, 1929-68* (Toronto: Deneau Publishers, 1981), 33.

22 Lord Garner, "Comments on Report on Conditions of Foreign Service," *International Journal* 37 (Summer 1982), 390. Another British diplomat, Sir William Hayter, called External Affairs "one of the highest-powered foreign services in the modern world." Quoted in Eayrs, "Canada: External Affairs," 97.

23 Hugh L. Keenleyside, *Memoirs of Hugh L. Keenleyside*, vol. 1: *Hammer the Golden Day* (Toronto: McClelland and Stewart, 1981), 233.

24 Stacey, *Age of Conflict*, vol. 1, 311-17; Skilling, *Canadian Representation Abroad*, ch. 5, 236-37.

25 *Documents on Canadian External Relations*, vol. 6: *1936-1939*, John A. Munro, ed. (Ottawa, 1972); *ibid.*, vol. 7: *1939-1941, Part 1*, David R. Murray, ed. (Ottawa, 1974); also Skilling, *Canadian Representation Abroad*, 249-54.

26 John English, "The professional diplomat in Canada," paper presented to Conference on Professionalization, University of Western Ontario, March 1981, tables A and B, 11-12.

27 Political I was responsible for international organizations; Political II for the Commonwealth, Europe, Africa, and the Middle East; and Political III for the United States, Latin America, and the Far East.

28 Department of External Affairs, *Annual Report, 1971* (Ottawa 1972), organization chart, 134.

29 Glen Williams, *Not For Export: Towards a Political Economy of Canada's Arrested Industrialization* (Toronto: McClelland and Stewart Limited, 1983), 157-61.

30 Freda Hawkins, *Canada and Immigration: Public Policy and Public Concern* (Montreal: McGill-Queen's University Press, 1972), 237-65.

31 James Eayrs, *In Defence of Canada*, vol. 1: *From the Great War to the Great Depression* (Toronto: University of Toronto Press, 1964), vol. 2: *Appeasement and Rearment* (Toronto: University of Toronto Press, 1965); postwar roles are discussed in vol. 3: *Peacemaking and Deterrence* (Toronto: University of Toronto Press, 1972) and vol. 4: *Growing Up Allied* (Toronto: University of Toronto Press, 1980).

32 A.F.W. Plumptre, *Three Decades of Decision: Canada and the World Monetary System, 1944-1975* (Toronto: McClelland and Stewart, 1977).

33 In 1945, Igor Gouzenko, a cypher clerk at the Soviet embassy in Ottawa, defected, bringing with him evidence of the existence of large-scale espionage activities directed at Canada's atomic research. J.W. Pickersgill and D.F. Forster, *The Mackenzie King Record*, vol. 3: *1945-1946* (Toronto: University of Toronto Press, 1970), ch. 2; Robert Bothwell and J.L. Granatstein, eds., *The Gouzenko Transcripts: The Evidence Presented to the Kellock-Taschereau Royal Commission of 1946* (Ottawa: Deneau, 1982).

34 It eventually evolved into a separate agency, the Canadian Security and Intelligence Service. Canada, Commission of Inquiry Concerning Certain Activities of the Royal Canadian Mounted Police, *Second Report*, vol. 1: *Freedom and Security under the Law* (Ottawa, August, 1981), 62-63; John Sawatsky, *Men in the Shadows: The RCMP Security Service* (Toronto: Doubleday Canada, 1980).

35 For a survey of the administrative apparatus down to the mid-1960s, see Keith Spicer, *A Samaritan State? External Aid in Canada's Foreign Policy* (Toronto: University of Toronto Press, 1966), 95*ff*.

36 In 1969, 1,030 officials from 19 federal agencies served in missions abroad; this number does not include Canadian Armed Forces personnel serving in Europe or the United States. Peter C. Dobell, "The management of a foreign policy for Canadians," *International Journal* 26 (Winter 1970-1), 206.

37 Michael D. Henderson, "La gestion des politiques internationales du gouvernement fédéral," in Paul Painchaud, ed., *Le Canada et le Québec sur la scène internationale* (Québec: Presses de l'Université du Québec, 1977), 86-87.

38 Denis Stairs, "The political culture of Canadian foreign policy," *Canadian Journal of Political Science* 15 (December 1982), 688.

39 For one view of DEA's self-perception during the 1950s, see Marcel Cadieux, *The Canadian Diplomat*, Archibald Day, trans. (Toronto: University of Toronto Press, 1963).

40 Quoted in Dobell, "Management of foreign policy," 202; also Bruce Thordarson, *Trudeau and Foreign Policy: A Study in Decision-Making* (Toronto: Oxford University Press, 1972), 91-92.

41 Trudeau to Pamela McDougall, 28 August 1980; see above *fn.* 4.

42 DEA's budget was kept constant, forcing the closure of missions, the redeployment of 74 diplomats, and the transfer, demotion, premature retirement, and dismissal of others. Peyton Lyon, "A review of the review," *Journal of Canadian Studies* 5 (May 1970), 34-47.

43 Eayrs, "Canada: External Affairs," 108.

44 Thordarson, *Trudeau and Foreign Policy*, 150, *fn.* 59. For a good examination of the Biafra issue, see Donald Barry, "Interest groups and the foreign policy process: the case of Biafra," in A. Paul Pross, ed., *Pressure Group Behaviour in Canadian Politics* (Toronto: McGraw-Hill Ryerson Limited, 1975), 118-23, 134-43.

45 Thordarson, *Trudeau and Foreign Policy*, ch. 5 and 177; Kirton, "Foreign policy decision-making," 291.

46 For example, in late 1972 and January 1973, two sets of negotiations were being conducted over participation in the international supervisory commission for Vietnam: Mitchell Sharp, the secretary of state for external affairs, was talking with William Rogers, the United States secretary of state, while Head and Kissinger held their own negotiations: see Charles Taylor, *Snow Job: Canada, the United States and Vietnam, 1954-1973* (Toronto: House of Anansi Press, 1974), 149-50.

47 Christina McCall-Newman, "Michael Pitfield and the politics of mismanagement," *Saturday Night* (October 1982), 24-44.

48 Peter C. Dobell, *Canada's Search for New Roles: Foreign Policy in the Trudeau Era* (Toronto: Oxford University Press, 1972), 21.

49 A.S. McGill, *The Role of the Department of External Affairs in the Government of Canada* (Ottawa, June 1976), vol. 3, 42.

50 G. Bruce Doern and Richard W. Phidd, *Canadian Public Policy: Ideas, Structure, Process* (Toronto: Methuen, 1983), 175-81.

51 Dewitt and Kirton, *Canada as a Principal Power*, 215-16.

52 Colin Campbell and George Szablowski, *The Superbureaucrats: Structure and Behaviour in Central Agencies* (Toronto: Macmillan of Canada, 1979), ch. 2 and 3.

53 "We trained hard, but it seemed that every time we were beginning to form up into teams, we would be reorganized. I was to learn that later in life we tend to meet any new situation by reorganizing, and a wonderful method it can be for creating the illusion of progress while producing confusion, inefficiency and demoralization." Thus did Petronius Arbiter, a Roman poet and novelist, assess reorganizations 1900 years ago. The quotation enjoyed wide circulation in External Affairs, or so we are told by the under-secretary whose task it was to oversee the 1982 reorganization. Gordon Osbaldeston, "Reorganizing Canada's Department of External Affairs," *International Journal* 37 (Summer 1982), 464-65. Although Osbaldeston was quick to decry the "latent cynicism" of those to whom this quotation appealed, his officials might be forgiven a measure of wry amusement at the durability of organizational behaviour.

54 Canada, Secretary of State for External Affairs, *Foreign Policy for Canadians* (Ottawa, 1970), main booklet, 39.

55 James Eayrs, *Diplomacy and its Discontents* (Toronto: University of Toronto Press, 1971), 39.

56 Ahmed Dahamni, "Quelques aspects du management du Ministère des Affaires extérieures du Canada," *Canadian Public Administration* 18 (Summer 1975), 184.

57 Eayrs, "Canada: External Affairs," 105.

58 W.M. Dobell, "Interdepartmental management in External Affairs," *Canadian Public Administration* 21 (Spring 1978), 83-102.

59 Jack Maybee, "Foreign service consolidation," *International Perspectives* (July/August 1980), 17-20.

60 James Rusk, "Straightening out merger mess first major challenge for Massé," *The Globe and Mail*, 3 November 1982, 9.

61 James Rusk, "New face on External gets lifted again," *The Globe and Mail*, 12 July 1983, 10.

62 *Ibid.*

63 Although, as Denis Stairs has so cogently put it, the effects of the Trudeau years may be longer term: "an older generation of mandarins, not a few of them reared and schooled in diplomacy, has lost its place, and with it the power to educate its successors." Stairs, "Political culture of Canadian foreign policy," 690.

64 John Kirton, "Managing Canadian foreign policy," in Brian W. Tomlin and Maureen Molot, eds., *Canada Among Nations—1984: A Time of Transition* (Toronto: James Lorimer, 1985), 19-21.

65 Harald von Riekhoff, "The structure of foreign policy decision making and management," in Brian W. Tomlin and Maureen Appel Molot, eds., *Canada Among Nations—1986: Talking Trade* (Toronto: James Lorimer, 1987), 29; for a description of the first year, see John Kirton, "The foreign policy decision process," in *Canada Among Nations—1985: The Conservative Agenda* (Toronto: James Lorimer, 1986), 25-45.

66 See von Riekhoff, "Decision making and management," 23.

67 *Ibid.*, 27-29; also David Leyton-Brown, "The political economy of Canada-U.S. relations," in Tomlin and Molot, eds., *Canada Among Nations —1986*, 149-68.

68 Mitchell Sharp, "Civil service recollections," *Ottawa Journal*, 12 and 13 December 1958, quoted in John Porter, *The Vertical Mosaic: An Analysis of Social Class and Power in Canada* (Toronto: University of Toronto Press, 1965), 427-28.

69 Sharp, "The role of the mandarins," *Policy Options* (May/June 1981), 43.

70 She delivered the initial address to the annual meetings of the Canadian Political Science Association in June 1980; revised versions were published in *Policy Options* and *The Globe and Mail*: see MacDonald, "Cutting through the chains," *The Globe and Mail*, 7 November 1980, 7.

71 Sharp, "Role of mandarins," 44.

72 Douglas G. Hartle, "Techniques and processes of administration," *Canadian Public Administration* 19 (Spring 1976), 32.

73 Robert Lewis, "Ottawa's power brokers," *Maclean's*, 24 May 1982, 20.

74 Quoted in Porter, *Vertical Mosaic*, 429.

75 J.W. Pickersgill and D.F. Forster, *The Mackenzie King Record*, vol. 4: *1947-1948* (Toronto: University of Toronto Press, 1970), 135-36.

76 John W. Holmes, *The Shaping of Peace: Canada and the Search for World Order, 1943-1957*, vol. 1 (Toronto: University of Toronto Press, 1979), 297-98.

77 For a discussion, see Kim Richard Nossal, "Allison through the (Ottawa) looking glass: bureaucratic politics and foreign policy in a parliamentary system," *Canadian Public Administration* 22 (Winter 1979), 610-26.

78 Jeffrey Simpson, *Discipline of Power: The Conservative Interlude and the Liberal Restoration* (Toronto: Personal Library, 1980), 145-59.

79 For an argument about the importance of this factor, see Michael M. Atkinson and Kim Richard Nossal, "Bureaucratic politics and the new fighter aircraft decisions," *Canadian Public Administration* 24 (Winter 1981).

80 Quoted in Granatstein, *Man of Influence*, 107-108.

81 Such was one contemporary characterization of senior officials in nineteenth-century Britain: quoted in Eayrs, *Art of the Possible*, 33.

82 Chinese differentiates between these levels: *lu xien*, or "line" (as in "the party line"), connotes the ultimate long-range goals of the state. *Feng zhen*, or "strategy" (the two Chinese characters literally mean "direction" and "pointing towards") are the general directions taken to achieve long-range objectives. *Zheng che*, or "political strategems," are the concrete and specific actions taken within the framework of *feng zhen*. See Franz Schurmann, *The Logic of World Power* (Toronto and New York: Pantheon, 1974), 18.

83 Excerpts from the Gray Lecture and the 1985 green paper are reprinted in J.L. Granatstein, ed., *Canadian Foreign Policy: Historical Readings* (Toronto: Copp Clark Pitman, 1986). Secretary of State for External Affairs, *Canada's International Relations: Response of the Government of Canada to the Report of the Special Joint Committee of the Senate and the House of Commons* (Ottawa, December 1986).

84 Thordarson, *Trudeau and Foreign Policy*, 167*ff*.

85 Secretary of State for External Affairs, "Canada-U.S. relations: options for the future," *International Perspectives* (Special issue, Autumn 1972).

86 Charles Ritchie, *Diplomatic Passport: More Undiplomatic Diaries, 1946-1962* (Toronto: Macmillan, 1981), 56.

87 Daniel Madar and Denis Stairs, "Alone on Killer's Row: the Policy Analysis Group and the Department of External Affairs," *International Journal* 32 (Autumn 1977), 727*ff*.

88 G.A.H. Pearson, "Order out of chaos? Some reflections on foreign-policy planning in Canada," *International Journal* 32 (Autumn 1977), 756.

89 Different "images" of the relations between bureaucrats and politicians are outlined in Joel D. Aberbach, Robert D. Putnam and Bert A. Rockman, *Bureaucrats and Politicians in Western Bureaucracies* (Cambridge: Harvard University Press, 1981), 1-23 and 238-62.

CHAPTER EIGHT

The Legislature

INTRODUCTION

In Canada, as in most parliamentary systems, control over the formulation and implementation of foreign policy remains vested firmly in the hands of the political executive in cabinet. Although responsible to Parliament, ministers of the Crown have, by convention and practice, relegated to the legislature a distinctly inferior role in the making of external policy. Decisions which set the course of Canada's involvement in world affairs are not made by the House of Commons or the Senate, as institutions, but by those members of Parliament who sit in cabinet. Unlike foreign policy-making in the United States, where constitutional authority over foreign policy-making is shared by the executive and legislative branches of government operating in separate institutions, and where decisions of the legislature can and do affect United States foreign policy,[1] in Canada the fusion of the executive and the legislature embodied in cabinet government has eliminated legislative foreign policy decision-making.

There are two reasons for this. First, the very nature of foreign policy precludes legislative decision-making. A legislature lacks the resources to conduct foreign policy. The interaction of a state in the international system demands an ability to respond quickly and decisively to external events and pressures on a wide range of issues; to participate in international negotiations, a process that requires both secrecy and flexibility; and to forge new policy initiatives, often within severe time constraints. A bicameral legislature, cleaved by party lines and with a membership numbering nearly 400, is simply not organized to perform these functions on behalf of the state. Even with its wide-ranging constitutional authority, the United States Congress periodically discovers its limitations in the making of American foreign policy. Similarly, the nature of foreign policy is such that it provides members of Parliament with only rare opportunities to indulge in the task for which legislators are most noted: law-making. Legislation rarely crowds a state's foreign policy agenda, though there are some notable exceptions. These are mainly in the economic, environmental, and resource issue areas, such as the Arctic Waters Pollution Prevention bill in 1970,[2] or Bill C-130, the legislation introduced in 1988 to implement the free trade agreement with the United States.

The second reason for the lack of a legislative role in foreign policy decision-making is that the political executive in Canada has been unwilling to grant Parliament any decision-making role, and Canadian legislators have proved unwilling to demand any. When Paul Martin, Lester Pearson's secretary of state for external affairs, wrote in 1969 that legislators "can discuss, but they cannot make, foreign policy,"[3] he was underscoring a half-century of executive dominance over the policy-making process.

It is true that prime ministers have been prone to proclaim that, on matters of foreign policy, Parliament would make the decisions. But rarely have they meant it. Mackenzie King used Sir Wilfrid Laurier's famous formula, "Parliament will decide,"[4] over the Chanak crisis of 1922, but it was proposed as an expedient way of deflecting an imperial request for Canadian troops by a prime minister in a precarious political position in cabinet.[5] Neither King nor R.B. Bennett, the Conservative prime minister from 1930 to 1935, was at all disposed to allow Parliament to decide on the foreign policy issues of the interwar period, however convenient at times they might have found the refuge afforded by Sir Wilfrid's formulation.

Postwar prime ministers have carried forward this tradition, although they have discarded the disingenuousness of the "Parliament will decide" formula. Despite the increased complexity and the growing range of foreign policy issues in the four decades since the Second World War, cabinets have jealously guarded the prerogative to decide on these matters. Parliament, as a result, has played virtually no part in the decision-making process that fashions external policies.

Members of Parliament who are not ministers of the Crown have not been inclined to challenge the executive's pre-eminence in foreign policy. We have not seen emerge in Canada the kind of feisty behaviour that has marked the conduct of backbenchers at Westminster on foreign policy issues.[6] The front benches of the opposition parties, for their part, recognize not only the constraints on decision-making authority that spring from the traditions of responsible government, but also the subsidiary location of foreign policy issues in the context of national politics. As a result, there has been little concerted effort to usurp the longstanding prerogatives of the executive in the formulation and implementation of external policy.

It is because the locus of foreign policy decision-making authority rests with the cabinet that Parliament must more properly be considered an "input mechanism"—a means by which pressure may be brought to bear on the policy process.[7] If Parliament is to shape foreign policy, James Eayrs has noted, it must do so by influencing the decision-makers.[8] Such influence is exerted both formally and informally. Members try to exert influence formally by interrogation and discussion in three fora: on the floor of the Senate or the Commons; in committees of both houses; or in party caucuses. Informally, members can make representations to ministers or bureaucrats, albeit privately and out of the glare of the public eye.

THE LOCI OF INFLUENCE

The Senate

The upper house of Canada's Parliament is often characterized as a final resting place for party faithful, troublesome or ineffectual cabinet ministers, or MPs who have outlived their usefulness on the government backbench. The prime minister is able to lure appointments by offering a substantial indemnity of well over $60,000 annually and a guarantee of tenure until the age of 75 to this political pasture where one's dotage can be spent comfortably. Given the manipulation of senatorial appointments by every prime minister from Macdonald to Mulroney, such a characterization of the Senate as the country's foremost pork barrel is neither unfair nor unwarrantedly cynical.

This is certainly not what was intended by the Fathers of Confederation. The Senate was originally designed to provide each of Canada's regions with representation in federal institutions. It was also intended to restrain whatever impetuousness might have been displayed by representatives in the Commons. The Senate, declared Sir James Lougheed, who was called to the Red Chamber in 1889, "is the bulwark against the clamour and caprice of the mob," or such was the intention.[9] But neither the representative nor the legislative review functions have evolved as envisioned by those who framed the British North America Act. Nor has the Senate secured a prominent place in the political arena. Since 1913, when the Liberal majority in the upper house killed the naval bill of Robert Borden's Conservative government, the Senate has left no significant mark on foreign policy. This lack of influence was to lead Sir George Foster, Borden's minister of trade and commerce who had represented Canada at the Versailles peace conference, to remark in 1921 when he had gone to his senatorial reward: "I have today signed my warrant of political death.... How colourless the Senate—the entering gate to coming extinction."[10]

In 1988, John Turner, leader of the Liberal opposition, sought to resurrect this institution's powers. In July, in an attempt to force a general election, he instructed the Liberal majority in the Senate, most of them appointed by Pierre Trudeau, to vote against Bill C-130, the free trade legislation. But the political legitimacy of the Senate as a "representative" institution has been completely eroded by its use as an instrument for patronage and Turner's attempt to use the Senate was widely denounced, by both supporters and opponents of the free trade agreement.[11]

However, to dismiss the Senate as harmless or ineffectual because of how its members achieved their seats would be to ignore the role it does play in the policy process in general and the foreign policy process in particular. Colin Campbell has characterized senators as either "business reviewers" or "social investigators" to underscore the evolution of the policy and investigatory roles of the upper chamber since 1960. In the process of Senate review of legislation dealing with financial or business matters, Campbell found that corporations and business groups would press for amendments more conducive to their interests: "Senators play crucial roles in the process. In a very real sense they are the lobby from within. They bargain and negotiate on business' behalf for amendments which are essential for a favourable financial and commercial climate."[12]

However, the influence of the business reviewers is offset by those senators who have initiated studies into aspects of social policy and whose recommendations have often been incorporated into government policy.[13] On foreign policy, the Senate has been as active but has been able to demonstrate little capability to affect the course of government policy. The main activity on international questions has not occurred on the floor of the Senate, where debate is usually perfunctory and question period desultory at best.[14] Not even when Senator Martial Asselin was appointed minister of state in charge of the Canadian International Development Agency and francophone adviser to Flora MacDonald in the Clark government of 1979-80 did discussion of foreign affairs improve in the upper house.

Rather, senators with international interests participate in the work of the Senate's Standing Committee on Foreign Affairs. Like its special committee counterparts, the Foreign Affairs committee has involved itself predominantly in investigatory work. Trudeau's decision in 1968 to conduct an extensive review of foreign policy provided the committee with the impetus to undertake its own review of selected aspects of external policy. Since 1969, the committee has conducted four area studies of Canadian foreign relations: the Caribbean (1969-70), the Pacific (1970-72), the European Communities (1969-70), and the United States (1974-82).[15] In the early 1980s, the committee began a series of studies of defence questions that resulted in reports on manpower and maritime defence.[16] In 1984, a special Senate committee on defence examined air defences.[17]

(Senators were also members of a special joint committee of Parliament that examined Canada's international relations in 1985 and 1986.)

The committee's reports during this period rarely took direct issue with existing policy, but recommended refinements and offered suggestions about how best to achieve the ends embraced by the government. The committee's recommendations often reflected the dichotomy within the Senate between business reviewers and social investigators, since both orientations were represented among the committee's membership. Thus the Caribbean report, for example, while addressing the complementary nature of Canada's trade and investment relations with the West Indies, also cautiously recommended that the government establish a Canadian Overseas Development Corporation to further aid the development of the nations in the region.[18] Perhaps the clearest indication of the business leanings of the committee was the recommendation in its 1978 report on Canadian-American trade relations that the government "consider seriously the option of bilateral free trade with the United States."[19] The committee then spent the next three and a half years exploring the feasibility of that option, concluding in its final report in 1982 that Canada had more to gain than it had to lose by negotiating a general, across-the-board free trade agreement.[20] However, the Trudeau government chose not to embrace publicly that advice: it contented itself with allowing its negotiators at the General Agreement on Tariffs and Trade talks in Geneva to work out a trade agreement that allowed Canada to come "as close as we could at this stage to free trade,"[21] and exploring sectoral free trade. The Mulroney government, by contrast, did negotiate a free trade agreement signed in 1987, though it was not motivated to do so by the Senate's views. (However, the Liberal chairman of the committee, George van Roggen, was still so committed to freer trade that he chose to resign the chairmanship rather than vote against Bill C-130 on Turner's instructions.)

Where there was a similarity in views between the committee and the government—as in the case of the committee's study of trade relations with the European Communities or its 1978 recommendations on free trade and the Mulroney government's policies—it appears to have been more the result of coincidence of approach than acceptance by cabinet of the senators' recommendations. On the whole, the government has been slow to act on most recommendations put forward by the Foreign Affairs committee. One reason for such diffidence is the very nature of parliamentary surveillance: *ex post facto* investigations are essentially reactive, and each of the committee's undertakings in the 1970s was in response to policy developments elsewhere. The Caribbean investigation, begun in early 1969, came in the wake of governmental consideration of establishing a free trade area between Canada and the West Indies. The report on the Pacific followed the publication of the foreign policy white paper in 1970 which, *inter alia*, forecast a more prominent role for the countries of the "Pacific Rim" in Canada's foreign policy.[22] The studies of Canadian relations with Europe and the United States came hard on the heels of the Nixon "shock" of August 1971 and the resultant rethinking of the relationship with the United States embodied in the "Options" paper adopted by the government in 1972.[23] The effect of such reactiveness was to render the committee incapable of affecting policy in a significant way: investigations inevitably trailed government action, leaving the senators with little option but to suggest a tinkering with established policy.

Another reason for the Senate's lack of influence lies in the constitutional and political inconsequence of the institution. A senator's importance to the government of the day diminishes considerably at the moment of appointment. Inattentiveness to senatorial concerns follows naturally, particularly when the majority in the upper chamber belongs to the opposition party in the Commons. Indeed, it appears that a senator's influence will be at its greatest when a favour is owed by cabinet. For example, Keith Davey directed the 1962, 1963, and 1965 election campaigns for the Liberal party, for which yeoman service he was elevated to the Senate in 1965. He directed his energies in the upper chamber towards his abiding policy interest, the mass media. The report of his special committee, published in 1971, called on the government to abolish the tax break enjoyed by both *Time* and *Reader's Digest* in an effort to promote the Canadian magazine industry.[24] It was a recommendation ignored by the Trudeau government. However, after Davey co-chaired the Liberal campaign in 1974—which resulted in a majority government—he again pressed his attack, this time with more success: the government finally agreed to abolish the *Time-Reader's Digest* exemption in 1976.[25] Davey's case is nonetheless unusual. Appointment to the Senate is normally regarded as reward enough. It is thus unlikely that, as long as the Senate remains in its present form, it will do more than pursue its present role as an investigator of government policy, providing decision-makers in cabinet with findings and recommendations arrived at through committee study.[26]

The House of Commons

The House of Commons, as we have noted, is not where the decisions that shape foreign policy are made. However, the House is a forum where a number of important political functions are performed. These include the functions of legitimation, representation, education, and policy.[27]

Legitimation. While all of the activities of the House lend legitimacy to the overall political system,[28] in the context of foreign policy we might define legitimation more narrowly: the conferring of authority on the executive by its ability to command the confidence of a majority of members of the House. While some students of Parliament have argued that in the foreign policy area, "the legitimizing function is not that important,"[29] it cannot be dismissed outright. Because the vast majority of foreign policy actions result from executive decisions—decisions that are taken without reference to, or discussion by, Parliament—the legitimacy of the government's foreign policy behaviour stems largely from the implicit confidence of the House of Commons. Such confidence is expressed both by periodic and formal votes of confidence and, more indirectly, by a continued willingness of MPs to approve the annual departmental estimates necessary to allow the government to function in the international sphere. But governments also use votes in Parliament on major foreign policy issues to create legitimacy for the course of action chosen by the executive, even when they do not need parliamentary approval.[30] Thus, the Commons voted to approve the declaration of war in 1939, Canadian membership in the United Nations in 1945, and the North Atlantic Treaty in 1949. Likewise, the government of Brian Mulroney introduced a motion endorsing the free trade initiative on 17 March 1987, even though they needed no formal parliamentary approval for the negotiations.

The executive can, of course, be deprived of this authority by a vote of non-confidence. This can occur either if the government party is in a minority position in the House, or if the government's own backbench revolts. While minority governments have occurred with some regularity, confidence in the government has been withdrawn formally only four times. Arthur Meighen in 1926; John Diefenbaker in 1963; and Joe Clark in 1979 were forced to seek dissolution. The successful vote of non-confidence in 1974 should be treated differently, since the Liberal government of Pierre Trudeau wanted to go to the electorate and engineered its own defeat. Only once has confidence in the government been withheld on an issue that could be broadly construed as falling within the foreign policy sphere. In February 1963, the Diefenbaker government was brought down on the question of its handling of defence policy. Indeed, it might be suggested that the government was brought down for a number of reasons, but that the nuclear weapons issue provided the catalyst.[31]

Likewise, the incidence of large-scale backbench revolts in the House of Commons is rare. On matters of external policy, it has occurred only over the issue of conscription (in 1944, 34 Liberals from Quebec voted against the King government's conscription legislation). Canadian governments have been fortunate (from their perspective at least) to have sitting behind them in the House a docile and placid group of MPs with a healthy regard for party discipline. Although Trudeau had to deal with an often dissentient Quebec backbench in the mid-1970s and early 1980s, and Mulroney had to cope with the so-called Dinosaur Club in the mid-1980s, there has never emerged in Ottawa the "foreign policy oppositions," with their willingness to bolt government ranks on key external issues, that are a tradition at Westminster.[32] Instead, the incidence of foreign policy rebellions is sporadic and involves only a few MPs, as the refusal of two Liberals to vote in favour of testing the cruise missile in June 1983 suggests.

The policy role. It is often claimed that the policy function of the House of Commons has been eroding over the years. In domestic policy, this is no doubt true; but in foreign policy, a caveat must be offered. There can be no erosion of something that was not there to begin with. In matters of external policy, so tight has been the grip of the executive on the setting of priorities and the formulation of policy decisions that other parliamentarians have been excluded since the beginning. Members of the House are thus left with an ability to affect policy outcomes that is marginal at best.[33]

There are, of course, exceptions. The expression of parliamentary opinion on matters of international affairs is, in a very real sense, policy-making, and here MPs have the capacity to influence the government by securing approval for parliamentary resolutions on foreign policy.[34] It should be noted that the government has often either acquiesced or even actively welcomed a backbench resolution, since these "could be used to convey views critical of foreign governments without having to make a direct government-to-government démarche."[35] On occasion, the government will even introduce its own motion to forestall a more critical one from the opposition benches. In January 1973, for example, the government's policy towards the United States and the war in Vietnam—and Canadian-American relations more generally—were directly altered by pressure from Parliament. In December 1972, the Nixon administration had responded to North Vietnamese intransigence at the negotiating table by bombing Hanoi and Haiphong. The government in Ottawa, like many other allies of the United States, had dispatched diplomatic notes expressing concern over what was seen as an excessive use of force. The New Democratic Party, however, wanted a stronger and more public expression of Canadian sentiment and announced its intention to introduce a motion "condemning" the United States when the 29th Parliament opened on 5 January. Even though the bombing had by then been terminated, the secretary of state for external affairs, Mitchell Sharp, moved a government motion when Parliament opened "deploring" the American action. It was a pre-emptive measure, for the NDP held the balance of power in this minority Parliament, but it shifted the government's position considerably. Had there been no legislative intervention, the government would have confined its opinions to the privacy of diplomatic channels for it had little wish to provoke the United States on this issue, however distasteful it might have found Nixon's tactics.

Representation. This is a central function of any legislature. In a parliamentary democracy, representative government implies both the periodic accountability of the representatives to the represented through the electoral system, and a continuing responsiveness to the demands and interests of constituents. The House of Commons is the locus of this representative function—a forum where MPs seek to translate constituents' interests and demands into policy. How MPs do this depends on which side of the speaker they sit. Opposition members tend to use the openness of the floor of the House, where parliamentary rules allow MPs to draw public attention to constituents' concerns. For example, in the mid-1970s, numerous municipalities, groups of environmentalists, farmers and fishermen, and ordinary citizens expressed considerable concern that the Garrison Diversion Unit, a mammoth public works project being undertaken in North Dakota, would cause pollution in their province. The Progressive Conservative and NDP MPs from Manitoba used all of the parliamentary techniques available to them under the rules at the time—motions under Standing Order 43; adjournment debates (the "late show"); and questions during question period—in a coordinated effort to persuade the government to press Washington to stop the project.[36]

Government members, by contrast, have no less interest in communicating the concerns of constituents to ministers in cabinet, but most are prone to keep this process hidden from public view. The imperatives of party discipline and the ambitions of backbenchers themselves combine to place a premium on the use of private channels for those who sit on the government side. In 1975, therefore, Liberal MPs from Ontario were eager to convey to the cabinet the degree to which their constituents were opposed to allowing representatives of the Palestine Liberation Organization into Canada to attend a United Nations congress on crime to be held in Toronto. If Liberal MPs had concerns over potential electoral retribution, they were not aired publicly in the House. What admonitions there were to cancel or postpone the congress were advanced in the relative privacy of the Liberal caucus.[37]

On most foreign policy issues, however, representing public concerns is problematic. Localized issues—such as the flooding of the Skagit valley in British Columbia or Soviet overfishing on the East Coast—or some issues in Canadian-American relations will inevitably prompt MPs to press these concerns.[38] But as we noted in chapter 4, most foreign policy issues remain sufficiently peripheral to the majority of Canadians that they do not seek to translate their interests into concrete political action. Where there is heightened interest in an issue, it tends to be geographically diffused, creating few imperatives for members of Parliament whose electoral bailiwicks are by nature and design geographically localized.

The educative function. Activity in the House is educative in the dual sense of increasing the knowledge, expertise, and understanding of members of Parliament, and of "educating and leading public opinion."[39] On the floor of the Commons, this pedagogic exercise usually takes place during question period and debates. Oral question period, dominated as it is by critical queries from the opposition benches, is a means of drawing public attention to foreign policy issues. It also seeks to elicit from ministers an indication of the government's position on those issues. It is not a means of increasing the knowledge of the members of the House, since most of the questioners know well the issue being addressed and often know in advance what the response from the government front bench will be.

Debates provide only limited opportunities for education in international affairs, for the simple reason that the House of Commons has traditionally spent little time discussing foreign policy. The loquacious spirit that pervaded the Commons in September 1919 on the occasion of the debate over the Treaty of Versailles and over what C.P. Stacey has termed Canada's "doubtful debut as a nation"[40] was soon to fade as Sir Robert Borden's successors found divers reasons for stifling parliamentary discussion of international affairs. Neither Mackenzie King nor R.B. Bennett was much disposed to promote parliamentary debate on foreign policy in the interwar period, frequently grounding their justification in the argument that discussion of international events unfolding in Europe and the Far East might upset the delicate balance of world power.[41]

Louis St. Laurent attempted to reverse this trend when he assumed the External Affairs portfolio in 1946. The following year, he used consideration of the estimates of the Department of External Affairs to present a full report on Canada's international activities to the House of Commons. This triggered an extensive debate on foreign policy.[42] Thereafter, when the House went into Committee of Supply for consideration of the External Affairs estimates, it became practice to have the secretary of state for external affairs apprise interested MPs of Canada's involvements abroad.[43] This exercise in public education—a practice continued by Lester Pearson—was not always seen to be successful. Pearson complained to MPs in 1950 that "I have pleaded for more interest in external affairs in the House of Commons to empty benches and empty press gallery seats.... Possibly we ourselves, in the House of Commons, are somewhat to blame for the lack of interest."[44] A quarter of a century later, with his years as foreign minister, leader of the opposition, and prime minister behind him, Pearson was to note in his memoirs that "much of the debating seemed artificial, a kind of play-acting. The words were for the record, not uttered in the hope that they would change the mind of anyone... [I]t often seemed that to talk in the House was not relevant or important enough to be given priority over other and graver business of government."[45] Nonetheless, debates on foreign affairs were regularly held when the estimates were considered, however dubious ministers of the Crown might have been about their utility.[46]

The practice ceased in 1969. The parliamentary reforms introduced by Pierre Trudeau in that year provided for the automatic referral of the government's main estimates to the various standing committees of the House, and the concomitant abolition of the Committee of Supply.[47] As a result, debate of foreign affairs on the floor of the House fell off sharply. "We did not get a chance to discuss foreign affairs," John Diefenbaker complained to the House in 1974, referring to the first six years of Trudeau's tenure. "Foreign affairs during that period were as foreign as the constitution of Timbuktu."[48] The former prime minister's awkward analogy did not much move the government. It was not until December 1977 that the Trudeau government sponsored its first full-scale debate on external relations.[49]

This attitude prompted much criticism from the opposition benches. "I have been in the House of Commons for almost two years now," Bob Ogle, an NDP member, complained to the House in March 1981, "and up until tonight there has not been a debate on external affairs."[50] However, responsibility for the paucity of foreign affairs debates in the 1970s lies only partially with the executive. The opposition parties, for their part, acquiesced in relegating discussion of Canada's role in the world to a position of secondary importance. The opposition has a number of opportunities to engage the government in debate on foreign policy. Rarely does it use them. The Address in Reply provides the opposition with an occasion to comment on the priorities laid out in the Speech from the Throne. But the focus invariably remains fixed on domestic problems. "There are many other areas I could touch on," Robert Stanfield, the leader of the opposition said during the Address in Reply in 1970, "areas such as external affairs. Because of the white paper [*Foreign Policy for Canadians*, issued that year] that was produced, probably the less said about that the better."[51]

Nor have the opposition parties made use of "opposition days" (time allotted to them under the standing orders[52]) to focus attention on foreign affairs. Debates initiated by the Progressive Conservatives on foreign trade policy in November 1976, and by the NDP on Canada's policy towards El Salvador in March 1981 and on the cruise missile testing issue in June 1983 and March 1987 are exceptions to the norm that opposition days are devoted to domestic issues.

In short, the MP who is seeking to acquire expertise in international affairs must look elsewhere in the legislative system for such education. Service on the various House of Commons standing or special committees that deal with foreign affairs is one way to secure this expertise.

Commons Committees

Of the score of standing, special, and joint committees of the House, the Standing Committee on External Affairs and International Trade (SCEAIT) is considered one of the more prestigious;[53] membership is much sought after as a result. Part of the attraction is doubtless the subject matter—the politics of international diplomacy, national security, and international development assistance. According to some MPs, however, another part of the attraction is that membership on this committee affords backbenchers unequalled opportunity for foreign travel— on committee investigations; to meetings of interparliamentary associations;[54] or as members of government delegations to international conferences or organizations.

The intimations of junketing notwithstanding, the external affairs committee does provide MPs with an opportunity, however limited, to enhance their knowledge of international affairs. Parliamentarians can question ministers and their officials, interview expert witnesses, and pursue investigations in Canada and abroad in an atmosphere far less partisan than on the floor of the House. They gain in the process a familiarity with the diverse issues of foreign policy. This educative function has been part of the committee's *raison d'être* since the Second World War.

The committee has gone through several incarnations. SCEAIT was created in February 1986, a result of the reorganization of Commons committees initiated by the Mulroney government; its progenitors, however, go back to 1924. In March of that year, Mackenzie King moved to create a Standing Committee on Industrial and International Relations.[55] Such an unlikely combination was attributable to King's desire to refer to this committee decisions of the International Labour Organization (ILO), whose conventions posed a thorny problem for the federal government (since labour matters fall under the jurisdiction of the provincial governments). Thus the committee's work on external relations during the interwar period was limited to an ILO draft convention on hours of work; a plan to use university scholarships as a means of promoting peace; and the question of employment of Oriental seamen on Canadian ships. The committee did not meet after 1936, although it remained a standing committee of the house.

With the end of the Second World War, John Bracken, the leader of the opposition, suggested to Mackenzie King that the government might consider splitting the committee and creating a separate panel for foreign policy matters. King declared himself "only too happy" to comply, and the Standing Committee on External Affairs was created in September 1945.[56] But old habits were to die hard. The first reference approved by the government for committee consideration was to examine two ILO conventions passed by that organization in the 1930s. Obviously not much stimulated by its investigations into the likes of the 1932 ILO Convention on the Protection against Accidents of Workers Employed in Loading or Unloading Ships, the committee's first report to the House recommended that "it be empowered to consider matters connected with external affairs and report from time to time any suggestion or recommendation deemed advisable."[57]

The government's first reaction was to deny the request. When the report came to the House for concurrence, the acting secretary of state for external affairs, Louis St. Laurent, claimed that such wide-ranging powers "would lead to a very serious disturbance of the order of business." The report was sent back to the committee to have the offending recommendation removed.[58] However, the opposition was unwilling to let the issue die. Howard Green, the Progressive Conservative external affairs critic, argued during the debate on supply for the Department of External Affairs a month later that "this new committee should not be crippled at the outset," and that the government might consider referring the estimates for External Affairs to the committee to give it an opportunity to explore various aspects of foreign policy. King was chary. "The committee," he replied, "might quite unconsciously, unless there was someone watching the situation very carefully, be going into some matter about which ... the minister in charge would have to take some responsibility." However, he did agree to the opposition request,[59] and in May 1946 the committee began consideration of the External Affairs estimates.[60] And so it remained. Until the reforms of 1968 that provided for the automatic referral of departmental estimates to the appropriate standing committee of the House, the external affairs committee alone was freed from the constraint of having to wait for an explicit reference from the House (which, in effect, meant a reference approved by the government).

It was, as a result, one of the more active committees of the House of Commons, particularly after 1968, when it became the Standing Committee on External Affairs and National Defence. One measure of its activity was the increased use of subcommittees. For example, there was a regular subcommittee on international development assistance, reflecting not only the growing importance of this facet of external policy, but also the increasing inability of the whole committee to deal adequately with this issue as well as matters of defence and broader issues of foreign policy. When the situation in El Salvador deteriorated in the early 1980s, for example, and the administration in Washington accorded growing priority to United States policy towards Central America and the Caribbean Basin, the committee in Ottawa was prompted to establish a subcommittee on Canada's relations with Latin America and the Caribbean. This panel conducted a well-publicized tour of several countries of the Caribbean in the winter of 1981-82, including a trip to El Salvador before the pivotal elections of 28 March 1982.[61] Yet another measure of the committee's activity was the number of reports submitted to the House in the 1970s and 1980s on issues as diverse as United Nations peacekeeping; the state of maritime forces; Canadian-American relations; Canada's position on the UN Conference on Trade and Development (UNCTAD); and the question of the renewal of the North American Aerospace Defence (NORAD) agreement.[62]

Such activity undoubtedly had a salutary effect on the expertise of those MPs who participated in the committee's work. But for all its activity, there is little indication that the committee had a substantive influence on the direction of government policy. To be sure, the committee's opinions often differed considerably from the government's own policy. Its 1970 report on Canada-United States relations, for example, was more nationalistic in its position on foreign ownership and American cultural dominance than was the Trudeau cabinet at the time.[63] A report by an all-party panel from the subcommittee on Latin America and the Caribbean claimed in February 1982 that it had the "gravest doubts that present conditions in El Salvador will allow elections ... to contribute positively to the making of peace" because the electoral system there was "gravely flawed."[64] (Such were not opinions held by the government, which was maintaining that elections should be supported.) Likewise, in 1987, the Standing Committee issued a report critical of many aspects of the government's international development assistance policies, for example calling for the abandonment of Canada's high volume of tied aid.[65] In short, members of the committee have shown no disinclination to disagree with the government over the years. By the same token, however, the government has not shown any disinclination to ignore unpalatable recommendations served up by the committee.

The government, for its part, has on occasion used the committee for its own ends. A telling example would be the persistent use of the committee to legitimate its decisions on the question of renewal of the NORAD agreement with the United States. On the four occasions that the agreement came up for reconsideration—in 1973, 1975, 1980, and 1985—the committee was charged with providing a recommendation to the government of the day. There is little doubt that on each occasion, the government had no intention of recasting its fundamental commitment to a system of joint air defence with the United States, regardless of the recommendations of the committee. A month before the committee began its investigations in March 1973, the minister of national defence, James Richardson, interviewed in *The Globe and Mail*, said that if Canada's role in NORAD did change, it would be as a result of decisions taken in the United States, not because Ottawa foresaw a change in its role.[66] Although members of the New Democratic Party dissented, the committee recommended renewal for two years.

When the agreement came up for renewal again in 1975, the situation had not changed. Negotiations were already underway with the United States when the reference was handed down to the committee, and it was clear to the members that they were not in a position to recommend anything but renewal if they wanted their recommendations to be accepted. "Your mind appears to be made up," Allan MacKinnon, the Progressive Conservative defence critic, complained to Richardson,[67] and so it was. The agreement was renewed again, this time for five years. And when the committee once again had the NORAD agreement referred to it by the Trudeau government in 1980 and the Mulroney government in 1985, it recommended renewal on both occasions.[68] It is clear, given the nature of the commitment to NORAD, that the executive was sending the issue to the standing committee not for advice but for ratification and legitimation.

Moreover, the government at times does not even use the standing committee for legitimation, advice, or public education. When Trudeau renewed his interest in North-South problems in 1980,[69] and wanted to increase public awareness of these problems on the one hand, and to gain parliamentary input on the other, the government chose not to have the issue examined by the standing committee or by one of its subcommittees. Instead the cabinet created a special parliamentary committee. The Parliamentary Task Force on North-South Relations was one of five special panels established in May 1980. Like the task forces on regulatory reform, alternative energy, the disabled, and "critical skills for the 1980s," the North-South panel was small, had a specific mandate, a nine-month reporting deadline, and was designed to maintain as high a public profile as possible.[70] When the Mulroney government sought increased public awareness for its foreign policy review in 1985, it created a Special Joint Committee of the Senate and of the House of Commons on Canada's International Relations under the joint chairmanship of Tom Hockin (PC: London West) and Senator Jean-Maurice Simard.[71] Although on both occasions, the government's intention was to focus public and parliamentary attention on these key issues by establishing new structures of parliamentary input, it might be noted that in bypassing the standing committees, the government was in effect commenting on the utility of the existing structures for investigation, debate, and advice.

THE INFLUENCE OF PARLIAMENT RECONSIDERED

One may with relative ease account for the absence of a parliamentary role in the actual process of making foreign policy decisions. The reasons for this lie in the constitutional conventions of responsible government and in the structural and organizational incapabilities of a legislature to participate in the conduct of relations between states. However, why Parliament has been unable to bring more influence to bear on the decision-makers is not as obvious.

One reason for Parliament's feeble influence, David Leyton-Brown and R.B. Byers have argued, is that the legislature lacks an historical tradition in foreign affairs. For at least half a century after its creation, Parliament exercised authority over domestic policy and over some aspects of Canadian-American relations. The government in London was left with formulating a foreign policy for Canada within the context of the Empire's global policies and objectives. As a result, it is suggested, there did not evolve within the new Canadian Parliament norms and expectations that would foster the emergence of a group of MPs knowledgeable in foreign affairs and prepared to define their parliamentary careers in the context of pursuing international matters. "While [contemporary] members of parliament may not consciously be aware of the historical background," Leyton-Brown and Byers conclude, "the early precedents clearly have had a continuing impact."[72]

A second, and related, cause of this lack of influence lies in the attitudes of parliamentarians themselves. Many MPs appear to believe that their constituents are not interested in foreign affairs.[73] Few of them, as a result, are willing to act on the assumption that political activity expended on external matters will bring rewards at the polls. Responsiveness to parochial concerns is believed to yield more tangible electoral rewards. Declaring one's position on the perennial issue of capital punishment, securing funds for the riding, or being available to handle the problems of constituents, it follows, become more valuable than discoursing on the effects of counterforce strategy, securing additional funds for an aid project in Tanzania, or travelling to Central America on a committee investigation. The parochialism is at once reinforced and reinforcing in circular fashion. "Let us conciliate Quebec and Ontario before we start conciliating Roumania and Ukrania," the House was told in 1923.[74] It was no doubt an expression of the pervasive isolationism of the interwar period, but also one which underscored the tendency towards introversion in that era. However, as we saw in chapter 4, this view has been given persistent expression.

Finally, one of the reasons for an enduring lack of parliamentary influence is the basic agreement on first principles found amongst parliamentarians about foreign affairs. "Bipartisanship"—in a foreign policy context, the notion that there exists between government and opposition a basic consensus on a state's external priorities—is somewhat too strong a term to describe Canadian foreign policy in the postwar period. But both the Liberal and Progressive Conservative parties have similar ends in mind, however much they may differ on the means.[75] When Leyton-Brown and Byers interviewed 251 members of what they term the

"Canadian foreign policy elite" (an admixture of government officials, academics, and parliamentarians), fully 79 percent believed that on foreign policy, the two major parties emerged as essentially similar. Indeed, of the 36 MPs—who, one might assume, would be the most aggressively partisan—only 45 percent thought that there was an essential difference between the parties on foreign policy matters.[76] Thus it is not surprising that on critical issues such as Canada's alignment in international politics, there should be a fundamental convergence between the Liberals and Progressive Conservatives.[77] Likewise, on the issue of trade with the United States, the two parties differ only on the means, not the ends.

Only the Co-operative Commonwealth Federation and its successor, the New Democratic Party, have stood out as the voice in Parliament which has historically offered both ends and means that differ substantively from those of the major parties. The CCF's leader, J.S. Woodsworth, as we saw in chapter 5, was a persistent exponent of pacifism in the interwar years, even opposing Canadian participation in the Second World War. This view was mirrored in the postwar period by the CCF and its successor. In particular, the pledge of the NDP to withdraw from the North Atlantic alliance (NATO) and NORAD, embraced in 1969, starkly sets the party apart from others in the mainstream. To be sure, the NDP's parliamentary leadership under Ed Broadbent has tried since the late 1970s to back away from the party's 1969 pledge to take Canada out of NATO, but without success: the party's rank and file have insisted that the NDP continue to embrace a withdrawal. In the 1980s, the parliamentary leadership, which will admit privately to being embarrassed by the pledge, has put forward alternative policy options. In the summer of 1987, Broadbent proposed that while an NDP government would indeed take Canada out of NORAD, it would then negotiate a new agreement with the United States for an all-Canadian detection and interception system, the cost of which, so he claimed, would be completely offset by the savings of bringing troops home from Europe.[78] However, the option of defence self-reliance[79] paradoxically flies in the face of the pacifism and anti-militarism of the party's rank and file that drives the anti-alliance stance. In order to achieve self-reliance, an NDP government would have to embrace a massive arms build-up and a huge increase in Canadian defence spending, for providing an adequate air defence for the United States would cost far more than the savings generated by the withdrawal of Canada's 5,000 troops stationed in Europe. Not surprisingly, therefore, the NDP has not been keen to publicize a policy option that not only finds little favour with the public at large, but would also be prohibitively expensive to implement. Instead, its parliamentary activity on foreign policy tends to focus on such matters as cruise testing; air defence; United States policy on Central America; Canadian policies towards South Africa; and Canadian-American relations, which find more support within the electorate as a whole.

The absence of profound differences on foreign policy between the major parties, and the reticence of the NDP on the issue of alignment, is reflected in parliamentary activity. It becomes more difficult to engage in debate when there is basic agreement on the fundaments. It could be argued that were the two major parties to articulate radically opposing views on foreign policy within Parliament, that institution would be far more engrossed in the foreign policy process than at present, and would, as a consequence, wield more influence than it does now.

NOTES

1 David Leyton-Brown, "The role of Congress in the making of foreign policy," *International Journal* 38 (Winter 1982-3), 59-76; Charles W. Kegley, Jr. and Eugene R. Wittkopf, *American Foreign Policy: Pattern and Process* (New York: St. Martin's, 1979), ch. 11; John Spanier and Joseph Nogee, eds., *Congress, the President and American Foreign Policy* (New York: Pergamon Press, 1981).

2 R. Michael M'Gonigle and Mark W. Zacher, "Canadian foreign policy and the control of maritime pollution," in Barbara Johnson and Mark W. Zacher, eds., *Canadian Foreign Policy and the Law of the Sea* (Vancouver: University of British Columbia Press, 1977); E.J. Dosman, "The northern sovereignty crisis, 1968-1970," in Dosman, ed., *The Arctic in Question* (Toronto: Oxford University Press, 1976).

3 Paul Martin, "The role of the Canadian parliament in the formulation of foreign policy," *The Parliamentarian* 50 (October 1969), 259.

4 In February 1910, in a debate in the House on the Naval Service Bill, Sir Wilfrid said: "If England is at war we are at war and are liable to attack. I do not say that we shall always be attacked, neither do I say that we would take part in all the wars of England. That is a matter that must be determined by circumstances, upon which the Canadian parliament will have to pronounce and will have to decide...." Quoted in C.P. Stacey, *Canada and the Age of Conflict: A History of Canadian External Policies*, vol. 1: *1867-1921* (Toronto: Macmillan, 1977), 135.

5 James Eayrs, *In Defence of Canada*, vol. 1: *From the Great War to the Great Depression* (Toronto: University of Toronto Press, 1964), 78-80.

6 William Wallace, *The Foreign Policy Process in Britain* (London: George Allen & Unwin, 1976), 93; Robert Jackson, *Rebels and Whips* (Toronto: Macmillan, 1968).

7 Denis Stairs, "The foreign policy of Canada," in James N. Rosenau, Kenneth W. Thompson and Gavin Boyd, eds., *World Politics: An Introduction* (New York: Free Press, 1976), 188.

8 James Eayrs, *The Art of the Possible: Government and Foreign Policy in Canada* (Toronto: University of Toronto Press, 1961), 103.

9   Georges-Etienne Cartier called it "a power of resistance to oppose the democratic element." Quoted in Robert J. Jackson and Michael M. Atkinson, *The Canadian Legislative System*, 2nd ed. (Toronto: Macmillan, 1980), 109.

10 Cited in W. Stewart Wallace, *The Memoirs of the Rt. Hon. Sir George Foster* (Toronto: Macmillan, 1933), 207.

11 See, for example, Peter C. Newman, "An exercise in Liberal arrogance," *Maclean's*, 8 August 1988, 29; Diane Francis, "A job for the hacks and bagmen," *Maclean's*, 15 August 1988, 9. Ed Broadbent, the leader of the New Democratic Party, despite his opposition to free trade, also criticized Turner's move.

12 Colin Campbell, *The Canadian Senate: A Lobby from Within* (Toronto: Macmillan of Canada, 1978), 10.

13 For example, the impact of Senator David Croll, and his special committees on Manpower and Employment (1960-61), Aging (1963-66), and Poverty (1968-71) would suggest that the "social investigators" are not without influence. *Ibid.*, 19-21.

14 Invariably, questions about foreign affairs asked of the government leader in the Senate during the few minutes that pass for question period are met with the standard answer that inquiries of the government have to be made before a proper response can be given.

15 Canada, Parliament, Senate, Standing Committee on Foreign Affairs, *Report...on Canadian-Caribbean Relations* (Ottawa, 1970); *Report on Canadian Relations with the Countries of the Pacific Region* (Ottawa, March 1972); *Canadian Relations with Europe* (Ottawa, July 1973); *Canada-United States Relations*, 3 vols. (Ottawa, 1975, 1978, 1982).

16 Canada, Senate, Standing Committee on Foreign Affairs, Sub-committee on National Defence, *Manpower in Canada's Armed Forces* (Ottawa, January 1982); *Canada's Maritime Defence* (Ottawa, May 1983). For a discussion of the latter report, see R.P. Pattee and Paul G. Thomas, "The Senate and defence policy: subcommittee report on Canada's maritime defence," in David Taras, ed., *Parliament and Canadian Foreign Policy* (Toronto: Canadian Institute of International Affairs, 1985), 101-119.

17 Senate, Special Committee on National Defence, *Canada's Territorial Air Defence* (Ottawa, January 1985).

18 Heath Macquarrie, "Canada and the Caribbean," in Peyton V. Lyon and Tareq Y. Ismael, eds., *Canada and the Third World* (Toronto: Macmillan, 1976), 225-27.

19 Standing Committee on Foreign Affairs, *Canada-United States Relations*, vol. 2, 124.

20 *Ibid.*, vol. 3, *passim*.

21 This was the assessment of Allan MacEachen at the conclusion of the Tokyo Round of the General Agreement on Tariffs and Trade negotiations in Geneva: quoted in *Maclean's*, 23 July 1979; also see Stephen Clarkson, *Canada and the Reagan Challenge* (Toronto: James Lorimer, 1982), 124*ff*.

22 Canada, Secretary of State for External Affairs, *Foreign Policy for Canadians* (Ottawa, 1970), Pacific booklet; for an assessment, see T.A. Keenleyside,

"Canada and the Pacific: perils of a policy paper," *Journal of Canadian Studies* 8 (May 1970), 31-49.

23 Secretary of State for External Affairs, "Canada-U.S. relations: options for the future," *International Perspectives* (Special Issue, Autumn 1972).

24 This was a 1965 agreement that allowed both magazines to claim exemptions from Canadian tax: see I.A. Litvak and C.J. Maule, *Cultural Sovereignty: The Time and Reader's Digest Case in Canada* (New York: Praeger, 1974).

25 Isaiah A. Litvak and Christopher Maule, "Bill C-58 and the regulation of periodicals in Canada," *International Journal* 36 (Winter 1980-1), 70-90.

26 For an assessment, see W.M. Dobell, "Parliament's foreign policy committees," in Taras, ed., *Parliament and Canadian Foreign Policy*, 29-34.

27 R.B. Byers, "Perceptions of parliamentary surveillance of the executive: the case of Canadian defence policy," *Canadian Journal of Political Science* 5 (June 1972), 234. For the views of one parliamentarian, see Gordon L. Fairweather, "The role of parliament in the review and planning of Canadian national defence and external affairs," in Thomas M. Franck and Edward Weisband, eds., *Secrecy and Foreign Policy* (New York: Oxford University Press, 1974), 161.

28 "When the activities of the legislative system produce acquiescence by members of the political system in the moral right of the government to rule...the legislative system is performing a legitimation function." Jackson and Aktinson, *Canadian Legislative System*, 27.

29 Byers, "Parliamentary surveillance," 234.

30 Peter C. Dobell, *Canada in World Affairs*, vol. 17: *1971-1973* (Toronto: Canadian Institute of International Affairs, 1985), 395.

31 Peyton V. Lyon, *Canada in World Affairs, 1961-1963* (Toronto: University of Toronto Press, 1968), 176-92.

32 Philip Norton, "The changing face of the British House of Commons in the 1970s," *Legislative Studies Quarterly* 5 (August 1980), 337-39; also Jackson, *Rebels and Whips, passim*.

33 Michael Tucker, *Canadian Foreign Policy: Contemporary Issues and Themes* (Toronto: McGraw-Hill Ryerson, 1980), 52, concludes that Parliament was not one of the "potent elements in the Canadian foreign policy making crucible of the 1970s." See also David B. Dewitt and John J. Kirton, *Canada as a Principal Power* (Toronto: John Wiley & Sons, 1983), 177. For a somewhat different perspective, see David Taras, "From bystander to participant," in Taras, ed., *Parliament and Canadian Foreign Policy*, 3-19.

34 A common way of expressing such concerns used to be by raising the matter under Standing Order 43, which allowed members to ask for the unanimous consent of the House to make motions without notice on matters of an urgent nature. Members seeking attention for an issue, or wanting to put statements into the record, would use S.O. 43. However, unless there was agreement from the government benches, or unless the government whip (who was charged with routinely saying no when the Speaker asked for unanimous consent) made a mistake, motions under S.O. 43 were regularly denied. The new rules of procedure in the House brought in on a trial basis in January 1983 did away

with S.O. 43. Under the new rules, S.O. 21 allows the Speaker to recognize a member "to make a statement for not more than one and one-half minutes."

35 Dobell, *Canada in World Affairs*, 399.

36 See Kim Richard Nossal, "The unmaking of Garrison: United States politics and the management of Canadian-American boundary waters," *Behind the Headlines* 37 (December 1978).

37 Bruce Thordarson, "Posture and policy: leadership in Canada's external affairs," *International Journal* 31 (Autumn 1976), 687.

38 The importance of Canadian-American issues in election campaigns is examined in Don Munton and Dale H. Poel, "Electoral accountability and Canadian foreign policy: the case of foreign investment," *International Journal* 33 (Winter 1977-8), esp. 220-22.

39 R. MacGregor Dawson, *The Government of Canada*, rev. by Norman Ward (Toronto: University of Toronto Press, 1970, 5th ed.), 305.

40 Stacey, *Age of Conflict*, vol. 2: *1921-1948* (Toronto: University of Toronto Press, 1981), 294.

41 Eayrs, *Art of the Possible*, 108; Paul Martin, Pearson's external affairs minister, would argue in 1969 that "over-participation on the part of Parliament...tends to hinder diplomacy. The public discussion of delicate international negotiations could well lead to detrimental consequences for the country and even for the world." "Role of the Canadian Parliament," 259.

42 R. Barry Farrell, *The Making of Canadian Foreign Policy* (Scarborough: Prentice-Hall Canada, 1969), 146-47.

43 See, however, the view of Robert A. Spencer, *Canada in World Affairs, 1946-1949* (Toronto: Oxford University Press, 1959), 403-406.

44 Quoted in Eayrs, *Art of the Possible*, 112.

45 *Mike: The Memoirs of the Rt. Hon. Lester B. Pearson*, vol. 2: *1948-1957*, John A. Munro and Alex I. Inglis, eds. (Toronto: University of Toronto Press, 1973), 12.

46 Franklyn Griffiths, "Opening up the policy process," in Stephen Clarkson, ed., *An Independent Foreign Policy for Canada?* (Toronto: McClelland and Stewart, 1968), 114.

47 Donald S. Macdonald, "Change in the House of Commons: new rules," *Canadian Public Administration* 13 (Spring 1970); John B. Stewart, *The Canadian House of Commons: Procedure and Reform* (Montreal: McGill-Queen's, 1977); Fairweather, "Role of parliament," 144-56.

48 Canada, Parliament, House of Commons, *Debates*, 30th parl., 1st sess., vol. 1, 3 October 1974, 81.

49 *Ibid.*, 3rd sess., vol. 2, 19-20 December 1977, 1993-2027, 2045-57.

50 *Ibid.*, 32nd parl., 1st sess., vol. 2, 9 March 1981, 8050.

51 *Ibid.*, 28th parl., 3rd sess., vol. 1, 9 October 1970, 27.

52 Jackson and Atkinson, *Canadian Legislative System*, 107-108.

53 See Allan Kornberg and William Mishler, *Influence in Parliament: Canada* (Durham, NC: Duke University Press, 1976), 164-69; it should be noted that when their survey was taken, this committee was called the Standing Committee on External Affairs and National Defence: see below.

54 Matthew J. Abrams, *The Canada-United States Interparliamentary Group* (Toronto: Canadian Institute of International Affairs, 1973).

55 Eayrs, *Art of the Possible*, 118.

56 House of Commons, *Debates*, 20th parl., 1st sess., vol. 1, 12 September 1945, 109; 18 September 1945, 244.

57 House of Commons, Standing Committee on External Affairs, *Minutes of Evidence and Proceedings*, 20th parl., 1st sess., #1, iii-vi, #5, iv.

58 House of Commons, *Debates*, 20th parl., 1st sess., vol. 2, 16 November 1945, 2182-83.

59 *Ibid.*, vol. 3, 17 December 1945, 3690-93.

60 Standing Committee on External Affairs, *Minutes*, 20th parl., 2nd sess., #1.

61 John R. Walker, "Foreign policy formulation—a parliamentary breakthrough," *International Perspectives* (May/June 1982), 10-12.

62 Tucker, *Canadian Foreign Policy*, 49; also Don Page, "The Standing Committee on External Affairs, 1945 to 1983—who participates when?" in Taras, ed., *Parliament and Canadian Foreign Policy*, 40-65.

63 House of Commons, Standing Committee on External Affairs and National Defence, *11th Report* (Ottawa, 1970).

64 Quoted in *International Canada* (March 1982), 5.

65 House of Commons, Standing Committee on External Affairs and International Trade, *For Whose Benefit?* (Ottawa, May 1987); for a discussion, see David R. Morrison, "Canada and North-South conflict," in Maureen Appel Molot and Brian W. Tomlin, eds., *Canada Among Nations—1987: A World of Conflict* (Toronto: James Lorimer, 1988), 136-58.

66 *The Globe and Mail*, 6 and 7 February 1973.

67 Quoted in Tucker, *Canadian Foreign Policy*, 50.

68 Douglas A. Ross, "American nuclear revisionism, Canadian strategic interests, and the renewal of NORAD," *Behind the Headlines* 39 (April 1982); for the 1986 renewal, see Ross, "Canada and the Strategic Defense Initiative: managing strategic doctrinal incompatabilities," in Lauren McKinsey and Kim Richard Nossal, eds., *America's Alliances and Canadian-American Relations* (Toronto: Summerhill Press, 1988).

69 Kim Richard Nossal, "Personal diplomacy and national behaviour: Trudeau's North-South initiatives and Canadian development assistance policies," *Dalhousie Review* 62 (Summer 1982), 278-91.

70 House of Commons, *Debates*, 32nd parl., 1st sess., vol. 2, 23 May 1980, 1356-57; also House of Commons, Parliamentary Task Force on North-South Relations, *Report to the House of Commons on the Relations between Developed and Developing Countries* (Ottawa, 1980).

71 For the committee's final report, see Parliament, Special Joint Committee on Canada's International Relations, *Independence and Internationalism* (Ottawa, June 1986).

72 David Leyton-Brown and R.B. Byers, "Parliament and Canadian foreign policy," paper presented to the Legislative Studies in Canada Conference, York University, October 1977, 3.

73 MPs' perceptions of the interests of their constituents in the Biafran crisis are surveyed in Donald Barry, "Interest groups and the foreign policy process: the case of Biafra," in A. Paul Pross, ed., *Pressure Group Behaviour in Canadian Politics* (Toronto: McGraw-Hill Ryerson, 1975), 138.

74 Quoted in Eayrs, *Art of the Possible*, 113; for a survey of parliamentary opinion at the end of the First World War, see Stacey, *Canada and the Age of Conflict*, vol. 1, 288-98.

75 Garth Stevenson, "Foreign policy," in C. Winn and J. McMenemy, eds., *Political Parties in Canada* (Toronto: McGraw-Hill Ryerson, 1976); also Martin, "Role of the Canadian Parliament," 259; and Robert A. Spencer, "Parliament and foreign policy 1960," *International Journal* 15 (Autumn 1960).

76 Leyton-Brown and Byers, "Parliament and Canadian foreign policy," table 2.

77 After Trudeau's resignation, the Liberal party had difficulty putting forward a coherent line on defence matters. During the 1984 elections, Turner's secretary of state for external affairs, Jean Chrétien, and the party's president, Iona Campagnola, joined a number of other Liberal candidates in embracing a nuclear freeze despite Turner's opposition: Kirton, "Managing Canadian foreign policy," in Brian W. Tomlin and Maureen Molot, eds., *Canada Among Nations—1984: A Time of Transition* (Toronto: James Lorimer, 1985), 20-21. These tensions did not dissipate. For example, in March 1987, Turner stated that he supported cruise testing because of Canada's "obligations" to NATO; his external affairs critic, Donald Johnston, and the Liberal defence critic, Douglas Frith, were both calling for an immediate ban on cruise testing, a position eagerly embraced by one of the members of the so-called "Rat Pack," Don Boudria. See *The Globe and Mail*, 9 March 1987.

78 Ed Broadbent, on "Question Period," CTV, Toronto, 26 July 1987: *International Canada* (June and July 1987), 14; see also *The Globe and Mail*, 22 July 1987.

79 See, for example, the response of Derek Blackburn, the NDP's defence critic, to the Mulroney government's 1987 white paper on defence, "Canadian sovereignty, security and defence: a New Democratic response to the defence white paper," (Ottawa, mimeo., 1987).

CHAPTER NINE

The Provinces and Foreign Policy

INTRODUCTION

In most states in the international system, governments other than the national government do not play an important role in the shaping of foreign policy. Normally, subnational governments would be considered as "nongovernmental inputs" to the policy process—little different than groups, firms, or other organized interests, lacking any autonomous political authority and capable of having higher authority exercised over them.[1] We cannot treat subnational governments in federal systems so lightly, however, as they have grown to play an increasingly important role in international affairs.[2] In Canada, the provincial governments play an even more important role in foreign policy-making, in part because of the uniqueness of the Canadian constitution.

SOVEREIGNTY, FEDERALISM, AND FOREIGN POLICY

The distinguishing feature of international politics has always been the existence of independent polities, or states, which seek to give expression to their autonomy. The ability of states to make autonomous decisions is one of the key ideals in the contemporary period. The history of the Eurocentric international system has been marked by a tradition of trying to give expression to this ideal state of autonomy that we know today as sovereignty. These attempts date back to the Peace of Westphalia of 1648

255

and the treaties that conceded the rights of the European states to make their own political decisions unfettered by the dictates of the Holy Roman Empire. Sovereignty refers to the ability of a state to make decisions autonomously from other states. In the latter half of this millenium, members of the states system have sought to give both political expression *and* legal meaning to the attributes of sovereignty. In international law, a sovereign state has three important legal and political rights: *jus belli*, a right to use force in defence of its interests, a right that has, to be sure, become more conditional and constrained; *jus legationis*, the right to send and receive diplomatic missions; and *jus tractatuum*, the right to negotiate treaties or agreements with other sovereign states. These rights and attributes of a sovereign state are possessed by a government within a defined territorial area, which exercises supreme authority over the population within those boundaries.[3]

Importantly, these rights and attributes are considered to be indivisible. Only one sovereign authority can exercise these rights for a given territory and population. The usage and definition of sovereignty precludes the possibility of two or more "sovereigns" exercising *legitimately* these rights for the same territory and people. To be sure, there can be rival claims to sovereignty. Since 1949, for example, two governments have claimed to be the rightful supreme and sovereign authority of both mainland China *and* the island of Taiwan, even though the government in Beijing clearly does not govern Taiwan and the government in Taipei does not govern the mainland. But the exercise of sovereignty is assumed to be zero-sum: other arrangements—such as a condominium, where two sovereign states share the powers of statehood—cannot be considered sovereignty.

Federations and Foreign Affairs

It is paradoxical that when the doctrine of sovereignty—with its assumption of one supreme authority exercising political power within a polity—was gaining legitimacy in the states system, a form of government based explicitly on the necessary *divisibility* of sovereignty was adopted in a number of national systems. After independence in 1776, the United States created a confederation[4] before finally adopting the federal constitution of 1787. In 1848, Switzerland, which had had a confederal system dating back to 1291, adopted a constitution which transformed the confederation into a federation. Federalism, by its very nature, precludes a single and supreme authority. It assumes that sovereign political authority can be exercised in the same territory, over the same people, by more than one independent political authority. It assumes that each level of government is immune from dissolution by the other and that each level is granted sovereign jurisdiction over responsibilities specified by the constitution. In short, federalism cannot work unless sovereignty is divided.

The indivisibility of sovereignty in the international system and the division of sovereignty domestically converge in a federal state's external policy. While a federal state is assumed by the international community to be a unitary actor, the realities of the domestic political structure provide the constituent parts of a federal state with a sovereign competence of their own in specified areas. The majority of contemporary federal systems have, however, anticipated this dilemma in their constitutions. While constitutional arrangements do not completely inhibit subnational international activity,[5] the constitutional setting places important parameters on the policy process.

A state marked by divided sovereignty internally can present itself to the international community as a unitary sovereign by assigning the power to exercise the rights of a sovereign state to the central authority. For example, the constitutions of Austria, Brazil, Burma, Czechoslovakia, India, Malaysia, Mexico, Venezuela, and Yugoslavia all preclude the constituent parts of those federations from exercising the rights of sovereign states by assigning these powers to the central government. Under Article 10(1) of the United States constitution, the states are prohibited from entering into any but the most minor agreements with "foreign powers"—and even then only with the consent of the United States Congress. Similarly, the constitution of the Federal Republic of Germany allows the *Länder* to negotiate international agreements with other foreign powers, but only "with the approval of the Federal Government."[6]

The constitution of the Union of Soviet Socialist Republics stands apart from this general tendency. In theory, the Soviet constitution allows each of the 15 republics the right to exercise all of the powers of a sovereign state; indeed, two—the Ukrainian SSR and the Byelorussian SSR—are charter members of the United Nations. But this unusual situation is deceptive. The formal trappings of sovereign status; the exercise of their legal rights under the Soviet constitution; and their seats at the United Nations; are all the result of a compromise among the great powers in the waning days of the Second World War. At the Yalta Conference of February 1945, Roosevelt and Stalin sought to impose on the new United Nations organization a system of weighted voting under which the United States and USSR would each be given three votes. While Washington eventually backed down in the face of objections from smaller powers, the Soviet government successfully insisted on the three votes agreed to at Yalta. Stalin had been prescient enough to facilitate such an arrangement by amending the 1936 constitution in early 1944 to allow the republics to engage in international relations.[7] But the Soviet constitution stands as an exception. The general tendency is for federal constitutions to retain that essence of unity by assigning to the central authority the rights of waging war, negotiating treaties, and engaging in diplomatic relations.

The Canadian Constitution and Foreign Affairs

While most federal constitutions explicitly assign exclusive power over foreign affairs to the central authority, the British North America Act passed by the Parliament at Westminster in 1867 was silent on the question. Sections 91 and 92 of the BNA Act (since 1982, called the Constitution Act, 1867), the provisions enumerating the division of powers, did not explicitly assign competence in foreign affairs to either the federal or provincial levels. Nor, importantly, did the BNA Act deny the provinces the possibility of an international role after the fashion of other federal constitutions. Indeed, the only mention of international affairs in the BNA Act was the now spent section 132, designed to extend to the new dominion the power to implement Imperial treaties:

> The Parliament and Government of Canada shall have all Powers necessary or proper for performing the Obligations of Canada or any Province thereof, as Part of the British Empire, towards Foreign Countries, arising under Treaties between the Empire and such Foreign Countries.

The silence was entirely understandable since such an explicit allocation of powers was, in the circumstances, entirely unnecessary. Perhaps somewhat short-sightedly, those who framed Canada's original constitution did not conceive that the new dominion might eventually enjoy the same autonomy in foreign policy as it was receiving in domestic affairs. Certainly, in 1867, Canada (as a member of the Empire) could have no independent international personality. Instead, the international community would continue to recognize only one sovereign, the Crown in London, and only one sovereign entity, the British Empire. Correspondingly, the rights and responsibilities of sovereign statehood would be vested in, and exercised by, the Crown—in other words, by the Imperial government in London. The constitution was thus framed accordingly. As Roff Johannson has noted, the BNA Act "was not designed to provide a constitution for an autonomous nation-state. Rather, what was involved was the sharing of authority between various levels of local government."[8]

And no effort has been made since that time to break the constitutional silence by amending the British North America Act to specify more clearly the powers and limitations of competence in international affairs. Although the patriation process of the early 1980s provided Canada's 11 governments with an opportunity to modernize the constitution by including a clearer reference to foreign affairs, the attentions of the first ministers and their delegations were fixed on far more pressing problems. As a result, the Constitution Act, 1982, leaves the question of the competence of the provinces in the area of foreign affairs as constitutionally unclear as the

BNA Act had in 1867. In the absence of any constitutional prohibition against international activity, Canada's provincial governments have sought to project and protect their interests beyond their—and Canada's—borders.

PROVINCIAL INTERESTS AND EXTERNAL AFFAIRS

Four distinct, but not unrelated, interests may propel provincial governments into the international sphere: constitutional; socio-economic; functional; and bureaucratic. The pursuit of these interests is part of a more general phenomenon known as "province-building"—the "emergence of the provinces as mature and complex institutions having the strengthened 'capacity to govern in the interests of regional communities'..."[9] But if all provinces have a degree of interest in international affairs, the province of Quebec stands apart in that the province-building interests embraced by the government in Quebec City are overlaid by *la question nationale*.

Constitutional Interests

Provincial governments have an interest in defending their constitutional prerogatives from federal encroachment. And, of course, they have a concomitant interest in expanding their jurisdiction as far as possible *vis-à-vis* the central authority. What is in essence a continuing struggle for constitutional power has occasionally manifested itself in the realm of foreign affairs. External provincial interests were pursued in an indirect way in the 1930s, with the Aeronautics, Radio, and Labour Conventions cases. A similar struggle occurred in a more direct way in the 1980s, with the attempts by a number of premiers to have the federal government's patriation package defeated by the British Parliament.

The feud in the 1930s between the federal and provincial governments over their respective jurisdictions under the BNA Act was played out in what then was the final court of appeal in Canada: the Judicial Committee of the Privy Council in London. At issue was the constitutionality of the extension of federal powers by means of implementing treaties to which the government in Ottawa was a signatory. In the Aeronautics Case, 1932, the provinces objected to the extension of federal power into the field of civil aviation. The dominion government argued that it was implementing an international convention signed at Paris in 1919 by the British Empire. The Judicial Committee concurred: clearly the Paris convention was an "Empire treaty," and section 132 of the BNA Act specified that the dominion government, in implementing a British Empire treaty, could infringe on provincial prerogatives.[10]

The Radio Case, 1932, also questioned the competence of the federal government to claim jurisdiction over the regulation and control of radio broadcasting in Canada as a result of Ottawa's ratification of an international agreement on wireless broadcasting. In that case, the Judicial Committee noted that section 132 was inoperative, since the Canadian government, and not the British Empire, signed the convention. But their Lordships were wont to note that they "think that it comes to the same thing" and decided that

> It is Canada as a whole which is amenable to the other powers for the proper carrying out of the convention; and to prevent individuals in Canada infringing the stipulations of the convention it is necessary that the Dominion should pass legislation which should apply to all the dwellers in Canada.

They held that because broadcasting was not assigned to the provinces under section 92, Ottawa's legislative competence derived from the residuary powers of the "peace, order and good government" clause of section 91.[11]

The effect of this decision was potentially detrimental to provincial prerogatives. The federal government could, by attaching itself as a signatory to an international treaty, impose a federal conception of the national interest on provincial rights. Indeed, the federal government sought to do precisely this in 1935. In seeking to implement agreements of the International Labour Organization, the government of R.B. Bennett introduced legislation governing minimum wages, hours of work, and weekly rest in industrial undertakings. Ottawa subsequently justified federal intrusion into the provincial realm by again invoking section 132. This view was upheld by the Supreme Court of Canada, but not by the Judicial Committee. In the Labour Conventions Case, 1937, the Judicial Committee held that "the distribution of legislative powers between the Dominion and the Provinces [regarding treaty implementation] ... is based on classes of subjects; and as a treaty deals with a particular class of subjects so will the legislative power for performing [i.e., implementing] it be ascertained."[12] In other words, unlike the Radio Case, the "peace, order and good government" clause did not apply because the matter in question fell under section 92. But the Judicial Committee established that section 132 could not be used to override provincial rights. The federal government could not enact legislation in an area explicitly given to the provinces under section 92, even if it was designed to fulfill obligations under an international treaty.

The quarrels over these cases in the 1930s did not involve foreign policy per se. At issue was a domestic dispute between two levels of sovereign governments testing each other's constitutional capacities, complicated and exacerbated by the general tenseness of dominion-provincial relations during this period.[13] The long-term effects of these judicial interpretations of the BNA Act on the conduct of Canadian foreign policy were not as significant as originally thought. It was feared that the Labour Conventions case would, in the words of the *Round Table*, "grievously injure" the conduct of Canada's foreign relations.[14] Commenting on the Judicial Committee's decision in 1937, Sidney Smith, who two decades later would become John Diefenbaker's secretary of state for external affairs, opined that "undoubtedly it serves to shackle the Canadian nation in its foreign relations."[15] As K.C. Wheare concluded ten years after the Labour Conventions case, "Federalism and a spirited foreign policy go ill together."[16]

In fact, these decisions did not seriously affect the ability of the central government to pursue an active, "spirited" foreign policy, as the ten years that followed Professor Wheare's assertion show. But the Labour Conventions case did and continues to circumscribe the ability of the federal government to enter unilaterally into treaties which involve provincial prerogatives. For example, in 1963 the federal government was hesitant to impose the Columbia River Treaty negotiated with the United States on the British Columbia government of W.A.C. Bennett since natural resources fall within provincial jurisdiction.[17] Likewise, the Mulroney government was careful to ensure that the free trade agreement with the United States of 1987 did not unilaterally impinge on those matters exclusively under provincial jurisdiction.

Concern over constitutional power launched several provincial governments into international activity in 1980 and 1981. They sought to defeat the Trudeau government's unilateral attempt to patriate the constitution by taking their objections directly to Britain. The "dissident" provincial premiers—mainly those from the West and from Quebec—lobbied vigorously in London for the defeat of the federal proposal. These attempts at provincial statecraft were singularly unsuccessful. Their first target, the British government, proved coldly unreceptive. Prime Minister Margaret Thatcher maintained throughout the patriation process that her government would deal only with the federal government in Ottawa. "Provincial premiers visiting London would, of course, continue to be treated politely, given a cup of tea, and shown the rose garden; but anything beyond that would violate Commonwealth protocol and so would not be extended to them."[18] British ministers and their bureaucrats accordingly refused to permit the premiers any formal hearing.

The premiers returned to Canada rebuffed, leaving their bureaucrats to continue lobbying ordinary members of the House of Commons at Westminster, hoping to influence their votes on the Canada Bill. While the dissident provinces did engage legal counsel and public relations firms in

Britain to aid in this task, the emphasis appears to have been on trying to influence British MPs mainly by an appeal to the palate. In what was dubbed the "battle of the dining rooms," most of the 635 members of the House of Commons were treated at some considerable expense to lavish affairs put on by the provincial agents-general resident in London. (When a compromise on the constitution was reached in November 1981, lobbying by all but one province ceased. Only René Lévesque continued to press Quebec's objections.) For all the provincially-sponsored cuisine, the constitutional bill was passed by the British Parliament without difficulty in March 1982.[19]

Socio-economic Interests

Provincial governments have external interests that stem directly from the wide powers granted to them by the Constitution Acts, 1867-1982. Section 92 gives the provinces authority to borrow money, legislative power over a wide range of economic issue areas and "Generally all Matters of a merely local or private Nature in the Province." Sections 92A and 109 give the provinces control over natural resources. Section 93 grants exclusive authority to the provincial governments in the area of education. Section 95 accords concurrent power over agriculture and immigration to both the federal and provincial levels of government.

Sovereign governments seek to exercise to the full their legislative competence; governments in federations, which also have a measure of sovereignty, are no exception. Provincial governments in Canada have thus been impelled to exercise their legislative competence, even when doing so necessitates going beyond their borders. When those issues under provincial jurisdiction, such as the provincial economy; resource development; health; or education have international ramifications, provincial governments have been disinclined to abandon these concerns at the provincial boundary line, relinquishing control to the federal authorities. Rather, such issues are seen as legitimate subjects of provincial concern, to be advanced and protected by provincial governments.

In the early years after Confederation, the external interests of the provinces—like those of the dominion government at the time—were quite limited. They lay primarily in the promotion of immigration and the expansion of trade.[20] The main means of promoting these interests was the provincial office abroad, justified by invoking section 92.4, which grants provinces authority over the "Establishment and Tenure of Provincial Offices."[21] Thus, the government of Quebec shared with the federal authorities their agent-general in 1882 until Fabre's death in 1910.[22] Ontario and Quebec both opened commercial offices in Britain in the early years of this century—Ontario in 1908 and Quebec in 1911.[23] In addition,

Quebec opened an agency in Brussels in 1915.[24] But this early activity, particularly on Quebec's part, was relatively short-lived. The government in Quebec City closed the provincial agency in Paris in 1912, because of lack of interest in Quebec on the part of the French business community. Both the missions in Brussels and London were closed in the early 1930s in an effort to trim provincial expenditures. When the Union Nationale under Maurice Duplessis came to power in 1936, all of Quebec's agencies abroad were abolished by law—perhaps because the new premier "préférait de beaucoup un Québec isolé et ainsi préservé des mauvaises influences du siècle qu'un Québec ouvert sur le monde."[25]

If the depression dampened the extension abroad of provincial interests, the Second World War caused a severe contraction in the ability of the provinces to exercise their legislative powers in a number of important policy spheres. The War Measures Act was invoked by the federal authorities at the outset of the war, centralizing government, increasing federal regulation of most spheres of activity, greatly enhancing federal jurisdiction, and stripping the provinces—temporarily at least—of many of their prerogatives. As a result, Mackenzie King and "[m]ost of his ministers came to view the provinces, not as rivals or antagonists, as they had been in the thirties, but as irrelevancies to be stroked or prodded according to whether they had a Liberal government or not."[26]

The end of the war, which brought both the relaxation of federal centralization and a plethora of new spending programs, restored to the provincial governments a more prominent place in Confederation.[27] But in the decade and a half following the war, the growth of the modern welfare state increased the burden on the provinces to provide social and other services. This created a concomitant imperative for provincial governments to promote the growth of their economies to provide the funds necessary for the provision of expanded provincial services—an imperative that had an implicit electoral connection. Thus, the expansion of provincial trade, and maintenance and expansion of a provincial infrastructure, and the raising of capital in foreign markets assumed increased importance in the postwar period. This economic imperative helps explain what prompted such a rapid expansion of provincial activities abroad in the postwar period. The most concrete expression of the provinces' growing international role was the blossoming of provincial agencies abroad and the frequent foreign travels of provincial ministers for the purpose of promoting their province's economic well-being.

Because of their size and economic structure, it is not surprising that Quebec and Ontario were the most active in establishing offices abroad to promote provincial interests, though other governments were no less prone to do so. By the early 1980s, seven provinces were operating over 35 agencies on three continents.[28] Likewise, provincial trade missions abroad, often headed by the premier, became more common as provincial governments sought to expand external markets for their products (particularly their agricultural and natural resources[29]); develop the secondary manufacturing sectors of their economies; or find new sources of capital. The favourite targets for provincial premiers have been American financial centres—New York, Chicago, Atlanta, Los Angeles—but there have also been provincial trade missions to Europe, and the newly industrializing countries of the Middle East, Asia, and Latin America in search of markets and capital.

A parochial concern with the economic health of the province drove each provincial premier and each provincial government into the free trade debate in the 1980s. No provincial economy would remain untouched by the effects of the free trade agreement negotiated by the federal government, and each provincial government sought to declare itself on the issue. As early as August 1985, all of the premiers but Ontario's had called on the Mulroney government to negotiate a free trade arrangement.[30] Throughout the negotiating process, the premiers were active in pressing their concerns publicly. David Peterson, alarmed at rumours that the Auto Pact of 1965 was going to be put on the negotiating table, flew to Washington in January 1987 to press American officials to keep it excluded.[31] And, as the implications of the agreement negotiated by the federal government were assessed by each provincial government, each of the premiers was to render his verdict. By the summer of 1988, all of the provincial governments except those of Ontario and Prince Edward Island had endorsed the agreement.

Functional Interests

A third, and related, factor that propels provincial governments into external activity is, very simply, geographic location, and the resulting mundane but functional needs of consultation and coordination with other governments. Local issues coming under provincial jurisdiction, such as coordination of law-enforcement efforts; forest fire-fighting capabilities; waterways management; power grid arrangements; and road, highway, and bridge management all prompt provincial governments to establish relationships with neighbouring jurisdictions—other provinces and American states. As a result, an extensive network of linkages between Canadian provinces and American states has emerged. There exists, for example, a regular "junior summit" of Eastern Canadian premiers and New England governors who meet to discuss matters of common concern; numerous transnational organizations, such as the Conference of State and Provincial Health Administrators of North America, serve to provide a forum for state-provincial contacts; Canadian provinces are members of such American bodies as the Northeastern Interstate Forest Fire Protection Commission or the Midwestern and Western Associations of State Departments of Agriculture.[32]

The Bureaucratic Impetus

The growth of the external activities of the provinces has been matched by an expansion of bureaucratic establishments—"foreign offices" of a sort—which are charged with the management of the province's international relations. But the degree to which provincial governments have sought to create bureaucratic agencies to support their burgeoning international activities varies considerably. At one end of the spectrum are those provinces which have eschewed anything more than the most rudimentary administrative and bureaucratic support systems for their international activities. The smaller provinces, such as Prince Edward Island or Newfoundland, have not created large bureaucracies to manage their international activities. Two or three officials attached to the cabinet or the premier's office oversee provincial activities abroad. This reflects in part the smaller budgetary bases of these provinces and their inability to fund such agencies. But lack of institutionalization may also be attributable to a simple lack of desire on the part of the premier and cabinet ministers to invest bureaucratic resources in international affairs. Until the creation of a special bureaucratic agency in the late 1970s, the Saskatchewan government's approach to international affairs was firmly ad hoc. A tiny percentage of the provincial budget was spent supporting Saskatchewan's international relations; officials in the Cabinet Office's Intergovernmental Affairs Unit devoted about five percent of their time to the coordination of the international activities of different departments of government.[33]

At the other end of the spectrum are those provinces which have sought to institutionalize the support system for their foreign relations. The growth of Quebec's bureaucratic capability is indicative of this trend. By the early 1980s, the most well-developed provincial bureaucracy charged with international relations was the Ministère des Affaires intergouvernement-aires du Québec (MAIQ). Created in 1965, Quebec's "foreign office" was originally an interdepartmental committee, the Commission interministérielle des relations extérieures du Québec. However, under the chairmanship of Claude Morin, then deputy minister of federal-provincial relations, the Commission grew from a coordinating body into a full-fledged bureaucracy charged with the development of external policy and the administration of a wide range of Quebec government programs abroad. Morin's nationalism (he eventually left the civil service to join the Parti québécois in 1971, and became the minister of intergovernmental affairs in

René Lévesque's cabinet) prodded him to develop a bureaucracy capable of identifying Quebec's interests abroad and projecting the Quebec government's presence internationally. In 1967, the Commission was absorbed into the Ministère des Affaires fédérales-provinciales, which was restyled the Ministère des Affaires intergouvernementales to reflect its expanded responsibilities for relations with governments other than that in Ottawa. From that time it grew apace under Morin's nurturing as both mandarin and minister. By the time he retired from politics after the 1980 referendum, the structure of the "foreign affairs" side of MAIQ—la Direction générale des Affaires internationales—mirrored that of any foreign office. The geographical divisions (France, Europe, United States, Africa, Latin America, Asia, and Oceania) reflect the global reach of the Quebec government's interests, while the functional bureaux (Affaires économiques, Affaires educatives et culturelles, and Affaires sociales et institutionnelles) reflect issues particular to provincial jurisdictions.[34]

Of the remaining provinces, Ontario and Alberta both have modest intergovernmental affairs agencies created in the late 1970s. Nova Scotia, New Brunswick, Manitoba, and British Columbia have not institutionalized to this extent, their governments content to conduct their international relations in an ad hoc and centralized fashion.[35]

Whatever the institutional arrangement, bureaucratic capability remains a key factor in explaining why the provincial governments have maintained their high level of international activity.[36] The greater the number of civil servants who have a specialized expertise and who are hired to devote their attentions to defining provincial interests externally, the more likely that provincial ministers will be encouraged to seek an expanded external role for their province, acting on the advice received from their specialized agencies. Thus, while provincial international activities do not spring from the creation of a bureaucratic establishment whose raison d'être is to define provincial interests abroad, these agencies of the provincial state, once in existence, tend to strengthen and perpetuate a provincial international presence.

QUEBEC: PAS COMME LES AUTRES

Prime Minister Louis St. Laurent's assertion that Quebec was a province "comme les autres" might have been politically useful in the federal government's squabbles with the government of Maurice Duplessis in the 1950s. But in the context of understanding what propels the provinces into the international sphere, the view that Canada's provincial governments have essentially homogenous interests masks those distinctive and unique interests the Quebec government wishes to project internationally.

On the one hand, Quebec does share with other provinces the desire to protect its constitutional, economic, and functional interests. Like other provinces, it is jealous of its constitutional prerogatives. So too is it concerned about the raising of foreign capital for investment; the sale of its hydroelectricity; the export of its manufactured goods in offshore markets; and the economic relationship between the province and the United States. And it is propelled into external relations with neighbouring jurisdictions by virtue of its geographical location.

On the other hand, the Quebec government has also been impelled into international activity by a desire to project abroad some sense of the province's cultural and linguistic attributes that distinguish francophone Québécois from other Canadians. The Quebec government's external impulses are, very simply, *nationalistic*, and its external interests as a result tend to be overlaid by *la question nationale*. No other province seeks to assert its interest externally for essentially "national" purposes. The Ontario government, for example, does not provide educational assistance to the Bahamas to project some sense of Ontario's "nationhood"; the same cannot be said of the Quebec government's education assistance program to Louisianna. Thus, while all provinces are, to a greater or lesser extent, motivated in their international activities by statism—or what some would refer to as the requisites of province-building—only Quebec is impelled by nationialism, or the requisites of nation-building.

The Nationalist Impulse: 1960-1976

Since the beginning of the Quiet Revolution in 1960, governments in Quebec City have sought to project into the international arena a special and separate (albeit not always an *indépendantiste*) personality for Quebec—the external dimension of the *statut spécial*. This marked a clear departure from the pattern under Duplessis. While eager to defend provincial autonomy from federal encroachment, Duplessis had no desire to pursue activist policies, particularly not in the external field. Instead, he had "un respect scrupuleux de la compétence fédérale en matière de relations extérieures," and, it has been argued, only attacked the federal government on foreign policy for electoral gain.[37]

By contrast, beginning with Jean Lesage, the increased statism evident in the expansion of provincial government functions was married to what Garth Stevenson has characterized as "a very intense provincially-centred nationalism."[38] In short order, the state in Quebec rapidly assumed the role of the primary protector of the francophone Québécois, the defender of Québécois culture, language, and ethnicity. The external dimension of this role—the establishment of a number of provincial offices abroad, the creation of a "foreign office," and more activist demands—complemented the internal changes occurring in Quebec society and politics.[39]

During this period, Quebec attempted to expand its international competence and the range of its international activities in areas and in ways consistent with the role of champion of Quebec nationalism. Enhanced relations were sought with Louisiana, the one American state with a francophone heritage.[40] A special emphasis was placed on relations with France, an emphasis, as we will see, reciprocated by Paris. Quebec began attending international conferences on education and joined multilateral francophone organizations, the most important of which was l'Agence de coopération culturelle et technique.

The governments of both Lesage and Daniel Johnson also began to claim for Quebec a special status in foreign affairs. The growing interest of the Lesage government in asserting a separate personality for Quebec internationally was most concretely manifested in the agreement on educational exchange concluded with France in 1965. There was little doubt of the Quebec government's desire to draw on the expertise of the French educational system. Reversing the traditional lack of emphasis on scientific and managerial training in Quebec's post-secondary educational system and developing an indigenous francophone cadre of Québécois professionals and managers were seen as critical to the ideals of the Quiet Revolution. In 1964, therefore, negotiations between the French and Quebec governments culminated in the signing in February 1965 of an "Entente" on educational exchanges between Quebec City and France.

But what began as an external expression of *functional provincial* interests was quickly transformed into an issue of *symbolic national* interest for the Québécois. Paul Gérin-Lajoie, Quebec's minister of education, heralded the Entente as evidence of the Quebec government's competence in international affairs. Lesage and Gérin-Lajoie began to assert Quebec's right to conclude sovereign agreements on issues under provincial jurisdiction, and to participate as an actor in its own right in international conferences on issues such as education and culture.[41]

Such assertions challenged the position of the federal government, which had agreed to the Entente in the expectation that it would be a functional agreement with no political ramifications. The acerbic debate that developed between the two levels of government was to intensify and would occupy the Ottawa-Quebec City-Paris triangle for the remainder of the decade. In short, Quebec's pursuit of functional interests—within jurisdictions granted them by sections 92 and 93—became overlaid by nationalist considerations. The implicit challenge to the monopoly desired by the federal government over the conduct of all foreign relations for Canada politicized the issue. The case of the Quebec-France Entente of 1965 underscores not only the nature of Quebec's definition of its "national" interest, but also the tensions inherent in a federal country's external relations. The Lesage government was not alone, however, in pressuring for an expanded international role for Quebec. The Union Nationale's 1966 election platform, under the slogan "Québec d'abord," claimed that the province should be given the international capacity to exercise the powers of a sovereign state in the two key areas under provincial jurisdiction: education and culture. Only with the election of the Liberals under Robert Bourassa in 1970 did the Quebec government take a more traditional approach to the province's international activities.

Some have argued that the growth of such activity in this period was an inexorable and natural outgrowth of nationalist demands within Quebec society. For example, Jacques-Yvan Morin, Lévesque's deputy premier, argued in 1981 that "L'activité internationale est en quelque sorte l'oxygène de notre société ... [C]'est une réalité quotidienne à tous les niveaux de notre société.... Les intérêts internationaux du Québec sont donc vécus d'abord à la base. Le Gouvernement du Québec n'a d'autre choix que de refléter ces intérêts...."[42]

It is, however, unlikely that cause and effect are as clear as Morin suggests. It is likelier that political leaders in Quebec City recognized that international activity was one means of legitimizing their role as the champion of special status for Quebec and Québécois, with the putative electoral rewards associated with such a role. Thus, for example, it is likely that claims for a special role for Quebec in international affairs, such as those put forward by the Lesage or Johnson governments in the 1960s, represented not so much a simple responsiveness by the Quebec state to nationalist demands as attempts by the state to reflect and draw on a provincial autonomism assumed to exist in the electorate.

The Separatist Impulse: 1976-1980

The nationalist impulses of the Quebec governments of the 1960s and early 1970s were predicated on the assumption that Quebec, however augmented its autonomy, would remain within Confederation. By contrast, the object of the nationalist impulse after the election of the Parti québécois in November 1976 was to secure independence for Quebec and international recognition of sovereign status. Thus, after 1976, the external dimension of provincial behaviour must be interpreted within the context of an attempt to influence the outcome of the referendum that would decide Quebec's position within Confederation. In this, René Lévesque and the PQ government were playing to two different audiences. First, Quebec's external affairs were directed at a domestic audience within the province. There was obvious value for the PQ in being seen by Quebec voters as able to operate effectively and successfully in the international community.

The government in Quebec City therefore tended to act as though it already possessed the attributes of a sovereign state. It tried to project the image of an independent international actor by attempting to acquire the symbols of statehood, such as diplomatic immunity for its representatives abroad, or "participating-government" status at international summits. It expanded the scope of its foreign policy pronouncements to include such issues as human rights and regional conflict. For example, to protest *apartheid* in South Africa, the Quebec Liquor Control Board imposed a boycott on wines from that country. Lévesque, quite understandably, called for the right of the Palestinians to "une patrie qui leur soit propre," and during the debate over the Clark government's promise to move the Canadian embassy from Tel Aviv to Jerusalem, Claude Morin roundly criticized Clark for damaging Quebec's interests in the Middle East.[43]

By 1979, the government had formulated a full foreign policy program for an independent Quebec.[44] It sought to demonstrate to the electorate that the PQ aspired to be a responsible member of the international community. Gone were the simplicities of earlier PQ foreign policy platforms which had called for a demilitarized Quebec, a policy of non-alignment, and closer ties with the Third World. Instead, the imprint of the professional bureaucrats in the Ministère des Affaires intergouvernementales was obvious. The Quebec government pledged to continue commitments to the North Atlantic Treaty Organization (NATO) and the North American Air Defence Command (NORAD), and even contemplated membership for Quebec in the Commonwealth. This conservative blueprint for the foreign policy of an independent Quebec might have offended the left wing of the PQ, but its purpose was to demonstrate symbolically the responsibility and competence of the separatist government.

The second audience was in the United States—both the government and the corporate elite. There was little doubt that the United States government was concerned at the implicit threat the PQ posed to the unity of the Canadian federation. The concern was not entirely altruistic: an independent Quebec would, apart from anything else, place the continental basis of American defence in jeopardy. If an *indépendantiste* government in Quebec City formulated its defence policy on the lines of pre-1976 PQ platforms, it would withdraw from NATO and NORAD, and eschew a military establishment. This would leave a large gap in both air defence over Ungava and maritime defence in the Gulf of St. Lawrence. As one defence analyst put it—none too subtly—in 1977, "an independent Quebec implies a fundamental change in one of the post-World War II military constants of the West, a strong and unified North America. The strategic reality demands that any attempt to make that change be thwarted—if not by Canada, then by the United States."[45] By 1979, the PQ government had abandoned its earlier attachment to neutralism. The government announced that an independent Quebec would contribute to the defence of North America by becoming a signatory to the NORAD agreement. One of the key reasons for this change was a recognition, somewhat belated, that the same constraints and imperatives that mold Canada's foreign policy would also act on Quebec. This policy attempted to convince Washington that an independent Quebec would pose no threat to the security of the United States.

There was a related impetus for such reassurance: the fear that American capital would follow the lead of Sun Life and flee the province, or worse, elicit the protective intervention of the United States government. Elected on a platform that featured nationalization as well as nationalism, the PQ had established itself as a party not entirely sympathetic to the interests of capital. Once in power, however, the implicit anti-Americanism evaporated. Instead Lévesque and his minister of finance, Jacques Parizeau, aimed much of their external diplomacy at reassuring the American business community that the prospect of an independent Quebec was no cause for alarm, and that the transition to independence would be marked by stability and continuity. The premier travelled widely in the United States carrying this message, meeting business leaders and newspaper editors, and appearing on TV.

The Role of France

A government, if it is to operate successfully in the international community, needs to acquire the symbol of formal recognition by other states. All states in the international system acknowledge the primacy of the federal government in Canada's external relations.[46] But it is important to recognize that the attempts of Quebec governments, from Lesage to Lévesque, to augment the province's role in international affairs were significantly aided by one state—France—which sought to provide the government in Quebec City with some of that symbolic legitimacy necessary for the conduct of foreign relations. Evidence for such a desire to aid the international aspirations of Quebec has ranged from the silly to the significant. On the one hand, the hunt for French indiscretions often took on the elements of *opéra bouffe*. For example, in February 1979, *The Globe and Mail* felt compelled to report that the Paris telephone directory listed Quebec's *délégation* under "embassies." For its part, the French foreign ministry felt obliged to issue the helpful statement that the Quebec mission could not possibly be an embassy since it was a *délégation générale*.[47]

On the other hand, the behaviour of the French government does suggest that from the mid-1960s to the early 1980s, it had an abiding interest in developing a special relationship with Quebec, even if such attempts interfered in Canada's domestic politics. The most famous of these was Charles de Gaulle's 1967 visit to Quebec. In a speech in Montreal, he claimed that driving from Quebec City to Montreal, "je me suis trouvé dans une atmosphère du même genre que celle de la Libération [of France from the Nazis]." It was at the end of this speech that he shouted "Vive Montréal, vive le Québec, vive le Québec libre, vive le Canada français, vive la France." De Gaulle followed this with an even more bizarre performance in November of 1967. In a press statement, he outlined how his desire for Quebec to be "maître de son existence nationale" might be attained.[48] In early 1968, Canadian-French relations were further soured by the "Gabon incident." Gabon, which was hosting an international conference on education, issued an invitation directly to the Quebec government, without either inviting or informing the federal government in Ottawa, apparently at the behest of the French foreign ministry. Indeed, when federal officials tried to secure an invitation to the conference in Libreville and the subsequent session in Paris, they were rebuffed.[49]

The death of de Gaulle had little impact on French policy. For example, as we saw in chapter 6, France delayed the holding of a francophone summit meeting by refusing to participate unless the government of Quebec was a full participating member. When Lévesque paid his first visit to France as premier in November 1977, Paris ignored a number of niceties of diplomatic propriety and gave him the kind of welcome normally reserved for leaders of sovereign states. At a state luncheon given by President Giscard d'Estaing, Lévesque was made a grand officer of the Legion of Honour.[50]

Much of the impetus for French support for Quebec can be traced back to de Gaulle's increasingly idiosyncratic search for an independent role for France in the Western alliance. Throughout the 1970s, the government in Paris struggled with the legacy of Gaullist policy, valuing the special relationship de Gaulle had helped foster with Quebec but uneasy about the implications for French relations with the central government in Ottawa. After the prospect of an independent francophone state on the North American continent dimmed with the results of the 1980 referendum, the French government appeared to lose interest in promoting the Quebec cause. By 1983, Prime Minister Pierre Mauroy was publicly rebuffing Lévesque's attempts to bolster flagging French support for Quebec's demand that it attend a francophone summit as a full participating government.[51] By 1985, with Brian Mulroney in Ottawa, the defeat of the PQ and the return of the Liberals under Robert Bourassa in Quebec, the French lost all interest in perpetuating the Gaullist dream of the 1960s.

The importance of French receptivity to, and encouragement of, Quebec's international role can perhaps best be seen by the significant shift that occurred in the public tone of Lévesque's own statements after French interest began to wane. By 1983, the premier was asserting that the emphasis of Quebec's relations with France was no longer on the cultural and linguistic affinities between the two societies. Rather, to avoid becoming a "museum piece," as Lévesque put it, the emphasis had to be on the economic aspects of the Franco-Quebec relationship,[52] a policy Bourassa carried forward after 1985.

THE FEDERAL RESPONSE

It should be noted at the outset that within the Canadian state, there are no constitutionally-embedded institutional mechanisms to provide provincial governments with the ability to express their parochial interests within the central government.[53] As a consequence, the style of interest articulation and aggregation has been largely ad hoc, with the central government responding with a variety of bureaucratic and political mechanisms to incorporate provincial interests and to attempt to coordinate policy. In external policy, this response has been a mixture of accommodation and intransigence. In particular, the federal response appears to vary with the degree to which its primacy in the foreign policy field is jeopardized. For example, because most provincial governments implicitly or explicitly recognize federal pre-eminence in the making of Canadian foreign policy, their international activities are not seen as a threat by central decision-makers. The result is that much of the activity is apolitical, in the sense that it does not engender political conflict between the levels of government. Provincial officials abroad, working to promote markets of tourism or investment, tend to work cooperatively with their federal counterparts. When most premiers embark on their frequent foreign travels, no one is much inclined to check the relative heights of the provincial and Canadian flags, or whether the arcane practices institutionalized at the Congress of Vienna are being rigorously followed. Simply put, since most provinces are not seeking to exploit the symbols of statehood in ways that would detract from the powers of the central government, those symbols become largely unimportant.

This is not to suggest that there are not differences of interest between those provinces who have predominantly economic interests abroad and the federal government. Certainly the provincial governments had a deep interest in the Tokyo Round of the multilateral trade negotiations in Geneva, but the view from the provincial capitals did not always accord with the view from the federal capital. However, the central government sought to coordinate its negotiations with the particular interest of provincial governments, complicating considerably the Canadian negotiating position. By 1980, this arrangement had been institutionalized, with regular federal-provincial consultations on trade policy.[54] However, when the premiers tried to insert themselves into the actual process of negotiating with the United States on the free trade agreement, the

Mulroney government refused: while the provinces were closely consulted by the Trade Negotiations Office under Simon Reisman during the negotiations, the premiers and their officials were denied a seat at the table.[55]

Similarly, the provinces continue to press to be allowed to open separate provincial offices in Washington to represent their interests. The federal position has been unrelenting. Canada will have only one voice in Washington, and hence only one office—the embassy. However, the federal government has tried to be more accommodating on other issues relating to provincial representation in the United States, possibly to compensate for its intransigence on the question of provincial offices. The provinces have seconded officials to work in the embassy; the Canadian ambassador periodically briefs provincial cabinets; and some material is copied to provincial capitals from External Affairs.[56]

Because Quebec's approach to international activity has been coloured by considerably different aspirations, the federal government's response has been more pointed. Ottawa has reacted (some would say overreacted) quickly and harshly to what it has interpreted as threats to its integrity by France or challenges to its primacy in foreign policy by the Quebec government. For example, after his "Vive le Québec libre" speech, de Gaulle was effectively declared *persona non grata* by a Pearson greatly angered at the president's implicit comparison between anglophone Canada and the Nazis. French-Canadian relations were soured for a decade. Likewise, Ottawa treated the Gabon incident with the utmost severity. As Ivan Head, who was later to become Trudeau's principal adviser on foreign affairs, noted at the time, the Gabonese invitation to Quebec was "one of the most serious threats to the integrity of Canada that this country has ever faced.... It contains the seeds of the destruction of Canada as a member of the international community."[57] Canada immediately severed diplomatic relations with Gabon, and issued some not so subtle reminders to other francophone African states that Quebec was unlikely to be able to match federal development assistance programs. The coercion worked. In 1970, at the inaugural meeting of l'Agence, the francophone states voted for Canadian membership alone, with provincial representation subsumed within the Canadian delegation.[58]

At the same time, however, the federal government has sought to blunt the claims of Quebec by effecting a number of changes in the content and process of policy. Lester Pearson and Pierre Trudeau after him devoted progressively more attention to *la francophonie*, increasing, for example, Canada's development assistance and representation in francophone countries.[59] Bureaucratic structures in Ottawa were created in an attempt to coordinate policy. To institutionalize the input of Quebec into the process of making policy, the federal government provided for provincial representation on Canadian delegations to international conferences, even arranging for provincial representatives to head the Canadian delegation when education was concerned. And on those two occasions when Robert Bourassa, with his more pragmatic approach to relations with the federal government, came to power, the effects were immediate. In the early 1970s, the Trudeau government responded by securing "participating government" status for the province in l'Agence in 1972. In the late 1980s, the Mulroney government ensured virtually equal participation for Quebec at the francophone summit.

CONCLUSIONS: THE STRUCTURAL CONSTRAINTS OF FEDERALISM

From the perspective of the central government in Ottawa, Canada's federal structure places considerable constraints on the development of a "national" foreign policy in a number of key areas. The existence of provincial governments with parochial interests to project and maintain, and a constitution that does not explicitly deny the provinces the possibility of an international role, has precluded unilateralism in any but the high issues of war and peace. (And even then, electoral demands will on occasion propel provincial governments into pronouncing on those issues.[60]) On those foreign policy issues which involve provincial jurisdiction, the imperatives of federalism demand that Canadian foreign policy-makers attempt to reflect the diversity of regional interests and concerns and try to leaven the impact of a centralist astigmatism. The nature of Canadian federalism also demands that in the process, the provincial governments at least be consulted, if not brought directly into the process of policy-making.

For their part, however, the provinces argue that *their* particular interests, important to the growth and health of the provincial economy and the provincial state (and of course to the electoral fortunes of their political elites), can best be protected by the provincial state. Often the "provincial interest" must be defended against competing conceptions of the "national interest," and there is an occasional disagreement on basic elements of policy. For example, the federal government's restrictive foreign investment policies of the 1970s might have well suited a central Canadian's concern with the degree of foreign ownership of Ontario's manufacturing sector; making it more difficult for direct capital investment to enter the country would hardly meet the needs of those provinces seeking foreign investment to finance industrial growth.

Nor can provincial governments always be sure that the federal government is willing (or able) to represent their concerns and interests abroad satisfactorily. When the PQ government in Quebec City wishes to project to the United States an image of itself as a responsible future member of the comity of states, it can hardly have confidence that the job will be done adequately by representatives of a government avowedly opposed to Quebec's secession. But such doubts are not exclusively Québécois, or limited to the particularisms of Quebec's position within Confederation. The premier of Alberta complained in 1969 that "[M]any Western Canadians are tired of going to Asian countries and meeting with well-meaning, but Eastern-Canadian-oriented civil servants who can relate the name of every major company doing business in Montreal or Ottawa or Toronto, but who have never heard of some of the international concerns of Winnipeg, Regina, Edmonton, Calgary or Vancouver. These people represent the interests of some Canadians, but they do not represent our interests."[61] Likewise, the premiers of Ontario and Prince Edward Island have persistently argued that their provinces' interests were not well represented in the free trade negotiations.

Both levels of government may seek to dampen the political impact of conflicting interests by institutionalizing consultative and coordinating procedures, anticipating problems, and trying to accommodate each other's legitimate interests. But the potential for conflict always remains, rooted as it is in shared sovereignty and constitutional imprecision. So too may the conflict between Ottawa and Quebec City vary in intensity over time, but the structural conditions that gave rise to the most serious confrontations of the late 1960s and late 1970s have not disappeared. In short, only a radical restructuring of the Canadian federal system would eliminate the constraints imposed on foreign policy-makers in Ottawa by the existence of provincial governments with not so parochial interests.

NOTES

1 The acid test of a government's autonomy is whether it can be legally legislated out of existence without its concurrence. On this measure, each of the provinces is autonomous; a municipal government, by contrast, is merely the legislative creation of a provincial government and could be legislated out of existence by an act of provincial parliament.

2 For an argument on the increasing role of subnational governments, see Brian Hocking, "Regional governments and international affairs: foreign policy problem or deviant behaviour?" *International Journal* 41 (Summer 1986), 477-506.

3 Jacques Brossard, "Introduction," in Jacques Brossard, André Patry, and Elisabeth Weiser, *Les Pouvoirs extérieurs du Québec* (Montreal: Les Presses de l'Université de Montréal, 1967), 12.

4 In a confederal system, the constituent units retain their sovereignty, but form a central authority whose autonomy is dependent on the constituent parts. By

contrast, in a federation both the central authority and the constituent parts share sovereignty.

5   See, for example, the articles on subnational activities in the United States, Germany, India, Nigeria, Yugoslavia, and Australia in the summer 1986 issue of *International Journal*.

6   Federal constitutions are surveyed in the Canadian government's white paper on federalism and foreign affairs: Canada, Secretary of State for External Affairs, *Federalism and International Relations* (Ottawa, 1968), annex, 49-56. Also the discussion in Annemarie Jacomy-Millette, "Aspects juridiques des activités internationales du Québec," in Paul Painchaud, ed., *Le Canada et le Québec sur la scène internationale* (Québec: Centre québécois de relations internationales, 1977), 520-29.

7   The 1936 Soviet constitution, as amended in 1944, establishes the three sovereign rights as concurrent powers: article 14 gives the Union government the right to decide questions of war and peace, to negotiate treaties, and to establish diplomatic relations; sections (a) and (b) of article 18 give essentially the same rights to the republics. Leonard Shapiro, *The Government and Politics of the Soviet Union* (New York: Random House, 1965), 83-89.

8   P.R. (Roff) Johannson, "Provincial international activities," *International Journal* 33 (Spring 1978), 359.

9   This is the definition offered by M.A. Chandler and W.M. Chandler, *Public Policy and Provincial Politics* (Toronto: McGraw-Hill Ryerson, 1979), 8. Province-building lies at the centre of the analysis in Garth Stevenson, *Unfulfilled Union: Canadian Federalism and National Unity* rev. ed. (Toronto: Gage, 1982).

10 The Aeronautics, Radio, and Labour Conventions decisions are reproduced in Howard A. Leeson and Wilfried Vanderelst, *External Affairs and Canadian Federalism: The History of a Dilemma* (Toronto: Holt, Rinehart and Winston, 1973), 65-77.

11 *Ibid.*, 70-73.

12 There is a considerable literature on the Labour Conventions case: Mr. Justice Bora Laskin, "The provinces and international agreements," in Ontario Advisory Committee on Confederation, *Background Papers and Reports* (Toronto: Queen's Printer of Ontario, 1967), 109-11; André Patry, "La capacité internationale des états fédérés," in Brossard, Patry et Weiser, *Pouvoirs extérieures du Québec*, 83-86; Edward McWhinney, "The Labour Conventions Case, 1937, revisited," in Leeson and Vanderelst, *External Affairs and Canadian Federalism*, 82-83.

13 Stevenson, *Unfulfilled Union*, 57.

14 Quoted in Leeson and Vanderelst, *External Affairs and Canadian Federalism*, 78.

15 Quoted in *ibid.*, 82.

16 K.C. Wheare, *Federal Government* (New York: Oxford University Press, 1947), 196.

17 Neil A. Swainson, *Conflict over the Columbia: The Canadian Background to an Historic Treaty* (Montreal: McGill-Queen's Press, 1979).

18 Edward McWhinney, *Canada and the Constitution, 1979-1982* (Toronto: University of Toronto Press, 1982), 72.

19 For a discussion of provincial lobbying activity in London, see *ibid.*, 69, 72-74, 133-34.

20 Leeson and Vanderelst, *External Affairs and Canadian Federalism*, 45, 48-49.

21 Patry, "La capacité internationale des états fédérés," in Brossard, Patry et Weiser, *Pouvoirs extérieures du Québec*, 68.

22 Wilfrid Laurier appointed Philippe Roy to succeed Fabre, but the Quebec connection was severed. As Robert Borden noted in 1912 in his recommendation to terminate Roy's connection with Quebec City, "It is undesirable that the representative of the Dominion government should represent one of the provinces as distinct." Quoted in Louis Beaudoin, "Origines et développement du rôle international du gouvernement du Québec," in Painchaud, ed., *Le Canada et le Québec sur le scène internationale*, 447.

23 For a discussion of early provincial representation in London, see A.B. Keith, *Responsible Governments in the Dominions* (Oxford: Oxford University Press, 1912), vol. 1, 343.

24 Jean Hamelin, "Québec et le monde extérieur," *Annuaire statistique du Québec, 1968-69* (Quebec, 1969), 19-26.

25 Beaudoin, "Origines et développement," 461.

26 Robert Bothwell, Ian Drummond, and John English, *Canada Since 1945: Power, Politics and Provincialism* (Toronto: University of Toronto Press, 1981), 74.

27 Alan C. Cairns, "The governments and societies of Canadian federalism," *Canadian Journal of Political Science* 10 (December 1977).

28 A.E. Blanchette, ed., *Canadian Foreign Policy, 1966-1976: Selected Speeches and Documents* (Ottawa: Institute of Canadian Studies, Carleton University, 1980), 302.

29 See Andrew Fenton Cooper, "Subnational activity and foreign economic policy making in Canada and the United States: perspectives on agriculture," *International Journal* 41 (Summer 1986), 655-73.

30 *The Globe and Mail*, 23 August 1985.

31 *The Globe and Mail*, 28 January 1987.

32 See, for example, K.J. Holsti and T.A. Levy, "Bilateral institutions and transgovernmental relations between Canada and the United States," in Annette Baker Fox, Alfred O. Hero, Jr. and Joseph S. Nye, Jr., eds., *Canada and the United States: Transnational and Transgovernmental Relations* (New York: Columbia University Press, 1974), 295-304; Gerard F. Rutan, "Legislative interaction of a Canadian province and an American state: thoughts upon sub-national cross-border relations," *American Review of Canadian Studies* 11 (Autumn 1981), 67-69.

33 Robert I. McLaren, "Management of foreign affairs reflects provincial priorities," *International Perspectives* (October 1978), 28, 30.

34 André Patry, *Le Québec dans le monde* (Ottawa: Leméac, 1980), 76-77.

35 Wayne Clifford, "A perspective on the question with particular reference to the case of the province of Alberta," *Choix* 14 (1982), 94-95; also other contributions to this issue of *Choix*.

36 J. Peter Meekison, "Provincial activity adds new dimension to federalism," *International Perspectives* (March/April 1977); Thomas Levy and Don Munton, "Federal-provincial dimensions of state-provincial relations," *International Perspectives* (March/April 1976); Johannson, "Provincial international activities," 363-64.

37 Patry, *Québec dans le monde*, 23.

38 Stevenson, *Unfulfilled Union*, 91.

39 William D. Coleman, *The Independence Movement in Quebec, 1945-1980* (Toronto: University of Toronto Press, 1980), 144-46.

40 For example, Jean Louis Roy, "Les relations du Québec et des Etats-Unis (1945-1970)," in Painchaud, ed., *Le Canada et le Québec sur le scène internationale*, 512-14.

41 The best account is in Charlotte S.M. Girard, *Canada in World Affairs*, vol. 13: *1963-1965* (Toronto: Canadian Institute of International Affairs, 1980), ch. 4.

42 Jacques-Yvan Morin, "Allocutions d'ouverture," *Choix* 14 (1982), 11-12.

43 On South Africa, see *International Canada* (September 1979), 206; on the Palestinians: Patry, *Québec dans le monde*, 148; on the embassy issue: *Le Devoir*, 27 juin 1979.

44 Québec, Conseil exécutif, *La nouvelle entente Québec-Canada: proposition du gouvernement du Québec pour une entente d'égal à egal: la souveraineté-association* (Québec: Editeur officiel, 1979), 62, 104-105.

45 Nicholas Stethem, "Canada's crisis (2): the dangers," *Foreign Policy* 29 (Winter 1977-78), 59.

46 Donald C. Story, "Government—'a practical thing': towards a consensus on foreign policy jurisdiction," in R.B. Byers and Robert W. Reford, eds., *Canada Challenged: The Viability of Confederation* (Toronto: Canadian Institute of International Affairs, 1979), 108-24.

47 *The Globe and Mail*, 27 February 1979.

48 For these incidents, see Girard, *Canada in World Affairs*, 153-67; Bothwell, Drummond, and English, *Canada Since 1945*, 304-308; de Gaulle's speech in Montreal reproduced in Blanchette, ed., *Canadian Foreign Policy, 1966-1976*, 304.

49 Beaudoin, "Origines et développement du rôle internationale," 456-57.

50 This prompted an External Affairs official to point out that under Canadian law no citizen is allowed to receive decorations from a foreign government without prior approval from Ottawa: *International Canada* (November 1977), 273-74.

51 At a dinner honouring Lévesque in June 1983, Mauroy stated that "France forbids itself from interfering in the affairs of others. This guiding principle [applies] to Quebec as anyone else." *The Globe and Mail*, 28 June 1983.

52 *Ibid*. See also René Lévesque, "Quebec independence," in Elliot J. Feldman and Neil Nevitte, eds., *The Future of North America: Canada, the United States and*

Quebec Nationalism (Cambridge: Center for International Affairs, Harvard University, 1979), 61-70.

53 This point is made about the province's external interests by Hans J. Michelmann, "Federalism and international relations in Canada and the Federal Republic of Germany," *International Journal* 41 (Summer 1986), 548-49, but it applies more widely.

54 Gilbert R. Winham, "Bureaucratic politics and Canadian trade negotiation," *International Journal* 34 (Winter 1978-9).

55 *International Canada* (October and November 1985), 4-5, and (April and May 1986), 4.

56 Stephen Clarkson, *Canada and the Reagan Challenge* (Toronto: James Lorimer, 1982), 302-10.

57 *Montreal Star*, 18 March 1968.

58 Michael Tucker, *Canadian Foreign Policy: Contemporary Issues and Themes* (Toronto: McGraw-Hill Ryerson, 1980), 53-54.

59 See the two federal white papers issued in 1968: *Federalism and International Relations*, and *Federalism and International Conferences on Education*; also Leeson and Vanderelst, *External Affairs and Canadian Federalism*, section 5.

60 For example, the Ontario government became embroiled in the 1975 crime congress issue discussed in chapter 4. Likewise, in 1985, with his Liberals in a minority situation, Premier David Peterson of Ontario invoked economic sanctions against South Africa, banning purchases and sales of those products exclusively under Ontario's jurisdiction.

61 Quoted in Johannson, "Provincial international activities," 364, *fn* 11.

FURTHER READING AND RESEARCH

The purpose of this brief bibliographical survey is to provide a guide to some of the literature in Canadian foreign policy. The works and sources cited here represent a suggestive, rather than an exhaustive list: the most comprehensive bibliography in the field is published by the Canadian Institute of International Affairs: *A Bibliography of Works in Canadian Foreign Relations*, in four volumes, the first two compiled by Donald M. Page, the last two by Jane Barrett, Jane Beaumont, and Lee-Anne Broadhead.

Histories of Canada's External Relations

C.P. Stacey, *Canada and the Age of Conflict: A History of Canadian External Policies*, vol. 1: *1867-1921* (Toronto: Macmillan of Canada, 1977); vol. 2: *The Mackenzie King Era, 1921-1948* (Toronto: University of Toronto Press, 1981) is the best comprehensive history to 1948; John W. Holmes, *The Shaping of Peace: Canada and the Search for World Order, 1943-1957*, 2 vols. (Toronto: University of Toronto Press, 1979, 1982) provides a full discussion of policy during the so-called "golden age" of Canadian diplomacy. James Eayrs's mammoth series is primarily a study of defence policy, but it is defence defined widely, and an important source for all students of Canada's foreign policy: see *In Defence of Canada*: vol. 1: *From the Great War to the Great Depression* (Toronto: University of Toronto Press, 1964); vol. 2: *Appeasement and Rearmament* (1965); vol. 3: *Peacemaking and Deterrence* (1972); vol. 4: *Growing Up Allied* (1980); vol. 5: *The Roots of Complicity* (1983). While not a history per se, mention should also be made of J.L. Granatstein, *Canadian Foreign Policy: Historical Readings* (Toronto: Copp Clark Pitman, 1986), which contains a number of important statements of government policy and eleven interesting and informative scholarly essays.

General Works on Canadian Foreign Policy

Some of the key works which have appeared over the last thirty years are: James Eayrs, *The Art of the Possible: Government and Foreign Policy in Canada* (Toronto: University of Toronto Press, 1961); R. Barry Farrell, *The Making of Canadian Foreign Policy* (Scarborough: Prentice-Hall Canada, 1969); Peyton Lyon and Brian W. Tomlin, *Canada as an International Actor* (Toronto: Macmillan, 1979); Michael Tucker, *Canadian Foreign Policy: Contemporary Issues and Themes* (Toronto: McGraw-Hill Ryerson, 1980); David B. Dewitt and John J. Kirton, *Canada as a Principal Power* (Toronto: John Wiley, 1983).

Interpretative Essays

Canada's premier contemporary essayist on foreign affairs was the late John W. Holmes. See his three collections: *The Better Part of Valour: Essays on Canadian Diplomacy* (Toronto: McClelland and Stewart, 1970); *Canada: A Middle-Aged Power* (Toronto: McClelland and Stewart, 1976); and *Life with Uncle: The Canadian-American Relations* (Toronto: University of Toronto Press, 1981).

Canadian-American Relations

A general introduction is provided by Edelgard E. Mahant and Graeme S. Mount, *An Introduction to Canadian-American Relations* (Toronto: Methuen, 1984). Stephen Clarkson, *Canada and the Reagan Challenge* (Toronto: Canadian Institute for Economic Policy, 1982, rev. ed. 1985) provides an exhaustive review of the early 1980s. Essays on a range of issues in the relationship can be found in Charles F. Doran and John H. Sigler, eds., *Canada and the United States* (Englewood Cliffs: Prentice-Hall, 1985).

Annual Reviews, Reports

The Canadian Institute of International Affairs published the biennial series *Canada in World Affairs*, which covers two-year periods from the late 1930s to the mid-1960s. An additional volume, for the period 1971-1973, was published in 1985.

An indispensable research source for the Mulroney period is the annual series edited by Brian W. Tomlin and Maureen Appel Molot, *Canada Among Nations*. Volumes from 1984 to the present feature essays on both the foreign policy process and key issues, and include an annual statistical profile and a chronology.

International Canada is a month-by-month report on Canada's foreign affairs. Until 1982, it was produced by the Canadian Institute of International Affairs with an annual index. Since then, *International Canada* appears as an insert to the bimonthly journal *International Perspectives*.

Periodicals

Interesting articles on Canadian foreign policy can be found in *Canadian Defence Policy*, *International Perspectives*, *Behind the Headlines*; also see *Peace and Security*, the journal of the Canadian Institute for International Peace and Security; and the periodical of the Professional Association of Foreign Service Officers, *Bout de Papier*.

Scholarly periodicals with articles focussing on Canadian foreign policy include *International Journal, Canadian Journal of Political Science, Canadian Historical Review, Journal of Canadian Studies, Etudes Internationales*, and *Canadian Public Administration*.

Government Publications, Collections of Documents

The Department of External Affairs publishes a series of *Documents on Canadian External Relations*. For recent statements, see Secretary of State for External Affairs, *Foreign Policy for Canadians* (Ottawa: Information Canada, 1970); Parliament, Special Joint Committee of the Senate and of the House of Commons on Canada's International Relations, *Independence and Internationalism* (Ottawa: June 1986). A three-volume series of selected speeches and documents is also available, the first one (1945-55) edited by R.A. MacKay, the last two (1955-65 and 1965-75) edited by Arthur E. Blanchette: *Canadian Foreign Policy: Selected Speeches and Documents*.

Diaries, Memoirs, Biographies

There are numerous diaries, memoirs, and biographies of the major political and bureaucratic figures in Canadian foreign policy-making. Of particular interest are *The Mackenzie King Record*, edited in four volumes by J.W. Pickersgill and D. Forster. Lester B. Pearson's memoirs are in *Mike: The Memoirs of the Rt. Hon. Lester B. Pearson*, in three volumes. Volume 2, *1948-1957* (Toronto: University of Toronto Press, 1974), covers his time as external affairs minister. Charles Ritchie, *Storm Signals: More Undiplomatic Diaries, 1962-1971* (Toronto: Macmillan, 1983), provides not only a fascinating glimpse into the policy process, but an entertaining one. For an historical treatment of the senior bureaucracy, see J.L. Granatstein, *The Ottawa Men: The Civil Service Mandarins, 1935-1957* (Toronto: Oxford University Press, 1982).

Index